INTERIOR FRONTIERS

Praise for *Interior Frontiers*

"What do we need in a moment of catastrophe: environmental, sanitary, cultural, democratic, pedagogic? Not pain relievers, but rage. But not only rage, also infinite subtlety and sensitivity. But not only sensitivity, also erudition, memory, inflexible conceptual rigor. All this, and more, we find in Stoler's collection of essays, which weaves together the sinews, elusive inequalities, and creative refusals of imperial democracy. I call this a book of necessity."
—Étienne Balibar, author of *Violence and Civility*

"At a time when questions of social, racial, and economic justice are as desperately urgent as they are contested, Ann Stoler's *Interior Frontiers* brilliantly points out the importance of the cultural, affective, and aesthetic undercurrents that both advance and limit the unfinished process of decolonization that has stretched from the last century into this one. Stoler's essays chip away at what she and Étienne Balibar term "internal frontiers," the less visible divisions within, as opposed to on the peripheries of, political and social entities. In her readings of Albert Camus's *The Stranger* and Pierre Bourdieu's *Distinction*, Stoler insightfully demonstrates how elisions of race and colonialism in the critiques by European writers on the Left are symptoms of hidden hierarchies. Crafting the idea of "colonial aphasia," Stoler unveils how apparently innocuous but sometimes even prized acts create shadow indices of worth with material political ramifications. In a time where the evidently unjust—even the obviously violent—is whitewashed into acceptability, Stoler shines a necessary spotlight on the softer, blurrier, and perhaps even more pernicious forms of erasure that undergird the divisions that govern our lives and values today. *Interior Frontiers* is a veritable tour de force."
—Bernard E. Harcourt, Isidor and Seville Sulzbacher Professor of Law and Professor of Political Science, Columbia Law School

"*Interior Frontiers* sheds brilliant light on the subtleties of social line-drawing. With these essays, Ann Stoler (re)establishes herself as the foremost theorist of affect. From the snobberies of the dinner table to the under-interrogated "instincts" rationalizing global carcerality, she dissects the complex, ineffable sensibilities and "gut" intuitions that inform hierarchies of taste, place, vulgarity, disgust, fear, temporal order, revenge, social death, and physical vulnerability. Greatly expanding the insights of Bourdieu's magnum opus, *Distinction*, Stoler presents an important fracturing of the binarism upon which so many political exclusions, colonial practices, and racialized regimes depend. This collection looks at examples ranging from zoning laws to statelessness to the revulsions of touching "alien" skin, and deploys them to question the shape-shifting nature of such invented division. Most importantly, Stoler asks what is fluidly emergent in the resonant depictions of "the frontier" itself—what motivates the regard that moves from "neither here nor there" and proceeds to a sense of bounded existence runneled by Janus-faced mechanisms of simultaneous certitude and ambiguity. In examining those quietly mobilizing edges, Stoler delivers a searing indictment of our greatest contemporary paradox, the democratization of human inequality."
—Patricia J. Williams, University Distinguished Professor of Law and Humanities, Northeastern University

interior frontiers

essays on the entrails of inequality

ann laura stoler

UNIVERSITY PRESS

Oxford University Press is a department of the University of Oxford. It furthers the University's objective of excellence in research, scholarship, and education by publishing worldwide. Oxford is a registered trade mark of Oxford University Press in the UK and certain other countries.

Published in the United States of America by Oxford University Press
198 Madison Avenue, New York, NY 10016, United States of America.

© Oxford University Press 2022

All rights reserved. No part of this publication may be reproduced, stored in a retrieval system, or transmitted, in any form or by any means, without the prior permission in writing of Oxford University Press, or as expressly permitted by law, by license, or under terms agreed with the appropriate reproduction rights organization. Inquiries concerning reproduction outside the scope of the above should be sent to the Rights Department, Oxford University Press, at the address above.

You must not circulate this work in any other form
and you must impose this same condition on any acquirer.

Library of Congress Control Number: 2022933394
ISBN 978-0-19-007638-2 (pbk.)
ISBN 978-0-19-007637-5 (hbk.)

DOI: 10.1093/oso/9780190076375.001.0001

9 8 7 6 5 4 3 2 1

Paperback printed by LSC Communications, United States of America
Hardback printed by Bridgeport National Bindery, Inc., United States of America

Heretical thinking is a constituent power born in the act of non-acquiescence, born in the estrangement from what we once imagined we were able to know, born in the leaching of confidence in the categories we call upon and the concepts of which we have lost the capacity to even ask after the scenes of their making.

Table of Contents

Without Whom   *ix*
Unquiet in the Polis   *xiii*

PART I: ON THE METRICS OF WORTH

1	Interior Frontiers	3
2	Weaponizing the Senses	35
3	(Dis)taste of Race	67
4	How Not to Know	108

PART II: OF DISSENSUS IN THE MAKING

5	Poetic Rage: Anti-colonial Avant-Gardes	141
6	Archiving Praxis: For Palestinians and Beyond	199

PART III: SHATTERZONES OF IMPERIAL DEMOCRACY

7	"All Things being Equal": Mobile Extractions in a Carceral World	237
8	Colonial Diffractions in (Il)liberal Times	272
	Bibliography	*301*
	Index	*339*

Without Whom

Without whom... writing these essays would have been a much harder and more lonely task. Instead, writing them has provided rare occasion to have dearest friends and new ones as interlocutors to think with me about what so matters. Writing what matters congeals political dissent and concept work, animates discomfort, compels a welding of content and form. Not least their support curbed fears, induced a more precise word, with tender if tough critique. They course through this work as inspirations.

I should perhaps start with one I've never met and who has never read my work. Not surprisingly, Foucault seeps in the folds of my thinking, his queries have compelled my own.

My debt to Etienne Balibar (who I refer to as EB throughout these essays) is at once personal, politically pressing, at times inscribed in bold font, sometimes subjacent but just as strong. I could say his support over decades as that of cherished mentor if I didn't already know that he would reject that assignment, in favor of that of a cherished friend. His breath-taking philosophical labor stops me short in work that has never veered from a concerted task: creating, at times reviving, a political vocabulary that assails, without cynicism, how deeply power is wielded in the violences of inequality. Still he tenaciously refuses that it cannot change, that it needs to remain as it is today. I owe to EB, the book's very title, *Interior Frontiers*, sometimes stretching the concept across other scales and terrains with his encouragement to venture further than where I thought to go.

* * *

Paul Rabinow has been a collaborator in absentia, a friendship perhaps nurtured by distance, by our stubborn dispositions that somehow didn't get in the way. Concept-work was a passion we shared. Both of us were taken by the concept and substance of "fieldwork in philosophy," both imagining its potential to transform the nature of social inquiry. He is present here, though he never saw these essays. Our styles of writing differed. Politics and poesis matter to me. Paul not so much. When asked, he said he saw them getting in the way. Still his style of thought seizes me. He is a much-missed interlocutor and friend.

* * *

An unexpected "without whom" emerged in my feverish effort to identify an anti-colonial avant-garde, and its distinctive expressions of "poetic rage." I sought out Henk Meier's help, a long lost friend and colleague with an uncanny capacity to convey the nuances and power of Indonesia literature. I sought out his help in working on that literature in a conversation that somehow we had never had before.

* * *

Nancy Lutkehaus, Victoria Ebin, Jay Bernstein, Seloua Luste Boulbina, Jean and John Comaroff, Bernard Harcourt, Nancy Hunt, Neni Panourgia, Richard Rechtman, Kate and Ed West, Pat Williams, are those long cherished confidants whose sharp insights remain always nested in a trust that could make me retreat from a too strident claim to embrace one more pointed and often more bold. Nancy Hunt patiently worked with me to pursue the spare, to remove the excess, and to delete, making way for less cluttered passage.

* * *

Many others also have guided me with care: Fady Asleh, Ariella Azoulay, Omar Berrada, Leonoor Broeder, Val Daniel, Beshara Doumani, Eric Fassin, Rema Hammami, Charles McDonald, Mohamed Amer Meziane, Gwenn Miller, Adi Ophir, Sherene Seikaly, Saphe Shamoun, Dominque Rousset, (Karib) Fathun Satrio. I thank Keith Foulcher for offering a counterpoint to what I see as a recalcitrant unnamed anticolonial Indonesian avant-garde literature. Erin Simmons editing skills carried me through the scorch of summer with attentiveness to every line of the manuscript, from punctuation to question marks next to awkward turns of phrase. She crafted the index as I imagined it should be: a conceptual map and key, guiding readers within and between essays.

* * *

And then, of course Bruno and Tessa (who did the cover photo) holding me tight through Covid. I'm not supposed to say they are guardian angels of sorts, but they are. They grace me both with gentle reminders that the political practice when I was their age configures differently today. Their generosity in the face of the time and attention I poach from them is precious—for work they know sustains me in dark corners of the everyday. Larry's presence is on every page: drafts read and reread, muddle cut, portals pried from a throw away phrase.

* * *

"Without whom" is my gratitude to them all.

Unquiet in the Polis

It takes strength "to be able to live and to forget the extent to which to live and to be unjust is one and the same thing."[1]

COLONIALISMS STAMP THEMSELVES INTO BODIES, into minds, in the creases of skin, in the pores of flesh. As Simone Weil and Frantz Fanon have insisted, those who imagine having escaped that inscription fool themselves.[2] This is especially true of the well-meaning, good-hearted among "us" who never wanted "them" to be colonized, but profited and continue to profit, nonetheless. As beneficiaries, subsidizing extractions—hailed as development—is the stock and trade of the well-meaning, a set of practices renewed at every turn. Philanthropy and humanitarianism are the goods parlayed in the process of feeling good about feeling bad while the well-intentioned, in their silence, endorse camps of containment, forests destroyed for mega-plantations, gated corporate-funded compounds, and ever more lethal tactics to render "sensitive quarters" more secure and well-heeled ones more safe.

---

1. Frederick Nietzsche, "On the Uses and Disadvantages of History," in *Untimely Meditations,* trans. R. J. Holliingdale (New York: Cambridge University Press, 1996), 76.
2. Simone Weil, *Contre le colonialisme* (Paris: Payot & Rivage, 2018), 33–35, from "Les membres palpitants de la patrie," *Vigilance* 63, no. 10 (1938).

Imperial formations are racial emporia, stacked with commodities and currencies of inequality—infrastructures that are unevenly distributed, resources that are generously allotted to some, meted out meagerly, if at all, to others. Imperial designs are drawn with measures of cultural capital that are both white defined and white infested—assuring blocked and privileged access. Those psychically and physically damaged by (what I refer to in these essays as) "imperial democracies" occasionally have their privations verbally acknowledged, but still left materially unaddressed. Those others, not counting among the counted, are subject to forms of duress that go unregistered or strategically lit upon then (willfully) ignored.

This extended early-twenty-first century conjuncture amplifies, as it refigures, implacable features of imperial democracies and their quasi-democratic struggles. On the one hand is a protracted moment of enflamed and threatened ultra conservative activisms; on the other hand is a fierce rejection both of racialized practices and those "colonial-like" inequities, recursively structured, recasting ones that have come before.

Baldly skewed and public attention-getting contests over the language and landscapes of pedagogy, politics, labor, and aesthetics rage. Sometimes the substance of the battle is on unrecognizable terrain to all interlocutors; sometimes the battle is explicitly over the same time and place. Those bent on prohibiting and denying the teaching of colonial histories of dispossession, massacre, and violence versus those asserting the palpable, urgent need for more specific and pointed such histories may be voicing mutually unintelligible claims. Or they may be positioned in hand-to-hand combat, in practiced pursuit over museum curation, dispossession of land, restitution payments; in short, over every object and inch of contemporary and historical terrain.

It is hard not to be struck by the disparate renderings of what democracies are built upon and what they do and need to do now. Even an agreed upon vocabulary calls up different phenomena and distinct understandings of the political stakes and underlying principles on which the social sphere of the polity is founded and expected to thrive. Affective allegiances too are distinctly oriented to the public expression of fear, shame, indignance, humiliation, anger—all emotives distributed differently, less often with resignation than rage.

IMPERIAL DEMOCRACIES ON THE LINE

We've got on slippery ground where there is no friction and so in a certain sense the conditions are ideal, but also just because of that, we are unable to walk. We want to walk; so, we need friction. Back to the round ground.[3]

British imperialism, built on the tenets of nineteenth-century liberalism rather than in contradiction to it, prepares us in many ways for what has followed: the terms of how liberal democracies are understood to protect its communities or sever them, each with distinctively different rights.[4] Even those who are critical of

---

3. Ludwig Wittgenstein, *Philosophical Investigations*, trans. G.E.M. Anscombe (New York: Macmillan, 1968), 46.
4. See Uday Mehta, *Liberalism and Empire: A Study of Nineteenth-Century British Social Thought* (Chicago: Chicago University Press, 1999) that was to become and still is required reading in any course on empire. I was on the board of *Politics and Society* in 1989 when Mehta's manuscript "Liberal Politics of Exclusion" (*Politics and Society* 18, no. 4 (1990): 427–54) arrived. Totally taken with his bold and pointed analysis, even as a fledgling, I took it on as my first manuscript to edit. That sense of wonder led to profiling its framing as the first chapter in the volume Frederick Cooper and I edited, *Tensions of Empire: Colonial Culture in a Bourgeois World* (Berkeley: University of California Press, 1997), 59–86. Mehta's appreciation of the interior frontiers and cultural competencies "molded" by liberalism (what I would later call the requisite "education of desire" of imperial governance) was already set out with respect to Locke in *Anxiety of Freedom* (Ithaca: Cornell University Press, 1992), where he wrote: "Locke is [was] concerned not merely with settling the boundaries between individuals... but also... with settling the *internal boundaries of individuals (emphasis added)*," a century before the German philosopher Johan Fichte used the term, "internal frontier" as described in my opening essay included here. Mehta, *Anxieties*, 3.

what democracy offers don't agree on the "democratization of violence" that underwrites it. John Keane, political theorist of democracy (and who has written for decades about eastern Europe and "the power of the powerless") questions whether violence is really at the heart of democracy, arguing that the "democratization of war" makes acts of violence "publicly accountable."[5]

Achille Mbembe, to the contrary, would hold that democracy, in its very making, nurtures violence and a "democratization of fear" in which "necropolitics" is not only a tool of democracy but its core (and a protracted death sentence for so many who have imagined salvation in its promises). This "society of enmity," about which Mbembe has long written, nourishes the explicit delineations of difference and the (sub) metrics of inequality.[6] There is virtually no democracy separate from the colonial condition and the displacements it inflicts. The dark spaces of democracy are not only penal colonies and prisons, strategically located for surveillance, isolation, and extraction. Extractions of land, labor, and produce shape governing policies, practices, and violences in the interior borderlands, and supposedly exterior territories of democratic racial states.[7]

"Imperial democracy" can be celebrated or derided but rarely is it understood to mean the same one thing.[8] Some treat it as the

---

5. See John Keane, "Does Democracy Have a Violent Heart," in *War, Democracy and Culture in Classical Athens*, ed. David Pritchard, 378–408 (Cambridge: Cambridge University Press, 2010); Vaclav Havel and John Keane, *The Power of the Powerless: Citizens Against the State in Central Eastern Europe* (Armonk: M.E. Sharpe, 1985), and a rich Wikipedia entry on his work on human rights at John Keane (political theorist), Wikipedia, accessed June 13, 2021, https://en.wikipedia.org/wiki/John_Keane_(political_theorist).

6. Achille Mbembe, *On the Postcolony* (Durham: Duke University Press, 2003); *Necropolitics* (Durham: Duke University Press, 2019); *Politiques de l'inimitié* (Paris: La Découverte, 2016).

7. See Part III, "Shatterzones."

8. See David Slater, "Exporting Imperial Democracy: Critical Reflections on the US Case," *Human Geography* 2, no. 3 (2009): 1–13. I hadn't known that Arundhati

joining of two opposed projects: one interior to the polity and its citizens; the other directed at the conquest and coercive management of subject peoples and sites of extraction, as if the imperial spaces were outside the nation's proper bounds. But this is not what most fundamentally characterizes imperial democracies, nor what they do on the ground.

It should not be necessary to repeat (but I would hold that it still is): The common image of a dichotomy between inside and outside, with respect to those infrastructures in democratic liberal policies that distribute rights and resources, dissembles, and misconstrues. It is not that access and resources are meted out sparingly in the imperial domain, "outside" national borders, but allotted with equity for those who are properly within. *"Interior frontiers" do not refer to inside and outside the nation. Rather they mark distinctions among the good citizen, the sub-citizen, and the non-citizen, those with a place vs. those who are superfluous and have no place, citizen vs. subject, refugee, migrant.*

Interior frontiers are at once fierce and fragile sites of struggle between differentiated populations, spaces, and persons—divisions that can be silently and violently enforced. Distinctions are drawn along multiple axes. The boldest are between those relegated to deprivations vs. those who feed off scarcities—of health, housing, education, and wealth. Interior frontiers can mark "osmotic borders" or a "no man's land" of "fragile limits" as André Green

---

Roy used the term "imperial democracy" nearly twenty years ago in a hugely popular broadcast at Alternative Radio on May 13, 2003, on America's purported "moral right to rule." Originally at https://www.alternativeradio.org/speaker/arundhati-roy [no longer available], there is now a DVD recording of the two lectures entitled "Imperial Democracy" followed by a discussion with Howard Zinn. For a much earlier and alternative use of the term to describe a U.S. in which its "greatness was thrust upon it" and on President McKinley, "reluctant" to annex and colonize the Philippines or intervene in Cuba at the turn of the twentieth century, especially see Ernest R. May, *Imperial Democracy: The Emergence of America as a Great Power* (New York: Harcourt and Brace, 1961).

writes, among persons or within persons themselves.[9] But Green's most striking observation, which Balibar placed as the subtitle to his 1993 text "What is a frontier?" reads: "One can be a citizen or stateless, but it is difficult to imagine that one is a frontier."[10]

Some would argue that today's template for imperial democracies is that of ancient Athens where Sophocles was lauded for crushing a rebellion on the island of Samos. Although there was no mass enslavement or massacre, as the renowned British classicist Mary Beard contends, subservience, dependence, and debt were the Samosians' lot.[11] The semiotic politics that lauds both Athens' imperial conquest and its commitment to internal democracy is a rhetorical ruse. Its resilient appeal clearly speaks to a confirming and comforting political imaginary for the demos today. The mythohistory is of imperial ventures as oceanicly distant, "outside," with respect to the democratic venture: democracy as the pre-eminent space of equalitarian justice, a firmly possessed place and foundational principle within the "nation's" fortified bounds.

But this characterization misses a critical point in this ever-ambiguous play and politics of comparison. Only a small fraction of those within Athens had voice or rights. The interior frontiers were sharply drawn with slaves, women, and immigrants excluded from the polis. In the early-twentieth century U.S., the "Ugly Laws" targeted removal from public space of those who were poor, beggars, lame, disabled, Black, or petty "criminals," those

---

9. André Green, "The Borderline Concept," in *On Private Madness* (Abingdon: Taylor and Francis, 2018), 63 [originally published in French in 1986]. In the earliest of Balibar's essays on "Interior Frontiers" Green is quoted in several places (referenced in the eponymous first essay of this volume), but in subsequent texts of the same essay, reproduced in French and English, reference to Green in the text and notes, and the quote above are absent.

10. See Green, "The Borderline Concept," 63.

11. Mary Beard, "Democracy according to the Greeks," October 14, 2010, in *New Statesman Podcast*, produced by The New Statesman, podcast, MP3 Audio, https://www.newstatesman.com/ideas/2010/10/athenian-democracy-athens. Beard called Athens' imperial democracy something akin to "an exclusive gentleman's club."

not altogether different from immigrants, underemployed, homeless, and superfluous persons cast out of the polis today.¹² Those not protected by the normative requirements of the community's protocols are reminded in every movement and everyday practice that they are outside both "invisible borders" and requisite competencies, deserving of full membership.¹³

BETWEEN THE BLATANT AND IMPERCEPTIBLE

Still, imperial democracy is not a world of clarities, not Manichean as some political positions might claim. How those who move across the edges of these divisions and distinctions, and how those distinctions are finely calibrated and discerned, open to core concerns of the essays that follow. Roland Barthes made a germane case in his exceptional thinking on semiotics where a specific issue guided his methodological work. As Evelyne Grossman parses it: his approach seeks to enlarge our "fields of perception and sensations . . . *to touch from a distance, to augment the threshold of sensibility (emphasis added)*."¹⁴ This piercing analytic and methodological insight is joined by another—akin to how Raymond Williams described a "structure of feeling" only a few years earlier; as that which is "at the very edge of semantic availability."¹⁵ Both point to a critical

---

12. Susan Schweik's powerful account of the career of what was to be called the "Ugly Laws" is discussed in various subsequent essays here. See *The Ugly Laws: Disability in Public* (New York: New York University, 2009).

13. Étienne Balibar, "Fichte and the Internal Border," in *Masses, Classes, Ideas: Studies on Politics and Philosophy Before and After Marx*, trans. James Swenson (London: Routledge, 1994), 83.

14. Evelyne Grossman, *Eloge de l'Hypersensible* (Paris: Les Editions de Minuit, 2012), 119.

15. Raymond Williams, "Structures of feeling," in *Marxism and Literature* (Oxford: Oxford University Press, 1977), 134.

space of *politicality*, where and when the emergent and potential political, can thrive.

Barthes posed his problematic in a semiotic lesson on how to read: "to render sensible to an imperceptibility that does not know how to know what it discerns."[16] Here, he stretches between what is linguistically unavailable and the "imperceptible" as that which one does not yet know how to know. It's a politically vital distinction addressed not only to what one *cannot yet say*, but to a "rendering" of the "sensible," as a practice attentive to sensory epistemics, a way of knowing that so textures the lived experience of disparate lives.

Williams rather looks to the "affective elements" that articulate the personal and the social as a politically emergent space.[17] Barthes opens to politicality in the "minutely detailed."[18] For those for whom reading is a political practice and literature a foundational site, the political seems to emerge on his every page.[19] Barthes offers the possibility of speaking to what constitutes the political with each point of pressure put on the imperceptible and how we might learn to see. Nuance replaces the rigid binarisms he rejects. In his accounting, emphasis is less on not yet having an adequate language to say something than on the dilemma of not even knowing "*how to know what one discerns.*"[20] Hans-Jorg

---

16. Quoted in Grossman, *Eloge*, 119.
17. Williams, *Marxism*, 132.
18. Roland Barthes, "Utopia," in *The "Scandal of Marxism": and Other Writings on Politics, Essays and Interviews, Vol 2* (Calcutta: Seagull Books, 2015), 106–107; and see Sam Maculiffe, "The Imagination of Detail: Barthes and Politics of Utopia" (paper, London Conference in Critical Thought, London South Bank University, London, UK, June 2017).
19. In a critically negative and snippety review of Barthes' *Mythologies* in *The New Yorker*, he is described as "an unrelenting opponent of French imperialism" whose "strongest essay in the book is 'African Grammar,'" missing from the 1972 edition of *Mythologies* and reinserted in the 2012 edition. Richard Brody, "The Uses of 'Mythologies'," *The New Yorker*, April 19, 2012, https://www.newyorkers/com/cult ure/richard-brody/the-uses-of-mythologies.
20. Barthes, in Grossman, *Eloge*, 119.

Rheinberger reposes that caveat again: "*One must know the method of knowing in order to grasp the object to be known.*"[21] It's a methodological guidepost not to be missed. Others have said it, but Rheinberger reduces the noise, conveying it in a sentence.[22] The succinct formulation stops one short, capturing why the *how* matters. Racial formations are steeped precisely in an assumed way of knowing expressed in loquacious and carefully muted registers. The relationship between what one knows and how one imagines to know informs each of these essays to follow.

Gaston Bachelard somewhat differently grounds the how of knowing in an "epistemology of detail" that he once described as the aspirational crux of his work.[23] That torque on the detail has guided my archival practice for years. The anxiety of not knowing how one should know was both a leitmotif of the nineteenth-century Dutch colonial archives and in turn of my anxious movements following the archives' own. Evidential truths derived from rumor, visual proof, hearsay, emotives, and the written word, each called upon as "fact" (or disparaged as unreliable) depending on who conveyed them, where and when. These "hierarchies of

---

21. Hans-Jörg Rheinberger, *An Epistemology of the Concrete: Twentieth-Century Histories of Life* (Durham: Duke University Press, 2010), 31.

22. This principle and imperative defined my reading of colonial archives as I sought what those governing thought they knew and how they thought they knew. *Along the Archival Grain* came out the year before Rheinberger's, *An Epistemology of the Concrete* where the citation is located, but his earlier *Toward a History of Epistemic Things* (Stanford: Stanford University Press, 1997) was already shaping my archival trajectory.

23. Gaston Bachelard, "une philosophie du détail épistémologique" in *La philosophie du non* (Paris: Presses Universitaires de France, 1940), 14. I render the phrase as an "epistemology of the detail," but it might better be rendered as a "philosophy of epistemological detail." In either case, both forms address what we imagine to know and how we imagine to know it. In my own thinking on race and empire, I have taken it as an insight of conceptual methodology, "crucial to understanding how, where, on whom, and with what intensity imperial relations impose and thrive" in Carole McGranahan and John Collier eds., *Ethnographies of U.S. Empire* (Durham: Duke University Press, 2018), 480.

credibility" were protean as contexts, urgencies, and imaginaries of subtle recalcitrance to subversion changed.[24]

Epistemological hesitance has served me as a political diagnostic. It can mark where and when problems of interpretation arise, where doubt confronts emphatic claims. Such issues are alerts to where interior frontiers emerge and reposition, how sentiments distribute social distinctions, how taste marks denigration, and how the forgotten and forgettable withhold social worth. In Part I, attentiveness to the "how" of knowing is key to idioms, comportments and sensory regimes of racialized attributions and the (sub)metrics of inequality.

Explicit and subjacent spaces of entitlement and deprecation make up racialized systems of credence. Those participating in these practices (that impinge on social ecologies) may barely know the discernments in which they invest. Anxiety and ambiguity aside, persons and peoples are still easily dismissed as if with unwavering clarity, the criteria imagined to be so self-evident, as if without intended political effects. This unflexing confidence, providing a willingness and an impulse to subscribe, circulate through these essays to locate different sites of application. The formulation speaks to an effort to make visible the conceptual and material practices that *concerted disregard* (and what the attentiveness that goes with it) entails. When disregard is sanctioned with certitude and by common sense, implausibilities about racisms' reason may be hardly questioned at all.

Reason can be turned from itself. Disregard depends on bodily and psycho-social requirements that are not always the same: sometimes disregard is a concerted effort, conscious but unacknowledged, or "innocently" processed as "inadvertently passing over," or in repulsion, looking away. For adverbs can point to ethical compromise, wavering intent, couched animus. Adverbs do lots of work: they can provide an excuse for one's *qualified commitment* to particular acts: those "unwittingly" carried out,

---

24. See Ann Laura Stoler, "Hierarchies of Credibility," in *Along the Archival Grain: Epistemic Anxieties and Colonial Common Sense* (Princeton: Princeton University Press, 2009), 181–236.

practices "hardly" visible, a declaration of innocence in "I 'simply' didn't know" alter the claims for an act, how it is judged, and the limits of accountability.²⁵ It was the philosopher and linguist John Austin in a "A Plea for Excuses," (his 1955 essay often taken as the manifesto of ordinary language linguistics) who reminded us to seize on, and not ignore protective adverbs that qualify claims.²⁶

This volume's final essay "Colonial Diffractions in (Il)liberal Times" turns less to the moral authority that disregard confers than to the conditions that recast liberalism's fundamental inequities as primarily colonial coordinates. If excuses are an "admirable" subject for exploring the range of withdrawals from ethical responsibility, as Austin held, imperial democracy might serve as one of its exemplary sites. "Colonial aphasia" as I have long suggested is an ultimate excuse, one that removes the need for excuses, with a lapse of knowing as a powerful occlusion, one almost shorn of accountability.²⁷ "Decolonizing" becomes almost a conciliatory gesture, turning the inequities of imperial democracy away from the liberal demos as if those inequalities might better be accounted for in the exterior sites rather than in the movement between these spaces and in the managed mobilities on which imperial democracies thrive.

A SET OF ÉTUDES

In the spirit of Barthes' sensory alertness, I think of the essays that follow more as a set of *études* than chapters, not as cases strung out to resolve into convergent points.²⁸ Each is part of studied concentrations on a domain in which interior frontiers are assiduously

---

25. See the final chapter of Stoler, *Archival Grain*, 237-79, "Imperial Dispositions of Disregard."
26. John L. Austin, "A Plea for Excuses: The Presidential Address," *Proceedings of the Aristotelian Society* 57 (1956-1957): 1-30.
27. Ann Laura Stoler, "Colonial Aphasia: Disabled History and Race in France," in *Duress: Imperial Durabilities in Our Times* (Durham: Duke University Press, 2016), 68-121.
28. The turn to études is not a linguist conceit but a call to the double meaning of études as essays that do work as well as studies that research.

and surreptitiously assembled—and defiantly dismantled (the latter is a focal point of both studies in Part II on *Dissensus in the Making*). I ask how these distinctions, denigrations, and dissensions are reworked and recharged. I think of an *étude* as used in apprenticeship and musical pedagogy, exercises intended to instill skilled patience, not always achieved. It is not a set of abstract skills. If anything, it is (and I am) tediously focused. An *étude* offers the occasion for practicing a technique, relinquishing any claim to mastery. I use it here to suggest a set of tentative takes on inequities written into seemingly benign designations packed with judgments of worth.

Enumerated chapters suggest a succession, a cumulative making, a narrative with crescendo and denouement. Anticipated resolution and forecasting conclusions afford good introductions, offering readers a path to make sense of a book's direction. These studies work in a somewhat different way. *Interior frontiers* offers neither a narrative nor seeks one. Rather, it pulls on a thick thread that courses differently through each essay. Each, of varied lengths, tracks how the distinctions of superiority and subordination, high and low, command and subjugation are forged in imagined measures and metrics of worth. In the essays that follow, I refrain from referring to them as *études*, with a sense that some readers might see it as mannered. Still, the term sticks with me to stress a poetics of politics, an undercurrent of what follows. Conceding to some convention, I rather refer to these conjoined thoughts as "essays/*essais*" throughout the volume.

ON (SUB)METRICS

The term "(sub)metrics" appears throughout these essays. I take it as a term that demands attention to what is actually measured, what is imagined to be measured, what is an imaginary measure, and what succumbs to the exactions of numbers (as in the obscene, meticulous documents of torture regimes from the fifteen-century Inquisition to twentieth-century Pol Pot massacres in Cambodia).[29] The sites of differentiation I explore are located in a more ambiguous space: some (hardly) acknowledged, (partially) subjacent, and (largely) evasive of measurement though they are "measured" all the time – not unlike Austin's attentiveness to the quiet power of adverbs to limit an ethical claim.)

Judgments of worth are made across the often obscure affective landscapes in which sentiments are joined in different composites that distribute worth. The "sub" here underscores what exceeds, evades, or is fundamentally outside measurement. But measures are still there, imagined to be there, denigrating, dangerous, and in their certitudes, blinding and defended in violence. Attention to what I call the (sub)metrics of inequality does not abide by a fixed frame in the essays that follow. Sometimes there is an almost hidden measure, often that which is imagined to be a "measure" is neither a quality nor feature of thing or person that can be measured at all.

Measures and "metrics" in these essays appear as palimpsest, subscript, and imaginary; calculations, despite incalculabilities, repeatedly take hold in gray zones where differences that count and those that don't are punctuated, erased, and assessed. These are not always measures primarily riveted on distinctions of worth and exclusions of access. They may operate in dimmer light, in lower register, in modulated speech acts, in practicing tentative distinctions that make a case.

Lower, quiet registers can hold silent or nuanced verbal court. Such is the case with the searing anecdote of Aimé Césaire about his first day in a white lycée in Port-au-Prince when he was a young boy (which opens Part II, "Poetic Rage"). A schoolboy, the son of a

---

29. On the state's meticulous record-keeping around torture, see Irene Silverblatt, *Modern Inquisitions: Peru and the Colonial Origins of the Civilized World* (Durham: Duke University Press, 2004); Michelle Caswell, *Archiving the Unspeakable: Silence, Memory, and the Photographic Record in Cambodia* (Madison: University of Wisconsin Press, 2014).

beké (as elite whites were called in colonial Martinique) dismissed him as nothing but a Black, having no place in the school and no worth. The assault was not shouted across the courtyard as a racial slur. It was spoken in the modulated voice that elite white boys in the colonies (and elsewhere) were groomed to practice as "second nature." Sufficiently soft-spoken, their teacher could pretend not to notice or hear. Thus Part I, "The Metrics of Worth," argues for an implicit metrics of difference and a recurrent epistemic dilemma that cannot quite capture what people imagine they know and how they know it.

The early-nineteenth century term, "interior frontier," which Étienne Balibar forged into a political concept some thirty years ago, has become an unexpected conceptual hinge for my thinking about racial formations across colonies and Europe's "raceless," racialized urban strongholds. It's a concept with political weight, cutting across affects and bodies, along soft and hard borders of community, and through the fault lines of polity. It complements biopolitics, with more specific emphasis on the frictions of fraught divides. As a political concept it demands a reckoning of unstable scales of demand and duress. Interior frontiers rest in no one place. They occupy person and polity, body, and body politic. They mark the interior workings and psychic spaces of bodies where there is permeability, seepage, opened pores, skin tightened against contagion. These metaphors and means of toxicities absorbed, cracked fissures, and unhealed closures define the changing contours of interior frontiers in their making.

The first essay, "Interior Frontiers" makes a move in that direction, reflecting on the paradoxical, quixotic quality of the concept in the practices it calls forth. On the one hand, to seal affiliations among "a people," and between person and polity, and ostensibly, as Johan Fichte put it in 1808, to bolster "moral armament" or possibly the opposite—tear at the inner seams of civic life, turn persons against one another. It may do what the singular French expression *"moi peau"* invites to thought about the skin as an "envelope:" a sensorial limit, site of excitation, a "protection against aggression," a "defense against effraction" and a sieve to the self. I think of it less as a metaphor of a "me," or ego (as *"moi"* is usually translated), but of the skin's capacity to activate the abrasions that mold one into a political subject refusing to be demeaned, a racialized. But that white skin, so easily contaminated and equipped with imagined protective features does more: it protects white time and space from lesser, or not quite human-kinds.[30]

"Weaponizing the Senses" (essay two) concentrates on distributions of sentiments, a subject that has directed much of my work on the toxicities of racecraft for some time. Here sentiments are broached as *relational measures of value* that may be articulated in speech, or mutely performed. Treated as *judgments in the making*, they may confirm what one already imagines to know, or they may provide the occasion to form a new assessment. Whether the sentiment is "remorse" or "longing," or "disdain," these are never freestanding internal states but elements of social dispositions, responses to relations, and contested arrangements. As importantly, they index inequalities, active in producing dispositions and conditions needed for inequities to flourish.

In moving among sentiments, sensibilities, and the senses, I look to how they politically matter, and what is entailed in making such a claim. These affective spaces provide the kinetic and arrested emotives that shape the tones in which subordinations are played out. Sensory intrusions and insights turn on smell, sound, touch, revulsion, and unwanted proximities. "(Dis)Taste of Race" (essay three) could be considered a centerpiece to the volume. It is exemplary of conversions from common noun to political concept I have in mind. It is where the sinews of discrimination take

---

30. The term *"moi-peau"* is used by Didier Anzieu. It is usually considered a psychic device constitutive of a "me" (it is mentioned in Green's text, not Balibar's). Didier Anzieu, *Le Moi-Peau* (Paris: Editions Dunod, 1985). Also see Charles Mill's powerful rendering of "white time" and its construction of stolen time in a white chronotopic world of ideal theory. "White Time: The Chronic Injustice of Ideal Theory." Du Bois Review 11,1 (2014, 27-42).

a rarely considered and strikingly powerful form. Like "gut feelings" and "intuition," "taste" (good and bad taste, or the "tasteless") can operate undetected, below the radar of identified and indicted hate speech and enmity, classified as racial crimes. Yet it is precisely these seemingly innocuous, even cherished, conceptually laden acts—to compare, to intuit, to forget—that are girded by, as they furnish—fierce senses of belonging and demarcations in our fractious racialized world. I treat them here as sites of potential danger, readily recast as cure rather than poison, caring rather than corrosion, enabling rather than destructive, inclusionary rather than the very bedrock on which exclusions rest.

They do something more. They address a multisensory overload that yields more than Pierre Bourdieu sought to address in *Distinction*, while taking more seriously the underside of aesthetic eminence that was neither Kant's subject nor concern. Here, the convention that sets taste and distaste—*goût* and *dégoût*—as subjects of different fields and methods of inquiry is not cast aside. Instead, the two are treated as mutually enabling, dependent and joined. In rebinding their common making, viral, visceral distinctions condone the making of social kinds and truth-claims as judgments.

Kant's *Third Critique of Judgment* is the founding text for the philosophical study of aesthetics; Bourdieu's study is poised as its "transgressive" counterpoint, an assault on elite aesthetics. If Bourdieu were with us today, we might ask about his seamless move between a critique of Kant's blindness and a pointed attack on French elite values. His acute sense of distinction draws on commodity consumption to demonstrate difference and confirm status. Still, Bourdieu and Kant could be seen as sharing some common ground. If, for Kant, disgust has no place, for Bourdieu, centuries later, the *dégoût* that underwrites *goût* is left in the shadows. *Dégout* is there in Bourdieu's formulation of taste but absent from the extensive surveys his team carried out or the commentary on them. As importantly, distaste and disgust are hardly accorded an analytic or political space.

Attending to the muted and glaring, and even low-key forms of exclusion exposes a sense that the psychic life of power is doing important and contradictory work. The material longings and distribution of resources offer a window on to disparate micro-ecologies in which so many live. That thought informs my discussion of Albert Camus' *The Stranger* in the essay "How Not to Know." Others have read the novel as retreating from and effacing the colonial situation in Algiers. But through another lens, one might consider the racial subtext (unremarked and treated as given by Camus), as the template for a broader racial imprint. As a racial common sense, endorsing an achieved racially calibrated lifestyle, this scene Camus offers is one that never forgets who is an impoverished *indigène*, who is a poor white, striving to be properly modern.

Racism in France is ever present in the minor details of gesture and speech, policing what it means to be "really" French.[31] If geared in a particular direction (toward Roma, Algerians, Islam in general), French racism engages familiar conventions as in the United States. Some might argue that in 1960s France it was a non-subject, one submerged, absent, erased, but this is a hard case to make with respect to the infrastructures and architectures throughout France: *bidonvilles* (ghettoized tenements), public school manuals with French colonial ventures applauded

---

31. And its ever presence, despite denials, has been there for a long time. Among others, see Michel Wieviorka, *La France Raciste* (Paris: Seuil, 1992); Herrick Chapman and Laura Fader, eds., *Race in France: Interdisciplinary Perspective on the Politics of Difference* (New York: Bergahn, 2004); Didier Fassin and Eric Fassin, eds., *De la question sociale à la question raciale* (Paris: La Découverte, 2006); *Cette France-la*, volume 2 (Paris: La Découverte, 2008–2009); Carole Reynaud Paligot, *La Republique raciale: Paradigme racial et ideologie républicaine (1860–1930)* (Paris: Presses Universitaires de France, 2006); Miriam Ticktin, *Casualities of Care: Immigration and the Politics of Humanitarianism in France* (Durham: Duke University Press, 2011); Marc Bernardot, *Captures* (Bellecombe-en-Bauges: Editions du Croquant, 2012); Eric Fassin, *Démocratie précaire* (Paris: La Découverte, 2012); Mayanthi L. Fernando, *The Republic Unsettled: Muslim French and the Contradictions of Secularism* (Durham: Duke University Press, 2014).

or erased, "overseas" (*d'outre mer*) policies, torture tactics during the Algerian war.

Racism was never peripheral. A racialized vocabulary defined the internal borders of French society, and as Aimé Césaire put it, an undeclared "racial war."[32] Bourgeois elitism and bourgeois arrogance have produced less aggressive ire—more willingly if begrudgingly recognized. In Bourdieu's exacting study of the details that command class and racial valuations, the clarity of difference might have been as much in the untranslatable etiquettes that dictate how and when to do what, as it was for Bourdieu in the life of things.

SCENES OF DISSENSUS IN THE MAKING

One of the most striking responses to imperial and colonial impositions derives from a poetics of dissent that is creative, crushing, energizing, and exceeding what is deemed "relevant." The two essays in Part II address a dissensual politics seventy decades apart, in some cases even more. There is no claim that they are the same. Both moments are marked by a creative energy not focused on colonial atrocities. More emphasis is on creating and finding a new space of aesthetic response, alliances that make that possible, and an explicitly dissensual poetics.

Philosophy has often been accorded (and claimed) the tribute of working toward "wisdom as practice."[33] I'm not sure about ceding that honor to philosophy. The anti-colonial forms of practice discussed here might be candidates for such acclaim. Likely

---

32. Aimé Césaire, *Non a l'humiliation* (Paris: Actes Sud, 2014), 11.
33. Peter Sloterdijk, *The Art of philosophy: Wisdom as Practice* (New York: Columbia University Press, 2012); Pierre Hardot, *Philosophy As A Way of Life* (London: Blackwell, 1995).

they wouldn't have assigned it themselves. "Poetic Rage: On the Anti-colonial Avant-garde" (essay five) looks to that flourishing of artistic production and a form of life spirited by anti-colonialism throughout the world from the 1920s in some places, through to the 1950s and 1960s in others. That flourishing suggests more than a reassessment of the locus of avant-garde practice. Although Europe and Paris clearly figured in the circuits of political recalcitrance and artistic production, the multiple centers of gravity for locating that work demands an adjusted optic and frame.

From Cuba, Morocco, Lebanon, Mexico, Egypt, and across the Antilles were courageous persons engaging creative thought and practice, whose signature one could argue was more organically political than some of the traditionally labelled avant-garde with which they have been linked. They often were forefront precisely because of the colonial constraints they sought to escape and were forced to reckon with. Europe was not their originary site or source of their visions of the future. Rather, Europe was a rich site of meeting and collaboration, *a way station*, a stop along the way. They seem to have been constantly on the move, creating new socialites and alliances. Such a perspective changes the points of articulation and orientation, changes what can be seen, and obliges us to rethink which tracks are critical to follow.

Essay six, on what has been happening in Palestinian collective work or among individual artists/activists/academics, builds on an earlier attentiveness to archives and the limited access of Palestinians to Israeli ones. Research devoted to when, where, and how Palestinian documents were seized and stolen is producing an intensely political project. Another set of ventures shifts the focus yet again, addressing the practice of archiving itself as a political and creative project. Here I look at a sliver of that practice, small scale and personal, and that on the troubled scale of one of the most important new museums in the Arab world, Ramallah's "independent" Palestine Museum.

THE LOWER RECESSES

These essays open to calibrations and metrics of inequality that move between the nuanced and blunt, the subtle and bold, the diffuse and concentrated, the boisterous and silent. Features of these often opaque measures, are sometimes elusive in words. Sometimes they are hard to see and label. As with most powerful idioms—conceptually they bear the "polyvalent mobility" that can work both to secure relations of power and undermine them.[34] For as many as have hailed a postracial society and asserted a resolutely postcolonial one, dissension also comes from other directions: from the far right, on one hand, and from those for whom enduring colonial conditions wreak destruction in the protracted past and overlapping present. There is really no "our" in these political scenarios. For as many condemning a contemporary racial history, are others who deny racial logic and the racial imaginaries stamped into national priorities and the contorted contours of interior maps.

These essays are about the conditions of imperial democracy—both the marked and unmarked racial inequalities folded inside seemingly innocuous distinctions that make up their conceptual grammars. Taste, remorse, and forgetting emerge as evaluative spaces that elicit *veridictions* about the differences between social kinds and their supposedly definitive and defining qualities. The temporal zones stretch across what might be considered past and present, refusing the clarity of those designations. Instead, they hover between what is not over but rendered forgettable—what is disregarded as irrelevant for the future and only a vestige, barely present. Sometimes these temporal and political claims are fought as wars of position that shift and sharpen the terms and practices

---

34. On "polyvalent mobility" see Ann Laura Stoler, *Race and the Education of Desire: Foucault's History of Sexuality and the Colonial Order of Things* (Durham: Duke University Press, 1995), 89.

of dissent. Sometimes the deep inequities of imperial democracies are treated as if in need of a dedicated colonial lexicon.

Bringing "imperial democracy" into focus undermines the conceptual and political artifice of interior and exterior, rendered as fixed and distinct rather than a strategic, conjured fiction. Imperial democracy makes sense of multinational resource extractions with consequences for the future. These wars on the disenfranchised follow the logics of illiberalism, emerging as a global phenomenon across the EU, the United States, Turkey, Israel, Hong Kong, Brazil, the Philippines, and India, to name just some of the most currently repressive.

COVID-19 and Black Lives Matter have riveted global urgencies over the year and a half (from early 2020 to summer 2021) during which these essays were written or revised. In that time, political cleavages have forged new and hardened censorships, in radically oppositional directions. Far right-wing parties, from France's *Rassemblement National,* Denmark's People's Party, the Alliance for Brazil, the Netherlands' two radical right-wing populist parties, and the U.S.'s white supremacist contingency are only the most obvious signs of how deep commitment is to racially infested and discriminatory politics.

Once claiming the extreme right mantle, the French FN and then RN led an advocacy of policing the poor, "foreigners," the underemployed, and the allegedly recalcitrant. But the extreme right was never alone in advocating for these demands. Social maps realign as a more extensive population assert that being truly European or American is their historical, sacrosanct right, their coveted possession. Those claims open to others; entitlement to put up "no trespassing signs" to exclude those who do not (and can never) comply with often opaque, proprietary requirements. Colonial conditions (as if set outside imperial democracy) have been repositioned as descriptive of a planetary phenomenon; not just the dark underside of the global economy but the equivalent of a predatory cyclops propagating death inducing conditions and captivities on an ever-broader scale.

A SHATTERZONE OF INEQUALITIES

Shatterzone, an eighteenth-century geological term, refers to an area of fissured boulders severed through with cracks, crushed stone under such weight and pressure they split from compression at their seams. Sometimes the fissures look haphazard; unevenly layered sediments—a cascade of folded rock. But shatterzones are made up of more than heaves of displaced rock and scattered stones.

Something extraordinary and precious appears in the crevices of the fissures, in the space of the cuts, in the fault lines of a racism that too often goes unnamed: what forms is a network of veins that are often filled with rich mineral deposits. It is an image that seems resonant in thinking both about what makes up Europe and North America, how to reconceive who has made up its "outside" in Palestine, Indonesia, and the Caribbean. Contrary aesthetic frames and political energies make up its veins.

Shatterzone as metaphor and model has a history of its own, most commonly used among political analysts and in international relations to refer to sites of constant ethnic conflict, "fracturing" in the Balkans, "splintering" in the Sudan, fractious hostilities in the Middle East, and borderland rebellions in Russia.[35] Shatterzones as in the "borderlands of Europe," can fulfill an Orientalist fantasy as conflict zones of Jordan, Lebanon, Syria, and Iraq. Europe

---

35. Michael J. Totten, "Shatter Zones," *Australia/Israel & Jewish Affairs Council Review*, July 31, 2015, https://aijac.org.au/australia-israel-review/shatter-zones/; also see Grace Lugo, "Shatter-belt Countries: They Affect the Rest of the World, Too," *StoryMaps*, February 2, 2020, https://storymaps.arcgis.com/stories/8cf2192b8 7cd4ad787086c30467e7d48; Omar Bartov and Edward Weitz, eds., *Shatterzones of Empire: Co-existence and Violence in Eastern European's Borderlands* (Bloomington: Indiana University Press, 2013). An exception is James C. Scott's use of the term in *The Art of Not Being Governed* (New Haven: Yale University Press, 2009), where it defines "places of resistance," (p.22) rather than marking zones of dense and persistent inequalities as I use it here.

is always positioned outside its circumference. As political metaphor, shatterzones are on the borderlands of civility where ethnic ferocities reach a pitch and degree of "random" killings—not in "the West." The press revels in those distinctions, a clash of civilizations that asserts, as Samuel Huntington did twenty years ago, that there really is only one civilization in the clash. In the Orientalist model, the rich mineral veins go unremarked.

Here I think of Euro-American imperial democracies as shatterzones of compressed inequalities, racial cleavages, and geopolities of distributed impoverishment, damage, and neglect, of exorbitant privilege and wealth. The figures are rampant and repeated: refugees, Roma, undocumented workers, and migrants described invariably with the same worn intimation of being a "problem"—lacking the agency to "rise above" crime, violence, and their consequences—on which the U.S. and Europe depend.

Both diagnostics and design are needed to confront the *dispositifs* of empire's continual remaking. Required are sharpened tools with which to challenge and garner conceptual and political traction to do something different, and better. Europe and the United States (and Israel should be included) are shatterzones of inequalities, studded with rich deposits of those who refuse to be governed in this way, here and now.

Critics of racialized Europe refer to a newly fractured social fabric (think the "outrage" in Germany over a swastika scrawled across a church). I would argue that it has been fractured in its very making; exclusions, dispossession, and racial infrastructures have defined the underside of European modernity all along.[36] My compass here is not pointed to the "hot spots" on the global international relations map. Nor is it pointed to the "turbulence" with which the Middle East is so inherently endowed. Rather it

---

36. Enrique Dussel, *The Underside of Modernity: Apel, Ricoeur, Rorty, Taylor, & the Philosophy of Liberation* (London: Humanities Press, 1998)is focused on the once current concept and material conditions of underdevelopment and colonialism, and less on the racial coordinates of those projects.

is directed at the distress caused by displacing Europe's foundational imperial history and the people on whom the privileges of Euro-American prosperity have relied, i.e., those who have been drawn on, recruited, expelled, recruited again, set aside, abandoned, reduced to second class citizenship or shorn of residence and citizenship and thrown outside the carefully guarded interior parameters of what Edward Said called the "imaginative geography" of Europe, and its distorted map.

The first essay in "Shatterzones of Imperial Democracy" (Part III), entitled "All Things Being Equal: Mobile Extractions in a Carceral World" calls on the common phrase to consider that things are never equal; that it is the assured inequality of things on which racecraft is based. In the case of imperial democracy, "all things being equal" (premised on the imperative that things should never be and never are) is a principle and substance of their radically racist histories, insupportable without those inequalities, vital to its organic growth. No institution of imperial democracy is more glaringly racially skewed and exploitative than the incarceration industry. Although today's abolitionist anti-incarceration movement has now spread to mainstream politics, race still defines a system designed to entrap, to bring into captivity a class of persons for whom the end of slavery was not guaranteed by the thirteenth amendment but ensured by it. This is a shatterzone of the United States.

ON STRATEGIC IRREVERENCE

Imperial democracy is predatory on holding fast to certain institutionalized practices: on producing internal enemies, democratizing fear, limiting social goods, and skewing their distribution, and broadly investing in insecurity.[37] As Fanon held, we are all implicated

---

37. Mbembe, *Politques*; Stoler, "Reason aside," in *Duress*, 205–236.

and affected by its making. But the "we" as Foucault insisted, cannot come before the problematic is posed and the question asked.[38] Some "we"—yet to be determined—needs to identify the new and renewed practices, disciplines, and institutions on which imperial democracy thrives. Imperial democracy impales the present, shot through with a longevity of inequalities that can neither be absolved in a generation nor in a calculable set of years. Foucault's warning implies something else: that some constitutive "we" must redefine what constitutes a recalcitrant politics—polyphonous and irreverent.

The project is vexed from the start, conceptually, practically, and in just about every way. Hierarchies of relevance, and the uneven valuation of what counts as knowledge, the conversion of veridiction into opinion, as Hannah Arendt warned, is the modus operandi of politics.[39] If life is always already potentially political, as Carl Schmitt claimed, and the political is always tethered to what constitutes a life and who has a right to one, then the visceral nodes of affect, taste, boundaries of the self, and the major nodes of incarceration and dispossession are implicated in setting out which borders are porous and resilient, which are not. For they delineate in an oblique register how one sees and forges oneself as a political subject and social being.[40]

Reconfiguring archiving projects has the possibility of distorting its principles of production, rejecting its logic, and redrawing the map. Again, my compass points elsewhere: to a politics of comparison that refuses some of the incommensurabilities on which the U.S. as an exception is based. The inner "borderlands" of race produced in Europe are not carved out by red lining but

---

38. Michel Foucault, "Polemics, Politics, and Problematizations," in *The Essential Foucault: Selections from the Essential Works of Foucault, 1954–1984*, eds. Paul Rabinow and Nikolas Rose (New York: The New Press, 2003), 114.
39. Hannah Arendt, "Truth and Politics," originally in *The New Yorker*, February 25, 1967.
40. Carl Schmitt, *The Concept of the Political* [1932] (Chicago: Chicago University Press, 1996).

the geopolitics of HLM's (habitation à loyer modéré, low-income housing) in cities and on their urban peripheries, as in France, are used in principle, if not in their specific practices, with similar effects.

In 2017, I went to the Quai Branly Museum to see its new exhibition, "The Color Line: African-American Artists and Segregation." I had an introduction in hand to meet its producer and curator, Daniel Soutif, who graciously shared his thoughts and time. I should have been prepared for what was sayable and unsaid. Instead of using the occasion to challenge the myth of a raceless France, there was no reference, neither an artistic, ethnographic reference, nor curatorial gesture to race in Republican France nor to the aptness of a comparison.[41] Soutif held that comparison with France would have been inappropriate where "real racism" was absent.

Many in France agree. Others hold that the erasure of the damages inflicted by French imperial pursuits and colonial history represent a refusal that extends to children, and subjects intentionally not taught the subject in public schools.[42] Still, rather than dwell on the catastrophic and most obvious denials, here I stick closer to the underside of damaging gestures, disdaining habits, and affronts that prepare the ground for and accompany

---

41. The Musée de l'homme set up in 1937 was *the* Anthropology Museum of Paris, whose holdings were transferred to the Musée de Quai Branly in 2012. Many who have worked on colonialisms and museum curation rightly imagined that the Quai Branly would articulate a radically different history of its collections than its earlier incarnation obscuring France's colonial history. Surprise, fury, and disappointment at the curation with lionization of French activities in Africa and description of objects and artifacts not as stolen but "given" to soldiers was not expected. See Sally Price, *Paris Primitive: Jacques Chirac's Museum on the Quai Branly* (Chicago: Chicago University Press, 2010)for an excellent account of the transfer to the Musée de Quai Branly.

42. For a brief recapping of the storm around colonial history at a local and national level see Itay Lotem, "A Decade After the Riots, France has Rewritten its Colonial History," *The Conversation,* January 25, 2016, https://theconversation.com/a-decade-after-the-riots-france-has-rewritten-its-colonial-history-50499.

disaster, sometimes before these conditions are given a name.⁴³ Overt and subjacent distinctions cling to the lower recesses of daily lives: where one walks by day, avoids by night; how one walks, at ease or at a clip; jobs impossible to get, buildings where one is asked to show an identity card, treatment in hospitals and government offices; waiting hours for a visa, then told the office is now closed; waiting for a restaurant table until none are left. The list is a fraction of the everyday.

These essays are efforts to take direct and oblique paths to the "rough ground" of imperial democracies. Certitudes are fragile. There is no smooth passage. My response is to the dissensions of these times. Nietzsche's warning can't be repeated too often. Here it serves as prelude to what follows: the strength it takes *"to be able to live and to forget the extent to which to live and to be unjust is one and the same thing."* It is both in the subjacent and frontal affronts of violating, subordinating practices—their verbal, gestural, and torqued expression—in which those damages thrive and where these essays uneasily rest.

* * *

---

43. Saidiya Hartman, *Wayward Lives, Beautiful Experiments: Intimate Histories of Riotous Black Girls, Troublesome Women, and Queer Radicals* (New York: Norton, 2019).

PART I

ON THE METRICS OF WORTH

Interior Frontiers

INTERIOR FRONTIER *IS A CONCEPT that has accompanied me for more than thirty years as I've been following the fault lines that racial states produce and the distinctions on which they depend. Étienne Balibar [EB] introduced me to his 1990 essay of that title when it was published just as my work was turning to the racial distinctions that colonialisms install.*[1] *On leave in Paris in 1987, I attended his small seminar on nationalisms and racisms while steeped in the Bibliothèque Nationale's collection of pamphlets, manuals, and newsprint on the French colonies, on the proper physical and psychological hygiene for those European whites preparing to leave for French Indochina and French West Africa, and for those already there. There were piles of thin, barely opened household manuals devoted to guarding one's white health in the colonial tropics; still not what I was after, those official, unofficial, miscellaneous documents that were "lost" among other concerns: about inappropriate intimate relations, about those who fell outside the neat racial categories imposed (or chose to stay precariously and sometimes insistently outside them). That year, I had just made my*

---

1. I refer in this essay to Étienne Balibar as EB rather than "Balibar" finding it awkward, as I long have, to refer to a close colleague/friend by a last name. EB's first use of the term "interior frontier" appears in Étienne Balibar, "Fichte et la frontière intérieure: A propos des *Discours à la nation allemande*," *Cahiers de Fontenay* 58/59 (June 1990), reprinted in his *La crainte des masses: Politique et philosophie avant et après Marx* (Paris: Galilée, 1997), 131–156. For the English translation, see Étienne Balibar, "Fichte and the Internal Border: On *Addresses to the German Nation*," in *Masses, Classes, Ideas: Studies on Politics and Philosophy Before and After Marx*, trans. James Swenson (New York: Routledge, 1994), 61–84.

way to the French colonial archives near Aix. Racial imaginaries in imperial pursuit occupied page after page sometimes in sotto voce, *sometimes with a fervent bold, white supremacy making up colonial common sense.*

I don't remember EB using the term in that 1987 seminar but when he sent his 1990 essay on "la frontière intérieure," *there was already an uncanny affinity in the turn his own work was taking and my own.. Neither Fichte in 1808 nor EB's rethinking of the term in 1990 were concerned with colonialisms. Still, the term and EB's treatment of it captured the ambivalent and ambiguous work that boundaries, enclosures, frontiers do when they occupy internal/interior spaces of polity and person, porously encased.* "Invisible bonds" was *a key term in Fichte's formulation for national regeneration— also recurrently present in the French and Dutch colonial archives when the subject turned to* "national belonging" *and race. The invocation of* "invisible bonds" *and who could not share in them marked a core* dispositif *of colonialism's racial infrastructures and imagination.*

I first drew on the concept in 1990 then again in Comparative Studies in Society and History *in* "Sexual Affronts and Racial Frontiers" (1992) *where it framed my thinking about* métissage.[2] *By the time* Carnal Knowledge and Imperial Power (2002) *appeared, the concept showed up in three chapters.* When the Political Concepts collaborative decided in November 2016 to devote our next annual conference and volume to EB's work, it was "interior frontiers" I turned to again. This time to follow the work it did in his writing, dovetailing with, and sometimes diverging from, my own. The revised version here opens this volume to underscore this unfinished work and to continue my pursuit of what it offers.

---

2. That first presentation was a raw version, in honor of Eric Wolf at an American Anthropology Association meeting, elaborated in Ann Laura Stoler, "Sexual Affronts and Racial Frontiers: European Identities and the Cultural Politics of Exclusions in Colonial Southeast Asia," *Comparative Studies in Society and History* 34, no. 3 (1992): 514–551, later revised in *Carnal Knowledge and Imperial Power* (Berkeley: University of California Press, 2002).

> In the practice of philosophical writing, the words and propositions around which aporias crystallize and inventions take place always belong to long signifying chains, most often they constitute its element of *Unruhe*, of uneasiness or uncertainty . . .[3]

AN "ASTONISHING" CONCEPT

This moment is not the one in which I first wrote this essay. It was in 2016: Donald Trump was on the rise, Geert Wilders was about to be eclipsed by an even more popular far-right populist party in the Netherlands, Marine Le Pen was not yet on the cusp of garnering a new anti-Macron constituency and winning a national election as she may today, Recep Tayyip Erdoğan was imprisoning more Turkish journalists by the day, and Jair Bolsonaro was preparing to win the 2018 Brazilian elections. I was convinced we should have been more prepared for the rightist, racist surge that could no longer be tracked as if on a distant horizon. It was, and remains, dead center in forging the political cleavages of our times.[4] These were singular crusaders but hardly alone.

---

3. Étienne Balibar, "The Infinite Contradiction," trans. Jean-Marc Poisson and Jacques Lezra, *Yale French Studies* 88 (1995): 147; originally presented at the jury for promotion to Research Director, January 16, 1993. I thank Jay Bernstein, Michel Féher, Lawrence Hirschfeld, Adi Ophir, and Richard Rechtman, Mathieu Renault, and Diogo Sardinha for their queries, as well as those at the occasions where this essay was presented: the *Political Concepts* "Balibar Edition," Conference, Brown University, December 2-3, 2016; the History of Science Department, Harvard University, October 26, 2016; Bertrand Oglivie's philosophy seminar at Paris 8, March 2017.

4. On the fact that the Front National in France, and the Le Pen "phenomenon" were not "marginal" twenty-five years ago nor was he "*nul*" (a hopeless nothing, of no import), but already recruiting political sensibilities and xenophobic dispositions, long entrenched and firmly French, see Ann Laura Stoler, "Racist Visions and the Common Sense of France's 'Extreme' Right," in *Duress: Imperial Durabilities in Our Times* (Durham: Duke University Press, 2016), 269-304.

Assaults on the fabulated dangers of "critical race theory" and "islamo-gauchisme" have ever increasing traction.[5] They operate too through racialized distinctions and fears in which a broader public now shares and to which a more vocal patriotic white public demands repressive policies, practices, an armor of noxious terms, and increased attention.

These divisive cuts through our social, political, and affective landscapes are not eruptions. Rather, they register tectonic shifts, viscerally felt by some, askew to others' radars. If prevailing political categories and concepts do not always seem adequate, might it be worth reshaping and reactivating those dormant with which we could do more? I think of "interior frontiers" as offering a number of possibilities to track the claims (and panics) raised to fortify inequalities. As a concept I treat as both *dispositif* and diagnostic, it may identify the often unarticulated criteria that binds and excludes. As a political concept affectively charged, it works through multiple sensibilities recruited to produce hardening distinctions between who is "us" and who is construed as (irrevocably) "them," across the intimacies of personhood and wider sliding scales.

5. For a useful summary of the sequence of publications, public pronouncements, and persons most directly involved in the attacks, see Yaser Louati, "What Does Islamo-Gauchisme Mean for the Future of France and Democracy?" May 14, 2021, Islam, Secularism, and the Culture Wars in France, Berkley Forum at https://www.google.com/url?sa=t&rct=j&q=&esrc=s&source=web&cd=&cad=rja&uact=8&ved=2ahUKEwiY7rmn8uj0AhUGjIkEHffVBbgQFnoECAMQAQ&url=https%3A%2F%2Fberkleycenter.georgetown.edu%2Fresponses%2Fwhat-does-islamo-gauchisme-mean-for-the-future-of-france-and-democracy&usg=AOvVaw19XN7d0O4S4ZBASylLE0wk. And see a some unusual place for a critique of conservative accounts of Critical Race Theory, at Opinion, Daniel Kreiss, Alicee Marwick, Francesca Bolla Tripoli, "The Anti-Critical Race Movement Will Profoundly Affect Public Education." https://www.google.com/url?sa=t&rct=j&q=&esrc=s&source=web&cd=&cad=rja&uact=8&ved=2ahUKEwiQ2oug9Oj0AhWtkokEHSDVCbgQFnoECAMQAQ&url=https%3A%2F%2Fwww.scientificamerican.com%2Farticle%2Fthe-anti-critical-race-theory-movement-will-profoundly-affect-public-education%2F&usg=AOvVaw1DSU7db6TXZwhxrmeX2HKh.

In reanimating "interior frontiers"—Johan Gottlieb Fichte's early nineteenth century concept—EB turned to its contemporary relevance and nuanced qualities.[6] The term, "interior frontier" ("*innere grenzen*") first appeared in Fichte's 1808 *Addresses to the German Nation*.[7] EB consistently has rendered it in French as "*frontière intérieure*"; in English translations as "interior frontier," but also as "interior" or "internal border," or boundary as well.

This "astonishing expression," as he called it in 1990, derives its force from its "condensation of contradictions," the term "itself a symptom" of those very contradictory qualities. The border, he writes, is what encloses, imprisons, and puts in touch. It is a "site of passage," both an "obstacle" to movement, and the "starting point of expansion." Those contradictions might be specified further: sites of arrest and attenuated movement, of transgression and exchange.

But *internal* borders occupy more ambiguous and less visible sorts of space. They may divide the "interior of a territory or empire," "isolate," and thus "individualize it," and serve "as *expressions of the very constitution of the subject (emphasis added)*."[8] The oblique phrasing in the final clause (equally opaque in French and in English) is difficult to grasp, in part, because it anticipates a fundamental feature of "internal borders" themselves. The clause

---

6. Throughout this text I refer to Johann Gottlieb Fichte, *Addresses to the German Nation*, trans. Isaac Nakhimovsky, Bela Kapossy, and Keith Tribe (Cambridge: Hackett Publishing, 2013). However, other (earlier) translations have been consulted and are mentioned as well.

7. "Border" and "frontier" are used interchangeably for the thirty years of EB's texts covered in this essay. One could imagine a generative distinction with use of "frontier" marking a more intensely racialized imperial history than "border" usually invokes. Here, however, I focus on the "interior" and "internal" qualities of these divisions, where I see the analytic traction to lie. In any case, as late as 2014, the two terms are not distinguished, even as he turns to an explicit conceptualization of the "phenomenology of the border" most recently to date in Étienne Balibar, "At the Borders of Europe: From Cosmpolitanism to Cosmpolitics," *Translation* 4 (Spring 2014): 83–103.

8. Balibar, "Fichte and the Internal Border," 63.

bears vital weight, pointing still only implicitly to the changing scale on which internal borders constitute subjects who do and will invest individually and collectively in them. If Fichte played skillfully on the term's multiple connotations as EB suggests, the latter has as well. The politically affective charge of "interior borders" seems almost to suspend and secure the tensions of a political condition with the very multiplicity and realignment of its potential adherents.

Taking analytic advantage of this slippage between what becomes internal both to the person and polity is a key to the term's diagnostic capacities and its opening to political effects. "Interior frontiers" are malleable, situated, and responsive—with opaque power. The term itself, EB claims, embodies "the non-representable limit of every border, as it would be seen 'from within' its delineation."[9] This is not a bird's eye view; it's a multiplex optic, proximate and intimate. It's a view from those hugging a border's edges and excluded from its protection, as much as from those seeking security and refuge in its sheltered space.

Both elements of the concept—"interior" as modifying adjective, and "border" as mobile noun—gain their force from their polyvalence and variant referents. The analytic challenge is to make room both for the tightening parameters of inclusion it announces, and the mobile practices to which it refers—exercises that a community and individuals have imposed but also practice on themselves. Potentially, those interior frontiers confer belonging for some, estrangement for others. Adherence and exclusion are conjoined—not sequentially in fixed order, nor necessarily at the same time. Ambiguous sites, milieus, persons, and investments that "interior frontiers" delineate are themselves key features of the political, affective, and epistemic qualities such a political concept affords.

---

9. Balibar, "Fichte and the Internal Border," 63.

"Interior frontiers" provide a succession of vantage points to identify the making of the "strangers and undesirables" in the matrix of citizen and subject and the affective alliances that go with them. Blurring distinctions between political rationalities and the affective economy where belonging and exclusion lodge, an interior frontier makes the personal fundamentally political, fortifying tenuous attachments that allow a "me" the sense of being part of a "we," an elemental feature in recruiting that "me" to invest in distinguishing "us" and "them."

"Interior frontier" is a commanding concept on which EB draws for decades, sometimes with similar emphasis, at times with equivocal inflection in a score of texts. But even *prior* to its use as a political concept—and to even passing reference to the term itself—the political condition that it speaks to is there. It is invoked with respect to (1) the *dispositifs* that maintain inequalities; (2) the delineations of difference that inform the racialized issues and political "accents" on which he will press; and (3) the political logics that make citizen, stranger, enemy, and foreigner unstable appellations. Security regimes invest in augmenting those fears of distinctions, what they are supposed to say about the loci of dissent, and "internal enemies" in the making.[10]

Tracking the appearance of "interior frontier" between 1984 and 2015 provides an occasion to situate the purchase the concept offers to identify the scales that filiations between person and polity make hard to untangle.[11] It disrupts any easy rendering of what marks off an interior from an exterior, accentuating their conflation. For EB, "it brings to the fore . . . the classical aporias of interiority and exteriority." An "interior frontier" raises the

---

10. This is not to suggest EB's deliberate calibration for each of the term's inflections. Nor does it matter to my task. I'm more interested in the richness of the concept as a political one that slips between the political and psychic spaces of power, as it reflects quotidian ways in which racialized differences envelope social relations and personhoods.

11. Often I date his use of the term, to the date of the text's presentation, not its final publication or later translation.

problematic of "purification," and vigilance around perceptions and practices that might render the "inside" vulnerable, "adulterated" by "foreign" contamination. It foregrounds the very "uncertainty" of the distinctions on which those identities—precariously wrapped around a purest reasoning—depend.[12] These issues permeated EB's work before his use of the term. In the mid 1980s, he was already working through what distinguishes "the interior" from "the exterior," and why it politically mattered to pose the question. His trajectory consistently returns to the state's investment in casting the interior differentials of rights to the exterior frontiers that ricochet back to the interior again.

Earlier still, in 1981 (when the terms race and racism were virtually banned), he was on the track of a racism central to the making of modern France. Writing in *Nouvel Observateur*, he did more than condemn an endemic racism in the French Communist Party (of which he was a member until officially expelled—one day after his text appeared). He called out an endemic racism in France, intimately tied to its colonial history and the resurgence of nostalgia for a "France for the French," just one symptom of what he was to call a *"racist syndrome."*[13]

We might note here an extraordinary passage in *Reading Capital*, composed by the collective around Louis Althusser and his seminar, EB the youngest member. In the volume's compelling

---

12. The full quote reads:

This expression ["interior border"] brings to the fore all the classical aporias of interiority and exteriority. In the context of a reflection on the identity of a people, of a nation . . . it necessarily refers to a problematic of this identity, the way in which the "inside" can be penetrated or adulterated by its relation with the "outside" which here we will call the foreign. . . . (Balibar, "Fichte and the Internal Border," 63)

13. Étienne Balibar, "De Charonne à Vitry," in *Les frontières de la démocratie* (La Découverte: Paris, 1992), 19–34. In response to the *Front National*'s "breakthrough" in regional elections, see Étienne Balibar, "Suffrage universel!" *Le Monde* (May 4, 1983), https://www.lemonde.fr/archives/article/1983/05/04/suffrage-universel_2833939_1819218.html.

introduction, Althusser writes as if addressing the very issues around interior and exterior frontiers and the "invisible bonds" to which Fichte referred and on which EB seized.

> The invisible is defined by the visible as its invisible, its forbidden vision: the invisible is not therefore simply what is outside the visible . . . the outer darkness of exclusion—but *the inner darkness of exclusion*, inside the visible itself. The other space is only defined by the denegation of what it excludes from its own limits. In other words, *all its limits are* internal, *it carried its outside inside it (emphasis added).*[14]

BEWARE THOSE "INVISIBLE BONDS"

"Interior frontier" does work as a *political concept*, its fluctuating parameters mark diffracted histories of the present; as *dispositif*, it is intangible, occluding a central feature of racialized states. As *diagnostic*, it points to where and how sites of anxious *over*-identification emerge. "Interior frontier" identifies the conditions that depend on nurturing, intimately and fiercely held dispositions that those conditions solicit, and on which they call. As such, an interior frontier has a corporeal and affective quality of body and mind: how one's body is disposed, where disgust is directed, shaping comportment and (dis)taste for what is construed to produce discomfort and dis-ease.

How these "interior frontiers" are positioned—and where one falls vis-à vis their gated space—mark some of the most

---

14. Louis Althusser, Étienne Balibar, Roger Establet, Pierre Macherey, and Jacques Rancière, *Reading Capital: The Complete Edition*, trans. Ben Brewster and David Fernbach (London: Verso, 2016), 26–27.

consequential and violently guarded racial fault lines in our world today. For some, ready inclusion is easily conceived: for others—foreigners, those deemed "strangers," immigrants, children of immigrants born in France (and whoever and however "dangerous" persons are at that moment defined)—those borders are checkpoints for some, trespassing warnings for others. No official papers are ever enough to guarantee passage for they are not secured by barbed wire but by unarticulated and often inaccessible conventions that grant no entry.

Those conventions may be boldly advertised, with easily decoded terms like "family values" serving to police who "knows" what family is, what kind of families count, and what living arrangements are considered abhorrent to (and beyond) any valuation. But paradoxically and crucially, whether invisible or displayed, the attributes of "interior frontiers" are *made* hard to decipher. They may be experienced as amorphous, narrow, and petty by those excluded, instilling more than *ressentiment*; rather a categorical refusal to accept the required compromises demanded by what in the end neither guarantee, nor even offer assurance of equity or refuge for all.

FICHTE'S USE OF THE TERM— AND BEYOND

Fichte developed the term "interior frontier" at a specific moment and in a despairing context: as a summons to the defeated German nation on the brink of ruination following the Napoleonic wars. Given as a series of lectures in Berlin in winter 1807–1808, *Addresses to the German Nation* was a provocation to take up moral arms rather than the militarized deadly weapons of war. Central to his visionary program, "interior frontier" was to be a unifying concept, an enabling intervention, and indeed by EB's account then, a potentially radical one.

If, in Fichte's hands, an "interior frontier" was a fortifying moral barricade against erosion of nation and self, one could be just as struck by its underside; the raw, visceral, and passionately protected distinctions it bears potential to activate and install. I think here of racisms' intimate and surreptitious dwellings—bodily, affective, and in the flesh.[15] Fichte's "Thirteenth Address to the German Nation" provides some sense of these multiple possibilities, worth attending to in his extended description and own words:

> The first, original, and truly natural boundaries of States are beyond doubt [*ihre inners Grenzen*] their *internal frontiers.* Those who speak the same language are, *immediately and naturally* linked by the very *multitude of invisible bonds* to each other [by nature itself], prior to any human artifice [*kunst*] they understand each other and are capable of continuously developing this understanding; *they belong together* and are *naturally one, an indivisible whole.* Such [a whole] cannot desire to absorb [*in sich aufnehmen*] or *mix with* [*mit vermischen*] another of a different heritage/descent [*abkunft*] and language without at least initially confusing themselves and *without profoundly disturbing the regular development* of their culture. The outer demarcation of residence [dwelling] only follows as the consequences of this inner border.[16]

---

15. The iconic work on the subject is Franz Fanon, *Black Skin, White Masks* (London: Pluto Press, 1986), and for a succinct statement on the importance that Foucault gave to relations of power passing through the interior of bodies, see, Michel Foucault, "Les rapports de pouvoir passent à l'intérieur des corps, entretien avec L Finas, *La Quinzaine littéraire*, no. 247, (January 1977) in Michel Foucault, *Dits Ecrits*, vol 3, (under the direction of Daniel Defert and François Ewald) pp. 228-236.

Among the many important recent works on the flesh and race, see Alexander G. Weheliye, *Habeas Viscus* (Durham: Duke University Press, 2014) and R.A. Judy, *Sentient Flesh: Thinking in Disorder, Poesis in Black* (Durham: Duke University Press, 2020).

16. Johann Gottlieb Fichte, *Addresses to the German Nation*, trans. R.F. Jones and G.H. Turnbull (Chicago: The Open Court Publishing Company, 1922), 158. Other

Italics may not be needed here but some of the claims are so strikingly dissonant with any notion of an inclusive polity that they seem to warrant added attention. (German) Salvation here is sought in a nationalism generated out of this "multitude of invisible bonds."[17] A people is constituted for Fichte not by the borders of the territory they inhabit but because "they speak the same language."[18] Here, EB disrupts a facile reading to underscore two of Fichte's "displacements": one, refusal to reckon descent through blood, and two, a rejection of language as an historical artifact. The strength of Fichte's insight, he insists, is that belonging is not derived from "the objectivity of language" in its originary cast but rather from how a language is "*lived,*" "in the subjectivity of speech," coalescing in an "ethical attitude" and "reciprocal belonging."[19]

EB's interpretation of Fichte's "interior border" seems to take sustenance from the future possibility it offers to fortify moral responsibility, an internal "invincibility" that can forge "a new history."[20] Here is where "interior border" as concept holds political promise for him, describing this possibility as "its most profound

translations give a slightly different sense to this last sentence. Thus a 1923 translation reads:

> From this internal boundary, which is drawn by the spiritual nature of man himself, the marking of the external boundary by dwelling-place results as a consequence; and in the natural view of things, it is not because men dwell between certain mountains and rivers that they are a people, but, on the contrary, *men dwell together . . . because they were a people already by a law of nature* (emphasis added) which is much higher. (Fichte, *Addresses*, 224).

17. The extensive debates among French and Anglophone political theorists on the nature of Fichte's brand of nationalism as chauvinist or cosmopolitan are only broached in this essay with respect to the concept of "interior frontiers." See Isaac Nakhimovsky's introduction to Fichte's *Addresses to the German Nation* where he understands Fichte's proposals as a salutary set of "moral limits on power politics." Fichte, *Addresses*, xxvi. Arish Abizadeh reviews these arguments in "Was Fichte an Ethnic Nationalist? On Cultural Nationalism and Its Double," *History of Political Thought* 26, no. 2 (Summer 2005): 334–359.
18. Balibar, "Fichte and the Internal Border," 78.
19. Balibar, "Fichte and the Internal Border," 78–79.
20. Balibar, Fichte and the Internal Border, 66.

import."²¹ It is here where language is conceived as the "essence of the social bond," the fabric of enduring connection that "speaks in the first person." Not least, it embodies a spiritual training and moral education where "an individual's interiorization of the patriotic community" is nurtured.²² For Fichte, sensibility and feeling are linguistically tethered, ancestrally generated, nurtured in speech that adheres to the person, and is community bound.²³

Nothing is inherently positive or inclusive about such attachments. On the contrary, EB halts before the paradox that the internal border produces, entailing both "division and unity," "closure and opening." *For the border is no longer marking territorial spaces but a newly "constituted" time" of projection and the future (emphasis added)*. Warily he notes that new "internal borders" emerge for Fichte in an educational system that "suppresses the differences between conditions" as it creates another "critical kind of internal border."²⁴

On a more somber, prescient note, EB seems to hesitate, asking "whether the whole education process does not tend to substitute for the historical division of social conditions, another division between the good and the wicked [*méchants*], an invisible border *between two species (emphasis added)* of men."²⁵ That last sentence is chilling—moving from a utopian, unifying project to the potential for a racially defining, violent one. His cautionary observation anticipates as it remembers those categories of person designated as disposable, exterminable, dangerous to the defense

---

21. Balibar, Fichte and the Internal Border, 81.
22. Balibar, Fichte and the Internal Border, 82–83.
23. This affective charge is even more pronounced in Fichte's Fourth Address: "'This language goes deep into *the most private feelings of the individual's thoughts and wishes*, limiting or giving them free rein; it binds together all those who speak it into one common understanding; it is the *true mutual junction of the world of sense and of spirit*, merging them into one such that it is *no longer possible to say to which it belongs (emphasis added)*." Fichte, *Addresses*, 55.
24. Balibar, "Fichte and the Internal Border," 83.
25. Balibar, "Fichte and the Internal Border," 83.

and well-being of society and the security of the state.[26] Even a passing familiarity with the racial inequalities both in French and U.S. educational systems, employment, and housing, leave little doubt where and how the racial geopolitics of these internal borders would be drawn. *Homo academicus* displays its foundational grounding not only in a figure of *homo hierarchus* in bold relief; here it portends one powerful Nietzschean installment of unequally valued human—and not quite human—kinds.

COLONIALISM, RACISM, AND INTERIOR FRONTIERS

Interior borders bear equivocal potentialities. They mark restrictive exclusions and new divisions, hierarchies of worth and privileged moral affiliation. EB's re-animation of the concept exceeds the prompt that Fichte provided, in part because of the ever more immediately divisive and discriminatory contexts in which he chooses to examine its contemporary application, consequences, and racialized effects.

The 1990 text is where the concept of "interior frontiers" is given its most analytic due, but he invokes the links between it and racism five years earlier in two telling contexts: in discussion of colonialism as an integral internal feature of French society

---

26. On persons made disposable, see Bertrand Oglivie, *L'Homme jetable: Essai sur l'exterminisme et la violence extreme* (Paris: Editions Amsterdam, 2012). Somewhat surprisingly, Balibar does not take that racially inflected direction as he does in so much of his writing before and after 1990. In fact, he names those "two species of men" as "those who live in egotism and those who live in the realm of the spirit" (Balibar, "Fichte and the Internal Border," 83). I would draw on his phrase "two species of men" more literally as he himself does a decade later when he writes of racial discourses as attempts at interpreting "differences within the human species" and at defining what and who is "properly human" in relation to "the possibility of the inhuman." See Étienne Balibar, "Election/Selection" (keynote, delivered at the Conference: *tRACEs*, University of California, Irvine, April 10–11, 2003), https://vimeo.com/album/1631670/video/25691025.

and the French state, and in discussion of the "interior" features of citizenship (in "Les habits neufs de la citoyenneté") where it is prominently featured as a subtitle in an discussion of citizenship as a "property" in the double sense of the term: as "intimate character" of the person and a legal disposition. In his telling, citizens and subjects are distinguished not only legally but by "these interior frontiers" whose layout and outline (*le trace*) are at once "mobile" and "constantly overdetermined"[27]: "the distribution of male and female roles, social rights, and distinctions between a national and foreigner" are all implicated in defining where the private begins and the public ends. The domains that "interior frontiers" cover are illustrations. There is no analysis or explicit definition of the term.

"Interior frontier" appears again in a 1985 version but with reference to an "interior *political* frontier" (*"la frontière politique intérieure"*), a critical historical shift on two fronts: marking the distinction between citizen and subject, and those kinds of people considered dangerous.[28] Invoked as if it were itself a political *dispositif*, the term creates new distributions and divisions: the "laboring classes" are replaced by a category of *étrangers* (foreigners), of immigrants and colonized subjects, making race the divisive wedge.

But something else emerges; the connotation of "interior" moves out (to describe segments of the population) and then is drawn in again to speak to character traits and characteristics

---

27. EB writes:

On voit que la notion juridique et para-juridique de citoyenneté est indissociable non seulement d'un espace constitutionnel (territoire, souveraineté) relativement clos, mais aussi de *ses frontières intérieures*, dont le tracé, mouvant, est constamment surdéterminé. La limite du "public" et du "privé" telle que la dessine la distribution des rôles masculins et féminins, la zone névralgique du "droit social . . . opposition du 'national' et de l'étranger." (Balibar, "Les habits neufs de la citoyenneté," in *Les frontières de la démocratie*, 105).

28. Balibar, "Racisme, nationalisme, État" [1985] in *Les frontières de la démocratie*, 93; in this instance of the term's appearance, Fichte is not cited.

of those personhoods making them up. Tying these—if still obliquely—is a formulation of racism as the "psychic structure of the state."[29] For these are racialized identifications on which governance amplifies and through which states manage their microsites of control. If conceptualization emerges with the problematic in formation, the conceptual and political coordinates of interior frontiers are still subjacent, *avant le lettre*, an exacting examination of Fichte's use of the term.

It is no surprise that in 1987, in "Racism as Universalism," as EB's writing compresses more around racism and subcitizens, we find less an endorsement of the felicitous possibilities of "interior frontiers" than a dis-ease; as he notes, the "radicality" of Fichte's address "does not protect him against the highly ambiguous political implications of his doctrine."[30] For if racism is understood not as an additive or complement to nationalism but its product and fundamental infrastructural support, then the concept takes on another valence, one dependent on institutionalized inequalities and discriminations that internally divide not only subject and citizen but each among and within themselves.

"Double consciousness" in such a political frame may not only be the fate of those who are explicitly raced, as W.E.B. DuBois argued.[31] A distinct double(d) consciousness may be the state of those endorsing racisms while denying their adherence—*to secure themselves*. Europeans in the colonies were not unique in practicing a "politics of disregard," trafficking between claims to "ignorance" and practices of ignoring, accentuating the unease that comes with subscribing to the fictive worth of those distinctions.[32]

---

29. The French reads, "une structure psychique d'Etat," Balibar, *Les frontières de la démocratie*, 87.

30. Étienne Balibar, "Racism as Universalism," *New Political Science* 8, no. 1–2 (1989): 9–22.

31. W.E.B. DuBois, *The Souls of Black Folk* [1903], ed. Brent Hayes Edwards (Oxford: Oxford University Press, 2007), 8–10.

32. This point is elaborated in Ann Laura Stoler, *Along the Archival Grain: Epistemic Anxieties and Colonial Common Sense* (Princeton: Princeton University Press, 2009), 236–278.

On first reading "Fichte et les frontières intérieures," I was struck by its resonance with colonial vocabularies evoking what constituted the "invisible bonds" of white colonial privilege, the moral distinctions, and select cultural competencies that European colonials reserved for themselves. The concept of *frontière intérieure* captured, in its almost oxymoronic quality, the sort of unspecified moral criteria used to distinguish which colonial subjects merited European equivalence in a court of law. That "merit" required a particular kind of familiarity and comfort in European surroundings, evinced in child-rearing, schooling, domestic management, house plans, Dutch proficiency, criteria deployed to bar those who did not display and could not adequately demonstrate that they felt "at home" in a European milieu.

As striking was Fichte's very emphasis in describing this intangible belonging as *"les liens invisibles"*—the very same phrase used in Dutch and French colonial documents to assert who would be accorded the entitlements of a white European status and who should not. These were part of an everyday that neither could be touched though unnamed, nor named but unseen. The concept of "interior frontier" seems to reach equivocally for something more than mere affiliation: more an interior landscape of personhood responsive to—as it shapes—one's dispositions, "most private feelings" as Fichte put it, and attachments in the social world. French and Dutch colonial archives seemed alert to animating and securing European interior frontiers at every turn. Thus a colonial judge in Saigon could determine that a *métis* mixed-blood boy in the 1870s be tried (more severely) in a Native rather than European court of law (despite having a European father) because he did not demonstrate the sort of visible and interior qualities that showed his love of country and moral respectability: he was illiterate in French, demonstrated no distaste for Germans (!), seemed to speak only a few French words, with the added slur that his intimate relationship with his "alleged" French father of lowly origin may have been not parental but of a sexual partner.³³ At issue was not the deed but the *kind* of person charged.

The convergence between Fichte's aim to fortify these interior frontiers based on the ethical qualities of participating in a speech community and colonial projects designed to secure racialized governance was probably not as similar as I imagined them in that first startling encounter so many years ago. But one could imagine the opposite: that the colonial archives offered unusual clarity of the racial grammars of exclusion that swept through imperial democracy as viewed on common metropolitan and colonial ground. Both were hardening "interior frontiers" in the making: the category of European embellished by imperial pursuits, the category of internal enemy emerging out of those racialized frontiers.

Insight into EB's political critique turns back to those earlier 1985 texts that see citizenship operating to insure and then declare certain kinds of people (mostly from former French colonies and protectorates) "inassimilable"; here were differences created and maintained between "real French stock" (*Français de souche*) and the ever resilient category of *les immigrés*, despite the fact that most of the latter had and have long been legally French. If citizenship is based on a principle of exclusion, EB asks whether it is more than a *right* but a *status*, neither fixed, nor permanent, but present "by degrees."³⁴ Here the term *frontières intérieures* of citizenship does some work to account for granting and withholding the tools for acquisition, incremental success at mastering and/or succumbing to conventions, "by degrees."³⁵

---

33. On this case, see Stoler, *Carnal Knowledge*, 85–87.
34. Étienne Balibar, "Propositions sur la citoyenneté," [1988] in Balibar, *Les frontières de la démocratie*, 113.
35. Balibar, "Propositions sur la citoyenneté," 109–23, 113.

A BORDER IS NOT A LINE

Two moves add further ballast to the term, intensifying its relevance as a concept in its own right for contemporary political thought, EB elaborating an even more compelling direction. Several years after "Fichte et les frontières intérieures," he makes a striking move, invoking the observations of the well-known (renegade Lacanian) French psychiatrist André Green's understanding of what constitutes a border in the treatment of madness.[36] In an astute, and brazen leap of imagination, he draws on Green's psychoanalytic treatment of "limit cases" and "borderline patients."

Taking on Green's extraordinary insight about "the border" and the "line," EB shepherds it into another context. In Green's rendition a border is a "line of demarcation that is never a 'line'" but "a vast territory where no precise division allows for the separation between what is [madness] and what is not."[37] In EB's rendering, "interior frontier" does away with the "state fiction" that a border is a "line." No clearly demarcated or fixed lines are there to cross, where the "other side" provides immunity. Immunity is unstable, unpredictably located, and hard to achieve. An "interior frontier" depends on a messy set of attributes, not always the same place. It bridges and makes a case for plural interior borders of person and polity.

Conceptually and concretely, an "interior frontier" defines the contours of a protective and tenuous threshold more than a line. Instead, we might think of thick and narrow corridors where uneasy comportments, sensibilities, sensory aversions, dress, and speech meet, *unarticulated but not*

---

36. Étienne Balibar, "Les frontières de l'Europe," [1993] in *La crainte des masses: Politique et philosophie avant et après Marx* (Paris: Galilée, 1996), 381–395; see also André Green, *La folie privée: Psychanalyse des cas-limites* (Paris: Gallimard, 1990), which was published in English as *On Private Madness* (London: Hogarth Press, 1997).

37. Green, *La folie privée*, 104–105, my translation.

ill-defined—where the standards of normalization and defiance are at war and, as it were, on the line. With intangible sensibilities and immeasurable measure, interior frontiers are affective zones as well, where feeling (experienced as fear, humiliation, threat, longing, or shame) is indexical of political positioning in the making.

"INTERIORITIES" AND PERSONHOODS ON THE LINE

One can be a citizen or stateless, but it is difficult to imagine that one is a frontier.[38]

Dismantling the state fiction that borders are clear cut lines reorients EB's analysis. But Green's second insight on which he amplifies is more radical, one of Green's most striking and prescient statements, the one above. In this single stark phrase, Green shatters the parameters of the term. "Having a frontier [borderline]" is not the same as "being one."

EB attends, asking whether it is just such a condition, in Green's "no-man's land" where so many people live, "that affect up close their 'being' in as much they are subject to being in a physical, legal, and psychic space that is neither 'this nor that' [*ni ceci, ni cela*]."[39] And with the clarity of that insight comes a rhetorical question: is it really only on the margins of society, the *banlieue*, where this frontier is recognized and drawn? Or is it that

---

38. André Green, "Le concept de limite," in *La folie privée*, 107; quoted in Balibar, *La crainte des masses*, 383.

39. Balibar, "Les frontières de l'Europe," 383. The French anthropologist, Gérard Althabe made a similar observation with respect to the relationship between the rise of the FN, the precarity of "popular classes" and the racism directed as those designated as "the Maghrébins" when he wrote: turned out from French society, they "camped at [its] doors, and constituted its frontier." Gérard Althabe, *Production de l'étranger, xénophobie et couches populaires* [1985] (Paris: Sorbonne, 2017), 31.

"the parties, the nations, the regions that we have habitually come to consider as *having* borders, *themselves are ones?*"[40] [emphasis added]

What is actually "interior" and "internal" about an "interior frontier" remains intentionally loose, an open problematic serving as a diagnostic of how persons are shaped into political subjects by the *dispositifs* of governance. Circling around these issues, EB addresses and skirts how states harness individuals' affective ties, marshaling distinctions that make up who they imagine themselves to be, need to be to secure presence and dwelling, what they need to master to know they belong in their surroundings, and not least what they need to master in themselves.

In returning to the adjective "internal" or "interior," the "internal" moves analytically again, and its political potential transforms. More demands are put on other "polysemic" features of the internal with a slight shift of political grammar: "interior" slides from adjective to an active verb, a set of practices and affective attachments imposed upon and embraced by those precariously perched or comfortably settled on this toxic frontier. Of more issue is what gets "interiorized by individuals" and "internalized" in citizens, subjects, and the stateless, never completely managed by the institutions of the state.[41]

With this semiotic shift, the internal border is rendered with more substance: equally shaped by and defined through the dispositions and habits of those who relish its delineations and by those who are relegated to its outside and on whom it bears. The "border" neither looks nor feels the same for the two. Relations of power and asymmetrical force assure that interior landscapes are implicated in the emotional economy on which enmity and fear are animated and secure their central place.

---

40. Balibar, "Les frontières de l'Europe," 383.
41. Balibar, "Qu'est-ce qu'une frontière?" 374.

"Frontiers of Europe" marks a return to "*frontière intérieure*," called out here as one of Fichte's "decisive formulations."[42] Two alternative formulations (offered in parenthesis) suggest further rethinking about how to render what transpires in this space. The first is *frontières intériorisées*—now a familiar if variant formulation. The second, *frontières* pour *l'intériorité*," is awkwardly phrased.[43] What work might these supplemental rephrasings do that need these two qualifications? The first turns to how persons in a polity construe these delineations and *take them in as features of themselves*. In the second, "frontiers for interiority," the "for" suggests another charge: an "interiority"—i.e., a sense for one's worth that invokes the boundary/border as a stabilizing force, providing the psychic ballast otherwise unavailable to garner. EB seems to be reaching for this, writing more incisively several years later of:

> the subjective interiorization of the idea of the border—the way individuals represent their place in the world to themselves . . . by tracing in their imaginations *impenetrable* (*emphasis added*) borders between groups to which they belong.[44]

Here the imagined protective border joins the cultivation of a body politic secured through a "cultivation of the self." Such "symbolic differences" (as EB calls them) are not in the service of flourishing communal well-being (as Foucault described them in Ancient Greece).[45] This is rather what I call a "circumscribed

---

42. Balibar, "Les frontières de l'Europe," 388.
43. Balibar, "Les frontières de l'Europe," 388.
44. Étienne Balibar, "At the Borders of Europe," [1999] in *We the People of Europe: Reflections on Transnational Citizenship*, trans. James Swenson (Princeton: Princeton University Press, 2003), 8.
45. Balibar, "Les frontières de l'Europe," 389; see Michel Foucault, *The Government of the Self and Others: Lectures at the Collège de France 1982-1983*, trans. Graham Burchell, ed. Frédéric Gros (New York: Picador, 2010); Michel Foucault, *History of Sexuality, Vol II: The Use of Pleasure*, trans. Robert Hurley (New York: Vintage Books, 1990).

civility" where participation for some human kinds is categorically foreclosed.⁴⁶ "Impenetrable" seals too dark a fate. It is not a community to which anyone should wish to belong.

AT THE HEART OF CIVIC SPACE

Such a regime of truth has ugly consequences: EB identifies these effects as "ultra-subjective forms of violence," nourished in this darkened space. In these corridors of "*la limite*" and its "extreme" forms of expression, blockades are built.⁴⁷ Infrastructures of violence remain central. But EB will call on André Green to identify them more ominously again where an "idealization of hatred," as he understands Green to be suggesting, prevails:

> a process of psychotic cast, that, at the level of collective behavior, is integrally bound up with the fluctuating representations of the enemy, who is both potential victim and mimetic persecutor, or the fetishized Other (this also holds for imaginary constructs of the "races," whether superior or inferior).⁴⁸

In this vision, those expulsed are rendered as "disposable waste" while the "fetishized figure of 'us'—embodied in interior frontiers—is reduced to a fiction of 'absolute homogeneity'." This socially damaging vision is not the making of those diminished by precarity and weakened will alone. Interior frontiers gain their leverage because they are inscribed in the "naturalization

---

46. Balibar, "Les frontières de l'Europe," 389.
47. Étienne Balibar, "Émancipation, transformation, civilité," *Les temps modernes* 587 (May 1996): 438.
48. Étienne Balibar, *Violence and Civility: On the Limits of Political Philosophy*, trans. G.M. Goshgarian (New York: Columbia University Press, 2015), 60–61, a text based on his 1996 Wellek Library Lectures delivered at the University of California, Irvine.

of domination," a formula EB attributes to the joined lexicon of Marx and Foucault.[49]

One might think here with Edward Said's political concept, "imaginative geography," that so productively and emotionally bifurcates what is deemed a threat (in his case Islam) and what is not, a formulation of space and a "method" as he put it "of controlling what seems to be a threat to some established view of things."[50] This "imaginative" geography is an affectively inscribed and ultimately violent material one that limits what I can care about, what invokes my moral disgust, and what and who falls outside the reasonable purview of my morally founded concerns.

On the cusp of the twenty-first century, EB accelerates and intensifies his condemnation of the political work done by the border. It is further indicted and renamed.[51] Nowhere has he stated it so boldly: the border, *"la limite,"* is *"the wholly nondemocratic condition of democratic institutions (emphasis added)."* This key displacement is underscored: the border is "accepted, sanctified and interiorized," transported from the exterior "to the *middle of political space.*"[52] One is reminded of Nicos Poulantzas's 1978 treatment of "the internal enemy" as that which is amplified when and where the "frontiers of the national space" are "internalized" and "at the heart of that space itself."[53]

Note here that the making of "interior frontiers" can never be just a state project and a manipulation on high alone. Emerging at the *"heart of civic space,"* they may create an invisible geography marking out who can walk which streets without feeling "out of

---

49. Étienne Balibar, "Three Concepts of Politics: Emancipation, transformation, civility" in *Politics and the Other Scene*, trans. Christine Jones, James Swenson, and Chris Turner (New York: Verso, 2002), 439.
50. Edward Said, *Orientalism* (New York, Random House, 1978), 59.
51. Étienne Balibar, "World Borders, Political Borders," trans. Erin M. Williams, *PMLA* 117, no. 1 (Jan 2002): 71–78.
52. Balibar, "World Borders, Political Borders," 71–78.
53. Nicos Poulantzas, *State, Power, Socialism*, trans. Patrick Camiler (London: Verso, 1978).

place," who can stand on a street corner without being suspect, narrowing down the spaces one has the right to inhabit, or in which one can feel "at home." In the U.S., racecraft, as Barbara and Karen Fields describe it, shapes the places where one is rendered "unsafe"—or is considered "unsafe" for others.[54] Selective surveillance and racialized punishment precede incarceration. Loïc Wacquant puts it precisely and takes it further, arguing that in the U.S. "race is a civic felony."[55]

"THE INNER DARKNESS OF EXCLUSION"

The analytic traction of attending to "internal borders" reappears with new force when EB sets out to mark Europe as itself a borderland, with what Althusser once called "the inner darkness of exclusion." [56] With hardening internal borders threatened by the prospect of European citizenship,"the category of the 'national' (or the *self*, of what it requires to be the same) also becomes split and subject to the dissolving action of 'internal borders' which mirror the global inequalities... [with]... disturbing resurgences of traditional patterns of exclusion."[57]

There are the unassimilated but also increasing numbers rendered unassimilable (as if to be really French was the goal); on the one hand, with the designation of "foreign" and the category of (forever) foreigner assigned to bolster traditional "interior frontiers"; on the other hand, those demanding equal citizenship rights in law and in the everyday, which may manifest as the right

---

54. Barbara Fields and Karen Fields, *Racecraft: The Soul of Inequality in American Life* (New York: Verso, 2012).
55. Loïc Wacquant, "Race as Civic Felony," *ISSJ* 57, no. 183 (March 2005): 127–142.
56. Althusser, *Reading Capital*, 26.
57. Étienne Balibar, "Europe as Borderland" [2004], *Economic Planning and Socia Space* 27, no. 2 (2009): 201.

to remain different (and defiantly indifferent) to the normative regulations of cultural and nationalized convention.

The lathe of the concept is turned once again to ask whether the "marks of belonging" that are "retrieved in the individual" and "interiorized by him" produce a "countereffect" or what we might describe as the underside of those designations.[58] Interiors and exteriors are turned inside out. That "countereffect" of belonging is "the *stranger* as *other* (*emphasis added*) within . . . an intruder, out of place." This *internal other* provides negative contour in everyday life to "interior frontiers."

But what is rendered as "foreign" and "strange" and unseemly is not always raced, or only so. There are "different modalities of '*contradicting*' *the norm* (*emphasis added*), i.e., of destroying normality or deviating from it." Turning from Fichte to Foucault, the "interiorized border" between the criminal and deviant, between being socially wayward vs. physically homeless, being "at risk" or "a risk" is made into a moral and dangerously political space. The potential criminal is deemed deviant, mobilizing a surveillance and security regime sanctioned by the legitimized mandate to defend society (against itself.)[59]

ON VISCOSITY AND "INTERIOR FRONTIERS"

EB's relentless efforts to identify the "extraordinarily viscous" and potentially vicious features of interior borders stop somewhat short of at least one of Green's observations. In "The Concept of *la limite*,"

---

58. Étienne Balibar, "Civic Universalism and Its Internal Exclusions: The Issue of Anthropological Difference," *boundary 2* 39, no. 1 (2012): 215.

59. Michel Foucault, "About the Concept of the 'The Dangerous Individual,' in 19th-Century Legal Psychiatry," *International Journal of Law and Psychiatry* 1 (1978): 1–16; Michel Foucault, *Il faut défendre la société: College de France lectures* (Paris: Gallimard, 1976).

Green questions the limit of a person, a question hard to consider without thinking the intrusive transgressions that racialized relations inflict on those subsumed by them. Green makes no reference to Frantz Fanon, but his conclusions are resonant with what Fanon saw as the psychic scars of a racial colonial machine burned into the future of Europe, and into the permeable membrane of flesh.

Imagining the limit of a person, Green writes, the envelope of the skin immediately comes to mind.[60] But no, he reminds us, the skin is discontinuous and porous. The tissue of flesh is interrupted by other tissues, it is full of holes (*"il est troué"*) that act as gates or better as custom inspectors, he writes: "eyes" [I think to the suspicious gaze], "ears" [to unwelcome music as irritant/noise], "nose" [to cooking smells rendered repugnant], "mouth, anus, genitalia." For Green two problems persist: the "consistency and the structure of the border," and "circulation in and out of its gates." "But what are the frontiers of my psyche," he asks?[61]

> There are different sorts of frontiers: those without circulation across them, or osmotic membranes that permit communication with a selection among that which should be introduced or held exterior in the case of perturbation, and more vigorously rejected if there is need. In the case of danger, the osmotic borders can enlarge to relieve what is inside, importune excitations. But other measures are possible, such as *a rigidification of the line, a sort of sclerosis or even a jamming up of the frontier which creates in the place of a fragile demarcation rather a no man's land* (emphasis added). To be a frontier, is to identify one as a

---

60. Indeed, that the skin is not only a "physiological envelope" but "has a psychological function which permits containing, delimiting, putting in contact and inscribing" is the insight of Didier Anzieu in *Le Moi-peau* (Paris: Editions Dunod, 1985): "the skin, through its sensorial properties retains a determinant role in the relationship to the other."
61. Green, *On Private Madness*, 63.

moving frontier to which one submits more than one which is in one's command.⁶²

In attending to "rigidification," "sclerosis," "the jamming of frontiers," Green seems to anticipate our collective, securitized present, as though in a future conditional tense. His observation forebodes and offers more: "To be a borderline implies that a border protects one's self from crossing over or from being crossed over, from being invaded, and thus becoming a moving border. This in turn implies a loss of distinction between space and time."⁶³

A disturbing passage on several counts, it revamps the work that making of an interior border entails. It is not work *on* a body but rather *through* one. Bodily exposures are part and parcel of the interior frontier as *dispositif*. And what of this "loss of distinction between space and time"? Does submission to the command compress into a transgression of my body and senses? One might think with Jacques Rancière here about *"la partage du sensible"* (the distribution/division/sharing of the sensible.)⁶⁴ Or with Judith Butler's senses of the subject, the invocation of partitions, impingements, willfully and unwillingly imposed on a subject, a reminder that no selves can be fully subsumed or hermetically sealed.⁶⁵ If Green leans on the metaphor of territorial borders to make his case, he does so to emphasize permeabilities, invasions, contaminations, fissures, penetrations to which one has no ready exit and from which one cannot be immune.⁶⁶

---

62. Green, *On Private Madness*, 63
63. Green, *On Private Madness*, 63.
64. Jacques Rancière, "Ten Theses on Politics," in *Dissensus: On Politics and Aesthetics*, ed. Steven Corcoran (London: Bloomsbury, 2010), 44.
65. Judith Butler, *Senses of the Subject* (New York: Fordham, 2015).
66. See Ann Laura Stoler, "Introduction: The Dark Logic of Invasive Others," *Social Research* 84, no. 1 (Spring 2017): 3–5; see also the essays in this special issue edited by Arien Mack and Miriam Ticktin, "The Invasive Other," *Social Research* 84, no. 1 (2017): https://www.socres.org/post/841-spring-2017-invasive-other.

The present moment is not alone in fortifying interior frontiers. The "inversion" of democracy (as Achille Mbembe puts it) is occurring on a new globalizing imperial scale.[67] "Our" racial emporium both exceeds nation-states as it instills ever more expansive and intimate xenophobias. What forms of sociality might produce common refuge, not anxious retrenchment? No matter how well understood the conceptual matrix in which these internal and internalized distinctions are drawn, what is left to learn is more about their vernacular making in things, feelings, infrastructural arrangements—in visual images, decibel levels, aesthetic conventions, in what is misconstrued as innocuous common sense.

The colloquial form that these battles take are deceptively straightforward: there is a "we" who no longer feel comfortable and feel safely "at home," a *"nous sommes plus chez nous"* heard on the lips of more than *Front National* supporters. "We are where we belong and at home" (*nous sommes chez nous*), the response of a defiant citizenry born in North Africa and in France.[68] "Home" is invoked or rather erupts again with *"pas de jungle chez nous"* (no refugees, no squatter/refugee/gypsy encampments in our backyards) when the Calais refugee camp was dismantled in Fall 2016, reverberating among a well-mannered populous in small Dutch towns, in Iowa's high school hallways, on the wrestling team of a prestigious New York City university (Columbia), and at a self-declared poorly endowed progressive one (The New School). In each of these locations, some students felt licensed and emboldened to shout (as some French would put it with no compunction, *"decomplexifié"*) "go home where you belong."

---

67. Achille Mbembe, *Politique de l'inimités* (Paris: La Découverte, 2015), 62.
68. See also Thomas Chatterton Williams, "The French Origins of 'You Will Not Replace Us: The European Thinkers behind the White-Nationalist Rallying Cry," *The New Yorker* (December 4, 2017), https://www.newyorker.com/magazine/2017/12/04/the-french-origins-of-you-will-not-replace-us.

Home repeatedly figures for those who spend so much of their lives in passage, pretending to want to "pass" just to be able to get through a frontier or guarded zone. As EB notes, "passing and repassing" occur "at the mercy of expulsions and familial regroupings" through this "viscous spatio-temporal zone."[69] With homing in and closing in on such distinctive features of interior frontiers, the mirror image is dark. It is no surprise then that those frontiers can emerge as such a hollow space. As EB comes to understand, it is "almost a home—a home in which to live a life which is a waiting-to-live, a non-life."[70]

These designations and demarcations of what is at home (and who can be) are colloquial and familiar with a history colonial through and through. The French military security apparatus in the 1950s that conceived controlling an "inferiorized" internal population has now imposed their attention on an inferiorized interiorized immigrant population, not immigrants but French citizens.[71] But the figure of the "undesirable element" as the Dutch called those colonized seen as a threat or potential threat to colonial authority, and an "internal enemy" as the French called their immigrant and French citizenry of other origin, have a much longer history. That we know.

Distinctions among the terms, mutually defining, superimposed, overlapping, are hard to maintain. "Internal enemies" are figured on the qualities that make for "internal frontiers;" the "stranger" and the "enemy" as EB notes are dangerously confused.[72] "Internal strangers" threaten "interior borders." There is

---

69. Balibar, "Qu'est-ce que c'est une frontière?" 379.
70. Balibar, "Qu'est-ce que c'est une frontière?" 379.
71. Mathieu Rigouste, *L'ennemi intérieur: la généalogie coloniale et militaire de l'ordre sécuritaire dans la France contemporaine* (Paris: La Découverte, 2009).
72. Étienne Balibar, "Strangers as Enemies: Further Reflections on the Aporias of Transnational Citizenship," lecture, The Institute on Globalization and the Human Condition, McMaster University Hamilton, May 2006, https://globalizat

"growing confusion," as EB puts it, between the "internal stranger," the "internal enemy," and between the "internal stranger" and the "foreigner."⁷³ These figures fashioned of fear are traced by what a citizenry takes as its defining features.⁷⁴

We know less about the ruinous qualities of life that interior frontiers foster—the ultimate *pharmakon*, curative and corrosive, protective and poisonous. While altered in density, composition, and form, these spaces of refracted ruination are the dark, infra-red corridors on which divisions rely. In *Let Us Now Praise Famous Men*, James Agee described impoverished white tenant families in the 1930s American South for whom there was no possibility of a buffered self—persons assaulted and slandered by a system that produced "slendering of forms of freedom" over the course of their lives.⁷⁵

Such "slendering" degrees of freedom in this current hyper-commodified world of fictive choice produce a negative space of "interior frontiers." Sustenance is crudely abbreviated among those who experience the obscene inequalities that provide fewer buffers or none. Interior frontiers puncture possibilities by assuring that the *unheimlich*, the strange, the stranger, the unfamiliar,

---

ion.mcmaster.ca/research/publications/working-papers/2006/ighc-wps_06-4_balibar.pdf.

73. Étienne Balibar, "Can We Say: After the Subject Comes the Stranger?" November 2014 Columbia Maison Française, posted November 20, 2014, YouTube video, https://www.youtube.com/watch?v=ACaXH-WW6Fo.

74. Akeel Bilgrami's insight that subjective identity is that without which I would no longer be who I conceive myself to be, something "one ought not to revise" sets out a moving target and complicates the temporality of subject formation with respect to interior frontiers. Akeel Bilgrami, "Identity," *Political Concepts* 1 (2011): http://www.politicalconcepts.org/identity-akeel-bilgrami. As Judith Butler's claim that identity is responsive to changing notions of who I think I am in a present shaped by what I had wanted to be, could have been, and in relations to what acts upon me (Butler, *Senses of the Subject*, 8).

75. James Agee, *Let Us Now Praise Famous Men* [1939] (Boston: Houghton Mifflin, 2001), 96.

the too familiar are assaults or potential assaults on "feeling at home." Wherever one falls, safety and security are elusive. It is a space buttressed by a vicious fantasy that freedom comes from stronger barricades rather than embrace of the Hegelian mantra—the radical dependency of us all.

* * *

2

Weaponizing the Senses

I OFTEN THINK I HAVE written for almost forty years, relentlessly on the same subject: on the politics of knowledge, on what counts as the political and what counts as knowledge in conditions of colonial governance and duress. Sentiments, emotion, and sensibilities have been key to how I have come to track how relations of dominance work. Their distribution—and to whom certain sensibilities are ascribed—repeatedly have figured in how racialized power produces its categories, wields its force, and fortifies the inequities it seeks to impose. Often this is without acknowledgement, in bureaucratic denial, that emotions or sentiments matter at all. That work has kept me close to the distorted intimacies of colonial relations and the subjacent racial grammar of sentiment in the archives of governance and their literary shadows.

In teaching seminars on "Affective States" and the "Politics of Sentiment" for some twenty years, wondrous students have pushed me to make clear why certain kinds of queries about the tangled rapport between sentiments and governance are hard to pose, why I depart from the stringent distinctions often made between sensibilities, senses, sentiments, emotions, and affect, pushing instead on the range of composites they offer and engage. With generations of students, I've sought out the furrows where relations of power boldly or barely make their mark, to ask about the space between coercion and care that can hold those relations in tension. Here, there are no lesson plans to follow nor schema to master. For each occasion strains how the inscription of insolence or the appeal to *rancor, or the work of contempt, or a quixotic politics of shame does its work there and then, here and now.*

So, it came as some surprise to find that these were subjects I had taught about for years- far more than I had explicitly written about them. Some were about the powerful and elusive political critiques that a contest of sentiments offers, how certain affective registers allow particular claims. I was taken by how much sentiments were calibrated, and persons were ranked by them, when those sentiments—their intensity, their effect, the "proof" of those ascriptions—were at once minutely calibrated and did not succumb to measure. Colonial archives have drawn me repeatedly to ask what affective charges were emitted or checked on those documents' unedited edges. And the convoluted question that always returns: how did their authors think they knew what they also knew they did not?

This essay neither rehearses nor attempts to recoup that earlier work so much as pause in some of the spaces I have taught and thought. There is nothing comprehensive about it. It neither does justice to the enormous range of work that preceded the "affective turn," nor does it offer a condensed "catch-up" of the profusion of creatively undisciplined work since. It is rather the record of a more idiosyncratic venture that has been my own. In the early 1990s, the politics of sentiment guided me through the marginalia, the minor change of words, and fine print of colonial archives in ways I had not thought to explore before. These were documents that inconsistently denied some kinds of feeling and made a fearful fuss over others. Those distributions were never benign. They often turned out to cleave to what counted as a political concern and how it was affectively framed.

The politicality of the senses does something else. It presses on the conditions for potential critique that affective evaluations make, not unlike what Raymond Williams named a "structures of feeling," inchoate and on the horizon. My focus had been on those embodied forms of dis-ease, discomfort, and arrogance, cultivated, activated, and named. The concept of politicality strikes me as a demand to be attentive, not only to the forms of the political already in place, but to a more attuned sense of forms that sit differently in the borderlands of inequality.

The demand may be to attend less to brazen, irruptive resentments, than to protracted, cumulative, and quieter ones, to accretions that hide in accumulated mental and material rubbish that is too costly to remove. Might we treat these scenes as sites that offer a "diagnostic in reserve," a sub-metric of the fault lines of social bodies cleaved and fractured? These are the shatterzones where affect molds the very core of regimes of disparate truths.[1]

Finally: Two extraordinary pieces of history in a semi-autobiographical, semi-fictional mode have provided counsel to how I have thought and taught about affect and archives for decades: Carolyn Steedman's Landscape for a Good Woman (1986) *and Marguerite Duras'* Un barrage contre le pacifique (Seawall) (1950). *Both hew close to the fierce rapport of forever disappointed daughters and bitter mothers living on the social margins. Each are written inside those wounded lives. And for each, sensibilities bear political claims. Not only humiliations and indignations, but envy, jealousy, and revenge make livid the sites of damage and critiques of inequities that most class and colonial histories hardly find within their grasp.*

* * *

Aimé Césaire's *Non a l'humiliation* opens with his first day at the elite *lycée* Scholcher in Port-au-Prince.[2] It is 1924. He is twelve years old. Upon entry, he is accosted by the blonde-haired son of a *Béké* (a Martinician appellate for the ensconced, despised white colonial planters, military, and French elite) who taunts him by asking:

> "What are you doing here, mon petit? Are you keeping our satchels for us?"

---

1. On shatterzones see the prologue and the final essay devoted to these sites of intense pressure.
2. Aimé Césaire, *Non a l'humiliation* (Arles: Actes du Sud, 2014).

He saw from my reaction that I didn't understand, and the others noticed it as well.

"Ah, I'm sure of it; we were sent a guardian to watch our satchels"

In the guise of a smile, a grimace drew itself on his peach-colored lips. The others giggled. They couldn't let it go. The French teacher was watching us. The provocateur adjusted his impeccable jacket over his white shirt. Head straight, looking toward our Prof, he slipped very low, with cool composure (sang-froid) that suffocated me:

"It's fine that he watches our bags, sure, but still, he should be wearing decent pants. This rice sack that comes to his knees embarrasses me, you know what I mean? Let's get together and buy him some pants, real pants."

I thought my legs would shrink/collapse under my weight. None of this matters because it was clear. I was the peon Black in service. Thus the attacks. *It was the racial war*, the most predictable, a practicing sport for all. I had let down my guard as usual so the blow hit me with exceptional violence. Everything became ugly in and around me. A city that blacklists you because of your skin color is an ugly city, hideously ugly.

CIPHERS OF SUBORDINATION, WRITTEN IN CODE

Interior frontiers find sustenance in measured dispositions, calibrated exclusions, porosities sealed, leakages rapidly repaired. Their self-appointed guardians are alert and attentive to subtle codings of what and who belongs inside and out. *Gossamer borders can mark slits of distinction more finely than piled stone.* The material and unworldly are joined in that craftwork and figure in their maintenance. Some of the most stringent lines of demarcation are those barely visible, barely audible, derisions down dressed in nondescript clothes, hard to say how blindly or pointedly they were made and imposed.

In the submetrics of inequality, there is little that confounds and asserts those inequalities more than clusters of feeling that seem ready to gel into recognizable sentiments, then dissolve before leaving their mark or claiming a space. There is little that expresses and hides distinctions being made more than those packaged sentiments that lure good feeling and then dissemble into unacknowledged hierarchy again. Their furtive forms may avoid the common gestures that call out intended denigration. The messages remain mixed—the "care" curtailed by its unctuous display and performative pose. It is where pity slips to the edges of oblique humiliations. In the account that Aimé Césaire gives of his twelve-year-old self, humiliation was not couched. It was a knife that eviscerated his pride and shredded his clothes.

The metrics are ambiguous, but these are more than "the small daily indignities" that have come to be called "mico-agressions." There is nothing in the affective charge that is "micro" at all. Being hard to see does not diminish how they operate, nor reduce to a diminutive form nor to a lesser structurally consequential scale. They fragment the body and fix on its parts, flesh, size, sound, and smell, skin, what is rendered "noise," dissonant tone, speech mumbled, too loud or soft, inappropriate volume.

This is a fantastical world of racial shadows. As James Baldwin saw, it is just another space bracketed and protected by law, "the evidence of things not seen"—never passing muster enough to be considered evidence or violence at all.[3]

Within these exercised domains of differentiation, the calibration and distribution of sentiment can be key: sentiments may follow the fault lines of power or, in surges of refusal, cut a gash

---

3. James Baldwin, *The Evidence of Things Not Seen* (New York: Henry Holt and Company, 1985).

through the neat divisions that place the superior on one side and the inferior on the other. Refusals to abide by racial convention may reduce the burden of the ascribed affect, but not easily. The cipher of subordination, written in code, avoids the patent but still finds its mark.

For those dispositions valued in a racialized polity are precious—esteemed indices of worth that can confer supremacist status. In excess or absence (as in, too much pride or not enough), those ascriptions can wordlessly reduce a subject, or expose the underbelly of white vulnerability, fragile and more rigid in the face of the very white protocols its devoted members impose on themselves.

Might we think this iconic, brutal colonial scene, endowed with a politicality that traverses the senses. It is located in 1930s French *"Indochine,"* in the ultra-white plush quartier of colonial Saigon.[4] The account is that of Marguerite Duras in one of her finest autobiographical novels, *Un barrage contre le Pacifique* (translated in English somewhat flatly as *Seawall*). The central figure is the strikingly beautiful, seventeen-year-old Suzanne, Duras herself as a schoolgirl. Both the narrator and the author born in Saigon, one of the many places where Duras and her mother and brother lived, impoverished after her father's death and her mother's unsuccessful efforts to cultivate rice on a concession she was conned into buying on a worthless flooded plain.

The account and the affect are raw, both the spare writing and the deluge of emotions and sentiments called up—both desperately couched and mercilessly displayed. It is five o'clock in the evening in colonial Saigon on the high street, an avenue with a row of plush cafes reserved only for white rubber barons and other well-healed and high-ranking military and colonial administrators. There they took their coveted places for late afternoon drinks and repose. Suzanne is staying at the second-rate hotel down the

---

4. *Indochine Française* was made up of what is now Vietnam, Laos, and Cambodia.

road, run by her mother's acquaintance, Carmel, who suggests she strike out on her own (from her overbearing mother) and take her first walk alone in the latter's borrowed clothes.

The exquisite, poorly dressed Suzanne's climb to the fashionable High Street turns into a colonial passion play (the trial is short, the suffering hideous, the death imagined).[5] White heads turn, smiles of pity follow her. As Duras writes, she is "a stray" (*egarée*), wayward, out of place: "she did not know that a rigid order reigned there and that the categories of the inhabitants were so differentiated that you were lost if you could not manage to be classified in one of them."[6]

She passes by "them" pretending to not see their smirks. Not a word is spoken to her. She is shunned, for not having enough pride to know she should not display herself at five o'clock in a man's straw hat and tattered evening dress. She is mocked for having too much pride to imagine she could do so, unscathed. She is shameless, and casts shame on a white colonial sovereignty that is so ubiquitous it need not be named. Too much pride and not enough. Hate, shame, derision, and white arrogance draw the affective contours of an unspoken racialized politics, so potent it needs no speech, just a din and derisive glare.

Duras writes that the girl "imperceptibly" (*insensiblement*) realizes that she is, and looks, utterly ridiculous. It's a strange use of the word in both English and French because in fact everything she realizes is not imperceptible but identified through discernible perception, a visceral, sensory assault: the sound of whispers, the smell of their expensive perfume when clusters of coiffed women pass, the unfathomable comfort each show in belonging on that street, in that dress.

And her own ugly, disreputable image is played out in her head. She knows how they see her. Elegant high street is a place to be seen. There is nowhere to hide. Pity and disdain descend

---

5. Trial, suffering, and death are the three key elements of passion plays.
6. Marguerite Duras, *Un barrage contre le Pacifique* (Paris: Gallimard, 1986), 149.

on her body and mesh. She asks herself which of the ridiculous things about her are the worst. Duras writes (because she knows it too well):

> Her shame mounts steadily . . . She hated herself, everyone and everything . . . the dress too short and too tight. The straw hat. No one had one like that. This hair. No one wore it like that. But this was nothing. It was she, she who was contemptible from head to toe. Was it because of her eyes, where she cast them? Was it because of her gross arms? These pieces of trash, her heart, an indecent animal, her legs, incapable of offering support?[7]

The published English translation of the passage leaves out the separate odious words, "*ces ordures*," collapsing them into the preceding phrase. It is rendered in English as "these heavy and awful arms." But Duras' double entendre does more nuanced affective labor. It almost seems to confuse subject and object, making these despicable arms at once apart from, and of, her. Looking at herself as would the white colonial elite, she asks herself what is ridiculous. "*Ces ordures*" literally means "garbage," with "*ces*" ("these") referring back to her bulky arms, these gross things in which she is as if encased.[8]

The separate phrase and composite image are a sensory and emotional overload. She hates herself and them. She ricochets between self-loathing, their loathing, and her desire to annihilate each woman and man poised on the verandas she dares not

---

7. My translation. And the French:

. . . *cette robe . . . trop courte, trop étroite. De ce chapeau de paille, personne n'en avait un comme ça. De ces cheveux, personne n'en portait comme ça. Mais ce n'était rien. C'était elle, elle qui était méprisable des pieds à la tête. A cause de ses yeux, où les jeter? A cause de ces bras de plomb, ces ordures, à cause de ce cœur, une bête indécente, de ces jambes incapables . . .* . (Duras, *Un barrage*, 187).

8. Duras, *Un barrage*, 187. I thank Richard Rechtman for thinking with me about the strange and strained French wording that the English translation leaves out.

approach. As distraction, she conjures a theatrical, stupendous scene of her death. She imagines herself "gently dying," "stretched out in the gutter" for them to see.[9]

White arrogance produces a toxic mix. An unequal contest of racial etiquette defied, displaced, and displayed. And what was this image and imaginary of Suzanne's that so offended the senses? Contempt is the ultimate feature, the one that comments upon and orders all the rest. But contempt is not a steady state that stays where it belongs. If it is a way of "contesting relative rankings," there is no contest here.[10] Why would these obscenely rich colonial thieves even bother to be contemptuous of her? Duras tells us that she doesn't make it into even the lowliest colonial rank. Suzanne is in contempt of the racial order, herself an infraction of the racial law.

Contemptibility travels. It adheres to the one on whom it falls, who is claimed to elicit it. But being in contempt of someone else risks sullying the one who makes the accusation, spoken or not. Ancillary senses of disgust and contamination adhere.[11] William Miller writes: "Contempt can be a kind of defense against a fear of the contemptible."[12] Silent contempt and derision of poor whites are the marrow of colonial racial orders. Duras and her family knew that order too well.

The potency of contempt derives in part from its mobility but also from the multiple affective forms into which it plays. It is at once an emotional stance and a cultivated sentiment, both visceral and of the senses. For Suzanne, it does not dissipate with distance. It clings to her skin, her body and movements, not letting go. It is

---

9. Duras, *Seawall*, 151, and *Un barrage*, 187. Should there have been the "Ugly Laws" geared to the hierarchies that ordered a French colony, like those in the U.S. during those same years (that targeted certain populations for being abhorrent for the middle class to view), they might have included her. I discuss the "Ugly Laws" in two of this volume's essays: "(Dis)taste and Race" and "All Things Being Equal."

10. William I. Miller, *The Anatomy of Disgust* (Cambridge: Harvard University Press, 1997), 207.

11. Miller, *Anatomy*, 209.

12. Miller, *Anatomy*, 209.

embodied, a violence stored. Contempt exceeds definitional limits and delineations.

Can we say there is a politicality in this affective scene to which Duras has us bear witness? Is it in what she stirs in her readers, or what it awakens in Suzanne whose mortification produces a new knowledge of the racial regimes in which she did not know she was submerged? Or is the politicality one for Duras' own private reserve, animating her disgust, moving her to write with ferocity about and against colonialisms writ large and small? Her aim is exacting. It is weaponized against a specific, infested French colonial regime she craved to be part of, and abhorred.

As we know, a study of the emotions need not and might better not start with an emotion, or a sentiment at all. Sometimes, the actual conceptual work draws from attention to conditions of being and becoming that induce and animate affective responses neither necessarily nor intrinsically associated with them. I think of the concept of "duress" which I've described elsewhere, as:

> a pressure exerted, a troubled condition borne in the body, a force exercised on muscles and mind. It may bear no immediately visible sign or, alternatively it may manifest in a weakened constitution and attenuated capacity to bear its weight . . . when one is stripped of the wherewithal to have acted differently or better.[13]

The politicality of duress resides where despair, indignation, rage, and exhaustion meet, on the borderlands where one's wherewithal is stretched, with little room for resolve or repair.

Or one might think to how invocations of breathing, suffocation, and oxygenation have insisted on joining the material, affective, and metaphoric idioms of racial justice and the unequal

---

13. Ann Laura Stoler, *Duress: Imperial Durabilities in Our Times* (Durham: Duke University Press, 2016). 7.

distribution of racial violence and unbreathable air today.[14] Eric Garner's killing by a police officer in Staten Island in July 2014 has become the iconic context of racial injustice in the U.S. not because it was exceptional but precisely because it was egregiously not. Repeating eleven times, "I can't breathe," Eric Garner was officially declared dead by suffocation. The affective power of suffocation and racisms to animate political fury has a history. It infused the work of Aimé Césaire and Frantz Fanon as well, reminding us that those associations are not new.

Césaire's retelling of the striking racial confrontation with the privileged white boys in his all-white school in colonial Martinique in the 1920s was an assault, but it was not what took his breath away. His capacity to breathe was cut off by the unquestioned entitlement of a *béké*'s son to degrade him with utter *sangfroid*, sure of his inalienable right to do so. The only response was the silent applause of the jeering student chorus. But the scene Césaire describes is not confined to a still-shot in time. It is a site of political unfolding, almost a birthing of a will to say "*non*" for always to humiliation.

Humiliation is the term he calls on to capture the colonial scene of racial power, but it hardly stands alone. Interior frontiers are acceded to, challenged, and fortified with every interaction; pride blasted by shame, shame by fury, embarrassment for himself but also for his blonde classmate for stooping so low to initiate such a stupid set of racist acts. Hierarchies of color and status saturate every move the schoolboys make— white on white, mulatto on white, "petit-bourgeois blacks parading before the former two," bent on "whitening" their speech, their gestures, and very (e)motions. Acutely attuned to

---

14. "When breathing is political," Erasmus University Rotterdam, accessed May 13, 2021, https://www.eur.nl/en/news/when-breathing-political; Derek R. Ford, "Air and the Politics of Resistance," *The Aggregate Website* 2 (March 2021), http://www.we-aggregate.org/piece/air-and-the-politics-of-resistance.

this dense, defiling space of politicized affect, Césaire vows his liberation.[15]

Achille Mbembe's persistent focus on the formulations of "breathing," and "suffocation" in Fanon's work make ever more sense of the latter's concept-work, political force, and volcanic writing. Fanon's political attention to respiration calls out a right and demand to breathe—not racially rationed. Mbembe guides us through Fanon's prescient attention to the "social metabolisms" that colonialisms effect, the life forces they work to cut short, and can only curtail.[16]

How the passions, the political, and power configure have been central to the arts of governance, have been often far better understood by those thinking that alchemy in earlier centuries than our own. Such diverse political interlocutors as Machiavelli, Hume, and Vico among others took the passions as a political pharmakon—one set of passions (said Bacon, Spinoza, and Hume) a cure for another (less desired set), and the poison that fueled tyrannical power and illiberal rage.[17] By Hirschman's account, the harnessing of the passions was "the major tenet of 19th century liberalism."[18] And could it be that a spurring of ever more capitalist greed has been the imagined cure to too many liberal social provisions and neoliberal malaise?[19]

---

15. Césaire *L'humiliation*, 12.

16. Listen to Achille Mbembe's mesmerizing WISER lecture from the series, "Fanon after Fanon" on "breathing" delivered at Wiser, April 2021. Also see his discussion of breathing in a conversation with Paul Gilroy, Achille Mbembe, "SPRC In conversation with Achille Mbembe," interview by Paul Gilroy, UCL Sarah Parker Remond Centre, June 25, 2020, audio, https://www.ucl.ac.uk/institute-of-advanced-studies/publications/2020/jun/sprc-conversation-achille-mbembe.

17. See "Habits of a Colonial Heart" in Ann Laura Stoler, *Along the Archival Grain: Epistemic Anxieties and Colonial Common Sense* (Princeton: Princeton University Press, 2009), 57–73.

18. Albert Hirschman, *The Passions and the Interests* (Princeton: Princeton University Press, 1977), 19.

19. See Wendy Brown's always astute analysis of investments in social inequalities in Wendy Brown, *In the Ruins of Neoliberalism: The Rise of Antidemocratic Politics in the West* (New York: Columbia University Press, 2019).

But our landscape has changed. Kathleen Stewart's declarative statement, "power is a matter of the senses" demands no caveats, nor needs them.[20] We are in the throes, and have been for some time, of tracking the ways in which our porous beings and political dispositions work through our senses to challenge and change the relationalities we inhabit and the stability of who we think we are. We are in the throes of dissatisfaction with the limited ways used to describe the radical inequities in which some are forced to live. The politics of emotions, and the senses are being called upon to do new work. As Sara Ahmed writes, "pain is involved in the production of unequal effects."[21] But of course, it is not only pain. Remorse, shame, fear, and humiliation are productive of those distributions as well, pressing on some with more intensity than others, barricading other bodies against the permeabilities that allow us to change.

When, where, and by whom sentiments are expressed are occasions when relations of power are performed and put to the test. Some expressions seem submerged in affective registers we barely know how to name. James Scott draws on the term "infrapolitics" for what he called "the creative subterfuges of the disenfranchised."[22] But we might think it here to tap another subjacent vein. "Infrapolitics" could also describe those conditions in which the political saturates intimacies, draws envy into the political fray, or takes irritability (as Sianne Ngai reminds us that Aristotle did), as "one of anger's . . . excesses."[23] "Infrapolitics" could give expression to relations of power that call into question the most visible sites because they were identified with a high-definition lens.

---

20. Kathleen Stewart, *Ordinary Affects* (Durham: Duke University Press, 2007), xx.
21. Sara Ahmed, *The Cultural Politics of Emotion* (New York: Routledge, 2006), 31.
22. James Scott, *Domination and the Arts of Resistance: Hidden Transcripts* (New Haven: Yale University Press, 1990).
23. Sianne Ngai, *Ugly Feelings* (Cambridge: Harvard University Press, 2005), 182.

ON GRIDS OF SENSIBILITY

Sentience, sensibility, and sentiments constitute foundational features of regimes of truth—sometimes acknowledged, more often not. These are grids of sensibility on which trust is meted out (as Steven Shapin has famously shown us), sincerity is intuited, remorse is made credible, death sentences are conferred, durations of imprisonment are determined, innocence is restored, and guilt is assigned to its proper persons and quarters.[24]

Those who have studied the logos and pathos of colonial relations have good reasons to target the *assessment* of feeling, imputed feeling, anticipated sentiments, and unruly passions as the font of colonial racial politics. Hovering in the corridors of the visible and unseen, the palpable and recessed, there are "dense transfer points of power" where gradations of affordance and access to privilege and resources are subject to intricately crafted calculations.[25] The thought here is not of the high crescendo of emotional performance designed for public attention (of the defunct Trump, or Geert Wilders, or Bolsonaro's outraged denials of climate destruction, and Marine Le Pen's bid for mainstream French favor). Rather one might turn to the painful quiet of *lower-case* sentiments at lower frequencies, that act as *judgments* of a different intensity, a promise of hidden knowledge, be that of violent intent or moral character.[26]

Children in the colonies were a flashpoint of a sentimental education, colonial subjects in the making, groomed and

---

24. Steven Shapin, *The Social History of Truth* (Chicago: Chicago University Press, 1994).
25. Michel Foucault, *The History of Sexuality*, Vol 1 (New York: Vintage, 1976).
26. Robert Solomon, "On Emotions as Judgments," *American Philosophical Quarterly* 25, no. 2 (April 1988): 183–191 is a key intervention. Also see Linda M. G. Zerelli, "The Turn to Affect and the Problem of Judgment," *New Literary History* 46 (2015): 261–286. Unlike Zerelli, I would hold that affect is a way of knowing "that" and "how" in itself.

educated to avert and avow certain desires.[27] Within this intensely racialized and intimate space, misplaced attachments were taken as harbingers of danger, political adversaries in gestation. Affects were neither "pre-conscious" nor *distractions* from, or *supplements* to, political reason. On the contrary, as in Dutch colonial politics, they provided one of political reason's guiding constituent elements.[28]

RELATIONAL MEASURE OF WORTH

Attending, then, to the political force of affect locates specific technics of governance and sites of their making. Sensibility and sentiment are not outside the conceptual framing of politics. I see them rather as the very ballast of political concept formation. The point is a crucial conceptual and methodological one. I take sentiments to be *relational measures of comparative worth and value.* They instantiate prior relations of unequal worth. But more importantly, they are *productive* of those assignments.

Some affective dispositions stand out as those that designate who is high and low more forcefully than others: impertinence, shame, disgust, and contempt do some of that normative work. They mark who *should* act subordinately to whom and who is eligible to transgress that normative assignment—without a word. They mark who is affectively beholden and who is not (tapping into unspoken breaches of social and sexual contract, transgressions, and hidden costs). They demarcate who can pity, who can be pitied (with a requisite distance affirming safety for the pitying,

---

27. See "A Sentimental Education" in Ann Laura Stoler, *Carnal Knowledge and Imperial Power* (Berkley: University of California Press, 2002); but also earlier in Ann Laura Stoler, *Race and the Education of Desire* (Durham: Duke University Press, 1995), 95–164.
28. See Stoler, *Archival Grain*, 57–104.

as Luc Boltanski underscores).[29] Arendt was equally condemning; for her, a loquacious pity secures its heartfelt and contemptuous grammar.[30]

It is a *relational measure* that sentiments install, a form of *appraisal and deliberative assessment*.[31] Politically this *deliberative* feature is key. It may be about where one stands in relation to others, the desert or lack of desert with which one is treated, looked at, touched, or physically avoided, spoken to, regarded, and in turn assessed.[32]

It is hard to miss a new appreciation that they are a font of judgment, deliberation, and subterranean critique. Robert Solomon's understanding of that relationship has encouraged that move. Still, there are features of his insight that go unremarked. For one, he reminds us that judgment and emotion do not enjoy a one-to-one correspondence. Two, emotions are not, as often assumed, the *effect of prior judgments* alone (though they may be). Rather, the enactment of an emotion is an assessment in itself. It is in the very fact of feeling shame, envy, or rage, where the judgment is inscribed.

The distinction is crucial to how we might consider what feelings do. Such a treatment gives something like "jealousy" more than the status of a mean-spirited, petty reaction. Rather than banishing jealousy as a poor source of reliable information, it might assume an informational status with political valence (as we'll see it does it for Carolyn Steedman).

---

29. Luc Boltanski, "The Politics of Pity," in *Distant Suffering: Morality, Media and Politics* (New York: Cambridge University Press, 1999), 3–19.

30. Hannah Arendt, *On Revolution* (New York: Viking, 1963), 80–81.

31. Martha Nussbaum addresses this feature of appraisal leaving, at once unstated but implied, the relations of power that emotion appraises and describes. See Martha Nussbaum, "Emotions as Judgments of Value," in *Upheavals of Thought: The Intelligence of Emotions* (Cambridge: Cambridge University Press, 2001), 19–88.

32. "Desert" here follows the philosophical use of the term, as the condition of being deserving or not.

Jealousy says much more than it is often granted. It emerges as that on the cusp of a right denied, *the quiver of a claim*. Jealousy becomes a diagnostic of things we are not supposed to long for because, "all things being equal," those of the same class are assumed to have similar access to what they want, in the dark borderlands of desires and deprivations.

This feature of embodied judgment is not unlike Aristotle's formulation of anger, for what he described is not that flash of non-containment (as anger is so often parsed). Rather Aristotle leads us to the affective perception that points to and is animated by *an offense*—against the assumed equality of a relationship and the stronger truth of disparity.[33] This discrepancy between what is and what was assumed to be the case carries political weight, well beyond a mere recognition that expectations do not align.

Might we not consider emotions as emphatic or incipient assertions of much more than information? Might they be considered rather as an evaluative veridiction and verdicts "in formation"? This is not the claim that the emotional outburst tells the truth of the self. Nor does it embrace the Freudian understanding that the most repressed emotion is the "real" and has the ultimate truth-telling properties and truth exposing function. Nor does a "veridiction in formation" imply indictment or closure. Rather it is to argue that emotion may be a veridiction about the very terms of a relationship of power, about the lower recesses of subordination—a testing ground of sorts with almost a juridical inflection.

For in the folds of a disagreement about how one should be treated is a contested judgment of worth, a scene that "dramatizes an order of truth."[34] At issue then is not only the disdain expressed

---

33. See Danielle Allen, *The World of Prometheus: The Politics of Punishing in Democratic Athens* (Princeton: Princeton University Press, 2000), 81.
34. Michel Foucault, *Wrong-Doing and Truth-Telling: The Function of Avowal in Justice*, eds. Fabienne Brion and Bernard E. Harcourt (Chicago: University of Chicago Press, 2014), 38.

but what assertion of the right to show that disdain says about the inequality of that relation and the broader structured inequalities in which it is sanctioned and lodged. That "right to show" rarely enters the equation of inequality. But it is foundational. It builds on the very conditions of possibility that allows you that affordance, and not me. Thus the "aboutness" of emotions is not just about an object but about an unequal relationality.

Emotions, we know, are not free-standing "things"—irruptive by-products of thought, "momentary intrusions." They might better be understood as accretions of stored deliberation, as elements in what we might call a "calculus of relational estimation." Emotions are relational practices, *demonstrative interpretative labor for others to witness as well as for oneself.* Sentiments may build on prior beliefs. Or, those beliefs may be forged, as with indignation, in the subjacent recognition of one's treatment as unworthy, registering a perceived injury that can morph into a politicized sensibility in the intensity of the emotion itself.

Such a treatment would do away with any notion of singular judgments attached to any singular emotion. For envy can fold into desire, conflating—as Sianne Ngai argues in *Ugly Feelings*—the "wishing to be" and "wishing to have."[35] Humiliations may morph into fury, registering the unjust or turn to self-loathing and silence. Shame may be refitted as pride as with Gay Pride (with pride not canceling out shame but fueled and transformed by it). And disdain manifests as well as with words, in a non-verbal register, pleasurable and satisfying at another's cost.

Sianne Ngai's pause between "wishing to be" and "wishing to have" counts among those insights that makes conceptual leaps, unadorned with jargon. Little can be more consequential in the dictions of inequality than this distinction. For it speaks to those ubiquitous white imaginings that everyone else in the world wants

---

35. Ngai, *Ugly Feelings*, 152. The distinction is one that Freud made, as Ngai notes, in a different context, 144.

to be white. The "wishing to be" is a white fiction, refusing the fact that what is desired is not who they are, only what they garnered but never earned. A past and contemporary colonial history of racisms could be written off that insight alone.

"Wishing to have" rather than "wishing to be" captures a political insight almost too straightforward to be taken up. It sabotages European colonial whites' fantasies, deflates the pretension that wishing to be white or wishing to have what white colonials had were the only choices and desires for those whose worlds were not dictated by those desires.

ON BEING "SHORN OF GRACE"

Carolyn Steedman's *Landscape for a Good Woman* takes a range of feelings as the bedrock of class belonging. And it is that very complicit and contradictory range that makes for the competing realities that go into the messy affiliations of class. I know of no work that so disrupts and disallows simple readings of what it means to be forever wanting, not dirt poor, nor middle class. It is where the privileges of class belonging are not felt, granted, or affirmed among those in the unnamed lower rungs, with the longing for certain things, shaping class and character.

Steedman's account is passionately spare and perhaps most nuanced in detailing the ways in which emotions, desires, sentiments are the very material substance of the landscapes she describes and the stories she tells. Hers is an account at odds with the conventional descriptions of class. For its acute points of access are precisely those feelings so often relegated to the non-political, gendered, petty and private. Not least they are feelings attributed to irritated women, obsessed by desires that made motherhood trying, that made having children burdensome, and that positioned those children as always in the way—of work, rest, romance, and a future. Housework, children, and factory labor made up the constraints, accentuated in harsh and dulled corners of a life, especially that of mothers. What Steedman calls the "structures of deprivation" to which her mother was subject were tinged with rancor because they were precisely the features of her life that excluded her from imagined pleasures and assured others how much they belonged.

The resonance with Marguerite Duras' account is uncanny, both hinging on an "envy of those who belong."[36] Envy emerges as a political concept, indeed a "proper envy" is "of those who possess what one has been denied."[37] The envy doesn't only fall on persons, it congeals around things that one can have, wear, be in possession of, stash away for an unexpected fabulated day: "But there are people everywhere waiting for you to slip up, to show signs of dirtiness and stupidity, so that they can send you back where you belong."[38]

Steedman's bitter fury is not only at a mother who resented that her daughter could not "pay back" the cost of her existence; every line her mother utters, every line Steedman remembers bears witness to an emotional and financial cost. "Never have children, dear, they ruin your life."[39] The "dear" is not intimate, not tender. It's more like a sword. It is the "dear" that sends shivers down the spine of middle-class friends, she would say. Still, she claims to find the warning an honest and good one.

By Steedman's own account, *Landscape for a Good Woman* was something of a "cathartic" project.[40] I saw it as the only work I knew that actually materialized what a structure of feeling might look like, as Raymond Williams described the term, deeply present but "beyond semantic availability," occupying both figure and ground.[41] But the book was also her response to those many

---

36. Carolyn Steedman, *Landscape for a Good Woman* (London: Virago Press, 1986), 17.
37. Steedman, *Landscape*, 123.
38. Steedman, *Landscape*, 34.
39. Steedman, *Landscape*, 17.
40. A CSST post-lecture conversation, University of Michigan, Ann Arbor, 1992.
41. Raymond Williams, "Structures of Feeling," in *Marxism and Literature* (Oxford: Oxford University Press, 1977).

middle-class readers who wanted to empathize with her (and with whom she could be curt, impatient and turn away, knowing, as she wrote in the preface, that if she hadn't "made it," any of her now university colleagues could have been one of the women for whom she worked, cleaning their toilets, doing their wash).

Nothing escapes her acute attention to the details of difference—and her contempt. No one can read her account without knowing that the politics of wanting is located in her mother's "terrible tiredness and her terrible resentment," and without knowing that Steedman knew it was because of her.[42] Steedman mocks these brave mothers and their sons who describe them as women with "flinty courage" they so admire and adore.[43] No one evades her knowing, sensory appraisal of the unstated distinctions that divide and exclude. None escape her gaze.

How does politicality manifest in this harsh sensorium? In every word, in every thread and fold of cloth. Steedman calls on her perception of "childhood experience" as the "lineament of adult political analysis."[44] That line still stops me short. Out on the borderlands, potentialities are crushed, sparkling impossibilities don't have room to happen. Steedman has us take longing so seriously there is no moment when it doesn't burnish relations and singe the flesh.

She asks us to look to longing and nostalgia for what one has never been afforded; instead of approval, one's neat shabbiness eliciting pity and disgust. It's the 1950s, on the outskirts of English propriety. It is where the yearning for the cut of a dress was not a metaphor for class desires but the substance of them. The cut of the dress was the materiality of that moment. It was the cut of a dress that dilated envy, the ample yardage that some could afford, the longing it instilled in those who could not.

42. Steedman, *Landscape*, 39.
43. Steedman, *Landscape*, 17.
44. Steedman, *Landscape*, 7.

Both yearning and yardage contrast the uncomfortable pull of a straitened skirt that prevented one from mounting a bus with grace. It was at once a trivial, unmarked marker of disparities of a class deprived of opportunity. A gesture that one could hide by turning one's leg in, so the tight fit was not as easy to notice. Steedman calls on her mother's words to pin the sense of things not being "really fair" out on the class margins where one is rendered envious and shorn of grace.[45] It is a societal foothold denied to one who always and never really feels to belong. Alienation as a class concept has hardly been made to do enough work.[46] What is not there? There are no heirlooms to pass down, only wants and longings passed between generations. There are no clothes to savor from another time, no family albums of all the occasions to remember and rehearse. I haven't even mentioned her ever present, hated, absent father and the illegitimacy that she and her sister bore, when they learned of their out-of-wedlock births.

Freighted with different degrees of presence and intensity, sentiment dissolves as a thing, emerging in cold light as a process of minute calibrations whose opacities may not adequately yield to ready political recognition—or to the mandates of epistemic or methodological clarity. In critical question is how we really *know* the sentiments and emotions of others and what is the political purchase invested in the misrecognition (and the assertive claim of resolute and unquestioned recognition) of what others are construed to feel?

---

45. Steedman, *Landscape*, 47.
46. In a very first essay on affect, "Thinking through Sentiment in Political Economy," I tried to tackle what it could mean to treat Marx's concept of "alienation" through the affective spaces it produced and responded. American Anthropological Association Meetings, 1990. Teaching a seminar on Affective States this year, I find myself back to "alienation" again with a richer sense of its affective weight and material implications.

Common treatments of sentiments in and outside academe have long shared an implicit understanding about sentiment's distinguishing feature: a mark which serves as a vague measure of the "distance" between emotion and deliberative reason. What is affective might be defined by the *gradations of deliberative reason* that it is hardly accorded, where different kinds of sentiments are construed to be located in a hierarchical scale of proper thought. Not only might certain affects be considered in contrast to "reason" and "rationality," and thus inappropriate in considering what constitutes "truth;" as such, they could be banished from the domain of real "cognition."

It was a misplaced move. Susan James rightly chided moral and political philosophers some twenty-five years ago for "systematically ignoring" the sentiments as "a central topic in the heartland of early modern philosophy."[47] The social sciences were not doing much better, but there are always exceptions. Albert Hirschman was a luminous one. Forty years ago, in *The Passions and the Interests* he constructed a genealogy of statecraft so remarkable and alien to those then writing on the subject that his book was not recognized as part of the same subject or conversation.[48]

Setting reason aside, Hirschman surveyed how improvements in statecraft and the arts of governance have been perceived over three hundred years, how the work of the sentiments, both the unruly passions and the more benign ones, were understood alternatively to be harnessed, diverted, or countervailed, in governing the self, and in governing others. Affect here is not ancillary but politically center stage. The modulation and calculus of its distribution (among governing and governed) is what Hirschman considered statecraft to be

---

47. Susan James, *Passion and Action: The Emotions in Seventeenth-Century Philosophy* (Oxford: Clarendon Press, 1997), 15–17.
48. Hirschman, *Passions*.

about. It was a critical insight that his many laudatory reviewers never mentioned.

Still, Hirschman must have shared some common assumptions about the capacities of learned men and gentlemen. Did he assume that discerning the passions of others was a non-issue? Or, perhaps, that interpretive labor didn't need to be mentioned? As Steven Shapin has argued for seventeenth century England, "All 'normal' gentleman were deemed to be *perceptually competent (emphasis added)*—indeed the reports of such people largely defined what perceptual competence was."[49] Gentlemen and political philosophers were endowed. "It was they ['normal' gentlemen] who were considered to be *competent sensory agents (emphasis added)*" and thus able to evaluate truth.

Those were consequential assumptions. For knowing other people's mind is a feat, a fiction, an illusion, and one of the richest fields in cognitive psychology. What is called "theory of mind" (though we might want to refer to it as "theory of other minds") is devoted to the subject. As a field, it addresses the interpretation and prediction of behavior based on the ability to attribute unseen mental states (of belief, feeling, intent) to others.[50] It is an ability and interpretive labor on which the politics of affect depends. For at the nexus of sentiment and power is knowing how to know, assess, with "perceptual" mastery being the ostensible source of interpretive authority.[51] It is somewhat extraordinary how little we who grapple with the history and politics of sentiment focus on the competencies required to make assessments about the "sincerity" of affective states, be they of remorse, "proper envy," or rightful rage.

---

49. Shapin, *Social History*, 75–78.

50. On "theory of mind" (that is the minds of others) see the classic formulation by David Premack and Guy Woodruf, "Does the Chimpanzee have a Theory of Mind?" *Behavior and Brain Sciences* 1, no. 4 (1978): 515–526.

51. Shapin, *Social History*, 75.

RECOGNIZING REMORSE

Assessments of affect in the law is where I began work on racial categories some thirty-five years ago: on how colonial authorities imagined they could measure the feelings, sensibilities, and intents of others and how they imagined these were properties and dispositions they could know. The display and distribution of sentiment were key to judgments of racialized essence and character, their ascription a form of judgment (and indictment) in itself.

A few Dutch words prompted me to pursue what I had not done before. They appeared in a 1884 official document stipulating what it took for a "native" to be granted the status of European equivalence in a colonial court of law. The nature of the evidence was impossibly vague; the requirement was that the person "no longer *feel at home* in his native being." My reaction was both to the imaginary behind and beyond the phrase and to what it said: the assumed capacity to ascribe how another felt. By what criteria one might demonstrate an adequate distance from being at ease and feeling "at home"? By what criteria could Dutch authorities imagine they could make that assessment? Who would be charged and qualified to do so, and what might count as sufficient proof?[52] Attribution of race, character, and capacities for feeling were called upon. Could we have ever imagined that they should remain dangerous disquiets of the law today?

Michel Foucault, in his 1981 College de France lectures, called avowal (as quoted by Bernard Harcourt) "the thorn, the splinter, the wound, the vanishing point, the breach in the entire penal system." For it demands confession not only of what a person did but who s/he is (or what s/he *must be*) in order to have done what s/he did.[53] As most etymological entries for remorse rehearse, the

---

52. For an earlier discussion of this document and colonial attributions to what someone else is imagined to feel, see "Sexual Affronts and Racial Frontiers" in Stoler, *Carnal Knowledge*, 79–111, and "Habits of a Colonial Heart" in Stoler, *Archival Grain*, 57–104.

53. Foucault, *Wrong-doing*, 228.

notion derives from the verb *mordere* to bite and from the Latin, *remord*, to bite again. Turning back on oneself, this reflection on one's deeds and an owning of them, render remorse as the ultimate expression of avowal and thus a critical site of jurisprudence.

Avowal may be the law's lynch pin, but remorse and remorselessness expose recurrent breaches in the penal and legal systems that give primacy to emotion by conflating its expression as an "authentic" source of character. Arguably, no emotional evaluations are more consequential than those that decide on the evidence of remorse in the law. Few tells us more about the arbitrary, irregular, incoherent nature of juridical decision-making. But the nature of how remorse is defined and adjudicated also tells us about something more: about race and the law and the changes that have not been made and are being sought in criminal sentencing.

The secular state does not look very secular when we look at remorse. Confession, repentance, and explicit, manifest signs of suffering are three of the key ingredients in sentencing. Again, the *OED* defines remorse as "a deep regret for doing something [morally] wrong, the fact or state of feeling sorrow for committing a sin, repentance, compunction."[54] Note that in the *OED* the question is about "having" remorse. In the law, it is about "showing" remorse through identifiable, culturally mandated display. For remorse there is no fixed or agreed upon measure. It is where the arbitrary submetrics of racial inequality is at its compromised low and biased best. Decisions on capital punishment are literally decided by an arbitrary "sense," "perception," for evaluating truth and "deep character."

But the decision that a defendant is remorseless does much more. It is a banishment from the social body. It is a cultivated sentiment and an emotive only guaranteed by displayed suffering. The sub-metric is so varied and subjective, it is hard to imagine that this is the site where veridictions are evaluated and put to the

---

54. *Oxford English Dictionary*, 2nd ed. 20 vols. (Oxford: Oxford University Press) Continually updated at https://www.oed.com.

test.⁵⁵ Racism thrives in this space. Morality is only recognized if it abides by the local conventions of assessment by these particular judges in this court of law.

In a striking essay on "Remorse and Demeanor in the Courtroom," Susan Bandes looks at the consequences of misinterpretation, condemning a justice system that relegates remorse to a non-issue.⁵⁶ As she argues, its role in the criminal justice system garners a rich literature, but HOW remorse can be evaluated has not. Note: remorse is key but has no agreed upon measure.

REMORSELESSNESS IS NOT THE OPPOSITE OF REMORSE

If the subject of remorse is unevenly present, remorselessness receives less attention. It is a striking omission, for remorselessness is something different all together from remorse. It is *not* remorse's opposite, a point never addressed. To be without remorse is considered more than a negative affect. It is conferred a different salience and indexical weight. Remorselessness almost stands in a world of its own, endowed with a fundamental and other sort of truth. It is a condition of being, a disposition that sticks to the person, not the deed.

Some argue that remorselessness is the absence of an emotion, an incapacity of feeling empathy that reflects not the act so much as the quality of the person that exceeds the act. But it could also be argued that remorse is not an absence of an emotion but

---

55. Rocksheng Zhong, "Judging Remorse," *New York Review of Law and Social Change* 39 (2015): 133–172.

56. Susan A. Bandes, "Remorse, Demeanor, and the Consequences of Misinterpretation: The Limits of Law as a Window into the Soul," *Journal of Law, Religion and State* 3 (2014): 170–199; and Susan Bandes, "Remorse and Demeanor in the Courtroom: Cognitive Science and the Evaluation of Contrition," in *The Integrity of Criminal Process: From Theory to Practice*, eds. Jill Hunter, Paul Roberts, Simon N. M. Young, and David Dixon (Portland: Hart Publishing, 2016).

a matter of having the wrong ones. The qualities associated with remorselessness cover an extensive list of negative features. They are deemed evident in character, disposition, and behavior, far more than those tied to remorse. They include rigidity, stubbornness, relentlessness, obstinacy, and unyielding behavior. Each association suggests a willingness to contravene or a refusal to comply.

And unlike remorse (which in contemporary use is no longer tied to its earlier sense of compassion and pity), a person without remorse is still associated with one who knows neither compassion, pity, nor compunction. Remorselessness expresses more than the negative of remorse's earlier definition. One is condemned for being a person who does not know remorse, and for having no remorse with respect to a given criminal act. Whatever the sentence may be for a misdeed, remorselessness doubles the indictment again.

If remorse is a promise to act in the future and feel in a particular way, remorselessness verifies something else. It is not and cannot be the opposite of remorse or its absence. In standard dictionaries, being "remorseless" is defined by being merciless and relentless first of all.[57] But various thesauri offer it as a synonym for a broader range of recalcitrant and hardened dispositions. Obstinacy, incompliance, obduracy, implacability, and cruelty are among them.[58] The list is an extensive and moral indictment. Remorse, on the contrary, is endowed with ethical approval whereas a remorseless person is outside the pale of societal norms and punished more severely on multiple counts. Being remorseless is a humanitarian and human affront, a heretical act before humanity and the law.

57. "Remorseless," Google dictionary, accessed May 12, 2021, https://www.google.com/search?q=google+dictionary&rlz=1C5CHFA_enUS840US840&oq=google+dictionary&aqs=chrome..69i57j0i51213j0i131i433i512j0i51215.2244j0j4&sourceid=chrome&ie=UTF-8#dobs=remorseless.
58. "Remorselessness," Thesaurus.com, accessed May 13, 2021, https://www.thesaurus.com/browse/remorselessness.

In the case of evidence of remorselessness (or the intuitively assessed sense of it), punishment may be for a lack of submission to the normative demands of the law, for being inept or incapable of showing contrition in the requisite forms that make the contrition legible, or for remaining non-compliant to society's moral demands. The law wants remorse demonstrated vis-à-vis a prior act, but the law also wants a show of shame before oneself, in the courtroom, the Levinasian evidence that one has not fled from oneself, a sign of redeemed character.

In the DSM-V, the lack of remorse was one of the key diagnostics of psychopathic behavior. It's a risk factor for future violence and evidence of an "antisocial personality disorder."[59] The moral condemnation of remorselessness is intense and pervasive in and out of the legal system, despite numerous studies finding no correlation between it and the propensity for future violence.[60] Still, it remains a firm justification for giving more severe sentences. Demonstration and recognition of remorse, versus its lack, mark the difference between a commuted death sentence vs. one righteously enforced. Remorseful defendants receive lighter sentences than those judged to be without remorse.[61]

Studies of how judges and jurors identify remorse are chilling. As Bandes and Zhong both argue "the role of remorse in the legal system remains unresolved."[62] It is "a poorly formulated concept,

---

59. John F. Edens, Shannon E. Kelley, Scott O., Lilienfeld, Jennifer L. Skeem, and Kevin S. Douglas, "DSM-5 Antisocial Personality Disorder: Predictive Validity in a Prison Sample," *Law and Human Behavior* 39, no. 2 (April 2015): 123–129.

60. Mark Warr, "Crime and Regret," *Emotion Review* 8, no. 3 (2016): 231–239; Ryan Charles Meldrum, Alex R. Piquero, Turgut Ozkan, and Zachary A. Powell, "An Examination of the Criminological Consequences and Correlates of Remorselessness During Adolescence," *Youth Violence and Juvenile Justice* 16, no. 3 (2018): 279–298.

61. Zhong, "Judging Remorse," 133, makes the crucial point that although judges agreed "that remorse was a valid legal construct they disagreed about . . . the indicators of remorse: behaviors that suggested remorsefulness to some judges suggested remorselessness to others."

62. Rocksheng Zhong, Madelon Baranoski, Neal Geigenson, et al. "'So You're Sorry?' The Role of Remorse in Criminal Law," *Journal of the American Academy of Psychiatry and Law* 42, no.1 (2014): 39.

lacking clarity and uniformity in both its definition and the characteristics that signal its presence or absence."[63] Some judges take "greater levels of detail" in verbal statements to indicate "greater levels of sincerity;" others depend on a gestural economy, where "breaking down, being overwhelmed, not paying attention, or being distant" are the telling cues.[64] The following were differently weighted in assessment whether remorse was present or not: "crying, facial expression, leering, sneering, remaining expressionless, tone of voice, eye contact, lack of eye contact, head hanging, putting one's head down, looking up, looking down, looking around, and fidgeting."[65] The list is terrifying, so arbitrary it is hard to fathom in a court of racial law. Or maybe not.

The most disturbing feature in the decisions about remorse rival colonial regimes of truth that imagined that Judeo-Christian criteria allowed one to "see" "deep character," with demeanor serving as the measure of "candor" and "credibility." Decisions about life are at stake: remorse is *the* crucial fact in determining whether the defendant is sentenced to death." More restrictive prison conditions and denial of parole, pardon, or clemency follow the same logic.

Remorse (unlike some other sentiments that garner more agreed upon, recognizable measures) is one whose truth-value remains opaque. It is where access to others' minds is assumed to be transparent if one is gifted with the necessary competencies. Few judges could pass that test. In such a system of standards, young men of color are most vulnerable to its quixotic and obtuse logic. In juvenile court, not showing remorse (something many youth never show, regardless of race) can lead to a felony charge and transfer to an adult court.[66]

---

63. Zhong et al., "'So You're Sorry?'," 39; and see Stephen J. Morse, "Commentary: Reflections on Remorse," *Journal of the American Academy of Psychiatry and the Law* 42 (March 2014): 49–55.
64. Zhong et al. "'So You're Sorry?'," 43.
65. Zhong et al. "'So You're Sorry?'," 43.
66. Martha Grace Duncan, "So Young and So Untender: Remorseless Children and the Expectations of the Law," *Columbia Law Review* 102 (2002): 1469; also see

Race is a critical factor in whether a death penalty is administered or not.[67] In the moral economy of remorse, countless studies show that "black defendants" "are always viewed as more likely to repeat a crime, regardless of the crime in question. The evidence of remorse is close to pre-emptive: both an *anticipatory judgment* and an evaluation of *affective disposition* that tells the truth of an irreparable flaw in one's "deep character." Compassion is limited to those undeserving of suffering. Those who are remorseless are treated as insufficiently suffering and thus deserving of harsher measures.

On the face of it, remorselessness has no explicit political valence. But it figures in a moral economy, counting as a charge against those not deemed to inhabit a moral habitus that is "our" own. But it is also an act as well as an inner state. Might it be an observant act among those who see the life conditions of privation committed against them as unjust, thus refusing remorse for what they refuse penitence? These are conditions in which a disavowal of acquiescence to remorse can be a truth-telling act.

Might we treat remorselessness not as a sure sign of immorality but as a rejection of another sort, as an appraisal of a subject, a set of judgments defiant, refusing to subscribe to to this morally bankrupt universe and to another ethical code? It might be considered a truth-claim in itself, an exposure of the subterfuges of the law. Might it even be considered a form of *paressia*?[68] If so, it would need to adhere to some of the basic requirements of the

---

Leanne ten Brinke and Sarah Macdonald, "Crocodile Tears: Facial, Verbal and Body Language Behaviors Association with Genuine and Fabricated Remorse," *Law and Human Behavior* 36, no. 1 (2012): 51–59.

67. See Bryan H. Ward, "Sentencing without Remorse," *Loyola University of Chicago Law Journal* 38 (Fall 2006): 131–167; Richard Weisman, *Showing Remorse: Law and the Social Control of Emotion* (Burlington: Ashgate, 2014); M. Eve Hanan, "Remorse Bias," *University of Nevada, Las Vegas School of Law* 83, no. 1144 (2018): 302–356.

68. Michel Foucault, *Discourse and Truth and Parresia*, eds. Henri-Paul Fruchaud and Daniele Lorenzini (Chicago: Chicago University Press, 2019).

ancient Greek definition of truth: (l) spoken in the agora of public declaration—here, the courtroom, (2) a rejection of a certain authority—of the state and its penal system, and (3) an act that puts one at mortal risk and subject to death. Remorselessness returns us not to the criminal deed but to the "deep character" of one whose assault on the normative requirement to genuinely feel or feign to feel remorse could be a political emotive in itself.

Affects bears political import in obvious and subjacent ways that still beg to be further explored. They figure at the crux of political claims because they are bodily, personal, and of the senses. Understanding humiliation as a political claim, and anger as Aristotle understood it, as a right denied, opens to a radically different methodology. As importantly, it challenges the definition of what counts as political, the means and measures of what asserts and deserves to be understood as a political demand and political claim. It may be that we need to be more brazen in calling out the political valence such sentiments express, and more humble about what we know and can politically assess about what we hardly know enough.

3

(Dis)taste of Race

Neither amnesia, nor disgust, nor irony produce even the shadow of a critique.[1]

"TASTE IS A SOCIAL RELATIONSHIP made flesh."[2] These are the final words of the English language translation of the postscript, and the final words of Pierre Bourdieu's five-hundred-page monumental study, *Distinction: A Social Critique of the Judgment of Taste*. One might imagine that "flesh" would figure prominently in a treatment of the judgments of high and low culture, their criteria of consumption, and their rankings of approval and disdain. For surely the flesh's portals, hues, porosities, and receptors are alive to the demands of taste. But that is only partly the case. For

---

1. Louis Althusser, *For Marx* (New York: Verso, 1965), 9. Friends and colleagues are to be thanked for helping me think through different parts and versions of this essay's making. I first wrote about the absence of race in Bourdieu's *Distinction* in "Colonial Aphasia" *Public Culture*, 2011. In 2017, Eric Fassin and Patricia Williams joined me for a short interlude to imagine what an ethnographic project on *Distinction* read through race might entail. Our respective, ongoing projects truncated the time we had to work together. I thank both for the excitement that moment generated in my pursuit of a deeper conceptual if not ethnographic encounter with the text. In 2020, I returned to the project with a different focus, both on Bourdieu's treatment of taste and race, and on the features of Kant's critique of judgment that has shaped how subsequent generations of commentators have understood aesthetic judgment and followed Kant's lead or dissented from it. The essay in this form owes much to the comments of Étienne Balibar, Jay Bernstein, E. Valentine Daniel, and Lawrence Hirschfeld. Thanks to Lewis Gordon who provided comments on the final version.
2. Pierre Bourdieu, *Distinction: A Social Critique of the Judgement of Taste* (Cambridge: Harvard University Press, 1984), 500.

the translation is misleading. In French, Bourdieu wrote: "taste is a social relationship *incorporé, devenu nature*," i.e., "embodied" and that, literally, "has become (second) nature."[3]

We might consider "made flesh"—the translation of *"devenu nature"*—constituting what Barbara Cassin has called "a symptom of difference" between languages or locating "a word situated within the measurable differences among languages."[4] Or it may simply display the license given to (or taken by) a gifted translator. In either case, the equivocal equivalence (or non-equivalence of the translation) does what the best translation does; it pries open a partially shuttered window, makes us notice and hesitate before a door ajar. Here, on that threshold, ambiguities about the faculties on which taste depends are drawn to our attention.

"Made flesh" seems to locate a feature that pulls at the seams of Bourdieu's frame, what one had not come to see, or ask, before. For if taste is "made flesh," it suggests that taste is acquired, constituted from what was not of the flesh before. Is it that "taste" comes to saturate the skin, to make taste a substance fused to the flesh? "Made flesh" invokes inscription, branding, imprints on the body, and scars. One may wonder how one of the most embodied forms of stigmatized social ranking, race, seems to garner no comment or place. Racialized sensibilities, those that confer esteem or distaste, status or disgust are somehow not present to the study's interlocutors responding to queries on taste, nor does it surface in the array of bourgeois disparities in value tracked when the first surveys were initiated some fifty years ago.

The effect today is almost startling where issues of race, disdain for immigrants, derision of headscarves, and a press and

---

3. Pierre Bourdieu, *La distinction: critique social du jugement* (Paris: Minuit, 1979), 585. The French reads: "On voit que le sens de la distinction philosophique n'est qu'une forme de ce dégoût viscéral de la vulgarité qui définit le goût pur comme rapport social incorporé, devenu nature."

4. Barbara Cassin, ed., *Dictionary of Untranslatibles: A Philosophical Lexicon* (Princeton: Princeton University Press, 2014), originally published as *Vocabulaire européen des philosophies: Dictionnaire des intraduisibles* (Paris: Seuil, 2004), vii.

large swaths of France's middle-class have no compunction about denigrating those of Muslim faith. One doesn't need to go as far as the (in)famous and provocative right-wing French novelist Michel Houellebecq, who declared that "reading the Koran is a disgusting/despicable thing," to appreciate how much what is "disgusting" or distasteful today is that which refuses to endorse secular (Christian) Republican family values.[5] "Good taste" remains surprisingly stable, but what constitutes tasteless behavior is shunned. Dinner party decorum where taste is adjudicated in understated repartee is a place for clever, muted erudition about religion and politics but not race.

The negative sanction on letting discussion of race "intrude" in practicing good social behavior is not the issue so much as the unacknowledged presence of race in coding what constitutes the proper comportments and competencies of social behavior at all. Little of this would have even been broached during the years of Bourdieu's surveys.[6] Although launched as a project near the end of the Algerian war, and just two years after the October 1961 vigil of more than thirty thousand Algerians, of whom two to three hundred were killed, *Distinction*'s interlocutors (as far we know) invoked no trace of (nor even mutely registered) that deadly night on a Paris bridge.[7]

---

5. Mohammed Aissaoui, "Houellebecq et *Plateforme:* 'La region la plus con, c'est quand même l'islam'," *Le Figaro*, December 10, 2014, https://www.lefigaro.fr/livres/2014/12/30/03005-20141230ARTFIG00159-houellebecq-et-plateforme-la-religion-la-plus-con-c-est-quand-meme-l-islam.php.

6. Most of the empirical research for the *Distinction* project was done in the 1960s, in 1963 and again in 1967–1968. For a discussion of the methods used, the groups, over and under-represented, and the range of surveys employed, see Appendix 1, "Some Reflections on Method," especially pp. 505–518.

7. It was first estimated by the French police that there were "a few deaths" following the protest of some 30,000 Algerians opposing the curfew imposed on them by the Paris police. Following French President François Hollande's acknowledgement fifty-one years later of what is now recognized as a massacre, the number of those killed has been more recently estimated to be close to 300.

Then, and long afterwards, it was decidedly in "bad taste" (and would have been contrary to the official silence) in many French circles to mention the massacre and

The treatment of taste as "embodied social relations" is bodily, thus, in only limited ways. In *Distinction*'s explicit emphasis on the "profits of distinction" that taste affords, those qualities that evoke distaste and disgust (revulsion, convulsion, physical withdrawal, gagging, vomit, or merely a shudder and turn away) hover in the shadows.[8] Unnamed they remain outside the metric, displaced beyond even the popular and "vulgar" by which Bourdieu rightly identified "taste" itself as a French bourgeois conceit, rejected by the working class.

French of color, *Harkis* sequestered in France's forest hamlets, North Africans, French Jews, and Roma, some on the borderlands of being French, some French citizens in their own right, are they not relevant to the problematic posed? Nor were the categories of resident, citizen, refugee, or migrant enlisted. Whether a racial calculus might have distributed "taste" along other faultlines was not raised or perhaps insistently excluded from the conversation. Subsumed into the classes where they were imagined to "belong" (as one might argue in defense of *Distinction*'s broad class rubrics), those wedged on France's interior frontiers had neither presence nor place.[9]

the number of Algerian bodies thrown in the Seine. To what extent Bourdieu and his interviewing team thought to (or thought it appropriate to) ask about the "mannerless" decorum of Algerian French is not recorded in Bourdieu's writing nor in that of others. If television shows and media outlets had different audiences with different "tastes," as *Distinction* chronicles, one would expect that news and information sources did so as well. As Bourdieu and his team show, on the subject of taste and "tastelessness," there was and could be no consensus.

8. Bourdieu, *Distinction*, 5.
9. This was the case even in the sections of *Distinction* devoted to describing the "underrepresented" groups where there is an important brief discussion on why those excluded from "legitimate culture" were not included in the survey. These largely consisted of "the most disadvantaged category, that of the semi-skilled workers and unskilled labourers, who are very uniform with regard to the object of the survey, i.e., very uniformly excluded from legitimate culture," Bourdieu, *Distinction*, 505. The conclusion is interesting: that the most important information gleaned from

But the omission is strange since Bourdieu himself underscored that the French criteria of taste rested "first and foremost on distaste, disgust provoked by horror or visceral intolerance [vomit-provoking], of the tastes of others."[10] The insight could be considered the key to the entire work, but the project and the hundreds of questions the interviewers posed to one thousand two hundred and seventeen people did not broach that observation. The project skirts *where* and on *whom* the distaste of the ugly resides. It offers scant guidance to how the abhorred, unsightly, or unseemly might inflect the distribution of those persons and things coveted or contaminating, and what degrees of disdain, humiliation, or envy went with those assessments. Circumventing how disgust demarcates space and sense of place in the discernments of the everyday, the segregationist geopolitics of race and taste are missed by *Distinction*'s radar. If *colonial aphasia*, as I have argued for sometime, describes something of the absented/present nature of racism and colonial history in France over the last sixty-five years, *Distinction* might serve as one site of its instantiation (a circumvention that fewer French would be wont to absent from their memory, speech, and everyday today).[11]

This essay pivots on the grammar of taste and distaste in the politics of differentiations, in the subterrain of racial distinctions, and in the (sub)metrics of inequality. If taste is at once "*a mode of knowing*" and one critical marker of community, as the philosopher Hans-Georg Gadamer argued, distaste sets out the distorted

---

a preliminary survey among farmers was their ready and "universal recognition of the dominant culture. "

10. Bourdieu, *Distinction*, 56.
11. See "Colonial Aphasia: Disabled Histories and Race in France," in Ann Laura Stoler, *Duress: Imperial Durabilities in Our Times* (Durham: Duke University Press, 2016), 68–121.

interior frontiers fortified by racial distinctions made too thick to breech—and yet too banal and too patent to be named.[12]

> *It's a rainy afternoon [*Distinction *is about to hit France's bookstore shelves] in March 1979. Paris is dark, cold, wet, and I'm working at home struggling to write my dissertation. My partner, L. is trying to affix a wire that runs across the ceiling of our rez-de chaussée, ground-floor apartment. We don't have a ladder. So, L. calls our dear, middle-aged neighbor (always correct in dress and demeanor) across the courtyard with his wife (who too is always neat and carefully coiffed.) He speedily comes over with his ladder, offering his* bonhomie *and help.*
>
> *The conversation turns to taste, that of those small* coquilles *in garlic and white wine sauce and how to cook them (we had just returned from Honfleur on the northern coast, collecting a bucket-full on an empty beach on a blustery day). L. and monsieur T. had become comrades in labor at that moment and with a gesture affirming their comradery our neighbor looks up at L. on the ladder and says, "Me, I don't like Jews. Do you?"*

Taste and distaste meld in the pursuit of affiliation. This sort of affinity that harnesses a negation—of what one is not—was not quite what Gadamer was after when he noted how closely taste and community adhere. But it was one that Bourdieu identified as key to the power of taste, at once foundational to the project but methodologically suspended. As a form of "data," *Distinction* does not pursue it further. Still, in avoiding what is deemed too disgusting to behold, touch or smell, *Distinction* succumbs to a particular French common sense that refuses to ask how the making and remaking of racial categories is and has long been threaded through the fabric of the Republic's governance and the self-fabrication of France.

---

12. Hans-Georg Gadamer, *Truth and Method* [1960] (New York: Continuum, 1999), 36, 35–48.

TENSIONS OF TASTES: KANT AND BOURDIEU

Bourdieu's affordance of primacy to taste in the making of power is staged in reference to and as an assault on the canonical notion of taste grounded in Kant's 1790 *Critique of Judgment*.[13] Moving between taste and distaste demands at least a preliminary turn to the distinctions that Kant drew between two kinds of taste and the kinds of judgment they required: one that offers an epistemic challenge and is a compelling subject of inquiry, and one that is neither. "Pure taste" is Kant's subject. "Vulgar" taste is not. That "pure taste" cannot be learned and cannot be taught is fundamental. This for Kant is a "taste of reflection." What Kant will call either "vulgar" (or sometimes "barbaric") taste in contrast is "taught and learned."[14]

Bourdieu's critique is both simple and multiplex. He will at once dismantle the artifice of two kinds of taste, as he destroys their distinguishing foundations, then reworks them as class dispositions, calling out the elitist interests that "pure taste" defends. His assault is less on Kant than on the then current conceits of aesthetic theory, the pretensions of philosophy, and the arrogant and entitled priorities and unacknowledged premises of academe and the French bourgeoisie.

The "disinterestedness" that "pure taste" demands is one of Bourdieu's targets:

> Objectively and subjectively aesthetic stances adopted in matters like cosmetics, clothing or home decoration are opportunities to experience or assert one's position in social space, as a rank to be upheld or a distance to be kept... transforming the basic dispositions of a lifestyle into a system of aesthetic principles, objective

---

13. Immanuel Kant, *Critique of Judgement* [1951], trans. J.H. Bernard (New York: Hafner Press, 1974).
14. Kant, *Critique*, 48.

difference into elective distinctions, passive options . . . into conscious elective choices are in fact reserved for members of the dominant class.[15]

Bourdieu levels his gaze on the requirement of "disinterestedness" that "pure taste" demands, looking to reveal the intense social labor of its production and the accretion of power it enables. For he was after something else: to show that both "pure" and "barbaric" taste were embedded in class dispositions transformed into principles: cultivated, and taught silently, yet explicitly, and emphatically by visual and verbal example in school, in the media, and in the home.

Still, his critique is not an all-out rejection of Kant's claims. Probably Bourdieu's most compelling insight about taste is shared with Kant. It is one, I would argue, on which the deepest forms of discriminatory power thrive. In Kant's rendition, taste is a form of knowledge that exudes certitude as it *evades what it is that actually is known. Certitude and ambiguity co-reside.* This insight will take us to places neither Kant nor Bourdieu found opportune or worthwhile to go.

To return to Bourdieu's sense of taste as *"devenu nature"* (has become [second] nature) or as translated in English, "embodied social relations, made flesh": the phrase points to the subjacent, implicit register in which taste is sometimes understood. Still, it barely captures nor seeks to explore the range of affective and epistemic features on which it depends that we shall see hew so close to those affective and epistemic features of racisms: *as something learned but that cannot easily be taught, again, a form of knowledge that evades what it is that actually is known, as a "feeling" that is not a proper emotion—a formulation hard to decipher.*

Elements of the instinctive that build on intuitive awareness and join with the play of the imagination are often invoked as crucial modes of knowing in Kantian accounts (always leaving

---

15. Bourdieu, *Distinction*, 57.

unspecified what it is that the instinctive or intuitive animate, or when they come to the fore, always seeming to remain immeasurable and indeterminant).[16] No explicit grammar of taste shows the way. In Kant's reckoning, concepts are not needed, nor legitimately convened for "pure taste." Concept-work is not required.[17] On the other hand, imagination—that capacity to synthesize sensibility, understanding, and intuition—must be strategically activated and deployed.[18]

Pure taste's requirement of "disinterestedness" in Kant's iconic telling entails other requirements and effects. Foremost, it is both a criterium and criterion explicitly barring the supplements of "charm" and "emotion," each of which would disqualify a judgement of "pure taste." "Barbaric" or "vulgar" taste in contrast, as he famously put it, "would" need (remembering that his is a normative script) and depend on those wholly unworthy supplements, especially deplored when serving as a "measure of assent."[19] Pure taste would call on neither. And finally, (though we have just begun) taste is something so engrained, it need not really call up labored thought—but a unique amalgam that activates at once understanding, intuition, and the senses.

Affect is excluded from Kant's equation. In Bourdieu's, where one might expect it to flourish, it remains unexamined. Not because it is not there on the social landscape; nor because he has not sought to measure its destructive force. As Bourdieu writes

---

16. The fact that the "intuitive" must be present without being "determinant" is one instance of the way in which the "presence" of intuition matters, leaving unaddressed *how it does so*. For a critical discussion of Kant's theory of the imagination see Donald W. Crawford, *Kant's Aesthetic Theory* (Madison: University of Wisconsin Press, 1974), esp. 79-89.

17. Kant, *Critique*, 45. By Kant's casting, "taste" is neither a "cognitive judgement," nor even a cognition. It is closer to a "feeling" and "thus is not *based* on concepts...." The italics are Kant's (or what form an italic-equivalent might have taken in the late-eighteenth century). A few pages later, he writes that it does not "presuppose a definite concept." Kant, *Critique*, 52. See also Kant, *Critique*, 142, 184.

18. Kant, *Critique*, 52.

19. Kant, *Critique*, 58.

with respect to taste, it needs to be secured by "finding the right distance":

> There is no better opportunity to observe the functioning of this sense of the place one occupies than *in condescension strategies* (*emphasis added*), which presuppose both in the author of the strategy and in the victims a practical knowledge of the gap between the place really occupied and the place fictitiously indicated by the behavior adopted.[20]

Still, humiliation, envy, indignance, anger, and scorn are barely present. This is so, despite the fact that this (sub)metrics of value (on what and to whom condescenion is directed) is as sharply distributed as the values assigned to the allocated commodities and the uses to which they are put.[21]

For Kant, there are no final lists on which to settle. Taste is circumscribed by a cascade of positive and negative attributes and special properties, in his authoritative (if much disputed) assessment, a *unique* way of knowing. With different intensities of emphasis, the judgment of taste must count on a mix of faculties and forms of knowing: feeling, intuition, imagination, and an always unspecified set of cognitions that are not conceptual.[22]

This finely tuned and ill-formed recipe for how this particular "knowledge-thing [is] assembled" cannot be benign.[23] As I argue

---

20. Bourdieu, *Distinction*, 472.
21. Bourdieu, *Distinction*, 21. As Bourdieu repeatedly reminds the reader, the value of the products is derived, not from the product, but the uses to which it is put.
22. Gadamer, *Truth*, 41. Gadamer credits this move of Kant's as "epoch-making," limiting "the concept of knowledge to the theoretical and practical use of reason" (Gadamer, *Truth*, 40n71) and thereby contributing to cast aesthetics and taste askew to the central concerns of philosophy.
23. "How knowledge things are assembled" was Paul Rabinow's elegantly parsed definition for "fieldwork in philosophy" in *Anthropos Today*, an analytic insight so understated by Rabinow that it has been too easily by-passed and unappreciated as a powerful methodological point of entry. See Paul Rabinow, *Anthropos Today: Reflections on Modern Equipment* (Princeton: Princeton University Press, 2003), 85.

here, its coordinates bear an uncanny and powerful resonance with the ensemble of knowledge practices on which racial regimes of truth and the crafting of race are based. This is not to claim they are sewn from the same cloth or necessarily aligned, except in the sense that subjacent regimes of power build on ambiguities, on essentialisms that are protean and subject to change.

These ambiguities and essentialisms carry criteria of exclusion which are insistently clear and elusive, demarcated by boundaries that expand and contract, neither fixed nor articulated.[24] Like racial regimes of truth, criteria of taste seem unequivocal, yet hard to grasp. At issue is an assertion of clarity and ineffability at the same time, intuitive knowledge taken as trustworthy because, in Kantian aesthetics, it is assumed to be almost involuntary, disinterested, shared, and more real. Not unlike "gut feelings," this is knowing "in the flesh," not tethered to the capacity to say *how* one knows.

KNOWING WHEN AND KNOWING HOW

Bourdieu's mapping of taste works off what he takes to be Kant's spurious distinctions, turning them against the pretensions he sees them producing and protecting. In his mapping of the dispositions and elements that make up taste, calculated investment and strategic differentiation are crucial criteria, measures of ascent [and assent], that shape one's proclivities—which concerts to attend, what foods "satisfy" and "taste good," what counts as appropriate dress, and from which stores they should be provided.

Both implicit and explicit education of sentiment and desire make for ways of being in the world and dispositions toward the things deemed worthy of being consumed. *How* to consume is as

---

24. See "Racial Regimes of Truth" in Stoler, *Duress*, 237–265.

important as *what* is consumed; as in Gilbert Ryle's important distinction between "knowing what" and "knowing how," where the former is so often overvalued at the expense of the latter.[25] Indeed "knowing how" is the mark of good taste, as is when, where, and with whom to do what. Timing, as with ridicule, is key, where the "when" is a subtle feature of "knowing how."

"Others" may be contemptuously identified by not getting these timings right, or by not knowing what they are and how they work. "Crass," ostentatious, fast expenditures can warrant a disdain for not knowing the "how." Differentiation, and contrast to those not so cultivated, is the searing mark of social hierarchies. These distinctions are predicated on minute, hard to decipher, and sometimes outright illegible metrics. Still, accessing legibility offers no automatic ticket for entry.

GADAMER ON COMMUNITY AND THE POWER OF TASTE

If Bourdieu finds a violence in taste, Hans-Georg Gadamer, master hermeneutician, finds a treasure. Indeed, Gadamer opens his 1960 opus *Truth and Method* with the power of taste strategically founding his analysis. Here the power of taste to make and seal community along with common sense are taken as formative steps in defining "an ideal of genuine humanity," where taste once was (and should be considered?) more than an aesthetic.[26] For Gadamer:

---

25. Ryle's famous distinction between "knowing what" vs. "knowing how" frames some of the issues raised in the next essay as well. See Gilbert Ryle, "Knowing How and Knowing That: The Presidential Address," Meeting of the Aristotelian Society at the University of London Club, November 5, 1945, 1–16.

26. To note: Kant's notion of common sense is perhaps unique and not one connoted today. His *sensus communis*, as Sofie Rosenfeld notes, is a "perplexing" one. She writes, it "is *common* sense only insofar as it is communal." In Kant's words, "a critical faculty which in its reflective act takes account (*a priori*) of the mode of

A sensory differentiation of taste, which accepts or rejects in the most immediate way, is in fact not *merely an instinct*, but strikes *a balance between sensory instinct and intellectual freedom* (emphasis added). The sense of taste is able to gain the distance necessary, choosing and *judging* what is the most urgent necessity of life.[27]

This amalgamation of feeling, instinct, and judgment joined with an unknowable form of differentiation make for a concept that almost falls outside the rubrics of a concept and any familiar conventional frame. No matter. For Gadamer, taste is a prime mover, a fundamental and critical site for what makes us human. By his reading of Kant, taste is what offers the true sense of community, at once an index of community and an "intellectual faculty of differentiation." When Gadamer argues that "taste operates in a community without subservience to it," it is not clear whether taste is prescriptive and authoritative or guided by its more intuitive qualities.[28]

Bourdieu may be the ultimate sociographer of taste, but it is Gadamer's understanding of taste that is more suggestive for treating taste and distaste in the same field. Arguing that before Kant, the "concept of taste was originally more a moral than an aesthetic idea," it is this earlier sensibility Gadamer is intent to revalue and restore. It is taste he argues that Kant shows to be an "obscure kind of judgment called *feeling*."[29]

---

representation of everyone else . . . to weigh its judgment with the collective reason of mankind." Rosenfeld comments: "In Kant's telling, all judgments of taste both depended on and were actually synonymous with *this kind of* (emphasis added) common sense." See Sophie Rosenfeld, *Common Sense: A Political History* (Cambridge: Harvard University Press, 2011), 223. Cf. to Gadamer who argues, "*The sensus communis* plays no part in Kant." Gadamer, *Truth*, 33. But also see Gadamer, *Truth*, 43–44 where he is more equivocal.

27. Gadamer, *Truth*, 35.
28. Gadamer, *Truth*, 37.
29. Gadamer, *Truth*, 35.

Gadamer rails against Kantian aesthetic categories, taking taste to provide the glue of shared values (which he does not see as unwelcome constraint) in the making and prescriptions of our social worlds.[30] But Gadamer is not on Bourdieu's radar, the key predecessor he addresses is Kant, who endows elite scholasticism with honors.[31] Gadamer gets no mention, in part because Bourdieu's arrow is—as he slyly admits—somewhat parochial. Aside from Kant, it targets the class posturing of his contemporaries—Paris' elite circles, highbrow affectations, self-satisfied liberal intellectuals, curated dinner conversations, manicured and polished with the right shade, shoes and club chairs with the patina of well-cured leather, music that tempers the evening with an unknown aria that evinces iconoclastic cultural breadth.

For Gadamer, on the other hand, taste can help us choose and judge "what is the most urgent necessity of life." Its chilling underside is that distaste can justify the urgent necessity for protecting that life against others. (Dis)taste marks out more than a "moral and social sentiment" as William Miller contends but a "moral judgment," far more invidious—a boundary making scission between us and them.[32]

DIVERGENT EXPERTISE ON TASTE AND DISTASTE

My interest here is in what taste and distaste each tell about the other and in how the two are joined. One of the striking features of treatments of taste and distaste/disgust (*goût* and *dégoût* that in

---

30. Gadamer, *Truth*, 34.
31. This is aside from Bourdieu's diatribe against Derrida's refusal "to withdraw from the philosophical game" and who too takes disgust to be the "true origins of pure taste." Bourdieu, *Distinction*, 494–495.
32. William Miller, *The Anatomy of Disgust* (Cambridge: Harvard University Press, 1997), 2.

French retains a proximity unavailable in English, and a reckoning that English seems more easily to evade) is how rarely they are approached as convergent, or even mutually relevant subjects of inquiry and forms of assessment.

Their historical ontologies are rarely broached in the literature of aesthetic philosophy. They inhabit different spaces of expertise (their experts groomed in different disciplinary quarters). They, literally, rarely meet on the same page.[33] Studies of taste and aesthetic taste typically—whether explicating, conversing, or disagreeing with Kant, or in considering those before Kant—make no mention of disgust or distaste. Aesthetics, dedicated to the beautiful (and only by minor accord to the ugly, not considered its opposite) is shaped by Kant's definition and the subjects it is imagined to preclude from rightful attention.[34] A narrow treatment of the ugly limits the possible objects and subjects of scrutiny, so much so that virtually anything that might be considered part of the aesthetics of race, rather than the "sociology of aesthetics," remains outside consideration.[35]

Can judgments of taste and distaste really be assessed with no reference to their contiguities and contingencies? Can they be treated as virtually incommensurable social phenomena? It is hard to imagine. Martha Nussbaum's excavation of the work of disgust is a nuanced if oblique take on the problem. In her perspective, prevailing assumptions about how disgust figures are a "determinant

---

33. Miller is among notable exceptions. He briefly reads Bourdieu and less so Kant, to agree with the latter that "Taste manifests itself by refusing, by turning away in disgust, by recoiling at that which bears the marks of the vulgar, easy, cloying and cheap. The disgusting is that which poses no resistance" (Miller, *Anatomy*, 169). Unfortunately, this insightful reference to Kant and Bourdieu is limited to a page.

34. On the ugly in Kant's treatment of taste, see H.E. Allison who briefly discusses it in "The Analytic of the Beautiful and the *quid facti*," in *Kant's Theory of Taste: A Reading of the Critique of Aesthetic Judgment* (New York: Cambridge University Press, 2001).

35. Keijo Rahkonen, "Bourdieu and Nietzsche: Taste as a Struggle," in *The Legacy of Pierre Bourdieu: Critical Essays*, eds. Simon Susen and Bryan S. Turner (London: Anthem Press, 2011), 126.

of both social norms and lawmaking."[36] She attributes disgust's appeal to its reliability as "an expression of deep-seated social conventions," a "warning sign," and most importantly as a "'wisdom' that lies beneath rationale argument."[37]

The problem of course, as she underscores, is the kind of "wisdom" that disgust supports and conveys. She compels us to ask whose reactions of disgust are being measured and what sort of "wisdom" social conventions yield. Disgust is a social disapproval rating, but approval ratings that good taste might confer are not her concern. Her analytics of disgust addresses sexual orientation and the norms fortified in constitutional law. The oppressive, patriarchal, heteronormative is deemed self-evident. Bourdieu's excavation of taste and the subjacent mode in which he signals its vulgar coordinates has no place in her references, nor does Kant's *Critique of Judgment*.[38]

Giorgio Agamben's 2015 essay, "Gusto" ("Taste"), although disappointingly slim, too underscores this "knowledge that is not known."[39] The move from Plato to Lévi-Strauss occurs in a few brief pages, but even with brevity, he too identifies the strange qualities of taste, as if beyond epistemic limits, "excessive" and out of reach.[40] Still, his treatment of *gusto* so bypasses *disgusto*'s coordinates that one almost wants to remind him of what he has insisted upon: that those to whom "bare life" is assigned (the diseased, deprived, derelict, disabled, those conjured as producers of squalor and dirt, who wear them as a "second skin") are the subalterns in the power play of taste. Alas, *disgusto* for Agamben has no place.[41] He neither breaches nor

---

36. Martha Nussbaum, *From Disgust to Humanity: Sexual Orientation and Constitutional Law* (New York: Oxford, 2010), xx.
37. Nussbaum, *Disgust*, 10–11.
38. Also see Martha Nussbaum, *Hiding from Humanity; Disgust, Shame, and the Law* (Princeton: Princeton University Press, 2004).
39. Giorgio Agamben, *Gusto* (Macerata: Quodlibert, 2017).
40. Agamben, *Gusto*, 43.
41. Agamben, *Gusto*, 27. Referring to Leibniz's suggestion that "Taste as distinct from intellect consists in *confused* (*emphasis added*) perceptions that we cannot sufficiently clarify." Agamben too suggests that "It is something close to an instinct."

broaches the affinities of the two terms, nor how and when they are severed or joined.

From one of the most luminous artisans of concept work, Raymond Williams, "Taste" merits but a brief entry in *Keywords*, bereft of the rich social etymology offered for other terms. Always attentive to the elitisms that vocabularies harbor, Williams notes taste to be a "quick discerning faculty," transformed into a "generalized polite attribute" by the eighteenth century—"equivalent to discrimination."[42] Of course Williams is right that inculcated habits and discriminatory rules are crucial. Still, the entry feels almost truncated, not subject to the deep political genealogies he usually offers, ending abruptly on a wanting and as-if-unfinished note, the consumer.

The disgust that taste harbors, the disdain and disparagement on which it thrives seems a missed opportunity to do what Williams always did best: to provide his reader with a seemingly innocent and innocuous word's unexpected genealogy and counter-intuitive features. Here it might have been to taste's counterpoints, to those "structures of [ugly] feeling" where contempt may be semantically out of reach but easily conveyed.[43]

Distinction, on the other hand, treats the social power that taste commands as the crescendo of dominance, as the condensed elements of power with only attenuated discussion of what one could argue is at the crux of his work: the abysmal and almost inescapable depths to which those without taste are assigned, the revulsion they elicit, the disgusting class of contaminating beings into which they fall. The point is crucial for his conceptual methodology and the discussion that follows.

Returning to Bourdieu, his account of taste rests longer with its seemingly simple but complex mode of discernment. *Le goût* is a marker and metric with enormous power precisely because its

---

42. Raymond Williams, *Keywords: A Vocabulary of Culture and Society* (London: Fontana, 1976), 264–266, 264.
43. On "structures of feeling" see Williams, *Keywords*, 128–135.

criteria defy easy articulation, while new sites and renewed habits can alter its calibrations and expand or contract its breadth. Adopting the appropriate disposition toward endorsed cultural artefacts, be they in the fields of music, the graphic arts, literature, or electronic media, is a trained inclination, cultivated by some classes and carefully not cultivated by others.

Clearly it was neither a phenomenology of taste nor distaste that Bourdieu was after.[44] Still, the fine-grained gradations of taste so carefully noted never open to gradations of distaste, poor taste, and tastelessness, or to those on whom those denigrations and contaminating properties fall. It would have been far more difficult not to include the issue of racialized subjects if the metrics of distaste had been treated with the same attention as was taste.

RACE, TASTE, AND "A SENSE OF ONE'S PLACE"

"... finding the right distance..."[45]
Taste is a practical mastery of distributions which makes it possible to sense or intuit what is likely (or unlikely) to befall—and there to befit—an individual occupying a given position in social space. It functions as a sort of social orientation, a "sense of one's place"... It implies a practical anticipation of what the social mean and value of the chosen practice or thing will probably be.[46]

"A sense of one's place" as Bourdieu described the proper and pernicious requirements of "taste" is precisely what distaste and

---

44. On what a phenomenology of taste might look like, and the distinct sorts of questions asked, see, for example, Barry C. Smith, "The Nature of Sensory Experience: The Case of Taste and Tasting," *Phenomenology and Mind* 4 (2013): 212–227.

45. Bourdieu also cites those interviewed who referred to "finding the right distance," (*trouver la juste distance*), (*garder ses distances*), (*tenir à distance*) by means of a sort of practical calculus (Bourdieu, *La distinction*, 550; Bourdieu, *Distinction*, 472).

46. Bourdieu, *Distinction*, 466.

disgust police: "knowing one's place."⁴⁷ Addressing taste as that "obscure kind of judgment called *feeling*," that is more than an instinct but viscerally charged, Gadamer might be said to add to taste's ambiguous status; for he enjoins us to question what is a "faculty" and what is not. In asserting taste to be "a faculty of differentiation," Gadamer joins the "faculties" as did Kant, naming taste's lustrous capacity "to strike a balance between the sensory and the intellectual."⁴⁸

Nothing could more succinctly describe the racial *dispositifs* in which regimes of governance invest. But Bourdieu's allusion to "a sort of social orientation" with respect to "knowing one's place" mutes the violence of that command when it comes to race. This is not a vague "social orientation." For a young Black/Algerian/Arab man it is a warning not to stray, not to show your face here, not to cross a line.⁴⁹ Don't run in Central Park without a runner's outfit and gear that shouts "runner" and assures the white world around you that you are not running from the police, a theft, or scene of rape, or something else conjured in common sense racist imaginaries.⁵⁰ But "being tasteful" does not come with getting the outfit "right," nor with access to racialized rules of knowledge that will neither threaten nor transgress "knowing one's place." Neither confer taste if you get it right (for the "wrong" kind of person), only the mortal danger that comes with getting "it" wrong.

Strikingly, Nussbaum's and Bourdieu's accounts of what disgust and taste demand are very much the same; hers

---

47. Bourdieu, *Distinction*, 467.
48. Gadamer, *Truth*, 35.
49. In a particular perceptive text on the 1992 LA riots, Lewis Gordon identifies a similar phenomenon as "illicit appearance—the absence, that is, of the right of appearance." In Lewis Gordon, "Of Illicit Appearance: The L.A. Riots/Rebellion as a Portent of Things to Come," *TruthOut*, May 12, 2012, https://truthout.org/articles/of-illicit-appearance.
50. See Melanie Eversley, "Running While Black: Ahmaud Arbery's Killing Reveals Runners' Shared Fears of Profiling," *The Undefeated*, May 8, 2020, https://theundefeated.com/features/running-while-black-ahmaud-arberys-killing-reveals-runners-shared-fears-of-profiling/.

focused on sexual orientation, his on class, neither addressing the racial coordinates of their observations. Both claim taste and distaste to be a metrics of demarcation and sites of power. Taste and distaste are each considered "visceral" responses. For Nussbaum and Bourdieu, distaste and taste enlist an imaginary—one of contagious and contaminating substances, one of fictively fashioned claims to expertise and superiority.[51] Both terms animate practices that attempt to constrain the geopolitics of movement and emit precautions about "overstepping" borders. Privileges are guarded, social frontiers are not to be crossed, protocols of mobility and arrest need to be honored.

NOT KNOWING HOW ONE KNOWS

> *Taste is an acquired disposition to "differentiate" and "appreciate," as Kant says—in other words, to establish and mark differences by a process of distinction which is not (or not necessarily) a distinct knowledge . . . since it ensures recognition (in an ordinary sense) of the object* without implying knowledge of the distinctive features which define it *(emphasis added).*[52]

This "distinct knowledge" that does not imply "knowledge of the distinctive features which define it" is the quality that Kant confers on taste as one of its defining features, its unique singularity. It renders taste an unwieldy sort of thing—at once a faculty, a disposition, a form of appraisal based neither on rules of logic, nor on a concept, but increments of feeling. As one particularly devoted Kantian commentator writes, "the major difference between judgments of taste and moral judgments is that, in the case of the

---

51. On "the distance to be kept," (Bourdieu 1979: 57) and a "sense of one's place" (1979: 471). On the designation of the disgusting as power, Nussbaum, *Disgust*, xx.
52. Bourdieu, *Distinction*, 466.

former, the rule grounding the judgment cannot be stated."[53] It is not only that it "cannot" be stated; it cannot function as "an objective principle," it is "unstatable," with no identifiable rule that governs its use.[54]

The conventions that often assign taste and disgust to disparate fields of analytic operation and practical application seem confused and contradictory. Both occupy abstruse epistemic ground for we don't know the rules of use. Taste is considered a faculty, distaste and disgust are not. Both rely on imagination. The intuitive and unreflective are crucial for both, but hard to discern despite the power they wield in ordering the evaluative worth of social kinds. Both act on the "lower frequencies" of inequity; that is, they may submit to a gestural economy in which they need not be vocally expressed, as in the making of racialized relations.

Thinking with and against many who have engaged how taste matters and the constitutive features that make it up, I continue to pull here on a translucent thread, a starkly perceptible and invisible stitching in which race as embodied difference is entangled. For taste, in this wondrous, fantastical regime of truth, has a peculiar quality: it is at once a "mode of knowing" (as Gadamer would call it) ironically that cannot be known, a faculty that cannot be subject to disagreement, but is nonetheless "curiously decisive."[55] Kant's "disinterestedness" loses its prime salience for Gadamer, who underscores the "surety" one has in accepting or rejecting that something meets the measure of good taste (with hardly a nod to the privilege necessary to meet his criteria). "Good taste" comes with "no hesitation, *no surreptitious glances at others* (*emphasis added*), no searching for reasons."[56]

Clearly Gadamer's taste is a social phenomenon but more tellingly, it is an eminently *performative* and therefore *relational*

---

53. H.E. Allison, "The Modality of Taste and *Sensus Communis*," in *Kant's Theory of Taste*, ed. H. E. Allison (Cambridge: Cambridge University Press, 2001), 147.
54. Allison, "Modality," 147.
55. Gadamer, *Truth*, 36.
56. Gadamer, *Truth*, 36.

one. It should be played out, and works best, in the presence of an appreciative audience: the phrase, "no surreptitious glances at others" speaks to an unspoken gestural grammar in which "glances at others" can compromise a display of assurance. The phrase deserves a discussion of its own. Taste here forms the basis of a curated scene borne of confidence, privilege, trust that one's own judgment is in accord with those of an audience equally invested in the credibility of status that "good taste" confers.

Taste then is more than a social phenomenon imbued with power. It is a social relation of seduction, "soft" coercion, violence, and force, a *dispositif* that takes on the task of unvoiced denigration. With a sharp attunement to distinction and with an inherent violence that its arbitrators enlist, it begs for a social mapping of whom, when, and where the possession of taste could be exercised and displayed.

"Taste knows something" (*Geschmack etwas erkeent*).[57] Each of taste's attributes point to the fundamental labor it performs, labors that endow it with a politicality of its own; namely, the capacity to adjudicate, judge, distinguish, crush, dismiss, humiliate, segregate, and ignore those who cannot meet its unspoken requirements. As such *taste might be considered a governing* dispositif *in the (sub) metrics of inequality*. When Gadamer contends that "taste knows something," and like Kant stipulates a knowing that "cannot be reduced to rules and concepts," it is a shared sense and sensibility on which it depends.[58]

---

57. Gadamer, *Truth*, 38. In German:

> Im Gegensatz zurNormierung des Geschmacks durch die Mode macht sich so die Idealität des guten Geschmacks geltend.Es folgt daraus, daß der Geschmack etwas erkennt-Freilich auf eine Weise, die sich nicht vondem konkreten Anblick, an dem ersich vollzieht,ablösen, auf Regeln undBegriffe bringen läßt. Hans-Georg Gadamer, Wahrhiet Und Methode: Grundzuge einer philosophischen Hermeneutik (Langnau am Albis: Mohr 1960) p. 43.

58. Gadamer, *Truth*, 38. How "sensibility" features in taste remains contested. On sensibility see Angelica Nuzzo, *Ideal Embodiment: Kant's Theory of Sensibility*

In Gadamer's spare words: "a true sense of community, for Kant, is taste."⁵⁹ The phrasing is awkward, and surprisingly contorted for Gadamer who so values clarity. This is not because, as one might expect, taste circumscribes the consensual judgments that make up a community. For Kant, "universal agreement" is counted upon, not empirical universality.⁶⁰ More than a faculty common to all persons, Gadamer is after a common sense of right and wrong.⁶¹ But who are those moral arbitrators? At issue, and much closer to the relationship between taste and race, is how Gadamer parses Kant's treatment of taste and community:

> Like reflective judgment, it belongs in the realm of that which grasps, in the individual object, the universal under which it is to be subsumed. Both taste and judgment evaluate the object in relation to a wider order to see whether it *fits* in with everything else—that is, whether it is *"fitting"* (emphasis added).⁶²

"Fitting" should set off an alarm. To be "fitting" is dictated by those racial regimes of truth that name dispositions that result from "inappropriate" aspiration: "insolence," "putting on airs," "presumptuousness," "uppity" are part of the vocabulary of white supremacy across the globe. Each of these derogatory terms make up the common sense of early twentieth-century European colonial ventures, where "inappropriate" was not about the style of European educated colonized persons.

(Bloomington: Indiana University Press, 2008) who "challenges the notion that Kant gives no right to sensibility," quoted in Laura Henghold, "Between Bodies and Pleasures: A Territory without a Domain," *Foucault Studies* 15 (February 2013): 149.

59. Gadamer, *Truth*, 34.
60. Kant, *Critique*, 37.
61. See Sofia Rosenfeld's superb discussion of Gadamer on Kant, *sensus communis*, and the common good, in Rosenfeld, *Common Sense*, 246.
62. Gadamer, *Truth*, 38. "Fitting" is often understood in Kant as "fitting" in accord with the other faculties such that taste "fits in" with them. Here, I treat "fitting" with respect to the social order of things.

What was not "fitting" is what the style signaled about a person's willingness and intent to act out of bounds, i.e., to not act within the rubrics of prescribed character, well aware of the political consequences that could follow. It was not just how they dressed (as we'll see in "Poetic Rage" on the counter-colonial avant-garde) but that the presumptions of equality could engender such a play with fashion in a colonial world.[63] For taste, in the context of race, subscribes to specific protocols. "Fit" is loaded: it follows "where one belongs" but more fiercely it demands an adherence to a violence-inducing restriction, as Bourdieu argued (for taste not for race), of "knowing one's place."

ON TASTE AND TRANSGRESSIONS

> *The science of taste and cultural consumption begins with a transgression that is in no way aesthetic: it has to abolish the sacred frontiers which make legitimate culture a separate universe, in order to discover the intelligible relations which unite apparently incommensurable "choices."*[64]

Though Gadamer too is explicit in stating that "taste is an intellectual faculty of differentiation," he has no citation in *Distinction*. It is precisely this task of differentiation that informs Bourdieu's

---

63. Indeed, how they dressed, what some Javanese intellectuals intentionally "flaunted" (as did Mas Marcodikromo, who outfitted himself as a dandy in 1920s Dutch-ruled colonial Java) sometimes mattered a lot. Marcodikromo ended up in a colonial internment camp and died there at a young age. That "performance" was indeed part of the danger of frontiers crossed, a creative part of "the anti-colonial avant-garde." (The subject of essay five.)
64. Bourdieu, *Distinction*, 6. And in French:
> *La science du goût et de la consommation culturelle commence par une transgression qui n'a rien d'esthétique: elle doit en effet abolir la frontière sacrée qui fait que la culture légitime un univers separé pour découvrir les relations intelligibles qui unissent des "choix" en apparence incommensurable*... (Bourdieu, *La distinction*, vii)

own elaboration of the subtle and crude violences of distinction that taste monitors and measures. His project from the outset is intent on "transgression," one that storms the "sacred frontier" separating "legitimate culture" from everyday taste.[65] He seeks to abolish the logic that accounts for why and how that division is made. But the transgression is even more a creative act of demolition. In defiance, he pairs literature and coiffure, Mozart and cuisine, and Delacroix and sport to show how similarly they work to affix status. He enjoins us to participate in his "barbarous" conflation of that which Kant held and made sacred, viz.—the distinction between the (ordinary/vulgar) "taste of sense" and the (pure) "taste of reflection." The latter, for Kant, is privileged as universal and *a priori*, demanding no conceptual elaboration; the former, subjective, "merely private judgments," of interest to some, but aesthetically of little interest at all.[66]

But there are other transgressions Bourdieu almost seems categorically to refuse to make, "sacred frontiers" not crossed. To state it again: strikingly in a book that he anticipates will be read as "very French" (and thereby too French) and purports to define what polices the social boundaries of French life more than profession or income per se, is an effacement of the racialized sensibilities that for long have vigilantly and violently secured the interior frontiers and borders of being French and of class.

Edward Said and the writing in his wake repeatedly have made the case that orientalist depictions saturated French literature, art, design, and architecture, assigning superiority to the West and an eroticized, racialized inferiority to the Arab, Muslim, and Asian Rest.[67] The point has been long belabored. But these

65. Bourdieu, *Distinction*, 6.
66. Kant, *Critique*, 48, 49, vii.
67. Edward Said, *Orientalism* (New York: Pantheon, 1978). Among many others, Malek Alloula, *Colonial Harem* (London: University of Minnesota Press, 1986); Ali Behdad, *Belated Travelers: Orientalism in the Age of Colonial Dissolution* (Durham: Duke University Press, 1994); Mary Roberts, *Intimate Outsiders: The Harem in Ottoman and Orientalist Art and Travel Literature* (Durham: Duke University Press, 2007).

exotic figures, images, and racist imaginaries (by Flaubert and Delacroix and so many other literary and artistic luminaries) did something more with respect to the dictates of taste, their racial coding, and coordinates. For these are the very artists and literary figures who long have made up the French "classics" in and out of school curricula—the font of cultural competence, the bedrock of what counts as foundational good reading, fine literature, and good taste.

Still, the more proximate site of racist France was being played out in humble and elite milieu, noted earlier: the French-Algerian War that had just ended in 1962.[68] It was also the year that Frantz Fanon's *Wretched of the Earth* (*Les damnés de la terre*) was published and immediately banned in France, that infamous and celebrated anti-colonial manifesto that put France's war machine and the racisms of European imperialism up for scrutiny, assault, and destruction.[69]

Indeed, France's colonial and metropolitan archive of cartoons, photography, film, and postcards devoted to a prolific stream of racist pornography provided the material, everyday objects and imaginary font of 1960s France, more explicitly than it does today.[70] Given that this was the habitus in which those

---

68. This war without a name sent 400,000 French soldiers to Algeria, brought back at its end nearly one million *pied noir*. Ninety thousand Harkis, a majority of whom were poor Algerians who had fought on the side of the French, were placed in remote detention camps. Cordoned off from French society, they were treated as repellent, renegades, and scapegoats for what was despicable and "disgusting" sell-outs in a war they fought for France.

69. Frantz Fanon, *Les damnés de la terre* (Paris: Maspero, 1961).

70. See Pascal Blanchard and Nicolas Bancel, eds., *Sexe, race et colonies* (Paris: La Découverte, 2018), a 544-page visual compendium of over 1,200 images with contributions from scores of academics (and an unnamed many who refused to be part of the project) with the aim of illustrating the ways in which colonial powers made use of colonized bodies. Outrage against the book came from many quarters, especially by those who saw it as an exercise in reviving the humiliations of coffee table colonial porn. Those who contributed to the project argue

surveyed lived (when the research for *Distinction* was carried out), it is hard to imagine how this living archive failed to figure, even in peripheral mode, as part of the iconography of taste and distaste. *Distinction*'s very first line almost seems to invite the reader to think racialization in its analysis of taste: "Sociology is rarely more akin to social psychoanalysis than when it confronts an object like taste, one of the most vital stakes in the struggles fought in the field of the dominant class and the field of cultural production."[71]

One could substitute "race" for "taste" in this opening sentence. It is precisely what Fanon did in *Wretched of the Earth* in his socio-political psychoanalysis of French colonialism, the force of racism in disabling subjects, inflicting physical and psychic damages, contorted truths, and vengeful desires.

With colonialism and racism so absent from *Distinction*, one could almost imagine that the omission contributed to making its otherwise scathing analysis of class domination in France acceptable and celebrated, both sufficiently transgressive and within normative bounds. Ironically, while directed at the aesthetic conceits of the French intellectual elite and others of privilege, it participated in effacing one of French society's founding political features.[72] If some interior frontiers were secured by *goût*, those distinctions were only part of the history and the story. In occluding "*dégoût*," the history of endemic French racism had no place in its anti-Semitic, Islamophobic, and colonial registers.

---

that these images make up a history of the present. A used copy in June 2021 goes for over $2,000 on Amazon.

71. Bourdieu, *Distinction*, 11.

72. The relationships among colonialism, bourgeois sexuality and the racial state, and desire and disdain, are subjects of Ann Laura Stoler, *Race and the Education of Desire* (Durham: Duke University Press, 1995).

TASTE, VIOLENCE, AND THE POLITICS OF DISGUST

> *Kant's principle of pure taste is nothing other than a refusal, a disgust—a disgust for objects which impose enjoyment and a disgust for the crude, vulgar taste which revels in this imposed enjoyment . . . Disgust is the paradoxical experience of enjoyment extorted by violence.*[73]

If race is absent in *Distinction*, *dégoût*, abhorrence, distaste, and disgust are as if written in invisible ink, as if the subjacent underside of the project. And then sometimes that ink is immediately legible, as if in bold font, the rehearsal of a recursive history embedded in an imperial politics of white arrogance. Still, *dégoût* is never actually named, nor the subject of Bourdieu's carefully crafted surveys, nor developed in its own right as a conceptual dispositif with a history and as a subject of analysis.

Claiming a "deliberate amnesia" with respect to Kant's distinguishing features for taste, Bourdieu rejects the "disinterestedness" on which Kant insisted it depends, showing its affordance by the habitus and conditions of possibility in which one lived.[74] But something else emerges.

It is in the seething postscript, to my mind the strongest statement of the project, that Bourdieu's "vulgar critique" of taste (with the "vulgar" underscored) becomes explicit and direct. For taste not only marks class differences and their cultural distinctions. It refracts a minutely calculated immeasurable metric for what is not valued, what is "*facile*" (easy, fast, cheap, effortless, light), what is denigrated and accorded diminished status.

Still, exercising taste depends on prescriptions; the concerted effort it takes to affirm the distance between those versed in the right dispositions and those who are not and cannot be fixed once

---

73. Bourdieu, *Distinction*, 488.
74. Bourdieu, *Distinction*, 485.

and for all. This is a political scene imbued with relationality. For this separation is shaped by the slippery nature of disgust, the quality of the object deemed disgusting and the person naming it. Such is the impossibly pervious distinction between what is abhorred and who is doing the abhorring, between being revolted and what is considered revolting, the viscous substance of defilement that joins Us and Them.

We know that racism is toxic for those on whom it is foisted but also so on those whose dispositions it contorts—knotted subjects, strangled in their own webs. Assigning "contagion" to the other opens the dangerous possibility that one has been contaminated, can be contaminated, soiled by proximities of breath, of smell, of touch.

Disgust in *Distinction* occupies a shadow presence, haunting virtually every evaluation of esteem and approval. Still, it surfaces rarely, and when it does, its uses are surprising and telling. It is in the postscript again that Bourdieu's "vulgar" critique reduces Kant's principle of pure taste to nothing but "an imperative refusal, a disgust for easy pleasures."[75] But disgust plays other roles, as in "a disgust for the crude, vulgar taste which revels in this imposed enjoyment." Kant is emphatic that real taste is not for things that "charm." Nor ought it appeal to the senses.[76] That which "charms" is refused entry; the "agreeable" and "common"

---

75. Bourdieu, *Distinction*, 490.
76. "A judgment of taste on which charm and emotion have no influence . . . is *a pure judgment of taste (emphasis in original)."* Kant, *Critique*, sec. 13, 58. And again in section 14:

> A judgment of taste is therefore pure only so far as no merely empirical satisfaction is mingled with its determining ground. But this always happens if charm or emotion have any share in the judgment by which anything is to be described as beautiful.

Also see the last line of Section 14: "pure judgment of taste has for its determining ground *neither charm nor emotion*—in a word, *no sensation (emphasis added)* as the material of the aesthetical judgment" (Kant, *Critique*, 62).

are also disdained.[77] As Bourdieu notes, the refusal is of "what is easy in the sense of simple, shallow, such as 'Casbah orientalism'."

Despite Kant's claim that the senses are not called upon to discern pure taste, Bourdieu is convinced otherwise, arguing firmly that "the theory of pure taste is grounded in an empirical social relation . . . as is shown by its allusions to the teaching and educability of taste."[78] How sensibility and "sense" (as in Gadamer's use) figure in Kant's estimation of taste remains in debate.[79] And as with respect to the contaminating qualities of race, how sensibility, and "sense" are played out in the everyday evaluations of contagion have produced a blaze of evidence.[80]

This underside of taste is not directly addressed. Rather it emerges in what Bourdieu cites as the "highest degree of tension." On the same page, he writes of a *"trained* sustained tension" produced by the "intensity of the impulse denied, and the vulgarity refused."[81] Repression and Freud slip in with hardly a nod. One might even consider whether Bourdieu's target is aimed at something more planetary and more mundane.

A hierarchy of value attributes "moral excellence" and "ethical superiority" to something of which Bourdieu can only write with contempt: namely, the capacity for *"sublimation (emphasis added)* which defines the truly human man."[82] In this sublime art of living, the "negation of enjoyment—inferior, coarse, vulgar, mercenary, venal, servile" will define everything the elite will not

---

77. Bourdieu, *Distinction*, 488.
78. Bourdieu, *Distinction*, 490.
79. See Nuzzo, *Embodiment*, n56.
80. See, for example, Frantz Fanon, *Black Skin, White Masks* (London, Pluto Press, 1986); Sara Ahmed, *Strange Encounters: Embodied Others in Post-Coloniality* (London: Routledge, 2000); Alexander G. Weheliye, *Habeas Viscus* (Durham: Duke University Press, 2014); Michelle Ann Stephens, *Skin Acts* (Durham: Duke University Press, 2014); Kyla Schuller, *The Biopolitics of Feeling* (Durham: Duke University Press, 2018).
81. Bourdieu, *Distinction*, 490.
82. Bourdieu, *Distinction*, 491.

value; "easy pleasures, fast rewards, cheap satisfaction" are for those below.

The formula is rather simple and familiar: a moral high ground predicated on delayed gratification, a capitalist ethic of profit accruing and accessible only to those "in the know." This is the moniker that defines taste. Elite disgust in Bourdieu's template might come with a different vocabulary today, but some of the elements look much the same: good taste defined against cheap pleasures, easy access, fast food and fast fashion, easy consumption, soothing melodics, simple, repetitious chords. The language valorizes a privileged work ethic, profits accrued, and hard intellectual labor. The metric mimics what sanctifies the elite's own just rewards. It is a mirror of what they pretend to master, an aspirational enhanced portrait of themselves.

Here Bourdieu leaps to another claim and another realm. Taste is not just about status and worth. Its violence is in the very boundaries it draws. For it may distinguish not-quite human and humankinds, or even "mark the difference between humans and non-humans" all together.[83] Again, there emerges a disturbing similitude between taste and disgust, both serving similar projects. Nussbaum calls out disgust as that which "imputes to the other, a subhuman nature."[84] In *The Anatomy of Disgust*, William Miller puts it this way:

> Disgust evaluates (negatively) what it touches, proclaims the meanness and inferiority of its object. And by so doing it presents a *nervous claim (emphasis added)* of right to be free of the dangers imposed by the proximity of the inferior. It is thus an assertion of a claim to superiority.[85]

---

83. Bourdieu, *Distinction*, 491.
84. Nussbaum, *Disgust*, xviii.
85. Miller, *Anatomy*, 9.

Law professor Anthony Paul Farley offers a horrific account of the contagion of race:

> One spring day in 1976, on a bus chartered for a junior high school trip to Washington, D.C, one of my schoolmates stood and began to comb her long, brown hair. She was tall and cool and pretty . . . After a long while she turned and addressed us all: "Whose comb was this? Thanks, I'm all done." No one responded . . . Just then, one of our classmates answered in a mirthful voice: "It's Farley's comb."
>
> I, Farley, was the only black person on this otherwise all white school trip. My classmates burst into laughter. The girl with the long brown hair turned crimson and began to cry in loud, long sobs. The sobs quickly turned into the sounds of retching, which were accompanied by shudders running through her now hunched form. She may have vomited . . . I said nothing.[86]

The girl's shudder of disgust repeats itself again and again in the fear of contamination that joins with disgust. (White) immunity, or the quest for (white) immunitas as Roberto Esposito calls it.[87] But it is an anxious desire that is simply impossible; it cannot hold. For race as an imaginary emits substances in this contaminating world. Contaminants are lodged not just in the person, but linger in where they have slept, sat, what objects they have touched, in the creases of their clothes. As with the disgusting, the risk is artificially produced, legitimating the policing of the distinctions that maintain control.

86. Anthony Farley, "The Poetics of Colorlined Space," in *Crossroads, Directions, and a New Critical Race Theory*, eds. Francisco Valdes, Jerome Culp, and Angela Harris (Philadelphia: Temple University Press, 2002), x.

87. Roberto Esposito, *Immunitas: The Protection and Negation of Life* (London: Polity, 2011), 7–9. He writes, ". . . the immunitary mechanism presupposes the existence of the ills it is meant to counter . . . Immunity . . . is the internal limit which cuts across community, folding it back on itself in a form that is both constative and deprivative: immunity constitutes or reconstitutes community precisely by negating it."

THE UGLY, THE DISGUSTING, AND RACE

> By the mid-century, being black, being Jewish, being diseased, and being "ugly" come to be inexorably linked. All races . . . were described in terms of aesthetics as either "ugly" or "beautiful." African blacks . . . became the epitomes of the "ugly" race.[88]

In what Bourdieu called out as a *"monopoly of humanity"* (his italics), he derides aesthetic discourse for its "attempted imposition of a definition of the genuinely human."[89] But surely aesthetic judgment is not alone in imposing definition and differentiation of those bodies, that flesh, that skin that does not "fit" and that is unfit for inclusion in the body politic.

For nowhere is the relationship between the ugly, the disgusting, and the racially inferior more boldly produced than in what came to be called the "Ugly Laws" that Susan Schweik brilliantly describes in her book of the same title. The late nineteenth-century "ugly laws," coterminous with Jim Crow legislation, as we know from the earlier essays here, were part of a broader set of coercive statutes that legislated against those identified as too disgusting to be present in the public sphere, to be looked upon, and to be seen by that respectable citizenry who might cross their paths.

It is easy to see this as exaggeration. Indeed the "ugly laws" were not called that at the time. They were mandated by city ordinances across the U.S. "to abolish street obstructions."[90] Initially and narrowly construed as directed at "unsightly beggars," the mandates broadened beyond begging. The misdemeanor, as

---

88. Sander Gilman, "The Jewish Nose," in *The Jew's Body* (New York: Routledge, 1991), 173.
89. Bourdieu, *Distinction*, 491.
90. Susan M. Schweik, *The Ugly Laws: Disability in Public* (New York: New York University Press, 2009), 1.

evinced from a thick archive of municipal records, was *exposure of the unsightly*: contorted, amputated, festering, and disfigured limbs, bodies engaged in a war with poverty and sustenance were forbidden from being "too visible" to the public eye. There was no "space of appearance" sanctioned. Being seen, and allowing them to be seen, became the crime.

Schweik's does more than describe the perverse assessments to which the poor, Black, and disabled were subject. More impressive is the non-reductionist way in which she approaches the phenomenon of what is deemed ugly, neither assuming what "ugly" entails nor the attributes that become associated with it. She identifies what kinds of persons threaten the fiction of democratic equalities that in turn put in place multiple stigmas on which exclusions were based. Relevance to contemporary categories of disability, exclusion, and abandonment is the story she seeks to tell, humiliations embedded in infrastructures that have not gone away.[91]

In Martha Nussbaum's rendition, disgust knows no boundaries but effectively draws them nonetheless with an extraordinary criterium: that which disgusts the "average reasonable [white] man." It is not only for what he *may see, but what he imagines*.[92] Each word warps the assessment into its own form of racial profiling. Granted, we do not have "ugly laws" installed to remove from public space those deemed deformed, poor, ragged, demanding, promiscuous, unseemly in behavior, or inappropriately dressed. But there is a common feature of those laws and the underside of Bourdieu's description of elites' "monopoly on humanity." With aesthetic judgement reserved for themselves as the true purveyors of taste, that monopoly on humanity is contingent on assuring its negative, that deemed disgusting. Coercive normative social

---

91. The imagination looms again as it did for Kant with respect to pure taste. As a "sequel" see Jasbir Puar, *The Right to Maim: Debility, Capacity, Disability* (Durham: Duke University Press, 2017).
92. Nussbaum, *Disgust*, 126.

conventions are designed to weed out, eliminate, negate the unwanted and unseemly. In the end, taste and distaste do similar legal, social, affective, and political work—to diminish and differentiate with racial effects much the same.

For Schweik, the disgusting traces a social topography of the "American ugly line" that "meets up" as she writes with what Anthony Farley has called the "poetics of colorlined space."[93] Ambiguous corridors in a fluid space that marked those outside the acceptable aesthetics of the everyday, the disabled, beggars, the maimed: "unsightliness lay in or on skin, skin 'exposed,' skin 'disfigured,' skin that disgusted."[94]

Such imagined parameters had powerful effects. As Nussbaum writes, disgust is a prominent feature in the law as it is in daily lives, and far after the ugly laws were largely disbanded. Disgust remains serving, "sometimes as the primary or even sole reason for making some acts illegal."[95] The ugly and disgusting were not personal attributions. They were legally enforced parameters of human kinds, a calibration called upon to reassert who was contaminating, what was abhorrent, who was disposable, and what sites of enclosure and containment need to be fortified or changed.

THE POLITICS OF GUT FEELINGS

Taste makes its distinctions and signs of limited access without showcasing violence. Distaste and disgust do otherwise; they set out who are to be excluded with embodied force. If taste depends on an "obscure kind of judgment" as Kant held, distaste harbors a similar opacity. Not unlike "gut feelings," both can be marshalled to make assessments for which no evidence is enough, and no

---

93. Farley, "Poetics of Colorlined Space," 97–158.
94. Schweik, *Ugly Laws*, 187.
95. Nussbaum, *Disgust*, 2.

evidence is needed. As in the cunning crafting of race, both truck in unassailable truths and conjured claims.

In *From Disgust to Humanity*, Nussbaum almost seems to suggest that the politics of disgust is over, that the politics of humanitarianism has taken its place. But not quite; she does say that "disgust has not gone away. It has gone underground."[96] Maybe, but it depends where you look. With respect to some people and places, it would be hard to argue that it has gone underground but rather is vividly mobilized in the sensory regimes of racial politics. Disgust occupies a spacious terrain: subjacently marked in what is intuited as "taste," to the lowbrow intuitive knowledge that "gut feelings" and colloquial common sense are thought to embrace. These are forms of knowing that call on an affective sensibility, one recruited in the making of evaluative codes that assign social categories of worth, and the graded distinctions among them.

Kant may have left "taste" unsullied by the forms of distaste it implied, but that is precisely where its darker features reside. For in arguing as he did that "feeling" was at once "an obscure kind of judgment," a "mode of knowing," and a sensory intuition that demands that one know less rather than more, taste, common sense, intuition, and gut feelings (as the most colloquial form of intuition) come to look like discernments with much in common.[97]

If Arendt could endorse "intuition as the highest and ultimate form of cognitive truth," her vision must have been on conditions far from the racialized landscape where intuitions harbor their toxic waste.[98] "Gut feelings" in psychology and cognitive science may be considered intuitive (the "intelligence of the unconscious" as Gerd Gigerenzer has it).[99] But in the fields devoted to

---

96. Nussbaum, *Disgust*, xv.
97. In Kant's formulation, "All thought must, directly or indirectly . . . relate ultimately to intuitions, and therefore to sensibility, because in no other way can an object be given to us" (*Critique of Judgment* [1781 first edition]).
98. Hannah Arendt, *The Life of the Mind* (New York: Harvest, 1971), 121.
99. Gerd Gigerenzer, *Gut Feelings: The Intelligence of the Unconscious* (New York: Viking Press, 2007). Gigerenzer's account is socially thin, with little attention to the learned social habits on which gut feelings depend.

politics, governance, social hierarchy, and for those designated as racial others or precariously perched on racial divides, these "gut feelings" are perilous beasts, armed with discriminatory ammunition.[100]

Gut feelings depend on fast assessment that "mistakes" toy guns for real ones, and Black youth standing "where they do not belong" as essentially criminals in the making. Gut feelings offer a poor map of others' intentions. They do more than instantiate inequalities. They prompt a confidence in knowing not only what is not known but a knowing dependent on unacknowledged prior social conventions, "Gut feelings" take refuge in the satisfaction of reliability, and thus create the conditions for those very evaluations.

"Gut feelings" have a defined repertoire and rules of unstated grammar, as Clifford Geertz once noted for common sense.[101] They carry forms of political truth and instantiate discriminations in the name of what are considered as trustworthy forms of knowledge. Antonio Gramsci might remind us that common sense is duplicitous and not benign. Like taste, gut feeling is a *judgment* based on rapid response, achieved knowledge, and learned behavior. And like taste it is an "embodied" appraisal in which a sensibility and a feeling are imagined to elicit something intuitive, instinctual, shared, natural, and therefore more true.

The relegation of "gut feelings" and taste to the intuitive and instinctual that manifests as "having" taste, and "being" disgusted secure something inherent and reliable: a credibility unmarred by self-interest. For "having taste," being "without taste," and being tasteless, are all sensate signatures of desire and disgust, forms of

---

100. This is precisely William James' description of the bodily component of emotions. I thank Lewis Gordon for pointing me to this similarity. See Katherine Lacasse, "Going with your Gut: How William James' Theory of Emotions Brings Insights to Risk Perception and Decision-making Research," *New Ideas in Psychology* 46 (October 2015): 1–7.

101. Clifford Geertz, "Common Sense as a Cultural System," in *Local Knowledge* (New York: Basic Books, 1983), 73–93.

discernment from which historical ontologies develop and racialized distinctions depend.

Both *goût* and *dégoût* do sanctioned boundary work. Both are *gatekeepers of the sensorium* with implicit exclusionary potentials that make them up. Commencing with the observation that *goût* is the "product of an education" and a "familial" one, good taste requires material discriminations that a hierarchy of "cultural goods" endorse. As importantly, taste turns on the "affective properties" animated by attunement to the feel of "velveteen skin or a delicate lace," as if these were the most telling signs of aesthetic knowledge and its exclusive ways of knowing. Omitted from the picture is the racial sensorium that so vigilantly policies the boundaries of far more than the French middle class.

The slip between *"sans goût"* (without taste) and *"dégoût"* (distaste) is subtle but not innocuous. Both remove one from the domain in which one's judgment is worthy of consideration. The devaluation here has a different cast than Nussbaum places on emotions. In her rendition, emotions are value laden with respect to that to which I attach value and that favors my prior well-being and potentially makes me vulnerable to harm, as with the expression of compassion.[102] Here, emotion works on and through different layers and forms of vulnerability, material and immaterial, that is, all the way down.

But valuation enters into the relationality of emotion in other ways. That some emotives are predicated on someone else showing a "lack of taste" does not derive necessarily from my prior vulnerability to harm but from *an imaginary* of harm, a hierarchical ordering that excludes and diminishes a whole set of practices and sorts of people unworthy of counting among those to whom I am responsible.

One does not have to travel far semantically or politically to have unworthiness take on an even more sinister cast. *Dégoûtant*

---

102. Nussbaum, *Disgust*, 43–49.

(disgusting) places one not only unworthy of inclusion in the "community of taste" that Kant so named. If we take on Gadamer's understanding of taste as a "sense" that is not "the ground but the supreme consummation of moral judgment" then a lack of that "sense" is a condemnation, a judgment that one does not meet the requisite moral standards and should be outside that communal terrain.

(DIS)TASTE AS DEADLY WEAPON

Taste is an arbiter of moral behavior and social kinds. By Bourdieu's account, good taste is a powerful weapon. But, as argued here, the epistemic politics of taste and distaste do similar work. For being *dégoûtant* may make one not only unworthy of inclusion, outside a community of taste, with more dire consequence: one lacking moral judgment, an unworthy social kind—not a proper human kind at all. As Nussbaum writes, "disgust imputes to the other a subhuman nature."[103]

How could Albert Memmi, the Jewish-Tunisian writer born in Tunisia, who died in 2020 in Paris at the age of eighty-nine, have imagined that "racism is a pleasure within everyone's reach?"[104] His statement is intentionally provocative, pithy, ironic, and counter-intuitive. But, even as a cynical quip, it wholly misses and dismisses the relations of power on which racisms depend. *Arguing that racism is "a pleasure within everyone's reach" equalizes fields of power that are never equal.* This is not to say that groups of people cannot and do not judge the dispositions, habits, and comportments of others in damaging ways. But racism is NOT in everyone's reach (though as a Jew in Tunisia, in a place he

---

103. Nussbaum, *Disgust*, xvii.
104. Albert Memmi, *Dominated Man: Notes toward a Portrait* (New York: Orion Press, 1968), 201.

deemed endemically "anti-Semitic," it makes sense that he could imagine that all and anyone could be dismissed and disdained).

The use of the term "disgusting" with respect to the smell, sound, sight, and mere presence of refugees, beggars in the street, Muslims at prayer on the sidewalk, homeless in the metro, those talking to themselves foraging for food in garbage cans, has its correlates in an affective landscape common to communities of privilege and power throughout the world. When not grounded in "common sense," they are grounded in the law.

French sociologist and activist Eric Fassin, who headed a research team on the precarities of Roma life in France, cites the televised Toulouse news story from May 2009 of twenty-odd Roma camped at the foot of a construction site, violently removed by those nearby who formed a quasi-militia in sanitized white coverups, armed with pulverisers filled with powerful disinfectant. As Fassin reports, they claimed themselves simply to be "cleaning up" [*faire le ménage*].[105] Ugliness and disgust bled across the indictments. Comparative worth and merit are always on the line—the ugly laws made that case with no pretense that taste could cross the colorline. Taste and beauty could never meet in the "confluence" of what it meant to be a woman and Black. But as with remorse and remorselessness, taste and distaste are both inflected modes of policing the borders of who counts and who does not.

Reworking Bourdieu's *Distinction* through the lens of race is a collective task whose inflection today awaits to be done. There are concepts and terms, as the philosopher Richard Bernstein has argued in thinking with Gadamer, that *make demands upon us*. How racism and (dis)taste figure already garners an archive of

---

105. Eric Fassin, Carine Fouteau, Serge Guichard and Aurelie Windels, *Roms & riverains: une politique municipale de la race* (Paris: La fabrique 2014), 109. Roma children are reported too dirty and full of fleas to attend public schools: teachers report that they are no dirtier than any other children. A three-year old disabled boy pees on the ground behind his caravan: a blog notes "you see, they're animals."

inequalities that speak to the urgencies of the day. For the outlines of distaste can be as subtle as they are blatant, as invisible as they are glaring, as unstated as they are appalled by those to whom those assignments are directed. Neither taste nor disgust are confined to personal inclination. They are potent social markers, affectively and politically charged, mobilized in distinguishing the comparative worth of human kinds.

* * *

4

How Not to Know

To examine excuses is to examine cases where there has been some abnormality or failure and as often, the abnormal will throw light on the normal . . .
If ordinary language is to be our guide, it is to evade responsibility, or full responsibility, that we most often make excuses.[1]

WORKING THROUGH THE WAYS IN which colonial detritus gives force and form to contemporary inequities raises a conceptual and political challenge: namely, how to treat the ubiquitous use and abuse of "forgetting" that accompanies the official, revisionist, and personal histories of colonial impositions, degradations, and violences—of lives lived at the vortex or on the edges of the colonial disorder of time and things.[2] Colonial "forgetting" is invoked to describe and account for a multiplex of phenomena: strategic apologies, inadvertent omissions,

---

1. John L. Austin, "A Plea for Excuses: The Presidential Address," *Proceedings of the Aristotelian Society* 57 (1956–1957): 4.
2. Originally delivered as keynote address for the conference "Forgetting Knowledge" in February 2018 at the Max Planck Institute for the History of Science (MPIWG) in collaboration with The Descartes Centre at the University of Utrecht, the Vossius Center in Amsterdam, and the Huygens ING in Amsterdam. I thank the organizers, especially Ohad Parnes for extending the invitation, and participants for their interventions. I thank E. Valentine Daniel for his comments on an earlier version. Revised as keynote address for the CSLC Symposium, "Vital Lies: The Aesthetics and Politics of Disregard," USC, Los Angeles, February 2019, I thank the organizers and audience for providing the opportunity to engage their thoughts with my own.

Interior Frontiers. Ann Laura Stoler, Oxford University Press. © Oxford University Press 2022.
DOI: 10.1093/oso/9780190076375.003.0004

"unintended" neglect, oversights, mass graves "hard to locate," dramatic revelations, and belated and "sincere" recognitions of colonial violences past and present and how they bear, unevenly and collectively now.

Here I broach the work that forgetting is called on to perform, to identify the heavy labor (explicit or opaque) that the term is intended, expected, and counted on to do. I have three points of access in mind: one, to think with John Austin's treatment of excuses, of which forgetting might be considered a specific genre.[3] Austin warns that excuses, are "breakdowns" as he awkwardly phrased it, breakdowns "signalized [sic] by the various excuses . . . of radically different kinds, affecting different parts or stages of the machinery, which the excuses consequently pick out and sort out for us."[4] The "machinery" is made up of those "mechanisms" that render the obvious non-self-evident so we may attend to the "excuse" (or act of forgetting) in its clumsy, uneasy articulation.

This acute attentiveness makes some tasks clearer: to reckon with the range of affective sensibilities to which forgetting responds and calls upon (think shame and fury and resentment and shame again);[5] to acknowledge that there is nothing self-evident about "forgetting" (beyond the repressive model on which a Freudian take depends). I think here of what it takes to submit forgetting to the range of temporalities (from a day to a decade) it can inhabit with respect to colonial acts and effects. Not least, are the scales that forgetting traverses, from person to state, from archival holdings (shorn of shredded military documents)

---

3. This is no warrant to dismiss everything forgotten about colonial contexts, events, and relations as bad faith, but to understand something about the conditions that surround the "forgotten" as a response and "forgetting" as an evocation.

4. Austin, "A Plea," 6.

5. For a nuanced account of how shame figures as a form of deficiency virtually impossible for colonial critique to capture, see Timothy Bewes, *The Event of Postcolonial Shame* (Princeton: Princeton University Press, 2011).

to attic stashes of one's grandfather's personal letters. The effort would be to submit the act of forgetting to an accounting that retains its historicity and plurality, that retains the messy space between ignoring and ignorance, where Wittgenstein thought research should be done, on everyday forms of "rough ground."[6] Even a thread of this work—explored here—would constitute what for Austin might be considered a "good site" for "fieldwork in philosophy."[7]

Austin here pries apart what Foucault would call the "ready-made syntheses" that phrases like forgetting bury within their folds.[8] My thought is that forgetting, like excuses, measures *failures* of various kinds (of awareness, circumstance, relevance, knowledge, proximity, and place). But as we shall see "failure" to do x, or to address y, or to attend to z may not be considered "failures" at all. Within an imperial democratic colonial order that nurtures forgetting some things and not others, the distribution of "forgetting" may work to measure something else pursued throughout these essays: the assessment of worth, a (sub)metric of value. Forgetting may be a shadow index, a greyed-out grid, a measuring of what should be dismissed as of incommensurate and unequal value. The weight given to "the holocaust" vs. successions of colonial massacres, the "lapse" of recognition of an event or a recurrent violence is already primed for, and productive of, disparate worth. Again, we might do well to attend to the adverbial form that Austin suggests, to "pick out the internal details"—the "modifying" caveats that range from "inadvertently" to "thoughtlessly" that can make of forgetting an insignificant rather than monstrous relational act.[9]

---

6. See p. xi, fn. 3.
7. Austin, "The Plea," 9.
8. Michel Foucault, *Archaeology of Knowledge* (New York: Pantheon, 1972), 22.
9. Austin, "The Plea," 13.

FORGETTING AS A POLITICAL CONCEPT

But this is almost too much work for a mere phrase to do. Here, I hold to Austin's uncanny insights, but take them elsewhere. In this second effort to locate not one but multiple points of application, we might do well to treat forgetting less as a descriptive term of a "wide field of actions" than as a political concept charged with instrumentality, a political concept that has the capacity to swing between its stolid register ("I forgot that pale blue pinafore I wore when a little girl in Java") and its possibly ambiguous but dismissive denial of knowledge—and worth ("I actually forgot that there were swimming pool signs in Java that read, 'no dogs or natives allowed,' I didn't even really see them"). I say "possibly" to note how the adverb "actually" and "really" might work to indicate that I surprise myself for having forgotten this (or feign that surpise). Or it may possibly point to a dismissal of that particular act of forgetting, I may have done that then, but it really doesn't matter much now.

To my mind, forgetting may operate not only as what Foucault once called a "working concept," but as a political concept and political phenomenon with grim power to adjudicate silently on what matters and what and who does not—to efface whose lives count, whose were crushed and what forms of governance made that easily so.[10] Political concepts are porous and plastic, their "politicality" contained in their polyvalence, dependent on the flexibility and contestations that ambiguity of use confers.[11]

---

10. Foucault, *Archaeology*, 9.
11. For an important discussion of the "politicality" of political concepts see Étienne Balibar, "Concept" and Warren Montag, "Introduction" on the relationship between "politicality" and the "polyvalence" of concepts in Balibar's work and beyond in Ann Laura Stoler, Stathis Gourgouris, and Jacques Lezra, eds., *Thinking with Balibar: A Lexicon of Conceptual Practice* (New York: Fordham University Press, 2020), 54–70, 1–13. "Politicality" is not Balibar's invention (the earliest use of it I have found is in the 1930s) but it is he who makes it so analytically powerful. In his formulation it registers a potential for something to be charged with new stakes and new demands. WikiDiff notes that "'politicality' is not English"!

Treatment of forgetting as a political concept must address what is rendered more intelligible by such a designation, what conflicts and contests of relevance are worked through by a claim to forgetting—marking a refusal or embrace. And when does it appear *as if* in its benign, innocuous form—as a term, a simple gerund, or a phrase? What matters is the political forcefield into which it, as a concept is recruited and how its very deployment announces the *capacity to alter the field of the political itself.* Thinking with Gadamer, Richard Bernstein in his spare precision prose, might challenge us to ask what demands that a way of thinking and thus the use of a particular political concept puts upon us?[12]

Concepts occur in constellations, as Deleuze and Guattari insist.[13] Forgetting does as well. Clusters of other concepts enter into its orbit, share some of its features, others hover on its edges. Forgetting may respond to a private trauma or a state prohibition, the public injunction not to re-member and what not to rehearse. It may require the setting aside of prior designations that do not meet the policed criteria of an authorized common sense. Forgetting may cancel out other appellations for a phenomenon.

Some re-labelings are insidious familiar obscurants: genocide as "national defense," a torture-infested and protracted colonial war as intermittent "police actions" or "the events," "pacification" standing in for murder. For decades, these were the operative terms of French officialdom with respect to colonial Algeria and France's "war without a name."[14] In the Netherlands, the ubiquitous phrase, "police action," covered the orchestrated murder of Indonesian freedom fighters just after Indonesia declared independence (not yet recognized by the Netherlands.) In its gerund

---

12. Richard Bernstein, *Beyond Objectivism and Relativism: Science, Hermeneutics and Praxis* (Philadelphia: University of Pennsylvania Press, 1983), 137; Hans-Georg Gadamer, *Truth and Method* (New York: Continuum, 1999).

13. Gilles Deleuze and Felix Guattari, *What is Philosophy?* (New York: Columbia University Press, 1994).

14. A major proponent who refused the euphemistic and degrading nomenclatures for the war see Benjamin Stora, *La gangrene et l'oubli: La memoire de la guerre d'Algérie* (Paris: La Découverte, 1991). For the Netherlands, see Paul Bijl, "Colonial

form and as a political concept, forgetting conceals as it points to the polyvalent nature of its labor. Forgetting depends on—as it draws—other concepts into its chiseled out memory and aphasic folds. If concepts are "centers of vibration" as Deleuze and Guattari hold, forgetting a political concept accentuates the potent intensity of those vibrations.[15]

FORGET-ABILITY

Thinking with Samuel Weber's enabling exegesis on Walter Benjamin's commitment to the suffix "-abilities," offers a third opening of a different sort.[16] It's one that again releases the concept from the assuredness of the act in a finite, fixed, and finished form. In what we might call Benjamin's political semiotics, "forgetability" would put the emphasis not on the emphatic, determined sense that things *must* be forgotten of colonial histories. Forgetabilities turn us to what could have been otherwise, but also to what "forgetting" harbors, what is "potentially 'at work' even where it seems factually not to have occurred."[17] This "reserve" of possibility may be a portal where deadened, inactivated, refused memories escape from the protected truths.

Benjamin advocates, as Weber writes, "the re-inscribing of established terms so that *they part company with themselves*."[18] The point is not to "dissolve" a term but to attend to its distinctive "spatio-temporal singularity." Parting "company with themselves" may incorporate elements that newly attach to terms,

Memory and Forgetting in the Netherlands and Indonesia," *Journal of Genocide Research* 14, no. 3–4 (October 2012).
 15. Deleuze and Guattari, *What is Philosophy?* 23.
 16. Samuel Weber, *Benjamin's -abilities* (Cambridge: Harvard University Press, 2008).
 17. Weber, *-abilities*, 6.
 18. Weber, *-abilities*, 9.

reconfiguring their ground. Benjamin's is a conceptual rescue operation for what we think we already know. "Forget-ability" resists the inevitability of what has occurred—as a release from the hardened forms in which "forgetting" is accepted as given, and assuredly named. We might think here of the vexed, imprecise English translation of the French "*oubli*," invariably translated as "oversight," "oblivion," "forgetting." As composite, these terms are so disparate they hardly adhere to the same phenomenon, nor inevitably congeal into a constellation. The range elides the political work that forgetting entails, confusing the Austinian "excuse" for an act of withdrawal from knowing with the act itself.[19] "Forget-ability" rather stays close to those "conditions of possibility" of potency and potential, not always or yet present.

Each of these openings widens the scope of the field—as it narrows the specificities of use and production. In earlier work I sought to identify the conditions of attentiveness and materiality forgetting elicit and require. "Colonial aphasia" attempts to make sense of how long and how viscerally colonial damages are pre-eminent and absent.[20] If, for some, colonial entailments are decidedly extraneous to mainstream European national histories, for others, these broader histories make up the very core of what constitutes Europe as a political fabrication and strategic entity. Distribution of colonial aphasia charts the politics of racially defined relevancies to spaces of democratic inequalities. But colonial aphasia is also a political condition in which occlusion of knowledge is at once a dismembering of words from the object to which they refer, a difficulty retrieving both the lexical components of vocabularies, a loss of access that may verge on

---

19. English Translation of "Oubli," Google Translate, accessed May 15, 2021, https://www.google.com/search?client=safari&rls=en&q=oubli+english&ie=UTF-8&oe=UTF-8.

20. Ann Laura Stoler, "Colonial Aphasia: Disabled Histories and Race in France," in *Duress: Imperial Durabilities in Our Times* (Duke: Duke University Press, 2016), 122–170. A shorter version first appeared in *Public Culture* 23, no. 1 (2011): 121–156.

active dissociation, a difficulty comprehending what is seen and spoken.

DIAGNOSING POLITICAL ECOLOGIES

The suggestion that the act of forgetting might explain a practice, describe a subject position, or provide a useful epistemological perspective has little currency among students of colonial formations and their histories of the present. It is often dismissed as a wry provocation. But like disregard, forgetting can be labor intensive even as a failed excuse for neither wanting to know nor the will to do so. There still remains more to ask about its timing, duration, and techniques of production. Appreciating how it has re-emerged as a "virtuous act," (and its promotion as ethical and radical intervention) enjoys little consensus in public and academic domains.[21] For the always strategic timing of celebratory forgetting by political pundits and prime ministers reads as a myopic dismissal of imperial damage.

Not surprisingly Nietzsche is the authorizing figure, his counsel recruited to serve this gestural economy, where an "excess of historical sense" is detrimental and the "unhistorical" fosters the power of forgetting. The counsel is taken as unambiguous: forget in order to live, to renew and remember. Nietzsche aside, the consoling arguments that humans are either hardwired to forget or that forgetting is a moral good come with other claims: history is too burdensome, the making of personhoods should be released

---

21. See Paul Muldoon, "The Power of Forgetting: *Ressentiment*, Guilt, and Transformative Politics," *Political Psychology* 38, no. 4 (2017): 669–683, for a strong critique of this position. From the "front-line" journalist in the Bosnian war, see David Rieff, *In Praise of Forgetting: Historical Memory and Its Ironies* (New Haven: Yale University Press, 2011), 144, who writes of the "ethical imperative of forgetting so that life can go on," as if this was an equally distributed option.

from that burden. Both blot out the inequitable possibilities of participating in that alleviation. The assault can be on identity politics but more directly on those for whom violating histories cling and won't let go—and where viral, intimate political lines are drawn.

The narrative is succinct and shared: that "contemporary political life is preoccupied with traumas of the past and ought to be reoriented back to the future."[22] Once condemned as a "cognitive vice," forgetting is now embraced, as a "characteristic of normal adult human beings ... eliminating 'clutter' from [a] memory store." The vocabulary is almost arcane, drawing on a long-rejected model metaphor of memory imagined to mimic "the inaccessibility of stored records."[23] The breezy reference to "normal" needs no comment. History as "clutter" is more than a misnomer: for many, it's a violent imperial assault. Enter "the Holocaust," remaining the ubiquitous, fiercely protected standard of what James Baldwin called the (Euro-American) *White Republic*'s managed fiction.[24] From a colonial perspective, "forget" here resounds as an imperative and command. As Maori are repeatedly told, contesting white New Zealanders' refusal to acknowledge "indiscriminate land confiscations" and consequent generations living in poverty, "stop living in the past," its in your interests to move on.[25] That injunction is incessant, repeated across the imperial globe.

---

22. Muldoon, "The Power of Forgetting," 670.
23. Kourken Michaelian, "The Epistemology of Forgetting," *Erkenntnis* 74, no. 3 (2010): 404. Locke's metaphor as a "storehouse of ideas" has long been discredited, a point Karen Strassler and I discussed in "Casting for the Colonial: Memory Work in 'New Order' Java," *Comparative Studies in Society and History* 42 (2000): 4–48. Also see Ashere Koriat and Morris Goldsmith, "Memory Metaphors and the Laboratory/Real-Life Controversy: Correspondence versus Storehouse Concepts of Memory," *Behavioral and Brain Sciences* 29, no. 2 (1996): 167–228.
24. James Baldwin, *The Evidence of Things Not Seen* (New York: Henry Holt, 1985).
25. Note these same phrases were used by then French President Nicolas Sarkozy in 2005 to Senegalese students in Dakar and French President Macron in 2017. On New Zealand see Vincent O'Malley, "What a Nation Chooses to Remember and Forget: The War for New Zealand's History," *The Guardian*, October 17, 2016, https://www.theguardian.com/commentisfree/2016/oct/18/what-a-nation-chooses-to-remember-and-forget-the-war-for-new-zealands-history.

The call to forget performs different kinds of political labor. It can be a *diagnostic* of faultlines of what is not forgotten at all. It can reduce one's witnessing as suspect: proof, credibility, evidence, sincerity invoked when in the end none of those matter in part because proof is never enough, when dispossession and violence are refitted, and reframed.[26] Forgetting intercedes in how the political is conceived at any one moment and place, muting or amplifying what is imagined as possible to no longer confidently claim to know.. But not necessarily. As both Freud and Foucault insisted, occlusions are opportunities, *displacements leave the imprint of what was effaced.* An insight follows: an appreciation of the relationship between forgetting and remembering that does not perform a reduction to an on/off switch, thereby cancelling out the muddier grey zones of partial recognition, harder to trace and more often the case.

FORGETTING AND SCENES OF ITS MAKING

It is with these thoughts in mind that I treat forgetting as a working political concept, not as possessing a unified sense, but as a grouping of "dispersed events."[27] What goes into that synthesis? How broad is the field of possible events for which forgetting is called to account? Does equating forgetting with an "oversight" or the "overlooked" (for *oubli*) reveal an implicit logic covered (over) by the term? Does it signal a way to demarcate a political lexicon that makes of these two alternatives (oversight and overlooked) not peripheral but pertinent modifiers to the excuses that forgetting affords, to its logic and affective grammar?

---

26. Fabian, "Forgetful Remembering," 499.
27. Michel Foucault, "Nietzsche, Genealogy, History," in *The Foucault Reader*, ed. Paul Rabinow (New York: Pantheon, 1984), 76–100.

Or might we ask the always generative Derridean question: how forgetting as political concept *conceals the scenes of its making*? Here it carries its plural referents: scenes of avoidance or contest over what we can know and how we can know it. At issue then is awkward confrontation with the opacities forgetting affords, displacements that may be neither fictive nor real. Subterfuges, blockages, and replacements encircle and flit on its epistemic edges. In the end, the political power of forgetting may not be an absence or evacuation of memory, nor an outright erasure of things. We might rather broach its work as a *recomposition of relevance*, a reconfiguring of political accountabilities.

Forgetting knowledge of racial perceptions, practices, and imaginaries is a feat, an achievement, given the breadth of its contemporary and ever-expanding archive. Knowledge production is basic to the infrastructure of imperial macropolities, forged from commanding categories and authorized systems of classification. "Seeing like an imperial state" demands a valorization of some kinds of knowledge and a selective winnowing of those bits and pieces of demotic words and deeds demoted as facts poorly founded.[28]

Category-making, not unlike comparison—as Nietzsche warned—is built on the equation of unequal things, on foregrounding some features, on the dismissal and rapid foreclosure, forfeiting, and forgetting of others—features made featureless, unremarked, unmemorable if not unremembered. Forgetting and category-making could be construed as basic to the architecture of knowledge production—elements in a conjoined parsing project.

Being wary and recalcitrant in the face of forgetting then is not to argue that forgetting may not be inherent to some cognitive acts. Nor need it hold that some forgetting is psychogenic and involuntary (the result of brain trauma) as opposed to what some psychologists refer to as the "folklore" of amnesia of traumatic

---

28. James C. Scott, *Seeing Like a State* (New Haven: Yale University Press, 1999).

events.²⁹).The challenge is pointed: to identify the affective dispositions and political conditions that produce forgetting as a violent and viable concept, conferring under cover, the attributes of what is benign and blameless, unfortunate, but reasonable common sense. We need a better inventory of the steps that produce its micro-ecologies.

To invoke forgetting may be a declaration of a coercive imposition (of a state), or motivated by barely recognized discomfort and shame, a reaction to knowing too much. It may mark the social absence of knowledge once readily available; endorsements withdrawn, new sanctions imposed. Descriptions of forgetting can verge on rage at the violations not remembered, rage galvanized to buttress an indictment, the ballast for a legal claim. Preceded by the adjective "social," the indictment of forgetting is softened and diffused, implicitly assuring that no one is blamed. The indictment is focused on the conditions that render it neither a desirable, nor safe option to remember. Thus the 2018 ruling in Poland making it a criminal offense to invoke or incite others to refer to specifically Polish concentration camps during World War II.³⁰ But the policing and polishing of memory as we know are not forgetting. Silence is neither symptom nor cause of forgetfulness. Veena Das's work should dissuade assuming we know what it entails. It may sustain knowledge and strengthen its connectivities and embodied force.³¹

"The great forgetting"—Adam Hochschild's term to describe the wholesale public annihilation of Belgium's treatment of King

---

29. R. J. McNally, "The Science and Folklore of Traumatic Amnesia," *Clinical Psychology Science and Practice* 11, no. 1 (2004): 29–33.

30. Rachel Donadio, "The Dark Consequences of Poland's Holocaust Law," *The Atlantic*, February 8, 2018, https://www.theatlantic.com/international/archive/2018/02/poland-holocaust-law/552842/.

31. See Parvinder Mehta, "Repressive Silences and Whispers of History: Lessons and Legacies of 1984," *Sikh Formations* 11, no. 3 (2015): 366–396, a special issue devoted to "the seemingly reformist ideology of forgetting the anti-Sikh violence of 1984 and moving on."

Leopold's atrocities in the Congo (despite well documented condemnation by Mark Twain, Roger Casement, and others at the turn of the twentieth century.) It was "great" because it required a massive machinery to do its work: archives burned, documents shredded. Researchers systematically were denied access to those remaining documents not turned to ash.[32] This was a state administered project, an active succession of sustained deeds, destruction by design that rendered remembered things murkier, unverifiable, and by evidentiary standards, suspect.

LEACHING THE CONTEXTS OF RELEVANCE

It's not difficult to miss what is ostensibly forgotten in the ever-charged political arena of imperial histories—of Germany, Portugal, Spain, Britain, Australia, the Netherlands, Japan, Belgium, Canada, Italy, France, the United States. The issue rises to presence and recedes from view in waves of *astonishing regularity*.

The sheer number of colonial violences, mass murders, gross human rights violations, claimed to be forgotten, are overwhelmin. The staggering number of orchestrated acts of mass killings and mass executions in the Netherlands Indies—one in 1947 in the village of Rawagede, only acknowledged by the Dutch state in 2011—has been a political hotspot in the Netherlands today as it was never allowed to surface before.[33] Chiara Cesari writes of

---

32. Adam Hochschild, *King Leopold's Ghost: A Story of Greed, Terror, and Heroism in Colonial Africa* (Boston: Houghton, Mifflin, Harcourt, 1999); Mark Twain, *King Leopold's Soliloquy: A Defense of his Congo Rule* (Boston: The P. R. Warren Co., 1905), https://digitalcollections.amnh.org/asset-management/2URM1TE32PY?FR_=1&W=1150&H=919.

33. See Remco Raben, "On Genocide and Mass Violence in Colonial Indonesia," *Journal of Genocide Research* 14, no. 3/4 (2012): 485–502; Manfred Gestenfeld, "How the Netherlands Hid Its War Crimes for Decades," *Besa Center*, August 31, 2020, https://besacenter.org/perspectives/netherlands-war-crimes; Joeri Boom,

the "carceral heritage of Italian colonialism in Libya in the 1930s where close to half of the hundred thousand Bedouins imprisoned in Italian camps were killed or died of starvation" as a memory "foreclosed."[34] The U.S.'s successive dispossessions, mass murders, and assault on Native Americans were incessant but barely acknowledged and named. The infamous small pox war that killed thousands is rarely tied to the military officer, Amherst, the namesake of one of New England's elite small colleges.[35]

With respect to that regularity: forgetting knowledge in this fractious space of imperial deeds knows no linear course nor adheres to a linear narrative. Those histories *rarely accrue cumulative credibility. Attentiveness may be as recursive as these histories themselves. Or new attention may be triggered by current violences resonant, though not mimetic with earlier ones.* As such, public political awareness can't be tracked along an enlightening path from ignorance to knowledge, sidelining to attending, forgetting to remembrance and discovery.[36] As students of colonialisms past and present have come to recognize inventories of colonial violences, discriminations, damage and debris expand and contract, mushroom and retract. They come in and out of political focus as often as they are pulled in and out of the "civilities" of public discussion and their selective bounds.

What forgetting to know something looks like, what terrain of knowing it occupies, what features of a person, an event, a situation remain vivid, defy hermeneutic prowess, nor are they resolved by more ready archival access. Events may be remembered and

---

"Nieuw bewijs van massa-executie in Indonesie, *Archiefmap 1304*," *De Groene Amsterdammer*, October 10, 2008, nr. 41.

34. Chiara de Cesari, "The Paradoxes of Colonial Reparation: Foreclosing Memory and the 2008 Italy–Libya Friendship Treaty," *Memory Studies* 5, no. 3 (2012): 316–326.

35. For a recent re-appraisal see, Elizabeth A. Fenn, "Biological Warfare in Eighteenth-Century North America: Beyond Jeffery Amherst," *The Journal of American History* 86, no. 4 (March 2000): 1552–1580.

36. As Val Daniel would argue, here there is no Kantian *Aude Sapere* to be had.

things preserved, but *contexts of significance may be leached from them*. We need scaffolding to situate and remember—as theorists as diverse as Dan Sperber and Walter Benjamin insist—relevance is required, however construed.[37] Thus master ethnographers Richard and Sally Price have spent decades in Martinique trying to make sense of how "one generation's powerful historical metaphors could so quickly become the next generations' trivial pursuit."[38] This shearing of significance follows criteria of changing revelance. What Price called the "folkorization of colonialism" was an embattled colonial condition, now absented for some, deeply resented by others.[39]

KNOWLEDGE SUSPENDED, NOT FORGOTTEN

By the logic of imperial governance, some knowledges are deemed verified and qualified, disqualifying others. For many of those knowledge producing artisans, archons, and collectors—doctors, geographers, map makers, educators, ethnographers, journalists—that disqualified knowledge fell outside their policed and politically inflected expertise as they peddled and sanctified their own. But even here the lines between qualified and remembered, and disqualified and disowned were not clearly drawn. Foucault's insight remains useful here: that disqualified knowledges neither disappear nor are they truly forgotten. They remain embedded as subjacent, as suspended possibilities, inside qualified ones.[40]

---

37. Dan Sperber and Deidre Wilson, *Relevance* (Hoboken: Wiley Blackwell, 1986); for a revised, more concise statement of their argument, see Deirdre Wilson and Dan Sperber, "Relevance Theory," in *The Handbook of Pragmatics*, eds. L. R. Horn & G. Ward 607-32 (London: Blackwell, 2004).

38. Richard Price, *The Convict and Colonel: A Story of Colonialism and Resistance in the Caribbean* (Durham: Duke University Press, 1998), 157.

39. Price, *Convict and Colonel*.

40. Michel Foucault, *Il faut défendre la société: Les cours au College de France, 1975-1976* (Paris: Gallimard, 1997).

Augustine figured it long ago: one cannot look for something forgotten unless it is partly remembered.[41] Mary Carruthers' striking study of medieval mnemonics too underscores that no forgetting of knowledge is not remembrance otherwise. There is none that does not invoke that which *one remembers to forget,* replacing those objects, images, and relations with others, buttressed by another set of associations, smothering one set of truths with a counterclaim.[42]

An allied principle underwrites imperial pursuits and the dispositions it animates, if not requires. I've referred to this as "a politics of dis-regard."[43] Dis-regard entails a turn from the object, a turn of the body, of eyes and mind, a recognition that the object, the person, the event, is something from which one needs, wants, feels compelled to look as if not to have seen, to partly register, and turn away. One of the "prompts" I have followed in asking more about the politics of disregard as a set of principles and practices derives from a tacking between the contexts of late colonial periods and the contemporary diffractions of (Euro-American) imperial pasts today.

Working on the itinerary of a would-be whistleblower in the Dutch colonial civil service whose truncated career spanned some twenty years in the late-nineteenth century, was one of the sites where disregard took on an arresting and intimate cast. Both he and his compatriots seemed to cultivate a capacity to both see and not see what was around them, to know and not know the

---

41. Saint Augustine, *The Confessions*, trans. Henry Chadwick (Oxford: Oxford University Press, 1992).

42. Mary Carruthers, *The Craft of Thought: Meditation, Rhetoric, and the Making of Images, 400–1200* (New York: Cambridge University Press, 1998); In reflecting and working on how forgetting operates in the urban-industrial region of Shaba/Katanga in Zaire/Congo where he has worked since the 1960s, Johannes Fabian too pursued the mix of remembering and forgetting and what might be understood as "degrees" of forgetting in "Forgetful Remembering: A Colonial Life in the Congo," *Africa: Journal of the International African Institute* 73, no. 4 (2003): 495.

43. Ann Laura Stoler, *Along the Archival Grain: Epistemic Anxieties and Colonial Common* Sense (Princeton: Princeton University Press, 2009), 237–278.

precarious and illegitimate conditions of their profits and privilege. These capacities were not what one might expect, sequentially activated, but active and present at the same time.

> Imperial dispositions are marked by a negative space: that from which those with privilege and standing could excuse [and recuse] themselves, an almost legal legitimacy that refusal confers... One might consider the blinding nearsightedness of circumscribed community that sets out the proper limits of care and why it makes ethical sense for a community not to concern itself more broadly. Ethics are not absent, rather they provide exemptions from what one need not do.[44]

They also provide exemptions from what one need not know. Disregard provides the opening chords, the prelude to what can be construed as displaced and forgotten.

FORGETTING AS STRUCTURED VIOLENCE

Such a process extends Nietzsche's indictment in "The Uses and Abuses of History" where he implicates us all. The allegation that opens these essays, is apt again; is that we take notice of the "great deal of strength" it requires "to be able to live and *to forget the extent to which to live and to be unjust is one and the same thing (emphasis added)*."[45] It's a chilling formula. How is it that Nietzsche's *apercus* strikes at the very heart of the present again and again? "To live and to be unjust is one and the same thing." Does that imply that living is already imbued with a violence

---

44. Stoler, *Archival Grain*, 256.
45. Fredrich Nietzsche, "The Uses and Abuses of History," in *Untimely Meditations*, trans. R. J. Hollingdale (New York: Cambridge University Press, 1996), 76.

of disregard and injustice—a refusal to acknowledge the consequences of surviving and flourishing each and every day? Forgetting is the hard labor of turning away from the inequalities in which we live. Nietzsche anticipates (and provides a template) for Foucault's biopolitical equation where the right to live and defense of society are equally contingent on turning from and condoning the bare boned precarities of others.

Imperial formations seem to provide the quintessential scenes of the crime, conditions taut between the politics of forgetting and those who are its agents and beneficiaries, groomed to look away. The concerted energy that European colonials once expended (and European settlers in Kenya, Israel, Canada, Australia, the U.S. deploy today) on crafting narratives to account for themselves raises the moral question again: is forgetting a response to an ethical dilemma, one way of withdrawing from the question?

In 2013, teaching a seminar on empire at a prison in upstate New York, students read Price's disturbing ethnography of a young Martinican generation not knowing the extent of French colonial violence and how impossible it was for the older generations to forget. Refusing to accept the collective amnesia ascribed to farmers and fishermen, Price went precisely after those who supposedly forgot (and found they had not). He did so through, what at the time were, unconventional methods. He went after fragments and debris, pieces of stories, a carved wood sculpture perched high on a bar shelf, postcards, unauthorized accounts, resonant rumors, and French criminal records.

One student, struck by the power exerted in forgetting, put his question this way: "Couldn't we argue that systemic forgetting is a form of structured violence?" The class went silent as did I. The clarity of the challenge deserved time of its own. The key terms, "systemic" and "structured," curved back to what it meant to implement strategic and endorsed deprivations. One could argue that his question condenses an entire field of critical colonial studies that targets the fiction that forgetting produces benign irretrievability where the two become indistinquisably meshed.

Sometimes forgetting is so structurally embedded in state policy and social norms that its provenance remains opaque: school texts that whitewash colonial wars, massacres labeled as progress: genocides effaced, rapes deemed inappropriate to discuss in schools, while others produce glitzy pornographic popular attention. These fall within the rubric of forgetting knowledge in exceedingly common ways. What we do know about colonial violences is that they get "rediscovered again and again," exposed and re-exposed as forgotten.[46] That quixotic enabling and disabling of recognition scrambles what ties words and things, leaving untouched the *forms* of knowledge susceptible to loss and why that repeatedly is so.

WHAT DO WE KNOW AND HOW DO WE KNOW IT?

Setting aside forgetting and memory as common sense opposites makes strong analytic and empirical sense. Emphasis turns to the space in between. Mary Carruthers' sense that forgetting is only remembering otherwise (with the "otherwise" contingent and subject to change), underscores how much that interstial space is shaped by what form knowledge takes, neither wholly remembered nor forgotten.

Might we consider then the *kind* of knowledge at issue and the ways of knowing implied? Perhaps *the more basic question is not whether there is knowledge forgotten, but why it becomes unavailable and inaccessible, neither easily retained nor retrieved*. With respect to colonial knowledge and knowledge of what is colonial,

---

46. Paul Bijl, "Colonial Memory and Forgetting in the Netherlands and Indonesia," *Journal of Genocide Research* 14, no. 3–4 (2012): 441–461.

Gilbert Ryle's distinction between "knowing that" and "knowing how" seems useful to make.[47] This might be a first step in assessing not only what is forgotten, but *what kinds of knowing* might be more easily retrievable, why some demand different work, why some things are attention-getting and then fall outside a readily accessible frame.[48]

Here the thought is to take Ryle's distinction a step further: it is to ask not only what these knowledge things are that mark off "knowing that" from "knowing how" with respect to structural inequalities. Equally important might be the sort of knowledge that goes into knowing not only *that* things matter but *how* they do so. Some commentators on Ryle's distinction treat it as a variant of the distinction between the ancient Greek notion of *episteme* and *techne*. I'm not sure that sufficiently covers what Ryle's "how" demands and can do. I would treat it rather as a closer affiliate of *phronesis*, an ethical clarity responsive to a situation. Indeed, "knowing how" might be construed as having the potential capacity to evaluate how something is to be judged with an ethical sensiblity that gives weight to the judgment.[49]

Or perhaps "knowing how" in this context of "forgetting" may be a practical wisdom in a politicized space of assent or dissension. Most commentators on Ryle's distinction never broach the political effects of the distinction. But that potential

---

47. Gilbert Ryle, "Knowing How and Knowing That: The Presidential Address," Meeting of the Aristotelian Society at the University of London Club, November 5, 1945, pp. 1–16.

48. For some of the key debates and extensive treatment of the distinction and arguments for and against Ryle's claims see, John Bengson and Marc A. Moffett, eds., *Knowing How: Essays on Knowledge, Mind and Action* (New York: Oxford University Press, 2011).

49. Mary Carruthers works with a similar distinction (underscored in italics) to Ryle's, but surprisingly makes no reference to him.. As she writes "What is 'truthful' about [*res memorabiles*] is not their content, that is *what* they remember, but rather their form and especially their ability to find out things, that is *how* they cue memories" (Carruthers, *Craft*, 35).

is where it effectively could be cast. British philosopher Jennifer Hornsby is among the few to question whether Ryle's notion of "knowing-how" is more than a craftsman-like knowledge (as in *techne*) but rather, "knowing *how to act* (*emphasis added*)."[50] As she notes, Ryle's discussions of "knowing how" turns to a vocabulary that reaches beyond "ability," to "competencies" and "capacities," or more specifically capacity to act ethically with respect to an historical claim. Ryle's own elaboration is compelling to "knowing how" as a "disposition . . . not a single-track disposition like a reflex or a habit. Its exercises are [among other things] the application . . . of deeds performed or deeds imagined."[51]

Tethering knowing-how to a disposition "to behave in certain ways" commonly is followed by a phrase that suggests "knowing how" is about "following the rules."[52] But it may also entail "knowing how" *to break the rules*, knowing when they need to be broken, recognizing when they need to be changed. Drawing on Ryle's distinction and valorization of "knowing how" (beyond the thinner reading where it marks an ability "to ride a bike"), we might consider where Ryle speaks to a different order of things— of "knowing how to apply truths."[53] This latter use is precisely what distinguishes "knowing that" (there were French colonies) from an incapacity of "knowing how to act." One manifestation of the latter would be a lack of discernment of what would constitute an ethical and political act. *It could be that one could remember*

---

50. Jennifer Hornsby, "Ryle's Knowing-How, and Knowing How to Act," in *Knowing How: Essays on Knowledge, Mind, and Action*, eds. John Bengson and Marc A. Moffett (New York: Oxford University Press, 2011), https://oxford.universitypress scholarship.com/view/10.1093/acprof:oso/9780195389364.001.0001/acprof-978019 5389364-chapter-3.

51. Gilbert Ryle, *The Concept of Mind* (New York: Penguin, 1949), 46, and see Section II "Knowing How and Knowing That," 26–60.

52. Jeremy Fantl, "Knowledge How," *The Stanford Encyclopedia of Philosophy* (Spring 2021 Edition), ed. Edward N. Zalta, https://plato.stanford.edu/archives/spr2 021/entries/knowledge-how/.

53. Hornsby, "Ryle's Knowing How," 4; Ryle, *Concept of Mind*, 6.

that something happened but set aside how it mattered and why it still does so.

I am not concerned with whether Ryle fully implies this—indeed none of the numerous commentaries on the distinction—and the conflicts over how the distinction might be thought—are concerned with addressing its political implications. But the distinction may underscore something crucial about the nature of the political *forms of forgetting* activated when the principles and practices of colonial violences recede from a viable frame of relevance. There is no need to posit that a general French public "forgot" or "have forgotten" that there was a military campaign in Algeria, one designed to hold on to what some French thought was rightly part of France. It might rather be that people were shorn of the capacity and bereft of the competencies to "know how to act," to know how to defy a state-sponsored forgetting, to know how to make judgements and cultivate dispositions contingent on "knowing how to apply truths."

For "knowing how" is not simply a competence in "doing" a physical act. It is as much an illocutionary, performative one. By Ryle's account it need not be said or done but thought and imagined. It is a relational knowledge that places weight on the ethos, and value on the pathos of a polis' constitutive members. The unspoken question: who enters my field of analytic and political vision? Who within and outside the boundaries of what I think I know can be part of where my discernments are directed? At issue is not whether "knowing that" is something that might have been labeled an event or remained a non-event. It is rather that knowing how something matters and how I should act with respect to that knowledge represents a particular political disposition. It calls into question the very "politicality" of knowledge and how it aids in assessing truth-claims. Cultivation of a (political) self, implicates how memory and forgetting are entwined, where the demands of having and gaining citizenship may be a criterium for my field of vision, or defiantly ignored with respect to my "knowing how to act."

Politicality manifests in divisive partitions. It puts person and polities on the line. This latter feature of knowing, where phronetic know-how seems most fully to reside, cannot be one of rational choice alone. *Phronesis* depends on a richer epistemic field in which sensibilities and sentiments equally make up the fabric of how we know what we know. "Knowing how to act" versus "knowing that" is morally and politically more demanding: the former authorizes the recusals one affords oneself for not needing to remember or to know more, to know more deeply, or to know better. But then there is another version to consider of knowing how, which is, "knowing what it is like" which brings to the fore, not only "knowing how to act" but having the political imagination to know how something is experienced and endured by someone whose choices are not my own.[54]

THE CONDITIONS OF IRRETRIEVABILITY

One of Walter Benjamin's iconic observations aptly identifies the problem here: that "every image of the past that is not recognized by the present as one of its own concerns threatens to disappear *irretrievably* (*emphasis added*)."[55] What is meant by recognition—and of what? Recognize here is an understanding of what is pressing, relevant, applicable, noteworthy in its semblance and dissemblance from contemporary concerns. Recognition then could be an interpretive act, identifying semblance to earlier

---

54. This is an almost impossible demand of "knowing how" and what something is "like." See Michael Tye, "Knowing What It Is Like: The Ability Hypothesis and the Knowledge Argument," in *Reality and Human Supervenience: Essays on the Philosophy of David Lewis*, eds. Gerhard Preyer and Frank, 223–38 (Lanham: Rowman & Littlefield, 2000).

55. Walter Benjamin, "Theses on the Philosophy of History," in *Illuminations*, ed. Hannah Arendt (New York: Schocken, 1976), 255.

colonial contexts, locating iteration without repetition of the same, appreciating dispersed events, not an originary conflict but multiple threads of a genealogy.

Omitted from the English translation of *Illuminations* and only in some of the French translations which Benjamin himself edited, suggests something else. It is where Benjamin invokes Dante's verse to underscore that irretrievability is not the consequence of a one-time erasure: it is produced by *multiple* erasures and forgettings.

> Immobile truth, which only awaits the researcher, in no way corresponds to this concept of truth applicable to historical matters. It rather rests on Dante's verse that says, "It [historical truth] is a unique image, irreplaceable of a past that vanishes with *each present* that does not know to recognize being targeted [vise] by it."[56]

That omitted paragraph makes irretrievability and forgetting the consequence of *multiple acts of omission and conjurings of irrelevance*. It is not a loss of the past cut off at a particular moment, but the repeated misrecognition—re-installed irrelevance, blocked again and again.

Weber's attentiveness to Benjamin's formulation of "-abilities" offers further clarity. The loss is potential not given, not a *fait accompli*. Each forgetting reinstalls and closes off access. The fact of being "irretrievable," as both Benjamin and Weber suggest, is not the same as the potential quality of "irretrievability." The former assumes an annihilation of knowledge, a finitude, rarely so. The latter leaves open the possibility that this lack of recognition of the past's relevance may squander the opportunity for critique.

---

56. See Michael Lowry, *Walter Benjamin: Avertissement d'incendie: une lecture des thèses "Sur le concept d'histoire"* (Paris: Presses Universitaires de France, 2001), 48–49.

Or it may seize upon the past differently through contemporary iterations, never repetitions of the same.

Rather than irretrievable loss, too finite, I see suspended recognition, roadblocks to awareness, knowings rendered as "unknowing," under arrest. Parameters of current concern resonant with the past, or in learned and motivated contrast to it. One is a history of the present; the other a history crafted as a radical difference from this present, relegated to the *passé composé*. With respect to imperial ruinations, *knowing how something matters* is key. We need structures of relevance and accountable frames.

ANOTHER RIP-OFF AND THE HUMAN CONDITION

Forgetting is usually taken to be a loss of knowledge, but could the studious effacement of persons and the depreciation of context be a more specific subject of forgetting? What's in a scene, the entirety of a situation, or rendition of significance in a war of position.? We might return to the student who refused to relegate forgetting to an inadvertent lapse. He held fast to forgetting as constituted of *repeated* acts, of structured violence. Michel de Certeau warned that the grit of history has the power to erode concepts and wear them out. Might the concept of forgetting fail and fall, succumbing to corrosive wear of fickle fashion, thinned by overuse?[57] Can it still capture the histories that take cover in its shadows?

---

57. For Michel de Certeau, "The Historiographical Operation," in *The Writing of History*, trans. Tom Conley, 56–110 (New York: Columbia University Press, 1992), "construction and erosion of units" are two operations, central to all historical writing. For thinking about "forgetting" as an organizing principle of historical writing, his attention to the "slow erosion of organizing concepts" is key (de Certeau, *Writing of History*, 98).

Albert Camus' *The Stranger* imagines the lapse as posing a challenge. Having written about this work elsewhere, here I rethink it through a different lens. By the reading of the Algerian journalist *cum* novelist, Kamel Daoud, Camus' 1942 novel was a rip off, and a scam. So, he writes in his 2013 novel, *The Contre-Enquête*, translated in English as *The Mersault Investigation*, a *contre-histoire* to the one that Camus told of a young Arab shot five times by a spineless French office clerk, Mersault, on an Algerian beach in the glare of an afternoon sun.

Here I think less about Daoud's rewriting than about the colonial figures on whom Camus draws, as a kaleidoscopic rendition of what defines the "modern condition" in Camus' account. The most visceral rip off, Daoud states, is that the victim referred to twenty-six times as "the Arab" in *The Stranger*, is never given a name. In Camus' telling, we know nothing about his family, what he looks like, his home, his voice. *The Mersault Investigation* does just that: His name is Musa, a tattooed body, his brother Harun an aged alcoholic still in Oran who tells his tale. Musa is long and lean, has a girlfriend, a job, and a mother who goes nearly mad with grief for her murdered son and his disappeared body.

But the swindle goes further and is harder to track; for Camus plays with mirrors, taking what is an eminently colonial condition of meager lives and mediocre desires as the universal anguish of modern man. The act of omission leaves traces, but not enough for most readers to recognize the racial infrastructure beyond colonial Algeria. Indeed, the reader is encouraged not to do so. Colonial knowledge is everywhere and nowhere. Camus uses the colonial *mis-en-scène* for the senseless murder of an unnamed victim, while Daoud in retribution casts the colonial at center stage.

Or maybe Camus does too: the very parable he writes of the human condition, that he literally *steals* from Musa and his family, is instead a colonial one through and through. The hoax is on us: colonialism is hidden in full view—omnipresent and absent at the same time. Camus complicates the notion of forgetting. For clearly Camus did not forget to mention where the novel takes place. He names it again and again. It is not the landscape but the colonial condition which is so brutally effaced.

It is not that Camus duped us all by writing an everyman's life off this aphasic colonial tableau. It is rather that the very *mis-en-scène* makes *the colonial situation itself the template of our contemporary world*. It is in the stark glare of a French Algeria that genealogies of inequality course back through colonial histories to span the racial predicaments of our times. What does it do to call this forgetting? When is omission a commission and a violent act? What kind of knowledge can follow such systematic effacement? Can one sustain a faceless nameless Musa and not read this as a violent imposed refusal of his person? Is it enough to grant him a name? Camus borrowed and buried the colonial situation of Algiers and Oran in a nameless place, as an allegoric fable.

The robbery was that *The Stranger* is NOT everyman. It is a place and a space shaped by a racial and colonial history that excludes, and targets, and surveils, as it evokes a racial condition that is our own. Forgetting can be configured as "to *let forget*" as well. Daoud does not let us forget. He reminds us that there is no reading *The Stranger* without recognizing how many of "us" remain in the heart of the beast as before the Algerian war. Despair, violence, and privations were only partially seen, during and after.

But the scam is deeper still. *The Stranger* is elevated to the iconic masterpiece of existential anguish, meaninglessness, emptiness, and boredom in a universal modern man, untouched by time and place. It ties a knot of complicity around us all. The violences made possible, and the remorse that was not, was not a universal story. It was situated and located in the underbelly of French colonialism in Algeria. And Musa's effacement made sense for a broader imperial world in which "the native" needs neither psychic space nor geopolitical belonging. The swindle is how easy it makes forgetting when one is licensed to not need to know or to ask.

The decades in which Camus' *The Stranger* has been hailed as THE existentialist novel might be seen as a sour joke. For it was that and not that at all. And perhaps that magical feat made it a rip-off more than anything else: a mundane colonial reality elevated to THE shared existential condition of modern man—a novel that twisted what was thought in France to be outside its proper court. What was imagined as a *lieu de mémoire* exterior to France was in fact, *modernity's underside, empire in its shabby, unheroic, violently mediocre register.*

With Daoud's merciless retelling, we might see the colonial condition Camus chose not to name, not necessarily the one he prepared for us. It could be read for its global banality, *a common structure of imperial violence* played out in the white heat of the everyday. Here is a racially inflected detachment, an aborted pathos, a structure of feeling endemic to the imperial order of things. In Camus' rendition is a politics of disregard as the fate of a White republic. The "universality" of *The Stranger* is lodged dead center in the racial ecology in which we live.

We might think here with Benjamin again to ask what counts as "recognition" of "the past" by the present. Can that recognition be perceived through distortions, double images, refracted light, reflecting mirrors that make it difficult to discern a recognition of ourselves in that past? Is it a matter of recognizing a contemporary world made by that past, or a contemporaneity of that past, vital and potent in this present? What is it that we might potentially retrieve as the "present's concerns"? And whose concerns among us? What is it that Camus erases along with Musa's being and name? The colonial making of the modern "forgotten" again and again.

Gadamer's notion of the "historicity of understanding" thinks these concerns where he sets out two related thoughts: that "understanding begins . . . when something addresses us," when "our own prejudice is properly brought into play by being put at risk." "When something addresses us" is not a substitute for recognizing in the past the concerns of the present.[58] Rather, it registers the quest for an attunement, what might be learned by recuperating what some left aside because it was not needed to know. Forget-ability is a dangerous beast, whose powers are amplified by measures and modes of being that demean value and worth and thereby delimit what constitutes what can be rightly, not just inadvertently, set aside, dis(re)membered, and forgotten.

ON FORGETFULNESS "IN THE FLESH"

Nietzsche writes in *Genealogy of Morals* about "forgetfulness in the flesh."[59] It's an enticing and a strange phrase, suggesting that forgetfulness is marked on our bodies whether we want it to be or not. Or it may be that it is "in the flesh" in the sense that there is something close-up and intimate about that which we forget, between those sensibilities we inhabit as human kinds and what we otherwise know we should respond to and witnesses as informers. Nietzsche holds hat memory must be painful, inflicted by scars and wounds on the body and "in the flesh." This ensures that something is not forgotten. But if forgetting is never far from what is remembered, it might also suggest that what we work hard to forget is inscribed as well—the script might be different but forgetting has no easy retreat. It is indelibly marked upon us.

Or maybe we should be thinking about forgetting not as a galvanizing political concept but rather what one might think of as a concept *manqué*, what Louis Althusser once described as a *conceptual failure*. As Warren Montag puts it, with a clarity beyond Althusser's, we might think of forgetting as a concept that is constantly invoked as a stopgap "whose only function in

---

58. Gadamer, *Truth*, 299.
59. Frederick Nietzsche, *On the Genealogy of Morals II*, trans. Maudemarie Clark and Alan Swensen (Indianapolis: Hackett Publishing, 1998), 3.

a new domain is to conceal the absence of the concept required by the [problems] that have emerged in it."[60] Might it be that forgetting as a placeholder, even a conceptual one, is marshalled to amalgamate, compress, stand in for too many other processes at work in an instant and over time? In the end might it bring us no closer to what sorts of omissions and erasures are actually at issue? And then of course the question remains what parts of our sensory regimes forget as we move from translations of the visual to verbal, from the visual act of witnessing to the stench, to the screech, to the silent and unseen and unheard.

Conceptual failure is an invitation to ask more about *the leaching of relevance that forgetting requires*. Forgetting as achieved labor, makes room for other realities, other narratives. It scaffolds the conditions for subscribing to other regimes of truth. Ignorance, ignoring, and forgetting have shared histories in the imperial order of things. Sometimes they share political genealogies. But they are not the same. Ignoring, disregard and inattentiveness effectively slip knowledge off the page of what one needs to know. They can be mutually sustaining, but the affects that sustain ignoring and disregard may call upon a politics of sentiments for which we have neither adequate concepts nor names. Indifference and disdain are not enough. Ignoring and ignorance, ignoring and aversion, aversion and "inadvertent" forgetting do nefarious and surreptitious work. They may be where the politics of our accountabilities are defeated, where they lay and lie.

* * *

---

60. Montag, *Thinking with Balibar*, 11.

PART II

OF DISSENSUS IN THE MAKING

5

Poetic Rage

Anti-colonial Avant-gardes

IN 2016 EGIDIO MARZON'S PRIVATE collection of avant-garde works was donated to the Staatiche Kunstsammlungen Dresden. It was to be made into a public archive and to be named the Archiv der Avantgarden. In the company of artists, historians, architects, literary scholars, and poets, I was invited to participate in the three-day event in May 2019, devoted to thinking collectively about this archive in the making.[1] I had been invited to address the making of an archive, but I was as taken with what I saw as an unquestioned sense of what and who constituted an avant-garde.

Steeped for some forty years in colonial archives and the creatively resolute forms that responses to colonial repressions could take, it should be no surprise that the subject took me to outskirts of the European avant-garde, innovative force-fields of political and aesthetic practice, not peripheries at all. Calling on colleagues from the fields of art history, literature, design, curation, and poetics, their deep and longstanding knowledge of avant-gardes in Martinique, Morocco, proto-Indonesia, Central Europe, Palestine,

---

1. See The Whole Life: Archives and Reality, Hause der Kulturen der Welt, accessed May 13, 2021, https://www.hkw.de/en/programm/projekte/2019/the_whole_life/das_ganze_leben.php. I thanks Stefan Aue, a coordinator of the Whole Life archive project who first invited, encouraged, and challenged me to reflect on an archive of the avant-garde with an extraordinary group of curators, artists, and art historians whose own work spirited my own.

Interior Frontiers. Ann Laura Stoler, Oxford University Press. © Oxford University Press 2022.
DOI: 10.1093/oso/9780190076375.003.0005

*and Egypt drew me to sites of politicality and aesthetics I had not gone before.*²

This essay distills what I see as a fugitive, peripatetic set of counter-colonial avant-gardes, innovative and mobile to different degrees, challenging both what avant-gardes do and who are included among them. I do not treat them as a movement but as convergent spaces of work and thought, of "counter-conducts," of co-practitioners in restless motion, figuratively in style and genre, literally in the range of places they travel, paths they cross, where they linger, meet, and move to and from.³ What joins them are the singularities of where, how, and when they press against the oppressive weight of racialized imperial governance, the counter-colonial refusals they share in melding political and aesthetic commitments and labor. Their geopolitics makes for a restless, borderless archive, dismissive of finitudes, wary of certitudes, but taken with manifestos, visionary, and in formation.

---

2. Among the many I thank and without whom I could not have written this essay are Omar Berrada, Henk Maier, Keith Foulcher, Stathis Gourgouris, Lawrence Hirschfeld, Nancy Lutkehaus, Victoria Ebin, Shannon Mattern, Seloua Boulbina, Nancy Luxon, and Olivia Harrison.

3. I use the term 'counter-conduct' here in the sense that Michel Foucault sought to develop it, not as an opposition to the conduct to which one is suppose to subscribe and which is foised upon one, nor is it misconduct (*inconduite*). Rather it is a form of refusal beyond the act of disobedience but productive of new modes of being in relations to others and to oneself. See Michel Foucault, *Securite, territoire, populations, Lecon due 1 mars 1978, Cours au College de France 1977-1978* (Paris: Gallimard, 2007), 197- 219. This "revolte de conduit" (revolt of conduct) does not reduce to the negative of power but rather exceeds that negative, producing a new space of its own.

Although many of this avant-garde professed themselves 'anti-colonial," it could be argued that "counter-colonial" more accurately describes the moves they made, their modes of living, and the forms of aesthetics and filiations they developed. Also see Arnold Davidson, "In praise of counter-conduct," History of the Human Sciences 24, no.4 (2011), 25-41 and Bernard Harcourt, "From Counter-Conduct to Critical Attitude: Michel Foucault and the Art of Not Being Governed So Much," Foucault Studies no.21, 7-21 (June 2016), and Bernard Harcourt, "Contre/Counter-" in *Thinking with Balibar*, Ann Laura Stoler, Stathis Gourgouris, Jacques Lezra, eds., (New York: Fordham University Press, 2020), 71-84.

Though emerging from that Dresden invitation, the challenge came askew and from elsewhere: to understand politicality in a different register and mobile place, an aesthetics of dissent defiant of colonial governance and its conditions of subsumption. Tracking the ambiguities of political and aesthetic choice—from the common format of the "small magazine," the disguise of folkloric content to the printing and paper sources—it is clear that whether decisions (and restrictions) were made under fierce colonial surveillance, under Vichy command, or in the imperial aftermath of purported independence mattered enormously.

Some of the ambiguities now strike me not as issues to resolve, but as willed and sometimes strategic in the aesthetic making of dissensus as it emerged—experimental, casting aside modes of expression, rebels against canons while other implicit mandates were installed. In Southeast Asia, the Mahgreb, the Caribbean, Mexico, Brazil, the Middle East, in the urban enclaves of Beirut and Cairo and Port-au-Prince, with stopovers in Paris and New York and London, are circuits of movement, neither in unison nor in progressive succession. They appear in multiple cascades of political vision and aesthetic innovation.

Much of these avant-gardes, so named, cross archipelagos of colonial detentions and dispossessions; they were experienced piecemeal, sometimes on a global scale. If "managed mobilities" were emblematic *dispositifs* of colonial governance (as I long have argued), a common signature of these anti-colonial warriors was to be *emphatically in motion*, neither to be immobilized by government decree, nor dissuaded in their transgression by colonial constrictions and their fictive borders.

RIPTIDES OF DISSENT

The paradox is there from the start, in the very juxtaposition of terms: an "archive" by nature and in its emergence assumes a will and force of its own. It surreptitiously imposes category making, creates sharply marked divisions between information and debris. It sets out draconian rules of engagement: no pens, no photocopying, no cameras, ultimately no access. Not least, it elevates its own criteria of relevance as sacred in wielding its command. An "avant-garde," on the other hand, is poised and poses itself consciously not to do the opposite but to resist the nomos of classification and the norm of order, transgress the restrictions and constrictions that common sense so easily imposes even without explicit command.

Whatever this archive already includes, there is good reason to be on guard against its demands. Such an alert defines part of my venture: to address what principles and politics of authorization name something or someone as "avant-garde" without assuming who might care or remain indifferent to claim membership. What unexposed scaffolding might be brought into view, what does the label carry and to whom does it apply?. What sort of archive might it summon and what might go into its curation? And in the spirit of an avant-garde, what are the subversions we confront and might perform in doing so? It is a query that takes in Adorno's warning that no concept comes without a surfeit, a remainder, an excess that spills beyond its declared edges.[4] *It is precisely those edges—both of a possible archive and of a possibly radically differently circumscribed avant-garde to which I'm drawn.*

INVERTING THE LENS

My thought is that we might, as did the wondrous Filipino novelist and polymath José Rizal (executed by the Spanish government) with his subversive novels on the cusp of the twentieth century, recalibrate both the directionality and the gravitational

---

4. Theodor W. Adorno, *Negative Dialectics*, trans. E.B. Ashton (London: Routledge, 1973), 5.

pull of the imperial compass.[5] Might we invert the lens that has the European gaze riveted on the colony, and the colonized gaze turned toward Europe for "inspiration." Might these gazes melt into movement, materiality, and proximities that defy fixed directionality? In motion, circulating, accumulating new ways of seeing as they turn. I think here of the aesthetics of dissent not as it emerged at the presumed Euro-American core, but on a broader imperial map marked by anti-colonial moments and mobilities that transversed and transgressed that assumed center.

For here were an astounding trans-generational series of successive interventions, similar but never quite the same. These riptides of dissent flooded plains, breached levies, and the manicured gardens of colonial decorum. In so doing, they produced strikingly disruptive and eruptive forms of popular global politics. Histories of empire, produced a mottled mix of famed and unacceptable artists—novelists, poets, illustrators, journalists, and editors—who mobilized their dissensions to produce an irreverent aesthetics and recalcitrant politics. The forms of recalcitrance were neither fixed nor necessarily agreed upon. At the edges of such a potential archive and in the outer folds of what might be considered avant-garde emerges an anti-colonial compendium of possibilities and visions.

Documenting these breaths of vision from a clogged and embattled space identifies a loose set of allegiances at best. They might be made up of an assembly of small groups carrying out minor ventures, committed to bold interventions, or confronted with failed efforts. It is not even clear when and how an avant-garde might be considered successful or effective. Was it by its visibility or how belligerently it faced off the imperial powers (though public throngs did not know about it)? Perhaps it was neither a story of failure, nor one of success.

---

5. José Rizal, *Noli Me Tangere* (Manila: Institute Nacional de Historia, 1978) which frames Benedict Anderson's *The Spectre of Comparisons* (New York: Verso, 1998), 2.

What was the material with which they worked? Short lived journals, as in the insurgent Dutch East Indies on the cusp of becoming Indonesia in the 1930s. Some, like *Légitime défense*, published in Paris in 1932 (only one issue) by six Caribbean students who themselves saw the journal as a "provisional tool," were virtually ignored by those to whom it was acidly directed—the placid youth of Martinique.[6] As one of its authors, René Ménil, was to put it in a re-edition of *Légitime défense* forty-six years later, the "cruel pleasure of aggression" was a "way of settling scores with colonial hideousness (*laideur colonial*), 'sadism'" (as he put in parenthesis). The pleasure [was] also of living the inflicted wounds to better announce the legitimacy of the cause,"[7]

Légitime défense was followed by *Étudiant noir*, another "small review" (le petit journal) whose credentials gave it more fame but still dubious success.[8] The range of myths and ambiguities about how long the former lasted—a single edition in 1932, or two, whether poetry was included (it was not), whether it was indeed the first place where one of its group, Aimé Césaire, used the word "negritude" (the word he actually used was "*Négrerie*") was only rivaled by the fact that no African students (besides Senegalese Léopold Senghor) contributed to its profile, if not success. So, a question: was more made of their impact later than they actually had at the time? Or did their notoriety derive from the originary story they provided, with

---

6. Nor did it help that it attempted to garner a subversive imprimatur by borrowing its title from Louis Aragon and André Breton's surrealist pamphlet, *Légitime défense*, while writing against it.

7. René Ménil, Preface, *Légitime défense*, (Paris: Editions Jean-Michel Place, 1978).

8. Jean-Claude Michel, *The Black Surrealists* (New York: Peter Lang Publishers, 2000). Michel seems out to disparage the young collective of *Légitime défense* in nearly every sentence for being Marxist with surrealism offering them little more than "an excellent break to (sic) cultural assimilation." Jules-Marcel Monnerot, he writes, was the real leader of the group and a "sincere Marxist believer" (Michel, *Black Surrealists*, 32–33).

a beginning, specific time, and place of creation—facilitating retellings and an accessible narrative line?

That might have been what so irked the Cameroonian literary critic Edward Ako, who tracked down a half-century later the succession of (often unintended) misquotes and misinformation that was passed down (even by Césaire and Senghor years later) and by those who never saw or read either the one (or two) issues of *Étudiant noir* that actually appeared before it was censored.[9] But maybe not. There were revues that circulated across the Antilles in the 1940s, collectives that envisioned the Caribbean as a direct affront to colonial mandates, taking on petty and powerful forms of Vichy censorship to decry, to mock, to deplore.

In the early 1960s there was *Souffles-Anfas*, a journal with flaming, raging poetry and politics from Morocco. There were books published and immediately banned (think Frantz Fanon's *Wretched of the Earth*, emptied from French bookstores shelves by censures a day after it appeared).[10] And simultaneous with these dispersed movements, the succession of Asia-African congresses sometimes overrun by performative posturing (think Bandung 1955) but studded more importantly with prominent public figures who took their anti-European and anti-white supremacy politics as their mandate and founding premise.

---

9. Edward O. Ako, "*L'Etudiant noir* and the myth of the genesis of the Négritude Movement," *Research in African Literatures* 15, no. 3 (Fall 1984): 341–354. Ako writes that one of the most notorious mythmakers was (1931–1918) a French-Belgium specialist in African literature, Lilyan Kesteloot Lagneau who taught for years in Dakar. He railed most against her extensive analysis of the journal's content that she admitted she had never seen, attributing to its authors a distinct attitude to surrealism and communism (about which nothing had been written). As interesting is whether the claim that it was of the avant-garde was not only because of its sweeping anticolonialism but because both Césaire and Senghor were associated with it.

10. Olivia C. Harrison and Teresa Village-Ignacio, eds., *Souffles/ANFAS* (Palo Alto: Stanford University Press, 2016).

THE FICTION OF "A LITTLE-KNOWN CHAPTER"

Understanding how these constellations of persons maneuvered the constrictions of imperial governance, as well as psychic and material accumulations of imperial detritus pivots in different directions. Colonial installations that still made up the makeshift infrastructures in which they lived, entails taking on the always contentious claims about European "influence." Foucault reminds us early in *The Archaeology of Knowledge* that such concepts as "influence" are pernicious "ready-made syntheses" with "links whose validity is recognized from the outset," before the nature of those "links" have been established.[11] They pose as critical concepts but get in the way. Assessments of the "influence" of André Breton on Aimé Césaire, or Picasso on the Cuban artist Wilfredo Lam, or French poetics on the lilt of the Balinese poet Putu Oka Sukanta may conceal more than they reveal about how mutual inspiration, radical pedagogy, and learning work.

The model of a global avant-garde with a sprawling periphery and a European core, now seems predictably ethnocentric, Occidentalism gone rampant, a colonial imposition on positions that in the twenty-first century are hard to accept. That was not always so. As Doris Sommer might warn, we should "proceed with caution" on several fronts.[12] Nationalist visions and avant-garde dissidence sometimes seem hard to reconcile, but they appear over and again and cannot be ignored. (Brazil's ulta-avant-garde protagonists, Tarsila Do Amaral and Oswald de Andrade, for example, held tight both to a nationalist project and international audience.)

---

11. Michel Foucault, *Archaeology of Knowledge* (New York: Pantheon, 1972), 22.
12. Doris Sommer, *Proceed with Caution, When Engaged by Minority Writing in the Americas* (Cambridge: Harvard University Press, 1999).

Entreaties to honor the making of a new nation seem to converge and collide with innovative and dissident postures of this avant-garde for whom a nation-framed project was never enough. Experiment is one of the features of the avant-garde always noted. The anti-colonial avant-garde embraced experiments in genre, taking to one and rejecting another. There were moments of adoring adherence (remembering how very young many of these artists and literary "figures" were), finding a voice, moving on, and movement again. But as importantly, they were shaped by experiences of colonialism that were fundamental to why politicality was in their raced being. Being raced not race (as colonial experts imagined) is what coursed through the aesthetics of their politics, *in corpore*, in their veins, pulsating in bursts of outspoken energy, sometimes just the pulse of their everyday . . . obstreperous and not.

Exploring the features of an anti-colonial avant-garde finds its mode in the very embattled conditions to which it responded. Antonio Gramsci's distinction between "wars of maneuver" and "wars of position" is apt. These counter-colonial avant-gardes did not engage in "wars of maneuver." Frontal attack was neither their mode nor aim. Theirs were instead "wars of position"— "slow displacements," indirect forms, everyday and diffuse.[13] Those to whom I look here sought, as did the long unrecognized Suzanne Césaire, unedited truths behind the lush tropical island floral of bougainvillea. Behind it they knew a colonial imposed impoverishment, grim, cumulative, its grit embedded, its violence in their prose. As Suzanne Césaire put it, (and as Gramsci defined wars of position) her quest was to define what constituted the real, to build and develop a new definition of reality.

---

13. Amador Fernandez-Savater, War of Maneuver vs. War of Position, P2P Foundation Wiki, accessed May 13, 2021, https://wiki.p2pfoundation.net/War_of_Maneuver_vs_War_of_Position. Or for one of Gramsci's own discussions of that difference see Antonio Gramsci, *Selections from Prison Notebooks*, ed. and transl. Quitin Hoare and Geoffrey Nowell Smith, (London: Lawrence and Wishart, 1971), 229-235.

How to understand avant-gardes that transgress their common Euro-American sites of authorization? I see them inhabiting imperial metropoles not as sources of definition and innovation as often imagined, but as *waystations* on broader circuits of movement, opportune sites to cull and to sharpen what Aimé Césaire would call a distinctive "poetic knowledge." This sort of knowledge derives its force and form from the asphyxiating conditions of colonial racisms, the bold and camouflaged confrontations with imperial power to which those recalcitrant harbingers of hope found new ways to reject, not to adapt. Poetic knowledge attends to the senses, experiential tools carved from mobilities and detentions on land and sea that in turn have molded a death-defying poetics that makes that knowing a basis of dissent.

What might an archive look like of an avant-garde not only askew to Paris, its celebrated center, but askew to Europe as the epicenter of aesthetic and political experiment and innovation? What epistemic protocols may be breached, what politics might be mandated by a naming and locating of an avant-garde oblique to Euro-American concentrations of aesthetic capital, museum culture, philanthropic largesse, artistic endorsement, and institutional wealth?

In culling an-other, alter-archive, some persons and practices remain opaque, some come to the fore, others bring a new wave of attention to the aesthetic politics of the Global South. Cuban artist Wilfredo Lam (1902–1982) in his later years associated with surrealism, is caught in what appears as a burst of laughter with Picasso in a 1954 photo. Algerian-born Baya Mahieddine (1931–1998) is "championed" by Henri Matisse.[14] Aimé Césaire (1913–2008) shines as a luminary with André Breton by his side. These were European friends and alliances but their aesthetic politics was not forever dependent on those relations. Césaire's

---

14. On Baya Mahieddine see Baya: Woman of Algiers, Grey Art Gallery NYU, accessed June 15, 2021, https://greyartgallery.nyu.edu/exhibition/baya-woman-algiers/; on Wilfredo Lam, see Amica Sciortino Nowlan, "Who was Wilfredo Lam?" *1843 Magazine*, September 19, 2016, https://www.economist.com/1843/2016/09/19/who-was-wifredo-lam.

wife, Suzanne Césaire, who some consider to have been the "soul" of the famously anti-colonial surrealist-based magazine they founded, *Tropiques*, has been featured by an array of young scholars as an extraordinary figure, until recently lost in European and Caribbean male shadows.

There was Sumatran Sutan Takdir Alisjahbana, founder of *Pujangga Baru*, what some have dubbed as the first Indonesian avant-garde "small" journal (1933–1942), by others rejected as too smitten with "western civilization" to properly garner that title. Tadkir was probably less important to the making of *Pujangga Baru* than Armijn Pane. The latter was an avant-garde on his own terms and bolder than Takdir, who nevertheless was the one who won scholarly praise and is usually cited as *Pujangga Baru*'s founding editor.[15] Then there is the "little known chapter in the aesthetic struggles and political activism" in Egypt between 1938 and 1948 (the subject of a 2017 exhibition in Paris and Madrid) among whom were the Egyptian "pioneering women" who used photomontage "to deconstruct the human form and created surrealist juxtapositions that were commentaries on colonialism and the Fascist exploitation of Pharaonic Egypt."[16]

Each of these collectives and sites of their production provide a clue to something else: that being "avant-garde," disruptive, unacceptable, out of sync with obsequious hierarchies of value and wealth, were defined anew at different sites of imperial formation. This *organic politicality* emerges from what constitutes an effort (however failed) to assert a counter-vision to imperial racial

---

15. I thank Keith Foulcher and Henk Maier for their generous tutoring, each making this point to me in their own unique ways (personal communications, June 19, 2020).

16. Charles Ruas, "'Long Live Degenerate Art': In 'Art et Liberté,' an Egyptian View of Surrealism Addresses Contemporary Issues," *ARTNews*, March 6, 2017, https://www.artnews.com/art-news/reviews/subjective-realism-an-egyptian-view-of-surrealism-as-an-expression-of-contemporary-issues-7905/. For a more comprehensive view of the images and politics that informed the exhibit in Madrid see Raphael Rubinstein, "Surreal Cairo," *ARTNews*, January 25, 2017, https://www.artnews.com/art-in-america/features/surreal-cairo-63237.

orders, with anti-colonialism and anti-capitalism providing the fulcrum and defining their coordinates. This point and the task here is not to see how much and in what way these "peripheral" artists and writers *adhered* to an avant-garde norm, but how much they altered what made up the aesthetics of dissent and shaped so much of what was once considered a "European," Paris-centered venture.

While young Black poets/activists/artists were a kinetic force in the early avant-garde/surrealist circles, praise is still often handed to the "French surrealists [who] *embraced (emphasis added)* their black and brown counterparts from the start." But poetry and politics were already organically part of what they did and who they were. The small journal *Légitime défense*'s (*Self-Defense*) first edition was written as a manifesto by six Martinican students who convened in Paris and self-identified as French Caribbean. They disidentified with the brunt of their contempt: "*We are speaking to those who are not already branded as killed off, established, fucked-up, academic, successful, decorated, rotted, provided for, decorative, prudish opportunists (emphasis added).*"[17]

Their message was geared to young Black Caribbeans and "*la bourgeoisie de couleur française*" that they declared "is one of the saddest things in the world."[18] But, as they insisted, it was equally an invite to anyone and everyone who had not sold-out and cared to create a collective anti-imperial set of practices and consciousness. Their inaugural issue offered their sharpest condemnation of Antilleans unwilling to move. Their wrath was directed against

---

17. *Légitime défense*'s declaration as quoted in Lori Cole, "*Légitime défense*: From Communism and Surrealism to Caribbean Self-Definition," *Journal of Surrealism and the Americas* 4, no. 1 (2010): 15–30. See the original inaugural volume of *Légitime défense* (June 1, 1931): 1. The opening statement lists the following collective authors: Etienne Léno, Thelus Léno, René Ménil, Jules-Marcel Monnerot, Michel Pilotin, Maurice-Sabas Quitman, Augusta Thésée, Pierre Yoyotte. French authorities virtually banned the journal by suspending the students' grants.
18. *Légitime défense* (1931), 2.

those passive in the face of imperial sovereignty in its multinational, myriad, intimate and excruciatingly detailed forms:

> *The Antillean, crammed-full of white morality, of white culture, of white prejudices, paraded with puffed up images of himself.*[19] . . . *to be a really good imitation of those pale men, social reason serves as much as poetic reason.*[20]

Some of these incandescent and darker figures declared themselves avant-garde. Sometimes others declared them avant-garde. At times they were performative, some were recluses, shunning a public profile all together. Appearance in the public sphere and an attempted usurpation of what was acceptable in it, was a partial duty and requirement: to make noise, to disrupt, to use language and visceral description in ways that they imagined an upright, uptight bourgeoisie would not want to see or hear. Then there were others: unconventional in creative style, excessive (vis-à-vis the colonial norms or cold-war idioms of the moment), elsewhere dismissed as derivative or "second-rate," others defiant even under repressive colonial governance, unperturbed by proper forms of dress or address. Still, those who professed and declared themselves to be "avant-garde" in these colonial contexts, were not always those who others adorned with the label.

But the declaration of being avant-garde and aligning with it was also important. Paris was more a point on a pilgrimage than a final destination. And a short or extended sojourn in Paris might produce similar effects, recalibrations of how to further the colonial disorder of things. For the Brazilian artists Tarsila

---

19. And in French at *Légitime défense* (1932), 2: *L'Antillais, bourré à craquer de morale blanche, de culture blanche, de préjugés blancs, étale dans ses plaquettes l'image boursouflée de lui-même. D'être un bon décalque d'homme pâle, lui tient lieu de raison sociale aussi bien que de raison poétique.*
20. *Légitime défense* (1931), 2.

Do Amaral and her husband the equally well-known and well-off poet Oswald de Andrade (who made his fortune in coffee and real estate), Paris was not the "source" of being avant-garde but where they experienced a *"prise de conscience"* (an awakening). They were to embrace a modernism "independent of European canons," one routed in Brazil's sense of its own local knowledge and cultural creativity.

It was Tarsila Do Amaral's painting *"Abaporu"* (a word she found in a Tupi-Guarani dictionary), that de Andrade said inspired him to write what is considered his most radical manifesto against *"la peste"* (the plague) of elite, bourgeois, and Christian values. It was against those values that he proposed *Anthropophage*, a political ingestion of everything from elsewhere, followed by a vomiting out of Brazil's own creations, digested and stinking. Like Breton's early circle, they embraced being cannibals, as Breton did being barbarian. And perhaps they shared the problems that imagery and imaginary and politics called forth.[21]

Below the radar of labels were figures whose names only regional specialists continue to guard. For the colonial Netherlands Indies, I think of Mas Marco (Kartodikromo) (1890–1932) who in the 1920s wrote with an obstinate bite and humor, a mockery of Dutch authorities. His writing was a mixture of Malay, Javanese, and Dutch with some Latin added (and sometimes in Javanese script), probably flummoxing the less well-educated Dutch colonial censors). His active life (a mere fifteen years) of blazing critique of Dutch colonial rule was too short. Interned several times, labelled "crazy" by Dutch authorities, he eventually died of malaria at the infamous Boven Digul prison camp, isolated in Papua.[22]

---

21. Beatrice Joyeux-Prunel, *Les avant-gardes artistiques, 1918–1945* (Paris: Gallimard, 2017), 324.
22. See Hendrik M. J. Maier, "Phew! Europeesche beschaving! Marco Kartodikromo's *Student Hidjo*," *Southeast Asian Studies* 34, no. 1 (June 1996): 184–210.

But I also think of the deluge of "others," avant-garde artists and writers who made up the circles and circuits of exchange. There were those who worked next to the famed Aimé Césaire, writing, drawing, doing the layout for publications in Fort-de-France. Or we might turn to those who copyedited the manuscripts in Arabic and French of Egypt's *Art et Liberté* who lived and worked close by and may have shared rooming houses as well as *ateliers*. Proximity and senses of affiliation mattered; as at the hub along Al-Khurunfish Street in Cairo at the turn of the twentieth century until they moved to what became known as *La maison des artistes* where the core of the community came to have rooms (or was it only studios) in that sacred space.[23] And have the chroniclers of North Africa's avant-gardes registered that "influence" and "inspiration" seem to have come less from Europe than from the density of community they shared? But it also came from Palestinians and the Black Panthers, as the introduction to the volume of *Souffles/Anfas'* dense cumulation of both colonized subjects and revolutionary spirits (when it was almost impossible to be both) makes clear.[24]

COMMUNITIES OF (AESTHETIC AND POLITICAL) SENSIBILITY

Numbers of art historians have focused on the European luminaries with whom artists and poets of the imperial globe met, conversed with, and by whom they were inspired.[25] Few have written

---

23. Ola Sief, "Hotspots of Inspiration: Art Hubs that Transformed the Egyptian Art Scene," *Rawi Magazine*, 2016, https://rawi-magazine.com/articles/hotspots_of_inspiration/.

24. Harrison and Village-Ignacio, *Souffles/ANFAS*, 11.

25. See Joyeux-Prunel's two volume (each 1000 pages) transnational history of the avant-gardes between 1848–1918 and then 1918–1945, extraordinary in its breadth, studded with insights, and still readerly for the uninitiated. See *Les avant-gardes artistique, 1918–1945* (Paris: Gallimard, 2017), 16–17. I have only been able to consult Volume Two in depth. Also see her "Provincializing Paris: The Center-Periphery

those histories from other littorals. Among the most synthetic and impressive accounts are those of the French art historian Béatrice Joyeux-Prunel who so forcefully argues that the "grand modernist narrative" of the avant-garde is a distortion that excises some of the most "decisive contributions born in Mexico, Brazil, Hungary and the Czech Republic." These were avant-gardes that recognized themselves as "counter-currents" to the domination of Paris.[26] We might also look to the edited volume, *Decentering the Avant-Garde*. Although it clings close to the edges of Europe (looking to Eastern Europe, Central Europe, "East-Central Europe," and with one essay on "coloniality"), it effectively makes problematic the "centre"/"periphery" model.[27] As one essay persuasively insists, it takes the avant-garde as a "proposal of any innovative theoretical strategy at the beginning of the twentieth century."[28] This notion of a "proposal," a project always in formation, speaks directly to the unfinished, to the *potentia* that these avant-gardes held.

Less work has conveyed the repurposed tools dismantled and reassembled by those who grew up in colonized conditions out of which they fashioned emergent political grammars and landscapes, feeding on local idioms that were not European-bound and were their infrastructural support. "Infrastructure" itself takes on a new sense and sensibility in the new sites it takes form.

Narratives of Modern Art in Light of Quantitative and Transnational Approaches," *Artl@s Bulletin*, 4, no. 1 (2015): 40–64 where she first directly disputes the historical fiction that Paris was the "core of avant-gardism" (51). On the importance of Cubofuturism, "indigenous expressions" in Latin American and the Antilles, and Afro-Indian avant-garde in Brazil, also see Serge Facuhereau, *Avant-Gardes du XXe siècle: Arts & Littérature 1905–1930* (Paris: Flammarion, 2010), Eastern Europe figures prominently.

26. In Volume Two of *Les avant-gardes artistiques* she emphasizes these "*contre-courants*" (Joyeux-Prunel, *Les avant-gardes*, 16).

27. Per Backstrom and Benedikt Hjartarson eds., *Decentering the Avant-Garde* (Amsterdam: Rodolpi, 2014).

28. Daina Teters, "Pecularities in the Use of the Concepts Centre and Periphery in Avant-Garde Strategies," in Backstrom and Hjartarson, *Decentering*, 75–96.

These avant-gardes are not only avant-garde because their canvases stretched across new images with unconventional pigments on differently treated cloth: they animated queries that questioned the criteria of inclusion in what constituted dissent, what constituted the relationship between aesthetics and politics, and why and how poetics was such a foundational medium of their anti-colonial indictments.

Made up and by communities of affiliations in friendship and politics, in craft, artistry, and exchange, they were not only working in formal art (nor should they have been, as some critics wrote with withering dismissal). There is something else that seems to define their habitation of the world, what they see as the broader, extra-national horizons of their projects. Might we see this anti-colonial, anti-racist avant-garde's aesthetic politics in the styles of living they embraced and rejected, in the very forms of living and recalcitrance they inhabit, poised on the fractious fault lines of colonialism and imperial racial violences?[29]

---

29. Certainly not all avant-garde artists and writers fit this description. See Anniker Culver's striking study, *Glorify the Empire: Japanese Avant-Garde Propaganda in Manchuko* (Vancouver: UBC Press, 2013), where formerly leftist literary and artistic movements of the 1920s and early 1930s were recruited, as they were in fascist Italy and Germany, to the service of the state and to promote racist stereotypes, in the "fascist satellite state of Manchuria" (23). This was despite its attack on "bourgeois society." For a discussion of "contradictory aesthetic forms and political thought" that highlights its "simultaneity," see Culver, *Glorify the Empire*, 27–33.

Against the argument that everything to which they subscribed was boldly dissident (as sometimes claimed), see Phyllis Clark-Taoua's critique of the exalted radicality of the anti-colonial avant-garde that rather describes a contradictory scene and "problematic tension" between, among other things, Surrealism's "vanguard primitivism" and "anti-imperialism." Her critique of André Breton is stronger still with respect to the discrepancy between his "safe radicalism in art" rather than (as with the case for those from the colonies who he otherwise admired) in "ethical intervention." See Phyllis Clark-Taoua, *Forms of Protest: Anti-Colonialism and Avant-Gardes in Africa, the Caribbean, and France* (Portsmouth: Heinman, 2002), the only book length research I know to date that explicitly addresses both anti-colonialism and the avant-gardes, not in Europe. It remains an incisive study, once rarely but now increasingly referenced with expanding research and writing on the subject.

"INITIAL UNACCEPTABILITY": AVANT-GARDE AS DISRUPTIVE CLAIM

What to do with this weighty appellate that both reveals and conceals, as namings do? What politics might be highlighted and indeed mandated by a naming and locating of an avant-garde elsewhere and otherwise? Susan Buck-Morss writes:

> From an empirico-historical, descriptive point of view, it is enough for artists to call themselves avant-garde for them to be it (the Western art strategy). *But from a philosophical viewpoint*, the artwork itself must demonstrate this claim, within (and against) its historical context. *Artworks not artists* (*emphasis added*) are avant-garde and even here the category is not constant.[30]

Thinking through the marginally relegated lens of the anti-colonial avant-garde might complicate the categorical nature of the claim and its philosophical justification. There is something to gain in a definition that makes room for the very form of radicality and its domain of aesthetics to remain more open. Some of a "philosophical" justification might consider a way of being in the world, a "regime of living" that such an aesthetic and political form of living values and invites.[31] The ethical and political question is "how one lives" and thus the practices that certain ways of living

---

30. Susan Buck-Morss, "Vanguard/Avant-garde," based on material from *Dreamworld and Catastrophe: The Passing of Mass Utopia in East and West* (Cambridge: MIT Press, 2000).
31. Agamben is one who returns to the Latin, "forma vitae," moving from Wittgenstein's "forms of life." But also see Stephen Collier and Andrew Lakoff, "Regimes of living," in *Global Assemblages*, eds. Stephen Collier and Aihwa Ong (Hoboken: Wiley, 2005) where they describe their own project as one that follows "Michel Foucault's method in his genealogy of ethics," in that it "seeks to identify the elements—techniques, subjects, norms—through which the question of 'how to live' is posed" (23).

entail. When we turn to the personhoods cultivated by those of the anticolonial avant-garde, what seems shared is a creative recalcitrance in life as in artistic labor. Too, there were informal apprenticeships (rarely discussed as such). For many of the anticolonial avant-garde this shared sense of alternative community and non-ordained commitments was key.

This is a place to take seriously social etymology, as it mattered to those doing the naming and those being named. We know that avant-garde derives from the French "advance guard" of an army, a small group of armed combatants moving ahead of the rest. Little more is usually said about weaponry. Certainly, for those of the anti-colonial avant-garde, it was not only an abstract aesthetics that was a weapon. Their poetics and use of language were battlefields in themselves. I'm taken with Omar Berrada's sense that to say something is avant-garde, or "alter avant-garde" as he would put it, is at once to make a claim, an intervention, attributing to it the capacity to bring about an interruption.[32] This notion of "interruption" is not dissimilar to Foucault's definition of an event as parsed by Paul Rabinow: a "breach of self-evidence."[33] Both verbs "interrupt" and "breach" as they put on hold the "common-sense" of things.

Common definitions of avant-garde describe it as innovative, unorthodox, or radical—enough of each to be endowed, as Richard Kostelantz's *Dictionary of the Avant-Gardes* put it, with

---

32. I thank colleague/curator/poet/professor Omar Berrada for one of my best introductions to thinking avant-gardes, an extended conversation about this archive and what features would characterize "alter" avant-gardes. Again, not everyone would agree. Some chroniclers of avant-garde(s) argue that the term is ponderous, predictable, too male-oriented, and could easily be replaced with other nomenclatures and metaphors that better capture "alternative, non-mainstream art and performance." See, for example, Claire MacDonald's review of Mike Sell, *The Avant-garde: Race, Religion, War* (Chicago: University of Chicago, 2012) in *Performance Research* 18, no. 5 (2013): 137–140. I would hold that "avant-garde" can still do work as a nomenclature where the very challenge is to alter the term's unassailed features.

33. Paul Rabinow, *Anthropos Today: Reflections on Modern Equipment* (Princeton: Princeton University Press, 2003), 41.

"initial unacceptability."[34] We might note the timing and the limited temporality of the description. What André Breton once called the first article of the avant-garde's charter gets to the heart of the summons as it invokes a temporal moment, a reaction to a prevailing norm again: to celebrate "a deliberate will to deal the *coup de grâce* to that which one calls 'common sense' (which does not stop short of calling itself 'reason')."[35] In the case at hand, the common-sense to which Breton alludes was a racial colonial common-sense about people, about differences, about distinctions that mattered and that were made to do so. These were the negative coordinates of anti-colonial critique and against which anti-colonial poesis aimed.

Clifford Geertz once defined common sense as a "relatively organized body of considered thought," neither instinctive nor based on experience, rather a set of "historically constructed judgments."[36] It need not be uttered or named. His treatment of common sense as a "cultural" system excluded its intense political features, characteristically sweeping aside any attention to the work of common sense as a an quotidien technology of governance itself. Aimé Césaire knew better. He drew out the principles of imperial common sense with one of his most incisive intimately political concepts, "thingification, targeting the body as racialized ascription. These were techniques of dehumanizing, minute and searingly present, a submetrics of degradations, humiliations expressed as "care," persons treated as body parts, fragmented, as things.[37]

Breton and the members of *Tropiques* valued dissent that was excessive and in *disproportion* to the even keel of the norm.

---

34. Richard Kostelantz, *Dictionary of the Avant-Gardes* (London: Routledge, 2001).
35. André Breton's preface, "Un grand poète noir," in *Cahier d'un retour au pays natal* (Paris: Arthème Fayard, 1947).
36. Clifford Geertz, "Common Sense as a Cultural System," *Local Knowledge* 33, no. 1 (1975): 73–93.
37. Aimé Césaire, *Discourse on Colonialism* [1955], trans. Joan Pinkham (New York: Monthly Review Press, 2000), 42.

"Disproportion" offers a useful guide through avant-garde channels that might otherwise not seem aligned. In a colonial context, every defiance of a racialized hierarchy—from (over)dress to speech, from an embrace of a multi-lingual aesthetics, to literary references which censures could not grasp—disrupted racial decorum.

"INFLUENCE" AT ISSUE AGAIN

Such common sense can invite its own alternatives as in avant-garde challenges that were neither uttered (too loud) or named. As Breton, and those chronicling his encounter with the Césaires like to tell it, he "discovered" *Tropiques* by chance on a brief layover in Fort-de-France on the ship that allowed him to escape Vichy's edicts and the banning of his writings. The ship was making its way to New York with Breton and other well-known exiles, fleeing France (Claude Lévi-Strauss, Yul Brynner, Wilfredo Lam). By mythohistory, Breton was walking through Fort-de-France one day, and stopped in a dry-goods store to buy a ribbon for his small daughter. The store, it turned out, was run by a sister of René Ménil, the latter one of Aimé and Suzanne Césaire's closest friends, literary and political collaborator, and himself a philosopher, adherent to surrealism and a powerful force in Martinique's independence movement. Together with Rene Ménil, Charles Péguy, and Georgette Anderson, the Césaires published that first issue of *Tropiques*, which Breton came upon in the shop.

The details are charming, an unearthing of aesthetic and political dissent secured by a hair ribbon for Breton's five-year-old only daughter.[38] But the story is one that is often retold as if Breton "discovered" a diamond in the (colonial) raw, rather than a situation in which the Césaires took on Breton and shaped their own sense of what surrealism could do for an anti-colonial

---

38. Breton, "Un grand poète noir."

project on hostile ground. Robin Kelley's passionate introduction to Césaire's *Discourse on Colonialism*, similarly, undercuts the "diffusionist" narrative of Breton's "influence" on Césaire, as if surrealism was a "European thought" to which minor peripherals latched on.[39] The Césaires' effect on Breton was profound. He was taken by *Tropique*'s force and sophistication. But more so by a "poetically rich and revolutionary deployment of language."[40] The poetic in Césaires' hands was a weapon and a call to arms. As Kelley notes in introducing *Discourse on Colonialism*, it was "a declaration of war."[41]

RADICAL HUMANISM AS A VORTEX OF DISSENT

Here has been a vortex of dissent, négritude, and anti-négritude, racisms under the radar and in bold font, anti-racism, communism (anti-communism and the CIA as well), Asian-African alliances, fervent, enabling, and crushing Marxisms. And not least were utopian visions that competed, crumbled, converged, and vied for ascendance.[42] They collided and sometimes collaborated

---

39. As Kelley put it, "this sort of 'diffusionist' interpretation leaves no room for the Césaires to be innovators of surrealism to have introduced fresh ideas to Breton and his colleagues. I want to suggest that the Césaires not only embraced surrealism—independently of the Paris Group, I might add, but opened new vistas and contributed enormously to theorizing the 'domain of the Marvelous'." Robin Kelley, "A Poetics of Anticolonialism," in Césaire, *Discourse on Colonialism*, 16.

40. Suzanne Césaire, *The Great Camouflage: Writings of Dissent (1941–1945)*, ed. Daniel Maximin, trans. Keith Walker (Middleton: Wesleyan University Press, 2012), xi.

41. Kelley, "A Poetics of Anticolonialism," 7.

42. On the work of the CIA in promoting a "cultural politics" of literary figures and artists that was anti-communist and amenable to a domesticated black and subaltern population see Juliana Spahr, *DuBois's Telegram: Literary Resistance and State Containment* (Cambridge: Harvard University Press, 2018), in particular her chapter, "Stubborn Nationalism: Example One, Avant Garde Modernism" where she describes when and how her own thinking was transformed when she came to

in their assertion of aesthetic forms and political claims. Many of the connectivities between these various strands of alternative visions and imaginaries from Negritude to Black Power were contradictory to say the least, but there remains a sense that poetics shaped a "radical humanism" which seems to have coursed through the commitments to which so many adhered.[43]

Then there was Richard Wright, who was so struck by the refusal to address "the race question" when he confronted his Asian and specifically Indonesian interlocutors at the Bandung Conference in 1955 (who were said to have been impatient with his singular focus on racism rather than colonialism). Wright was as impatient with their denial of a colonial racism so blatant in what he called "a racial feeling... [evident] in a thousand subtle forms." In the essay "Racial Shame in Bandung" he describes both a general euphoria and safety conveyed by so many finding themselves in the midst of a "colored" congress, while a colonial language still pervaded Indonesian lesson books designed to teach new Dutch colonial recruits how to give petty orders to their gardeners and cooks, prepared with only crude phrases of command.[44] White knew white paranoia, a sense of white fear, Black fear of a white enemy. For him racism cut through the center and edges of the whole event. Wright was not a formal participant in the conference, but a journalist commissioned to write about it, as he did with a telling title, *The Color Curtain*, a year later.

---

understand (via her Hawaiian students) that "avant-garde modernism was a literature written in and out of empire" (62).

43. Cornel West's introduction to the collection of three of Wright's books entitled *Black Power* (New York: Harper, 2008), ix, refers to a "progressive secular humanism" that Wright lived and expressed in his writing. Also see Stathis Gourgouris, "Rethinking Humanism," in *Edward Said and Jacques Derrida: Reconstellating Humanism and the Global Hybrid*, eds. Mina Karavanta and Nina Morgan (Cambridge: Cambridge Scholars Press, 2008).

44. See Richard Wright, *Black Power: Three Books from Exile: Black Power; The Color Curtain and White Man, Listen!* (New York: Harper, 2008), introduction by Cornel West.

It is difficult to write about these figures without the accounts being about them and their visions rather than the communities of the named and unnamed with whom they worked and mounted their creative and political assaults. McKenzie Wark, writing about her avant-garde successors, the Situationist International, at once reminds us that reducing these aesthetic explosions to biographical accounts betrays the nature of their venture. And to give the reader that sense, she carries her reader through a set of avant-garde European activists, each one more excessive in style and more unconventional in the form of their claims, each linked to and in some cases the informal apprentice of another, from an earlier generation.[45]

Again, these anti-colonial avant-gardes were global but not an ensemble. Nor were they "movements" in some coherent sense.[46] Rather they show repeated evidence of a set of commitments that came out of colonial conditions, situations borne of repeated experience, embodied in sensibilities, sensory regimes, locale, and lived in bodies with parts cut off and in repeatedly scarred flesh. Colonial disfigurements are the landscapes of the anti-colonial avant-garde. From the avant-garde *Art et Liberté* exhibit on surrealism in Surreal Cairo, subtitled "Rupture, War and Surrealism in Egypt (1938–1948)," the paintings and drawings of mutilated and deformed bodies in the section of the exhibition titled "Fragmented Bodies" were overwhelming to the many who came to the exhibit.[47]

---

45. McKenzie Wark, *The Beach Beneath the Street: The Everyday Life and Glorious Times of the Situationist International* (New York: Verso, 2011), 3. As she wrote: "to reduce a movement to a biography or two is to cut a piece away from what made it of interest in the first place."

46. Sophia Setia makes a helpful distinction, writing of them as "provisional networks of affiliation" not firmly demarcated groups in *Provisional Avant-Gardes: Little Magazine Communities from Dada to Digital* (Stanford: Stanford University Press, 2019).

47. The section of the exhibit entitled "The Woman of the City" is too full of images of "extreme physical deformation." On the exhibit, see Rubinstein, "Surreal Cairo."

Colonial conditions unsettle the boundaries of bodies but also the certitudes of ordered temporalities. Their grammars of time condense, collide, and intensify in how those conditions have shaped the local micro-physics of social life. Within this anti-colonial archive in the making were conditions shared: primary, prioritized, and recursively present, in different locations, providing strongholds of thought and dissensual practices across the world. I've called that condition "colonial duress," thinking here with its rich political etymology so fundamental to the aesthetic expression it produced and the force of dissent it called for. They too were focused on "the hardened, tenacious qualities of colonial effects; their extended protracted temporalities."[48] But here I would underscore more the "endurance" entailed, countermanding duress' damaging qualities.[49] Official transfers of sovereignty have been more than disappointments: they've been strategic failures. Perhaps the amplifying interest in early radical colonized actors and practices today, is how much they stand as prescient resources for grappling with new forms of racecraft now.

"Independence" was never the finality of any anti-colonial venture: sometimes it was a false step on uneven ground, sabotaged from within, scattering critical energy in different directions. No one imagined it was an end. Often it was not even a beginning, but an intensified, recognized moment of dissidence built on decades of recalcitrance. Racialized afflictions prompted those who lived them to seek out a guiding politics. Jacques Rancière's definition of the political would have made immediate sense: perhaps as a confrontation but more so as a "gap in the sensible" a *partage du sensible*, a "making visible that which had no reason to be seen."[50]

---

48. Ann Laura Stoler, *Duress: Imperial Durabilities in Our Time* (Durham: Duke University Press, 2016).
49. Stoler, *Duress*, 7.
50. Jacques Rancière, *Dissensus: On Politics and Aesthetics* (London: Bloomsbury, 2010), 38.

That is, no reason to be seen under a particular colonial regime of truth.

Appearance emerges from the shadows of colonial surveillance. Appearance is heralded here in multiple sites and terms: through manifestos of declaration, poetry in unseemly prose, poster art, film, small magazines, appearances at exhibitions, international events, conferences. Few of these women and men would have seen themselves as amateurs of the conference mode, but they did show up not so much to "make an appearance" but for the space of worldliness to be occupied by their appearance rather than a European-someone-else.[51]

Such a joining of politicality and aesthetics could make sense of Ruba Salih's argument that Palestinian refugees should be considered avant-garde with respect to their radical claims, and their rejection of narratives that "territorially bound" access to rights are fundamentally flawed. Pointing to Hannah Arendt's insight that refugees are "the vanguard of their people," Salih argues that this new configuration of the political invites other questions: whether exile imposed by colonial and racial logics is a condition of a politically charged aesthetic innovation?[52]

ON "NASCENT OXYGEN"

An affirmation of the urgent reason and demand to be seen is precisely what those dissenting from the colonial order of things did through their visual and verbal poetics, novels, plays, editorials, and slim revues. No one has received more attention than Aimé Césaire, generating an almost infectious contemporary sense of

---

51. I owe my rethinking of Hannah Arendt's "space of appearance" to Shen Chang-Chen's incisive dissertation chapter on "stealth immigrants" and their creation of spaces of appearance.
52. See Ruba Salih, "From Bare Lives to Political Agents: Palestinian Refugees as Avant-Garde," *Refugee Survey Quarterly* 32, no. 2 (2013): 66–91.

political urgency and poetic force, that doubles on Césaire's own sense of urgency.[53] As Gary Wilder has argued in a stunning and carefully researched study of decolonization, primarily through the lens of the two extraordinary persons, Aimé Césaire and Léopold Senghor, theirs was a rejection of instrumental reason in favor of what Césaire would call "poetic truth."[54] Césaire's iteration of "poetic truth" and "poetic knowledge" are seductive entreaties borne of his own practice and the power he saw and sought in imagination. The journal *Tropiques* was the signature of the group with whom he worked. It thrived between 1941 and 1943 with several attempts by the French Vichy authorities to shut it down, a move eventually ensured by the Chief of Information Services, Bayles, withdrawing *Tropiques*' eligibility

---

53. Those many who have written about Aimé Césaire and his comrades in arms make some of my task here easier . . . and at times more challenging. Among these are André Breton, Bashir Souleymane, Robin Kelley, Gary Wilder, Bernard Harcourt; when writing about Césaire or Senghor, they are as if ignited themselves by the crystalline clarity of his words, "Poetic knowledge" and "poetic truth" capture the fierce and fearless unbounded . . . I think here of André Breton's rapture in recounting the effect of Césaire's person and writing on him in André Breton, "A Great Black Poet," in Aimé Césaire, *Notebook of a Return to the Native Land*, ed. and trans. Clayton Eshleman and Annette Smith (Middletown: Wesleyan University Press, 2000); Gary Wilder's *Freedom Time: Negritude, Decolonization, and the Future of the World* (Durham: Duke University Press, 2015); Bernard Harcourt, "Aimé Césaire: Poetic Knowledge, Vitality, Négritude, and Revolution," *Columbia Law Blog*, December 22, 2016, http://blogs.law.columbia.edu/nietzsche1313/aime-cesaire-poetic. Among the countless works on his life and work, the most powerful are those that that are in his voice and words. I think here of Aimé Césaire: *Ecrits politiques, 1935–1956* (Paris: Jean Michel, 2016) these are the short speeches and essays from which Césaire's *Discourse on Colonialism* was drawn. Most recently, see Aimé Césaire, *Resolutely Black: Conversations with Françoise Vergès* (New York: Polity, 2020) based on interviews that Françoise Vergès carried out in 2004, just four years before Césaire's death. First published in French as *Nègre je suis, nègre je resterai* (Paris: Albin Michel, 2005), in an interview in June 2020, Vergès graciously thanks her translator Matthew Smith for suggesting the brilliant title, *Resolutely Black*, reaffirming the power and politics of translation and the salience of Césaire's thinking before he became *the* famous tamer poet and political activist of his time—and now.
54. Wilder, *Freedom Time*, 30.

to get (what was then heavily rationed) paper on which to print.[55] Their response to Bayles is now famous, printed in *Tropiques* and directly addressing the racism that generated Bayle's indictment where he accused the journal of being "revolutionary, racist and sectarian." And their response: " 'Racists,' yes, Racism like that of Toussaint-Louverture, Claude McKay, and Langston Hughes— against the racism like that of Drumont and Hitler."[56]

"Poetic truth" was a truth about the colonial racial order of things and rejection of that order in these anti-colonial and anti-fascist alternative imaginaries and potential worlds. Aimé and Suzanne were not alone in the late 1930s while studying in Paris, as they mixed with expatriate colonial students, "Black surrealists" (among whom they were subsequently included) and the literary avant-garde.[57] The cultural and political project of Negritude indeed emerged from that mix, but only one albeit thick node of dissent in the making: young Vietnamese revolutionaries were produced in other amalgams of confrontation. In that same Parisian space were those who were to become Asia's young anti-imperialist revolutionaries.[58]

---

55. How little we know of that materiality and wish we knew more. For it was part of their anti-institutional sensibilities and practices that materialized in how they collated, printed, and disseminated their work.

56. Réponse de *Tropiques* à M. le Lieutenant de Vaisseau Bayle, Fort-de-France, May 12, 1943, *Tropiques* 1941–45. Collection complete (Paris: Editions Jean-Michel Place, 1978) quoted in Kristen Tromberg Childers, "Aimé Césaire's *Notebook of a Return to the Native Land*," Fiction and Film for Scholars of France, https://h-france.net/fffh/tag/cesaire-aime/ ; Among other places, we might find this response of *Tropiques* translated see, Kristen Stromberg Childers, *Seeking Imperialism's Embrace: National Identity, Decolonization, and Assimilation in the French Caribbean* (New York: Oxford University Press, 2016).

57. Wilder, *Freedom Time*, x.

58. This is a story written and rewritten many times. See Michael Goebel, *Anti-Imperial Metropolis: Interwar Paris and the Seeds of Third World Nationalism* (New York: Cambridge University Press, 2015), which the author describes as tracing "the spread of a global anti-imperialism from the vantage of Paris where countless future leaders of Third World countries spent formative stints." Goebel treats the lives of these revolutionaries in the making as not only products of the networks they engaged, but as importantly emerging from the experience of being *not intellectuals but migrants* (and treated as such) in France.

As Wilder writes, these "were the spaces from and in relation to which he [Césaire] helped to fashion the cultural and political project that would become known as *Négritude* [and] to refigure imperial France." Césaire's *Notebook of a Return to My Native Land*, published in 1947 on the cusp of his return to Martinique after studying in France, famously captured that "poetic knowledge" he so embraced—a rare, organic appreciation of the melded power of aesthetics and politics.[59]

Césaire was exemplary but he was hardly alone. Suzanne Césaire in her own right was a central force in the making of *Tropiques*. She studied at France's pre-eminent *Ecole Normale Superieure* as well, where she majored in philosophy and would later meet Aimé. Depending on how the story goes, they met via his sister with whom she shared a class, or through Léopold Senghor (the more favored narrative). If long muted in avant-garde and anti-colonial history, it is not clear that she was so muted at the time. One doesn't need to cast a strong light on her to sense from her writing and visual presence that her voice and disposition were crystalline sharp and bolder than has been recognized or, until recently, acknowledged.

A collection of her writing in *Tropique*s (that appeared for the first time, could it be, in English in 2012?), now available in a slim volume under the title *The Great Camouflage*, honors her best-known work. It suggests nothing derivative. Hers was a vivid, fresh cosmopolitan vantage on work that the trope of camouflage did in targeting the sordid system of post-slavery debt, "political smokescreens . . . and bad faith." Her anticipatory response was an emergent vision, as yet unarticulated by others, of a pan-Caribbean archipelago, not isolated islands, as the source and site of a poetics of liberation.[60]

---

59. Wilder, *Freedom Time*, 22.
60. See Annette K. Joseph-Gabriel, "Beyond the Great Camouflage: Haiti in Suzanne Césaire's Politics and Poetics of Liberation," *small axe* 50 (July 2016), and the translator, Keith Walker's Introduction in Césaire, *Camouflage*, vii. I thank Nancy Luxon for sharing her thinking about Suzanne Césaire with me.

The groundedness in the aesthetics these anti-colonial soldiers shared is rooted in Morocco, the "Indies," and the Caribbean's light and the habitations of place. But there is something else common in their dispositions that convey mobilities and restless movements: currents and currencies of translocations and motion—voluntary and involuntary displacements. There was Césaire learning from and leaning on Senghor, André Breton captivated by the fierce power of Césaire's poetics, the latter's voice in Breton's words "beautiful like nascent oxygen."[61] And then Césaire animated by Breton, Fanon turning back to Césaire and with Baldwin later adamant in turning against the essentialism of Négritude. Eduardo Glissant built on both, and Abedellah Latif in Morocco held up his pen to the light of Fanon.

And there was Blackness unspoken and shouted, present and absent, joining those across generations who have turned back to the 1950s, less to Richard Wright at Bandung and more to the Conference of Black Writers and Artists a year later in September 1956 at the Sorbonne in Paris. It was sometimes referred to as "the cultural Bandung." Wright was there but so were Aimé Césaire, Léopold Senghor, and Franz Fanon.[62] This was a feted "space of appearance," of sixty-three delegates from twenty-four countries. Strikingly, only one unnamed woman appears seated at the center of the famous, still circulating photograph that was taken at the time. No report on the congress (or in celebration of that congress today) mentions her name.[63]

Also see Joseph-Gabriel, "Subverting Empire: Gendered Narratives of Anti-colonial Resistance in Francophone Literature and Politics, 1939–1960" (PhD Diss., Vanderbilt University, 2015).

61. Breton, "A Great Black Poet," xviii.

62. See James Baldwin's report on the Congress and the enormous weight he gave to Aimé Césaire's analysis of confrontation with colonialisms in contrast to Richard Wright's concessionary one in Ntongela Masilela, "The Very Beautiful African-ness in Baldwin: In Memoriam," *Pitzer*, accessed May 13, 2021, http://pzacad.pitzer.edu/NAM/general/essays/baldwin.pdf.

63. See Merve Fejzula, "Women and the 1956 Congress of Black Writers and Artists in Paris," *Black Perspectives (AAIHS)*, November 3, 2016, https://www.aaihs.org/women-and-the-1956-congress-of-black-writers-and-artists-in-paris/.

EMERGENT INDONESIA'S
DISRUPTIVE AVANT-GARDE

There were waves from other shores, of movement in Asia that at times barely made contact with these Caribbean sites of volcanic poetics; at other times, Paris became a hub of cross—fertilizations. Still sometimes a tenor of impatience and rage, however submerged, was resonant if not the same. How much those I look at here, those proto-Indonesian authors and artists were actually avant-garde because they proclaimed themselves so or were more nationalists precariously poised between accepted new allegiances in a newly fashioned more travelled world is difficult to say. Assessment by those who have immersed themselves in Southeast Asian literature for decades narrate the constrained political space in which anti-colonialism could be expressed.

There were those from the contested affiliations of artists who wavered between passive supporters of Dutch colonial rule, like those who wrote under the aegis of *Balai Pustaka* (the Dutch colonial government's sponsored organization promoting Malay-language and later Indonesian literature from 1907 through to independence and after). Many slipped across and between different affiliations—writing for *Balai Pustaka* while rejecting the notion that Malay literature should be Dutch-sponsored. Others were viral in refusing that endorsement, holding to the politically precarious position that the colonial Dutch had no proprietary claims on them.[64]

Some of those from pre-independence Indonesia were peopled with persons who were incandescent, ironic, and fierce as was the case with the brazen Indies *pergerakan* (*movement*) that included on its journal mastheads young activist poets and novelists far

---

64. Doris Jedamski, "*Balai Pustaka*—a Colonial Wolf in Sheep's Clothing," *Archipel* 44 (1992): 23–46.

before independence. They did not label themselves "avant-garde" but their brazen practices suggest they were, absent that appellate, without assuming that name. It's hard not to return, again, to Mas Marco from that earlier period between 1912–1926 when he wrote. I would agree with Henk Maier that Mas Marco (dikromo) was probably avant-garde *avant le lettre*—more bold, innovative, and recalcitrant in the face of colonialism than those who later made those claims and gave that title to themselves.[65] Mas Marco never proclaimed himself to be "avant-garde." Rather, he fought a war in and of language that was violent and more than a war of "just" words, as the historian Takahashi Shiriashi put it. In the latter's unparalleled *An Age in Motion*, he documents and archives an incipient anti-colonial cultural politics between 1912 and 1926 that left almost no form of inscription, no sort of activity or opportunity for incitement untouched.[66]

And even the title of Takahashi's book takes its inspiration from Mas Marco's small journal *Dunia Bergerak* (*A World in Motion*)—bold and short-lived. Newspapers, journals, strikes, novels, songs, theater worked at twisting words—and world-plays in sundry ways. The political (and philosophical) played through mistranslation, retranslation, and non-translations, as master craftsperson of untranslatabilities and translations. Emily Apter helps us see the politicality in these moves.[67] Inverting the pomposity of Dutch colonial soliloquy to the language of the gutter, they labeled the obsequious bowing and scraping requisite in high Javanese circles as the "custom of frogs" (*adat kodokan*).[68]

Mas Marco made monolinguism obsolete. His repertoire unsettled the most confident and arrogant, rocking the fictive calm of Dutch rule. He was recalcitrant, playful, and brazen in

---

65. Henk Maier, personal communication, 21 June 2020.
66. Takahashi Shiriashi, *An Age in Motion: Popular Radicalism in Java, 1912–1926* (Ithaca: Cornell University Press, 1990).
67. See Emily Apter, "Afterword: Towards a Theory of Reparative Translation," *Cultural Inquiry* 19 (2020): 209–228.
68. Shiriashi, *An Age in Motion*, 62.

ways that would be hard to imagine, even years later. He challenged the Dutch court, he wrote "inappropriately" erotic stories, he was jailed several times (once for a year), and still refused to succumb to how he was supposed to be. As importantly, some notion of fostering a critical community of readership was key: a *community* of readers and authors for whom critique of Dutch rule was crucial and for whom obsequious Javanese behavior to power—Dutch or indigenous—was rendered "disgusting" and relegated to the past (long before such customs became so).[69]

The Indonesian and proto-Indonesian anti-colonial avant-gardes that came after are ones that I should know best, but accounts of their histories are contradictory and contested.[70] And perhaps that is a lesson in itself. Take the now oft-cited, self-declared, and commonly referred to avant-garde Indonesian language publication *Pujaanga Baru*. In the genre of the small magazine, yet again, published between 1933 and 1942 and from 1948–1954, it had no more than one hundred fifty paying subscribers. *Pujaanga Baru* was far from a household name, but then virtually none of the anti-colonial avant-garde aspired to such a distinction—or could have attained it.[71] They sought to counter a stalemate, a colonial infused blockage, that constrained the making of their literary world. But one important feature was shared among them, the connection between art and life was considered an important one for them.[72] One of its most important members,

---

69. See Hendrik M. J. Maier, "Phew!"
70. Here I thank Henk Maier and Keith Foulcher for taking the time and energy to lay out the disputed assessments of who might be actually considered "avant-garde" or even "anti-colonial" among those literary figures and artists who might otherwise be associated with both.
71. See Keith Foulcher, *Pujangga Baru: Literature and Nationalism in Indonesia, 1933–1942* (Adelaide: Flinders University, 1980), a publication unfortunately barely more significant in the academic hierarchical scheme of things than the small magazine about which he wrote.) Both are oversights sorely borne by those many who have tried to understand the bellicose possibilities of literature though not named "avant-garde."
72. See Heather Sutherland, "Pudjangga Baru: Aspects of Intellectual Life in the 1930s," *Indonesia* 6 (Oct 1968): 106–127. Theirs was a shared striving for a new "form of life."

Armijn Pane was said to have stated that "what distinguished *Pudjangga Baru* . . . was a *certain attitude towards life* (*emphasis added*) and culture rather than a single literary style."[73]

Another important sense was shared: "art for art's sake" was never endorsed among those who fought for social justice in the colonial and neo-colonial world they inhabited.[74] The act of writing was a political act, not always to the same extent, nor with the same bravado and sophistication of critique. There was a range. Henk Maier dismisses the claim that *Pujangga baru* was an avant-garde journal as Sutan Takdir Alisjahbana was always maneuvering a space of compromise before the war and more so after. Other members, like Armijn Pane, seemed to have a more robust politics, more aesthetically to offer, and a richer historical imagination and sense of the history of which he was a part.[75]

The 1940s—harsh years of an extended war of independence, and famine, and forced labor (1942–1945) under the Japanese occupation—put Indonesia's literary world on hold. But in the early 1950s, the literary became one of the fierce battle fields of politics, not only because the use of *Bahasa Indonesia* (the Indonesian language) was to unify those of the archipelago speaking hundreds of local languages, but because it was to become a centerpiece and powerful dispositif when the political face and force of that nation was under contestation. The pre-war avant-garde *Pujangga* artists and writers were set against what came to be known in 1950 as the *Gelenggang* artists, followers of Anwar Chairil, now a national

---

73. Referred to by Sutherland, "Pujangga Baru," 11.
74. As Keith Foulcher writes: "the outright rejection of art for art's sake has never really been questioned by any members of the artistic community," in "A Survey of Events Surrounding Manikebu: The Struggle for Cultural and Intellectual Freedom in Indonesian Literature," *Bijdragen tot de Taal-, Land-en Vokenkunde* 125, no. 4 (1969): 433.
75. See Keith Foulcher, "Culture and Colonialism in the Eessays of Armijn Pane, 1933–1953," in *Lasting Fascinations: Essays on Indonesia and the Southwest Pacific to Honour Bob Hering*, eds. Harry Poeze and Antoinette Liem, 131–152 (Stein: Yayasan Kabar Sebarang, Yayasan Soekarno, 1998).

hero whose commitment to political radicality is far from clear. That year also saw the formation of LEKRA, the cultural institute (and cultural arm) of the Indonesian communist party (PKI) whose adherents, artists and literary figures were encouraged to turn to socialist realism.

Whether LEKRA squeezed out a more innovative and subversive aesthetics is still disputed among those versed and immersed for decades in Indonesian literature. Keith Foulcher suggests that LEKRA authors were so impossibly curtailed by PKI political priorities that little room was left or made for aesthetic creative insubordination.[76] They too held that "art for art's sake" was not a position to defend. Aesthetic choice, content, and form were long recognized as political issues in themselves. But a reduction of literature to political signposting was rejected as well. What was embodied were positions born from living a deep colonial history of coercion and censorship.

The "small journal" or "little magazine" that Sophie Setia explores in a study of the "provisional avant-gardes," was a format that emerged from the 1930s through the 1950s in avant-gardes around the world. It embraced a provisionality that was part of its very form. It was not provisional in the sense of providing a format to be superseded by high gloss, high-cost publications. Instead, a more modest and home-grown sense and scale of publication mattered.[77] These were small collections not only supporting

---

76. Foulcher, "Survey of events surrounding Manikebu." The 1963 cultural manifesto of those writers and artists supporting "universal humanism" and not supporting LEKRA was banned in 1964 by presidential decree. Among those who Keith Foulcher parses as supporting the manifesto were those arguing that "art must serve humanity and not a political ideal" (434).

77. See Setia, *Provisional Avant-Gardes*. Setia's otherwise unique address stays confined to Euro-American sites, but her insights dovetail precisely with reflections I would endorse on the nature of what constitutes the "avant-garde" features of these communities: namely, that they were not only avant-garde in the poetry they produced. It was equally in a politics that came from the little magazine's production, distribution, and reception (192), a distinctive feature of the anti-colonial avant-gardes discussed here.

publications on second rate paper for small distribution on a local scale, but as importantly providing the material glue that allowed communities to be shaped around them.[78]

THE BANDUNG EFFECT AND "LATE BANDUNG"

And then of course there was what is often called "the watershed" of Bandung in 1955.[79] Hailed as the "inaugural moment," it was the first congress of non-aligned Asian-African leaders in a new world order to which former and contemporary colonizing states were not invited.[80] Of course, it was not the first, numbers of associations and conferences preceded it with the *League against Imperialism* in Berlin forming one prominent "hub" and the Brussels Conference of 1927 generally recognized as Bandung's predecessor. Anti-colonial groups were formed everywhere, in London, Liverpool, Berlin, Hamburg, Paris.[81]

---

78. Erick Bulson makes a similar point, tracing the form and materiality of the "little magazine" through a world-wide range of modernist and avant-garde ventures in *Little Magazine, World Form* (New York: Columbia University Press, 2019), arguing that "little magazines made modernism, and that the material conditions of its production in the avant-garde world was a recognized elem

79. The proliferation of writing on Bandung in the last decade is an historical event in itself. See Quynh N. Pham and Robbie Shilliam, eds., *Meanings of Bandung: Postcolonial Orders and Decolonial Visions* (London: Rowman and Littlefield, 2016); Amitav Acharya and Tan See Seng eds., *Bandung Revisited: The Legacy of the 1955 Asian-African Conference for International Order* (Singapore: NUS Press, 2008).

80. For an outstanding collection on Bandung's later effects see Christopher Lee, ed., *Making a World After Empire: The Bandung Moment and its Political Afterlives* (Athens, Ohio: Ohio University Press, 2010) and Antoinette Burton's epilogue, especially attentive to the "romance" of "interracial brotherhood it continuously deployed." "Epilogue: The Sodalities of Bandung: Toward a Critical 21st-Century History," 351–361. Not all agree. Dilip Menon critiques her suspicion of Afro-Asian solidarity in Dilip Menon, "Bandung is Back: Afro-Asian Affinities," *Radical History Review* 119 (Spring 2014): 241–45.

81. Wildan Sena Utama, "From Brussels to Bogor: Contacts, Networks and the History of the Bandung Conference, 1955," *Journal of Indonesian Social Sciences*

But Bandung was what and where the world was watching and were invited to do so and where those at Bandung were watching themselves being watched. Held in the west Javanese city of Bandung, once known as the Paris of the East, the city was renowned for its plush art deco colonial era hotels, spruced up for the attendees and the three hundred some odd journalists sent out to document the event. Attendants included stately sorts—Chou Enlai, Nehru, Sukarno (cameras focused on them)—and leaders from twenty-nine states and quadruple the number of journalists from all over the world. For those nascent countries just out of, or in the throes of independence, it announced an unprecedented anti-colonial anti-imperialist mandate—the manifesto was in their very vibrant co-presence alone. What was marked, in contrast to the anti-colonial avant-garde was the muted racial politics of the event and among most participants.

The recent number of accounts of global anti-colonial movements traced back to the 1930s and after the 1955 Bandung moment through the 1960s is staggering. Their trajectories and inspirations searched out in dissertations, essays, exhibitions, and books, each study picking up another thread of connectivity without positing unity, each documenting idioms of refusal and grammars of recalcitrance that reverberate across continents. Histories of avant-gardes often cover the same temporal breadth. But their persons and expressions of the political are in uneven alignment as some sought to be "non-aligned" and others took alignment with socialism, communism, or radical humanism as only partial restrictions in their quest for modes of dissent.

What is less clear, and for which there seems less evidence, is whether Bandung 1955 animated an aesthetic politics at its time or in its aftermath? The term "inspirational," so often used

and Humanities 6, no. 1 (2016): 11–24 and Fredrik Petersson, "Prelude to Bandung: Anti-colonialism between the Wars," *Imperial and Global Forum*, October 20, 2014, https://imperialglobalexeter.com/2014/10/20/prelude-to-bandung-the-interwar-origins-of-anti-colonialism/.

with respect to the "spirit of Bandung," should invite the same caution that Foucault urged with respect to "influence." It is not clear what it meant and whether what was "inspirational" was what happened at Bandung or its promise, or what did not happen and what those failures offered for rethinking the collaborations that mattered for the future. It could be argued, and has been, that Bandung gave weight to more overt anti-colonial expression, offering a precedent for making new claims. But there are few concrete cross-references to Bandung as an aesthetic inspiration, more a cumulative recognition that the overlapping agendas of the anti-colonial avant-garde poets and artists were resonant, but not the same.

The exhilaration of Bandung partially conveyed in Richard Wright's *Indonesian Notebooks*, written on the night train from Paris to Madrid, is, in many ways, a surprise—a conventional and somewhat caricatured—almost naively ethnographic—account by a rather parochial "American abroad" who thought he could describe an "Asian mentality" and an Asian type from three weeks among government dignitaries and a small literary elite in Indonesia.[82] As some have noted the "bare-breasted" women he claimed to have seen along the road from Jakarta to Bandung was an embarrassing mis-remembering in the strongly Muslim region of West Java (some have thought he probably saw women traders in his earlier trip to Africa) weighed down with wares on their backs and heads, walking on the sides of roads—a touch of the distracted tourist moving too fast, a glimpse of the scenery (that women too often are for foreign tourists) in Asia and Africa.[83] Wright insisted that it was the profusion of persons of color from so many places that grabbed and stirred everyone and held him fast.

---

82. See Wright, *The Color Curtain*; Brian Russell Roberts and Keith Foulcher eds., *Indonesian Notebook: A Sourcebook on Richard Wright and the Bandung Conference* (Durham: Duke University Press, 2016).
83. Roberts and Foulcher, *Indonesian Notebook*, 12.

But the story is more complicated. Who he met and what he "saw" was limited at best. As we now know, the group to whom he was introduced was select and carefully selected. And Wright was more than myopic. His time and curiosity too were limited and constrained. In the post-war independence period of Indonesia opening to the Bandung Conference, the tenor and nature of what constituted an Indonesian avant-garde was contested and charged. The well-known Indonesian novelist, essayist, and poet Sitor Situmorang was one of the foremost interlocutors of Wright, with whom he spent time before and during the Conference. Pramoedya Ananta Toer, by far the most well-known, widely read, and widely translated Indonesian literary figure, imprisoned at Boven Digul for some seventeen years as a part of the left-wing communist affiliated LEKRA, was not part of the small group of Indonesian writers to whom Wright was introduced.

This story is told in detail elsewhere, focused on Wright's meeting, arranged by the author Mochtar Lubis. It would be hard to claim that this group made up an avant-garde. Some would argue that the pressures of meeting the needs of Indonesia's then powerful communist party (PKI) would annul any possibility of those who were part of LEKRA to make that claim. Still, some of those committed to social realism found ways of breaking through the strictures that the Cold War divide and party politics imposed.[84] We might rather consider what it took to write at all.

---

84. See Leah Feldman's excellent treatment of this entangled history in "Global Souths: Toward a Materialist Poetics of Alignment," *boundary 2*, 47, no. 2 (2020): 199–225. There she takes on the impacted space in which Marxist-Leninist anti-imperial thought and a "materialist poetics of (non)alignment developed in the work of thinkers from Frantz Fanon to M. N. Roy" (201). Feldman points to "structures of feeling that crossed the Cold War divide," evident in the networks that emerged around 1955–1956 (203). She quotes Said:

> to speak here only of borrowing and adaptation is not adequate. There is in particular an intellectual and perhaps moral community of a remarkable kind, affiliation in the deepest and more interesting sense of the word (Said, 2000, 452).

Years later, the narrative artistry of Pramoedya Ananta Toer would cut through the darkness of internments with his stories whispered between cells in the night—orality, the carceral, and writing melding in the stories he told and how he told them, and how they were passed on. It is still unclear why he was not among those with whom Wright met. There is no indication that "Pram" as he came to be known, preferred not to meet with Wright. But there is good evidence that Wright turned with some contempt against those writers for whom socialist realism was their ideal, as well as to those advocating "universal humanism."[85]

Both Situmorang and Toer were imprisoned first by the Dutch and later by Soeharto for decades. The historian Rudolph Mrazek has called the infamous camp of Boven Digul where they were interned a site of "concentrated modernity" precisely because those held there were well educated, "urbanized, westernized," and endowed with cultural capital that few others could accrue or afford. If some like "Pram" were creative figures, all were exiled for their politics. Clustered together for years, they nourished one another with their politics of obstinacy, cultural literacy, creative talents, style, and recalcitrant prose.[86] Would that we might know more about what gelled into unrehearsed and unwritten prose and poetics and what evaporated in the waft of cheap clove cigarettes on sleep deprived nights.

Still, it is hard not to be skeptical of what has been conjured about the reverberations of Bandung, the embrace of "anti-colonial humanism" and what was actually part of the agenda at the

---

This too gets at something about the literary figures of an emergent Indonesia forged on a collective, if differently conceived notion of being "anti-colonial." It deserves to be considered "unacceptable" and avant-garde.

85. See footnote 43, where in West's introduction to *Black Power*, he celebrates Wright's "progressive secular humanism" nevertheless.

86. See Rudolf Mrazek's compelling commentary on a "concentrated modernity" at the Boven Digul internment camps of the Dutch East Indies and fascist post-war Indonesia under Soeharto. *The Complete Lives of Camp People: Colonialism, Fascism, Concentrated Modernity* (Durham: Duke University Press, 2020).

time.[87] Stathis Gourgouris and Amir Mufti argue that what they call the "Bandung effect" gave rise to a flourishing of multi-lingual literary journals that thought of themselves as avant-garde and part of a universal and *radical humanism* embraced by Fanon, connectivities fervently examined and curated today.[88]

Dipesh Charkrabarty has been more dubious about what was actually shared. He holds that Bandung participants were neither "of the same mind on questions of international politics, nor did they have the same understanding of what constituted imperialism."[89] As he wryly notes, they hardly even liked one another. No surprise. It was a supremely performative space after all. Hundreds of cameras were focused on their verbal and visual prose. Some responded with pedantic pronouncements, others were cut down as "dogmatic" by other participants. Nor is it clear from all that has been written, whether common folk had any more participation in the event than to gaze from a distance behind barricades at the ethnically attired royalty of what was to be called the "non-aligned Third world."

It was dazzling. An internationally feted political photo-op on a scale that had never been seen before. Still, one is hard-pressed to find considerations of how Bandung effected anti-colonial aesthetics on the ground. Although publication of Edward Said's

---

87. They are not alone. The number of books that refer to the "political afterlives" of Bandung, the "Meanings of Bandung," "The Bandung Moment," "Reviving Bandung," and "Bandung Revisited" speaks to failed visions as well as new ones. See, for example, Luis Eslava, Michael Fakhri, and Vasuki Nesiah, "The Spirit of Bandung," in *Bandung, Global History, and International Law: Critical Pasts and Pending Futures*, eds. Luis Eslava, Michael Fakhri, and Vasuki Nesiah, 3–32 (New York: Cambridge University Press, 2017); "Reviving Bandung" in Pham and Shilliam, *Meanings of Bandung*, 3–19.

88. I thank Stathis Gourgouris for sharing with me his compelling work about radical humanism and some of the intellectual itinerary of his five-year project with Aamir Mufti on the aftermaths of Bandung. See his "Humanism, Human/Animal, Human-Being" in *Nothing Sacred* (forthcoming).

89. Dipesh Chakrabarty, "The Legacies of Bandung: Decolonization and the Politics of Culture," in Lee, *Making a World*, 49.

Orientalism (1978) is often hailed as the incisive moment of anti-colonial studies and the radical humanism he sought and defended, others look to the post-Bandung fluorescence, dated some twenty years earlier. Such journals, *Lotus* among those best known, made Syrian poetry available to anti-colonial dissidents in a (post) colonial world elsewhere, a trilingual quarterly in Arabic, English, and French. It was a journal that was uprooted time again by politics that cut across the Afro-Asian nexus, insistently eschewing nation-based priorities and assiduously bypassing European metropoles as it travelled.[90]

WAYS OF BEING IN THE WORLD

These movements were not necessarily coordinated so much as animated by similar anti-colonial and anti-imperial impulses, that their participants increasingly were aware they shared. This was a protracted conjunctural set of cascading moments and persons whose aesthetic does not reduce to their artwork and never did. As those well-versed students of Indonesia's early literature contend, Indies literature, in Malay or Dutch, was never not tethered in some way to an anti-colonial politics.

Colonialism's impositions produced conditions of psychological and physical duress. A diffuse anti-colonial politics permeated what many of these local and worldly persons thought, what they read, how they wrote, how they produced their work, the music they listened to, how they spoke, how they moved, and dressed. One can almost see the casting and carving of a set of

---

90. See Hala Halim, "Afro-Asian Third-Worldism into Global South: The Case of Lotus Journal," *Global South Studies*, November 22, 2017, https://globalsouth studies.as.virginia.edu/key-moments/afro-asian-third-worldism-global-south-case-lotus-journal; Hala Halim, "Lotus, the Afro-Asian Nexus, and Global South Comparatism," *Comparative Studies of South Asia, Africa and the Middle East* 32, no. 3 (2012): 563–583.

dispositions in formation in this world they worked to unhinge from its certitudes and propel into motion. Strangely, this feature of *comportment* is hardly noted I take that feature of bearing as fundamental. Perhaps it is seen as awkward, smacking of too much westernization, a non-fitting concession to European style—of unadorned elegance in manner, bearing, and dress. But to reduce it to "European" is to miss its creative cast. For it was at once "cosmopolitan," what Edward Said might have called a "worldliness"—a capacity to remain mobile, taking sustenance from exile, rejecting a nostalgia for what was, while for some, still commtited to making possible a new kind of return. If hinged to European political and aesthetic movements, it was never defined only by them.

Strikingly clear in the visual archive was a confident demeanor, a clarity of regard, humored critique sometimes instead of rage, other times unleashed and exacting fury in the spoken and written word. Each of the Césaires, Aimé and Suzanne, epitomize that clamorous regard. The young anti-colonial Javanese author, Mas Marco, noted earlier, playing the dandy in the 1920s Netherlands Indies to an unappreciative audience, and to a Dutch colonial state that puts him in prison for what he wrote, what he did (and how he looked?), and what he said.

It was crystallized then in how this obstinate avant-garde was and what they cultivated in themselves. Confidence was in their prose and posture where being of color was luminous, not a detriment as it was in a racialized imperial world. There were radical visions and an abiding adherence to a recalcitrant politics. Imagination conceived as "the property of a collective," a "community of sentiment" captures something of one, as Arjun Appadurai puts it, "that imagines and begins to feel things together."[91] But the sensibilities that joined the anti-colonial

---

91. Arjun Appadurai, "Topographies of the Self," in *Language and the Politics of Emotion*, eds. Catherine Lutz and Lila Abu-Lughod, 92–112 (New York: Cambridge University Press, 1990).

avant-garde are sharpened and weaponized by racisms, its sundry forms, in which they lived and traveled— stop signs erected just for them, red lights flashing, more brightly by their refusals to succumb.

Their aesthetic was grounded in their politics but with care not to be confined by a rigid frame. It was a politics shaped by a battering colonial ethos but also by what other faces would come into view, what alliances they sought to activate, the questions they sought to address. They stood firmly, if not always successfully, on the conviction that critique was not to win out over poetics. There was a spoken and unspoken mandate that art and artistry mattered to define and redefine politics.

"TO HELL WITH FRANGIPANI"... OF SUZANNE CÉSAIRE

In writing about Aimé Césaire, the concept that drives the power of the response, that pushes to new heights, transforming the notion of "politics" is clearly Césaire's embrace of "poetic knowledge" and "poetic truth." Capturing the imaginations of those who followed his itinerant words, Cesaire was singled out as the one who conveyed the power of anti-colonial refusal, drawing in many who followed in his wake. Living in the COVID-19 pandemic amidst Black Lives Matter in New York City since mid-May 2020, I can't help but think that what actually galvanized so many and so many of us now, has been the Césaires' embrace of "poetic rage."[92]

A recent account of the Paris protests in support of Black Lives Matter uses the phrase, but it is one borrowed from, and captures the fierce poetics of the Césaires. Aimé is there at the forefront.

---

92. Many who write with fierce dedication to the Césaires' projects, and especially to Aimé's, seem taken by their capacity for fearless speech and their call to arms, so evident and still stymied today.

But it was Suzanne Césaire who was a force of her own. Her brilliance was breath-taking, as was her beauty (on which few who met her did not comment). Schooled in philosophy with Aimé at the *École normale supérieure* that pinnacle of French education, she cultivated the capacity to concentrate her rage in words that barely held to the page.

There is something else uniquely evident in this avant-garde, epitomized and named by Suzanne Césaire's essays. It was an astounding capacity to write "in code" in precarious times. It was a movement around censorship, seized books, shut down, and internment. Some have even argued that their *petit revue Tropiques*, now infamous and renowned, was camouflaged as a poetry journal dedicated to Caribbean folklore. Some claim that the surrealist movement was a mere cover as well. The first conjecture is only likely if Vichy officials never read what she wrote (which they surely didn't). For *Tropiques*' January 1942 edition, she was fearless and dismissive of what she called "hammock," "tourist literature," calling for "the death of [the] sappy, sentimental, folkloric . . . to hell with hibiscus, and frangipani, and bougainvillea. Martinican poetry will be cannibal. Or it will not be."[93]

For she and her comrades, publishing during the fascist Vichy government required writing "in code." With Aimé's writing already banned from publication in France, *Tropiques* required an attunement to political surveillance and to what demanded being said nonetheless. As striking to my mind was Suzanne Césaire's assault on colonial common sense. Her terse assessment of a "willful blindness" of history and of "the work it takes not to see."[94] "The work it takes not to see" has provided the colonial condition in its governmentality throughout the world. The terms of disengagement take many forms. They may emerge as "skittish seeing," of an "averted gaze," that imperial dispositions cultivated. Those

---

93. "Poetic Destitution" in Césaire, *Camouflage*, 26–27.
94. The phrases are those of Suzanne Césaire's translator, Keith Walker, in his introduction to Césaire, *Camouflage*, ix.

terms of disengagement were invariably followed by a turn away.[95] Suzanne Césaire's writing repeatedly expressed this "disposition of disregard"—a touchstone and measure of racial politics, an active dissociation, uncomprehending what is seen and spoken. That disregard describes yet something else, marked by a negative space, "that from which those with privilege and standing could excuse themselves."[96] This ability to excuse oneself from wrought engagement joins refusal to witness and the almost legal legitimacy recusal confers.

Breton shared another observation in his exuberant, almost ecstatic 1943 preface to Césaire's *Notebook on a Return to the Native Land*. The poetics of dissent was captured in the very lettered being of Césaire. It's a quite amazing passage in which Breton in turn regales the reader with Césaire's appreciation of the young trilingual gender bending poet, the Comte de Lautreamont—born in Uruguay, schooled on Baudelaire, Bryon, and Poe, and like Césaire, impassioned by a form of poetry that in itself was a "writ of expropriation." For here was a poet who understood, again as did Césaire that "poetry starts with excess, disproportion, quests deemed unacceptable."[97] These transgressive and radical moves condu embrace the very definition of what constitutes an avant-garde.[98]

Anti-colonialism and critiques of imperialism were not absent from European avant-gardes, but it would be difficult to argue that the politics of anti-racism provided the backbone of their being and the sinews of their assaults. It took several decades for Breton to come out forcefully in an anti-colonial position, far after Césaire. Anti-colonialism was there for some of the European avant-garde but could never be as central as it was for those whose

---

95. Ann Laura Stoler, *Along the Archival Grain: Epistemic Anxieties and Colonial Common Sense* (Princeton: Princeton University Press, 2009), 255.
96. Stoler, *Archival Grain*, 256.
97. André Breton, "A Grand Black Poet," xviii.
98. Breton, "A Grand Black Poet," xviii.

lives were framed by its constraints. When in 1925, Breton wrote the First Surrealist Manifesto—it was the year in which he notoriously, as James Clifford noted, made a stance on the side of anti-colonial rebels in Morocco when France was engaged in what Clifford wrote was a "minor [colonial] war."[99]

Actually, it was not so minor. Some historians consider the Rif War, which brought colonial Spain and France together to defeat a Moroccan army, the first war to use tanks and aircraft, a "harbinger of the decolonization process in North Africa"— or as some put it, the "last colonial war." Not least it could be considered, as by some historians, precursor to the Algerian war of independence three decades later.[100] Invariably accused of trespassing and transgressing norms, the militant poets of the anti-colonial moment did just that repeatedly. I'm not even sure that one can say that their "origins" were in Morocco or Martinique, in Indonesia, or Paris. Originary narratives were antithetical to their practices and projects. Their poetics and politics were firmly situated but not their imaginations. We might do better to be swept up with them in itineraries of meeting and inspiration.

EMPIRE AND THE AVANT-GARDE AS "HALLMARK OF THE MODERN"

Such itineraries make sense of something else. Should we think to other reasons for turning an account of the avant-garde to colonial conditions and imperial formations, we might also invoke again Breton, one of many who considered the avant-garde a "hallmark

---

99. James Clifford, *The Predicament of Culture: Twentieth-Century Ethnography, Literature, and Art* (Cambridge: Harvard University Press, 1988), 122.
100. David Slavin, "The French Left and the Rif War, 1924–25: Racism and the Limits of Internationalism," *Journal of Contemporary History* 26, no. 1 (Jan 1991): 5–32.

of the modern." Should it be the multiple "moderns" we are after, then it is unequivocally colonial conditions and imperial formations that offer points of access that a European origin story— once so comfortably endorsed—would not make. I've referred to this as a speculative project, but in other ways it was decidedly not—for it traverses a breadth of thinking and practice that questions the very making of what might be considered "modernity" and even why it should be a goal to be part of the "modern" age.

It has taken some two decades of a scrutinizing critical colonial studies to pry the concept of the modern from its hermetically sealed European home to ask what that protective shielding has displaced. Just a very brief partial detour through these alternative histories. We might look to the work of the historian Uday Mehta, who has insistently argued for nearly thirty years, since his first essay on "Liberalism and the Politics of Exclusion," that the rise of liberalism and the exclusions built into its structure were built into the pragmatics of empire from the very start.[101]

Race insured that no matter what the *de jure* requirements of access to citizenship might be, there were always unspoken credentials that were prescriptive, exclusionary, and implicit but essential. They could be language, comportment, rearing, or dress, those elements of everyday life through which dispositions are trained. These were gatekeepers that insured that citizenship was a liberal ruse, constrained by racial coordinates. In places like the Dutch East Indies and for those from there, few could possibly garner the cultural competencies and credentials that would make them eligible (and worthy) of the European equivalence they (might have strategically) sought in the legal domain. And even if they excelled in the requisite education achievements, these were never enough.

---

101. Uday Mehta, "Liberalism and the Politics of Exclusion," in *Tensions of Empire: Colonial Cultures in a Bourgeois World*, eds. Frederick Cooper and Ann Laura Stoler (Berkeley: University of California Press, 1997), first published in *Politics and Society* and later richly expanded into what is now considered the primer on liberalism and empire.

Or we might look to the work of the Argentinian philosopher Enrique Dussel who for decades has pursued a critical argument—building on dependency theory of the 1960s that there really was no modernity without what he called its "underside" —i.e., of a rapacious system of territorial conquest of expansive imperial formations. Here the underside of modernity is the extractions of imperial pursuits. The very technologies of bureaucracy, state racism, and documented torture, so defining of modern states and the global inequities on which they depend were honed in the imperial corridors of the inquisitions and incarcerations.[102]

And finally, but not least, has been a well-rehearsed formulation of colonial studies that the colonies were the actual and most robust laboratories of modernity where experiments could be conducted, materials were tried out, labor was cheaper, and no protocols were in the way to protect those subjected to them. The first museums in Indochina were filled with local art salvaged as railway construction sites felled forests and drained strategically placed swamps. Such selective conservation and managed restoration turned the colonies into "laboratories of modernity"—not only for architectural enhancement as the notion could be (mis)construed, but for the infrastructure of extraction, unfettered experimentation in segregated sewage channels for Europeans, urban organizations that kept Vietnamese from Whites. Displacing people and ignoring micro-ecological fragilities were fundamental to the choreographies of apartheid—they were colonial things.

This constellation of perceptions and practice that depended on "the peripheral colonial world" was clearly not peripheral at all.[103] So how does this refigure how we might recalibrate what

---

102. Irene Silverblatt, *Modern Inquisitions: Peru and the Colonial Origins of the Civilized World* (Durham: Duke University Press, 2004).

103. "Cultural" anthropology students of my generation, groomed on political economy and imperial world-systems, took Sidney Mintz's insights to heart: namely that the first sites of industrialized factory production were not Lancaster's wool mills but the sugar factories of the Caribbean where mills, turbines and industrialized colonized workers and European colonial labor made sugar the elixir of an overworked

constitutes an avant-garde and its locations? Of course, the sustained argument is that there is nothing peripheral about colonialism except a Europe-bound vision of it. In this peripheral vision we find not the margins of Europe, but the very conditions and relations that gave Europe material substance and shape as an entity. What it was and what it still is.

THE DIFFERENCE THAT MATTERED

This is not to say that there is no work on the avant-garde that notes some of its outlying practitioners on Europe's fringe. But something else has rarely been addressed; namely the conditions that made the counter-colonial avant-garde not only more political but endowed with an *inherent radicality* that could neither be borrowed nor cloned. Theirs was an embrace of refusal that alters the concept of the political. Endowed with a politicality borne of the "loose earth" (*la terre meuble*) into which they were borne, their political grammars evince more grounded substance than some of Europe's avant-garde's well-known central adherents and advocates.

For these activist artists and writers there was no avant-garde that could subscribe to or entertain the option of a muted politics. As Suzanne Césaire wrote in *The Great Camouflage*, subterfuge, fictive history, deception were hallmarks of colonial rule that had to be called out by their name. This was the politics of poetic

---

industrial labor force in Europe and on whose profits the luxuriant country estates of the British gentry were built. See Sidney Mintz, *Sweetness and Power: The Place of Sugar in Modern History* (New York: Penguin, 1985).

knowledge. Naming was a way of "laying bare," exposing the disguises of colonial contortions, making graspable and visible for all to see.[104]

For she and the constellation of extraordinary Black artists and poets with whom she worked, thought, and collaborated, politics was not only articulated with "poetic knowledge" but more fundamentally and consistently with "poetic rage." This was a brash poetics, constitutive of how they would understand their arts and their politics. Among these multiple generations of persons were some with family genealogies steeped in the histories of slavery, some not. But even the latter were marked with the sort of interpellations Fanon would take as a founding moment of a racialized identity—humiliations as Césaire would also describe, not surreptitious but in verbal and visceral assaults on one's presence, clothing, and being invariably out of place.

Among others like the Césaires, it was not in Europe where the most denigrating affronts were directed at them. Their defiance was against an imperial imaginary that theirs was a world of color, craving and anguished by wanting to be white. It was a white fiction dispelled by, and countered in their very being. In "Weaponizing the Senses," I referred to Sianne Ngai's concise take on the difference between "wanting to have" and "wanting to be" and the misrecognition that the affective politics of the two was the same.[105] But it was more than a white fantasy, but part of the micro-physics of colonial rule, built into the architecture of security regimes, household arrangements, and public space. It was and is fostered, regenerated, and unacknowledged by a white sovereignty extending far beyond the blatantly racist far right.

---

104. Again, I thank Omar Berrada for sharing this thought with me on the work of "naming" to which the anti-colonial avant-gardists were so committed.
105. Sianne Ngai, *Ugly Feelings* (Cambridge: Harvard University Press, 2005).

Perhaps that in part accounts for why so many histories of the avant-garde seem to harbor a subtext that those of the Global South sought to embrace European culture in toto, rather than distinguishing between those elements they saw of value and those from which they turned away. Gary Wilder makes the crucial point that theirs was not a rejection of European culture creativities, but of Europe as a political entity. Their interest was more in winnowing what they needed, what could be transformative on other soil. They neither relinquished being French nor claimed that the Caribbean was their only home. Their cosmopolitan breadth was a rethinking of the world map and the abundance of places that were "of them" and they belonged.

ON THE PROSE AND POLITICS OF INSPIRATION (*SOUFFLES*)

One of the prolific, "peripheral" avant-gardes rarely included in the non-European centered accounts I've read was Moroccan, a nexus where language is riven with furious grace. I think here of the initial stanzas of Mostafa Nissabouri's poem "Manabboula" ("Manpower"):

> *So that you may doubt our origins even more*
> *We offer you bodies for the salvation-of-humanity factories*
> *With ablutions*
> *Peaceful bodies on the sand placement offices*
> *Leathery bodies*
> > *Tubercular history*
> > > *us dogs the perfidious ones*
> *us of paleolithic brain squinty eyes thermonuclear liver*
> *bodies with wooden tables where it is written that underdevelopment*
> *is our congenital disease*
> > *and sir*
> > > *and madam*
> > > > *and thank you*

without forgetting our interminable procession of yellow teeth
and stupors
our blood half blood half tree
bodies nourished on locusts and camel piss
we are not
    even epileptic

Here's a poetics that shirks the indirect, blasting the ugly, blind perceptions of hollowed out European minds. The poem appeared in the journal *Souffles* (later *Souffles/ANFAS*) first in French, then in French and Arabic. *Souffles* referred literally to "breath" or "blast" and figuratively to "inspiration."[106] And it was just that.

When it appeared in the mid-1960s, nearly twenty years after *Tropiques*, it did so with an urgency that was no less. Its founder and editor in chief, Adbellatif Laabi, watched over the production, making sure that *Souffles* instilled itself as a form of "hand to hand combat"—at once an assault on milquetoast poetics (so reminiscent of Suzanne Césaire's scathing critique of tame Martinican poets.) Impatience was shared and cut across North Africa, the Caribbean, and Southeast Asia. Like Fanon, who was so adamant against "the bards of Negritude," this community of Moroccan artist activists was impatient with stale Moroccan stories and their folkloric authors, from the Carib to Algeria.[107]

Some have argued that *Souffles* itself was a precursor, an "inaugural spring" . . . "that anticipated and made a space for today's revolts against authoritarian regimes." But the lineages of dissent are resolutely there. As Olivia Harrison and Teresa Villa-Ignancio, editors of the beautifully translated collection of *Souffles*' writing state, it was never just a Moroccan affair but "an example of tricontinental aesthetic practice" that embraced

---

106. Harrison and Villa-Ignacio, *Souffles/ANFAS*, 1.
107. Wilder, *Freedom Time*, 134.

Haitian writers, Syrian poets, and the ten-point program of the Black Panthers.[108]

THE MANIFESTO

The Manifesto was a preferred genre of the avant-garde and for the anti-colonial avant-garde perhaps more so. These were summons to action, invitations to practices, and demands to do more than attend. It was by no means only Frantz Fanon who Laabi so admired for wielding the sharpened edges of language as a weapon. One need only look at Laabi's prologue in *Souffles*' first issue to get some sense of the political passion of his prose. For Laabi, poet, playwright, editor—in—chief for six years, *Souffles* was a place of unfettered words. *Souffles* seemed to embody precisely what Foucault would borrow from the ancient Greeks, *parhessia*, truth that translates as "fearless speech."

Laabi's prologue to Souffles' first issue is cutting, a manifesto condemning a "scelorosis" of creativity, the prance of Moroccan poets showing up and applauded at tame international gatherings to sell their tepid wares. The poet Mohammed Kahir-Eddine, often referred to as the Moroccan Rimbaud, too was known for his explosive expressive prose. In a letter to Laabi that appeared just after Laabi's prologue, Kahir-Eddine's turbulent tone might be taken as the poetic truth of their collective project. He wrote:

> *Tous ceux d'ici qui se réclament de l'avant-garde se leurrent. L'avant-garde c'est tout ce qui se fait en Afrique.* (All of those from here [Europe] who claim to be of the avant-garde fool themselves. The avant-garde is all happening in Africa.).[109]

---

108. Harrison and Villa-Ignacio, *Souffles/ANFAS*, 11.
109. The last line is ambiguous. Less literally and more accurately it could be, "the avant-garde is really only happening in Africa." (I thank Clara Beccaro for thinking through these possibilities with me.)

The "ici" is emphatically not here in Europe or elsewhere. It's an undaunting declaration, an assertion and a refusal, an unmitigated claim! It did more than put Europe and its originary myths in question. Here was the identification of another fulcrum, a counter knowledge drawn on another map.

POWER AS RECALCITRANCE: APPRENTICESHIPS OF THE AVANT-GARDES

Disruption, disproportion, and subliminal threat are all recurrently alive among the anti-colonial avant-gardes. They promise and offer other configurations of horizontal movements of which colony to metropole is only one interlude rehearsed along the way. Here are other locations to map, translocations to follow, a mobile, protean archive that slices across continents to reconnect them, that reimagines the Caribbean not as cut off islands but as Suzanne Césaire did early on, and Eduardo Glissant after her, as an archipelago of creative political innovations that move between a description of the Caribbean and the globe.[110]

Prominent in this possibly new archive of these avant-gardes is how many threads are tied without producing a weave of duplication. The Black Panthers show up as love child of the Pan-African Movement, of *Légitime défense* (1932), of the "Black surrealists," and Negritude, with varied models of militance in different medium, on paper, on walls, with weapons in hand,

---

110. Eduardo Glissant, *Traite du Tout-monde* (Paris: Gallimard, 1997) and *La Cohée du Lamentin* (Paris: Gallimard, 2005), where he writes "le Monde tremble, se créolise . . . La pensée archipélique tremble de ce tremblement" (75). I draw here on Richard Scholar, "The Archipelago Goes Global: Late Glissant and the Early Modern Isolario" in *Globalizations in the Making*, eds. Eva Sansavior and Richard Scholar, 33–57 (Liverpool: Liverpool University Press, 2015) where he notes how difficult it is to translate Glissant's "Le monde entier *s'archipelise* (*emphasis added*) et se creolise" Glissant, *Traite*, 194.

again and again. But as we know there are other threads that might celebrate the Cuban-born artist Wilfredo Lam and his own mixed heritage of African, Spanish, and Chinese kinships, none of which he sought to claim, eighteen years in Paris, Italy, Venezuela to return to Cuba. His painting, as he described it, bent on "disturb(ing) the dreams of the exploiters."[111] Or one might trace an Egyptian surrealism that joined "aesthetic struggles and political activism" between 1938–1948 and the manifesto, "long live degenerate art" as a direct response to Hitler's condemnation of "modern art."

These were interlaced maps of three and four dimensions with apprenticeships that make new political and aesthetic connections. "Apprenticeships" here emerge at central because of the evident scent and multiple scenes of a learning and leaning on those who came before, an admiration, a critique, and admiration again. Once again, vague concepts like "influence" are pallid and ineffective in describing the forms of learning and appropriation, resources, funds, dinners, lovers, and lodging, that were shared. These appear as lines of errant flight to what were imagined as a newly conceived sense of the political and its aesthetics. Might this be a new way of writing both a colonial history of the present and a history of an anti-colonial and counter-colonial future, with this protean archive as touchstone, in formation?

These luminous souls of the anti-colonial avant-garde who defied the rules of colonial decorum, racial subordinations, and a gender proper place, remind us of what it takes not to be subsumed by racial practices of silent, degrading force, unspoken violence, blatant clarity, white protocols, and their fearful imaginaries. Mas Marco, Armijn Pane, Putu Oka Sukanta, Pierre Yoyotte, and so many whose names remain in the shadows were as much the ballast of these powerful communities of political

---

111. "Wilfredo Lam: A Sketch by Paulette Richards" *Callaloo* 11 no. 1, 90-92.

and aesthetic acuity, of judgments, and violences in the name of a future equality still not yet theirs. We owe them much more than is often acknowledged. Awe can be the only response to the fearless truths that Mas Marco was willing to utter on threat of prison and death; of the members of *Souffles* in the 1960s, of Pramoedya Ananta Toer who suffered and celebrated a different fate. I think of James Baldwin, raging in a cage of tepid politics against those of Richard Wright and later even against Aimé Césaire for founding and endorsing Negritude, and the descent of Césaire's imagining that "departmentalization" was an appropriate step toward liberation from France.

And then there is again Mas Marco. It's hard not to be taken by his audacities. Dutch authorities wrote of him at the turn of the century as "mad." But perhaps his novel entitled *Mata Gelap* hints at something else, an inherent radicality that was always in "excess" of what was, and what should not be. *Mata Gelap* translates as "going amok," out of one's mind, but also could be translated as "blind rage."[112] Might this be similar to Suzanne Césaire's poetic rage, or James Baldwin's fury in the face of the U.S.'s foundational adherence to an insistent racial and sexual inequality that made him flee? Or the film makers who wanted to film a documentary extolling his love of France? As Baldwin put it in "Meeting the Man: Baldwin in Paris, "he couldn't care less about France beyond the fact that he didn't need to confront that in the U.S. he could be killed for walking a street where he did not "belong"—on any day. Ironically that flight was to a France that could not (and still does not) reckon with the depths of how race has constituted its "interior frontiers."

James Baldwin was considered by some a difficult and ornery figure who turned against monsters and heroes alike, "abrasive" in his writing and being, with hate in his heart. Unable to

---

112. Mas Marcokartodikromo, *Mata Gelap* [1914] (Yogyakarta: Pataba Press, 2021); "*mata*" translates to "eye," and "*gelap*" translates to "dark."

transform this world in motion must have made some suffocate, driving them and successive others to be consumed by the poetic rage that racisms' toxicities create. They rot out future visions. But rarely with success. Dissent's creative force builds on those for whom defeat is not an option.

* * *

6

Archiving Praxis

For Palestinians and Beyond

A kind of ur-Utopia exists in the desires of the imaginary despite the torturous environment that looms nearby in fences and towers and barbed wire.[1]

ON A HILLSIDE OUTSIDE RAMALLAH, are two distinct archival ventures years in the making. One, part of The Palestinian Museum, has garnered international attention. Its signature exhibits, conceived by the Palestinian curator, Jack Persekian, were prepared for the museum's opening. Neither were finished nor displayed: both were suspended in cold storage when Persekian was fired as Museum Director in 2016. The other archival venture, the *Birzeit University Digital Archive* (often referred to by its Arabic name, *Awraq*), was initiated by the historian Roger Heacock who taught at Birzeit University for some thirty years. Opened earlier but without adequate personnel, funds, and profile, it has languished. By 2015 it was superseded by the mammoth physical expanse (a 40,000 square plot of land) and fiscal support of the richly funded museum next door.[2]

1. Bruce Ferguson, "Preface," in *Otherwise Occupied*, Venice Biennale 2013, eds. Ryan Bishop and Gordon Han (Jerusalem: Palestinian Art Court—al Hoash, 2013), 7. This essay is a revised and longer version of "Archiving Praxis" in *Critical Inquiry* 48, no.3 (spring 2023): 1–25.

2. Lila Abu-Lughod describes her father's 1993 vision of the museum, suspended and re-animated with a focus on cultural heritage seven years later (see her "Imagining

Only fifty meters apart, there was virtually no communication, much less collaboration, between them. Those who had worked on the museums' exhibits during the overlapping years had barely heard of *Awraq*. Some not at all. The two intrepid persons laboring to gather and digitize *Awraq*'s holdings knew virtually nothing of the Museum's activities, nor their principles of collection. Little knowledge of their respective archival activities and practices have been shared. Both mark the fragmented Palestinian archival field, within and beyond the borders of occupied Palestine.

As two radically different, simultaneous, and adjacent archival ventures, their contrasts would undoubtedly make for a good story: distinctly different origin narratives, proximity and unaccountable "distance," a disconnect and connection, nevertheless. Still, this is not the most compelling story to tell, nor a fair rendering of even a small slice of the Palestinian archival scene. For in the space between these two ventures have emerged a spectrum of other archival projects, varied in content and form, mixed media making up a disparate, creative, and politically distinct turn in archival practice, reshaping an archival terrain that bridges occupied Palestine and Palestinians in Palestine, Israel, and beyond.

It is a small slice of this spectrum of projects, diverse in medium and scale, that make up what I call today's *archival surge* of Palestinians and Palestine. This surge is deeply political, emphatically anti-colonial, and bold in its methods of requisition.[3] *Archiving*, rather than working *in* and *on* archives, redefines terms of engagement. Instead of expending energy on countering authoritative inscriptions of state and institutional command, *archiving seems to be offering an imaginative rethinking of political praxis*. The challenge is directed at what constitutes custodial

---

Palestine's Alter-Natives: Settler Colonialism and Museum Politics," *Critical Inquiry* 47 (Autumn 2020): 1–26.)

3. I think of a "surge" here as in an accretion of stronger, increased motion preceded by smaller wave swells.

control, guardianship, access, medium, rubrics of order, digital coding, entry requirements, a pedagogy of use. All are in question, not necessarily by the same practitioners nor all at the same time. Still, they are all premised on turning away from colonial regimes of truth, and their epistemic, political, and bare aesthetic foundations.[4]

These projects include individual ventures: academics/artist/activists (and sometimes combinations of all three) challenging the aesthetics of politics, reworking archiving practice in modes of non-compliant dissent. These projects tend to start small in scale, few with institutional affiliation, most with limited profile; few are well backed by NGO benevolence or local wealth. Some derive from personal documents, family papers that have inspired a wider community (of common residence, background, or ethnic affinity) to share their own. Others have sought to cull material objects, significantly insignificant things—a porcelain plate, a shredded piece of clothing—that have survived dispossession and been stored.

A distinctive feature in this turn joins in the expansion of multimedia installations throughout the world: photographic montage mixed with film, video recordings mixed with material things. If distinct, it is in palimpsest screen images, overlays of past and future, temporalities played through things. Uneven with respect to small and larger publics, some are expressly dispersed and diasporic, others not. The Palestinian Museum figures here not because it is a museum nor because of the turbulent politics of the museum's making. Rather my interest is in it as a site

---

4. Palestinians, from 1948 onwards, and especially since 1967 with the radicalization of the PLO, also developed creative archival practices. With neither archies nor museums readily at their disposal (nor would there have been any presence of Palestian villagers' experience in them), they turned to oral histories erased by Israel. Palestinians haave been writing alternative forms of knowledge production for a long time. Wee, for example, Mezna Qato, "Forms of Retrieval: Social Scale, Citation and the Archive of the Palestinian Left," International Journal of Middle East Studies 52, no2 (2019), 312-15 and "Returns of the Archive," The Nakba Files, 1 June 2016. Nakbafiles.org/2016/06/01/returns-of-the-archives.

of seemingly ordinary, but uncommon, archiving ventures that succeeded as visions, and in execution failed.

What makes up this archival surge? Colonial archives are being pushed off center stage. Content and form come from wholly different styles of thought, and techniques of critique drawing sustenance from elsewhere.[5] The past matters and is active but with an optic and sonic less preoccupied with the flood of violent and fictive Israeli narratives needing to be disproved. Certainly, interest in archives has been there long before; as Rosemary Sayigh, one of the earliest academic/activists to collect oral histories of ordinary Palestinians since the 1970s, would hold, "making archives" is endemic to being Palestinian as every Palestinian steals away documents and photographs for their families, themselves, in groups or on their own.[6]

But the last two decades of reckoning with the durability of Israel's settler imaginaries and their hardened inequalities is ceding to another set of prominent tasks. Counter imaginaries and

---

5. This reflection began from a speculative exercise: to envision the shaping of what I was to learn was a rather particular Palestinian archive housed in Ramallah, incipient in form, disparate and unwieldy in content, with rubrics of access not yet in place. The task, put before me in 2013, was to imagine the possibilities of The Birzeit University Digital Palestinian Archive (*Awraq*, its self-assigned acronym honoring its Arabic name) created with the vision of being unfettered by authorities, energized from below, allergic to the strictures imposed by archival command. But in late summer 2020 when I thought to revise those earlier reflections, something different happened; I was swept up by a live current of those in creative movement, breaching archival protocols, working solo and independently, with a changing young staff in movement and exchange. A speculative experiment became a quasi-ethnographic one, over several months on a set of archivally anchored projects among activists/artists/academics, marking the uneven emergence of a new archival surge among Palestinians in and beyond Palestine. Initially focused on how *Awraq* might expand, here it refigures as but one node within a set of archiving scenes with multiple sites and scales of activity—congruent, in contest, at times set intentionally apart. This is not ethnography in colonial archives but closer to an (ethnographic) encounter with archiving, and with those actors and agents who are its protagonists.

6. See Beshara Doumani and Mayssun Soukarieh, "A Tribute Long Overdue: Rosemary Sayigh and Palestinian Studies," *Journal of Palestine Studies* 38, no. 4 (Summer 2009): 6–11.

counter movements of documentation are ever more spirited efforts to *displace* (rather than only disprove) colonial truths, to identify and reckon with claims they still have upon Palestinians now.[7] The conceits of what counts as archiving and archival labor—and who can do it—are poised to implode. For those of us who have long sought to identify the logic of archiving practices it is hard not to see them as war zones.[8] Battles over recognition of attenuated, arrested, and protracted time contest the tenses in which they are inscribed and should be read. The grammar of the archive is open to contest too, and like the archive itself, temporalities may be stretched and rendered undisciplined and unbound. Archiving Palestine is emerging as a political project where Palestine's designation as a "shatterzone" takes on a positive rather than a politically pathologized valence. In tapping the veins of submerged sensibilities where dispositions are shaped, archiving Palestine creates a zone that fissures the fictions of power politics.

AN ARCHIVAL TERRAIN

This lively attention to archiving has come in a rush from many quarters, both inside and significantly outside Palestine's political borders. In 2011, the same year *Awraq* was established, the American University of Beirut initiated its now well-known

---

7. In November 2020, Gil Hochberg (professor of Hebrew and Comparative Literature at Columbia) and I were to learn that we had each been writing this thought for some time; she in preparing her book, *Becoming Palestine* (Durham: Duke University Press, 2021), I in rethinking "On Archiving as dissensus," Comparative Studies of South Asia, Africa, and the Middle East 38, no1 (2018): 43-56..

8. Kirsten Weld, Rosie Bsheer, and I share this similar sense. See Kirsten Weld, *Paper Cadavers: The Archives of Dictatorship in Guatemala* (Cambridge, MA, 2014) and Rosie Bsheer, *Archive Wars: The Politics of History in Saudi Arabia* (Stanford, California: Stanford University Press, 2020). My own emphasis, more on the battle of tenses, treats those battles as diagnostic of imperial politics.

Palestinian Oral History Archive project, self-described as a "grassroots digital archive" of "over one thousand oral history testimonies by first-generation Palestinian refugees residing in Lebanon."[9] Given the interest in archiving, though, it's hard to say if Awraq is a representative archiving model given its meager funds, limited personnel, and minor public presence. Still, the issues it confronted and raised over the last decade speak to the creative, financial, and political demands of an aspiration to reconfigure new archiving space. In 2012, the *Palestine Poster Project Archives* for the first time was presented in Palestine. The possibility of digitization changed its presence on a broader global and Palestinian map. Its long-time curator Daniel Walsh contends that posters have not been accorded their due: long rolled up in the back of closets, with no outlet, or legitimation in the "Western" art world (where they were often disparaged as anti-Semitic and anti-Israeli). They were given a global stage when the digital archive was produced. With posters and digital replicas contributed from Cuba, the U.S., Brazil, France, archiving here speaks to the rich political matrix through which an expansive Palestinian presence has resonance around the world.[10]

Others hold that the independent archive projects have emerged precisely because of disappointments of post-Oslo among artists/academics/activists who have come to distrust institutional forms. Even with meager funds they have sought to circumvent full dependence on those associations. Some of these modest collections have been efforts to restore family histories fragmented by dispossession and diaspora. Monaster Tarazi, born into a Christian family in Gaza, basically sidelined his day job

9. See Hana Sleiman and Kaoukab Chebaro, "Narrating Palestine: The Palestinian Oral History Archive Project," *Journal of Palestine Studies* 47, no. 2 (2018): 63–76.

10. The Liberation Graphics Collection of Palestine Posters/Memory of the World (Nominated), The Palestine Poster Project Archives, accessed May 20, 2020, http://palestineposterproject.org/liberation-graphics-collection-of-palestine-posters-memory-of-the-world-nominated. With over 11,500 posters digitized to date, 1,600 made up the "Liberation Graphics" collection nominated to UNESCO's memory of the world program 2016–2017.

in 2013 to begin documenting his own family's history, an effort that grew to include the spread of Christian Palestinian families.[11] Helene Kazan's on the other hand, worked through "a collection of photographs taken by [her] father on the eve of [the family's] flight from the Lebanese Civil War in 1989." From them she produced a short film *Masking Tape Intervention: Lebanon 1989* (2013) which she describes as:

> an effort to reconstruct and reactivate the space of our home ... to stage my parents' first conversation on the material conditions of living through conflict, and *the spatialized nature of warfare*.

The film is as disquieting as is her description of reconstructed images of empty rooms in a house that appears almost gossamer in the film, one to which they could never return.[12]

This agile move between film, still, photo, video, installation is a hallmark of the current moment. Kazan is not after "proof" so much as to make legible "the limited frames of accountability" that underwrite international law. Not surprisingly, her contributions have become part of more extensive projects, like that of "Documentary World-making" initiated to profile the relationship between film and the digital archive as a political intervention. The intense and generative work of Sherene Seikaly also pulls in a powerfully intimate and political direction. She reflects on "a decade of research, contingent, accidental, and unconsciously autobiographical, to explore archival practices and the writing of history" where she "stumbled across family papers" that traced the financial world of her grandfather, of privilege and loss that

---

11. Yousef Alhelou, "Palestinian Archives: A Reflection of a Rich History," *Middle East Monitor*, February 7, 2019, https://www.middleeastmonitor.com/20190207-palestinian-archives-a-relfection-of-a-rich-history. I know of no further comment on Tarazi's archival project.

12. Helene Kazan, "Dossier\Decolonizing Archives and Law's Frame of Accountability," *Documentary World-Making* 4, no. 17 (2020): https://vols.worldrecordsjournal.org/04/17.

sealed her own trajectory (at once academic and passionately personal and political) through her family's papers.[13].

A melding captured in the aesthetics of dissent resonates in the part Palestinian, Israeli artist-activist Dor Guez, who finds a suitcase of his grandfather's photographs kept under his bed. Beginning in 2006 with a project to document his own Christian Arab family's history, Guez sent out an open invitation to Christian Arabs wherever they might be to partake in an archive of thousands of digital images. His archival labor and the very naming of his project as an "archive," opens to material layered and reused in a media explosion of intimacy and aesthetic dissent. Starting with his grandmother's childhood in Jaffa and expulsion in 1948, he combines videos with digitally manipulated archival materials to produce "scanograms," both a term and technique he applies to layer, restore, and create artifacts that cut across temporalities.[14] His pieces work both as art and as "new historical documents." His mismeasure of time is stunning: clinging fast to the quotidian activities of his grandmother Samira prior to 1948, he expands to wider histories shared, told, and untold. Some of his projects are explicitly "political," but it is his strategic overlays of temporal sequences that seem to become political statement in themselves.

---

13. Sherene Seikaly, "How I Met My Great-Grandfather: Archives and the Writing of History," *Comparative Studies of South Asia, Africa and the Middle East* 38, no. 1 (2018): 6–20. As Lila Abu-Lughod has noted Seikaly writes with "exquisite and uncomfortable detail," finding herself implicated and her family archive echoing her book on Palestinian "men of capital," published two years earlier. Lila Abu-Lughod, "Palestine: Doing Things with Archives," *Comparative Studies of South Asia, Africa and Middle East* 38, no. 1 (2018): 3–5. See Sharene Seikaly, *Men of Capital: Economy and Scarcity in Mandate Palestine* (Palo Alto: Stanford University Press, 2016).

14. Christian Palestinian Archive: A Project by Dor Guez, City University of New York, accessed May 20, 2020, https://www.gc.cuny.edu/About-the-GC/Building-Venues-Particulars/James-Gallery/Exhibitions/Detail?id=35554; Sarah Peguine, "Profile of the Artist: Dor Guez," *The Seen*, April 23, 2014, https://theseenjournal.org/profile-artist-dor-guez/. For a thoughtful interview with Guez see Helen Mackreath, "Interview with Dor," *The White Review*, November 2015, https://www.thewhitereview.org/features/interview-with-dor-guez/.

The Dar Jasir family project is something wholly different. Describing itself as "a grass-roots artist-independent artist-run initiative." It's located in the nineteenth-century family home in Bethlehem where an activist descendant, Emily Jacir in 2014 began working through holdings that included nearly three thousand Palestinian newspapers.[15] The richness of these collections is beyond my hardly rudimentary Arabic, though some were translated for me. Fortunately, many others are working with them and attending to their charge. There is a relish for this archiving mode in quest for a form of documentation that pushes on the bounds of received aesthetics as they define dissensus on their terms. This new creative substance alters what counts as witnessing—above and beyond images of Israeli atrocities—as ways of being present in the world.

Consider Fady Asleh. While studying Palestinian historiography at Hebrew University, he became drawn to Israeli archives, with what was and was not in the accounts and documents about Palestinian lives. First working with Israeli archives, he then spent three years on the team working with Persekian at the Palestinian Museum. When the projects on which he had worked were abruptly shelved and Persekian was fired, he was devastated. A year later in 2016, Asleh began a venture about which he had long fantasized: the construction of a material (and digital) archive built by Palestinians themselves from villagers first and urban dwellers after. Starting with his own family's ephemera, he then spread out to families of his small team of collaborators and eventually to eager volunteers who collected materials across the Arab world.

He calls the project *Khazaeen*, describing it as a voluntary independent association centered in Jerusalem, committed to archiving people's stories and "ephemera"—brochures, theater stubs, receipts—that would otherwise be thrown away, ineligible

---

15. For a description of their project see "About Us," Dar Yusuf Nasri Jacir for Art and Research, accessed May 21, 2020, https://darjacir.com/About-Us.

as archive-able documents. The aspiration is an archive that would "document [the daily life . . . people have lived in all its intensity."[16] *Khazaeen* derives its name from the term once used for libraries in Islamic history but it also captures something else: the imagined protective and sovereign space that *Khazaaen* would offer to those who have no other. "This imaginary," as he writes on the website, "is to make a societal archive where everyone could contribute and . . . would keep his/her contribution in a special *'cabinet'* . . . these cabinets or lockers together would form the people's *khazaeen*." Here too the digital form is hoped to animate "discussion[s]" around "critical political and societal issues."[17]

With focus on the future, the scope is now broadened with volunteers from seven countries with a Palestinian and Arab presence: Jordan, Lebanon, Algeria, Tunisia, Syria, and Palestine. Each "cabinet," *curated by its individual proprietor,* is Asleh's dream space for which he supplies acid-free paper (that he can hardly afford) and cardboard boxes with openings that allow the contents to breathe. Some items are marked "not to be opened" in sealed envelopes if their "archons" decide not yet to make them available. Otherwise most "cabinets" are there for anyone to examine and use. In 2020, thirty thousand visitors perused the website, fifty to sixty ephemera were downloaded by those consulting the site every week. To date (Dec 2021) Khazaaen has scanned 50,000 materials with 6,000 uploaded on their digital website (khazaaen.org). Khazaaen now has 138 personal archives.[18]

---

16. Khazaaen, "About Us" www.khazaaen.org/en/node/1113. I thank Rana Anani for introducing me to *Khazaaen*'s archival initiative. See "Who are we?" *Khazaaen*, accessed February 21, 2021, http://www.khazaaen.org/en/node/1113. Khazaaen participated Its most rin the "2020 social innovation summit," devoted to what has become a pervasive NGO theme: "Radical Imagination."[this link is no longer active]

17. Ibid: my emphasis

18. These statistics can be found in the attached booklet (personal communication with Fady Asleh, 9 December 2021. https://drive.google.com/file/d/1QqVPGQoH0x9k4I68Pcxz_dX6u9-JSh58/view?usp=drive_web.

While *Khazaaen* still awaits the profile it deserves, and credit for its creative form, part of what this Palestinian researcher is after is something he has imagined since he first went to an Israeli archive a decade ago. His practice and that of those with whom he works is geared not only to those he hopes to instill with "a new archival awareness" but first and foremost to a political project that is emphatically for a younger generation and for the future.[19]

TIME WARPS AND THE IMAGINARY

Some of these archiving projects are contesting earlier accounts of colonial projects, defying myths while plotting out political interventions that rewrite histories of the present.[20] But other new strategies of refusal and dissent are exuberantly transdisciplinary, adisciplinary, and undomesticated by normative standards of what counts as history and rule-driven documentation. As in many efforts elsewhere to capture subaltern lives effaced or erased, the imagined and fabulated are seen as speculative sources, gracing and grounding new practices, scrambling temporalities, opposing linear sequence or "proper" tense.[21]

---

19. Fady Asleh's lecture (April 2017) at the Doha Institute in Qatar. The title of the talk: "Khazaaen: an attempt to build a new archival awareness" In Arabic, "خزائن: ديج يفيشرا يعو ءانب ةلواحم" I thank Saphe Shamoun for translating it from the Arabic and for his research support. I think Fady Asleh for the time he spent sharing the project's making and trajectory..

20. As anthropologist Rebecca Stein writes, in *Screen Shots: State Violence on Camera in Israel and Palestine* (Stanford: Stanford University Press, 2021), disqualifying Palestinians as "impossible witnesses" is the norm.

21. In Black studies, in Native American studies, and in colonial studies broadly conceived, there is engagement with what a wider set of agents and citizens choose as their own histories and with how they want to be part of these newly arranged composites. See Hortense Spillers, "Mama's Baby, Papa's Maybe: An American Grammar Book," *Diacritics* 17, no. 2 (1987): 64–81; Saidiya Hartman's fabulating figuration of young Black women as champions of liberty in *Wayward Lives, Beautiful Experiments: Intimate Histories of Riotous Black Girls, Troublesome Women, and Queer Radicals* (New York: Norton, 2019); Jenny Sharpe traces how Caribbean literary and visual

As participants in the "unofficial" Venice Biennale 2013 project, "Otherwise Occupied," curators Bashir Maskhoul and Aissa Deebi offered a piercing reflection: that "clearly the imaginary is the place that people without human justice seek."[22] Ariella Azoulay turns from the imaginary to call for new "contracts" between archival practice and its citizenry, in politically creative work to revise, revamp, and reassess that relationship between colonial archives and a citizenry on which its rubrics and vocabularies are imposed. Those oppositional gestures may be crafted with good intentions and bold ressentiment; sometimes with only minimalist repair.[23] Vernacular idioms are sought from those reluctant to share their own duress or believe it of insufficient pertinence to be included at all. Frames are sought to enable unrecognized connections, to regather what has gone astray in habits disappeared in the clutter of the everyday. Processes of assemblage promise to make room for the unforeseen, bits and pieces of debris, the *éclat* of a parody, a macabre joke that plays off vernaculars, and visions of what was and could be.

The questions are different as well: they address strategies to consider, sites of attention, techniques of care. In Jacques Rancière's now iconic formulation, politics makes "visible that which had no reason to be seen."[24] James Baldwin's outraged articulation of this premise permeated his writing, as he gravitated toward "the evidence of things not seen."[25] A mandate of dissensus presupposes an equalizing of persons and things with a query: How agile would such an archive need to be to cross the multiple minute and oversized scales of *designed destruction*? Will its critical and political

---

artists "bend the categories of archival knowledge" in *Immaterial Archives: An African Diaspora Poetics of Loss* (Evanston: Northwestern University Press, 2020).

22. Ferguson, "Preface."
23. Ariella Azoulay, "Archive," *Political Concepts* 1, no.1 (2017): http://www.politicalconcepts.org/archive-ariella-azoulay/.
24. Jacques Rancière, *Dissensus: On Politics and Aesthetics*, trans. Steven Corcoran (London: Bloomsbury, 2010), 38.
25. James Baldwin, *The Evidence of Things Not Seen* (New York: Holt, 1985).

breadth make room for those trapped spaces in which Bedouins and otherwise impoverished North African Jews are recruited as the Israeli state's cannon fodder? Will measures of achievement, aspiration, and generosity speak both to Palestinians and forms of justice that invite the rest of the world to consider as exemplary sites of active dissensus? And does the latter really matter?

POLITICAL POTENTIALS IN ITS FOLDS

Archiving is never about documents alone. I refer to the potentialities and the political possibilities that inhere in them as documentality.[26] Documentality is a promise—a summons of sorts and form of address.[27] Archiving practices may serve as prescripts for the present or proscriptions for the future. They might incite anticipatory occasions to locate the evidentiary fragments of papers, things, and sensibilities that their new guardians hold tight. A potential to be animated with a political claim entails a conversion of sorts that redefines what counts as a document and what counts as politics.

---

26. The term "documentality" is that of Italian philosopher Maurizio Ferraris. In my use, its key attribute is *potentiality* and the political possibility lodged in how content and form construe what witnessing entails when "proof is not enough." Mimi Onuoha, "When Proof is not Enough," *Five Thirty Eight*, July 1, 2020, https://fivethirtyeight.com/features/when-proof-is-not-enough/. See Maurizio Ferraris, *Documentality: Why It Is Necessary to Leave Traces*, trans. Richard Davies (New York: Fordham University Press, 2013). Ferraris defines a document as "any inscription with *institutional value (emphasis added)*" (Ferraris, *Documentality*, 249). I rather would argue that it is precisely the *non-institutional* that opens to new kinds of political value.

27. The "anticipatory" tenor of archiving as future was also evident in earlier cultural heritage and political mobilization post-Oslo projects. See Chiara de Cesari, "Anticipatory Representation," in *Reimagining the State*, eds. Davina Cooper, Nikita Dhawan, and Janet Newman, 153–70 (London: Routledge, 2019).

Was Derrida in *Archive Fever* able to claim that documents are "mute" because his analytic attention wasn't about archives (as in catalogued state documents, "secret" reports, bundles of documents, and misplaced entries)?[28] Derrida wrote about archives rather than the *use* of them, which is extraordinary given that he had never worked in them—certainly not colonial ones. No matter. His "lessons" are rich: to approach "the archive" as a seat of command, its guardian archons endowed with the sole authority of interpretation. What so deeply affected historical work was the force he gave to the art of layered, palimpsest reading and the provocative figuring he did of "the archive's work against itself."

But if archiving convenes a new assemblage of political subjects and political will, it would be hard to think of it as mute. I think of these subjects and objects otherwise, as *dormant*, fragments that escaped pilfering soldiers. The thought here is that documents and objects remain dormant until a new relationship is established with them. One might think of them *awaiting a present that may do justice to them*.[29] As noun, term, and quasi-concept, emphasis is on the possibility for a figure, inscription, an object, a scene to animate a critical perception. But it also makes a demand, disregard becomes more conspicuous, disallowing a looking away. These artists/activist/academics seem to be extending an invitation and making a demand. "Stay with what you imagine as banal and trivial. Details matter. Don't look away." Social objects can become plausible and empowered candidates of worth that may be called upon for proof or claim—or for something more. The "life" of the document is a reserve weapon.

---

28. Jacques Derrida (*Archive Fever: A Freudian Impression*, pp.10,100. The French title, *Mal d'archive*, has its own ambiguity (somewhere between the sense of "sick with desire," "lovesick," "compulsively obsessed with" but also *mal de* as in "ache" or "pain") doing work that historians could recognize in their own archival desire to access, extract, miss, and long for.

29. I share in Alia Al-Saji's formulation and pursue its implications. See Alia Al-Saji, "The Past," unpublished working paper presented for the, *Political Concepts* conference, The New School for Social Research, New York City, NY, April 18, 2014.

Activation sustains its capacity to endure the weathering of being stored.

THE POLITICS OF ARCHIVAL DIGITIZATION AND *AWRAQ*

Digitization in the last decade has come to be a virtual replacement for collections of paper documents (despite and perhaps in response to the "digital occupation" which Helga Tawil-Souri has tracked for the last fifteen years, creating of Gaza a "political, physical, and digital enclave" of enclosure).[30] But digital power, usurpation, blocked portals, and militant censorship are not confined to Gaza. Archival ventures like *Awraq* were indeed made possible by digitization: among the special items in the collection were documents from the Arab National Committee since 1948, newspapers since 1909. It was open access that was paramount and part of *Awraq*'s self-defined mission.

Its founder, the historian Roger Heacock, thought to make a digital archive unencumbered by the command of Palestine Authority. Only one major restriction was imposed: the order by Palestinian authorities not to collect "official" documents, a restriction that was converted into a signature of the collection, in what was to be called, "the archival globalization of Palestine."[31] Years were spent contacting scores of individuals door to door, and with numerous organizations, seeking their photographic collections and papers.[32] Aside from forays to Istanbul for Ottoman

---

30. Helga Tawil-Souri, "Digital Occupation: Gaza's High-Tech Enclosure," *Journal of Palestine Studies* XLI, no. 2 (Winter 2012): 27–43.
31. See "Book Launch Marks Seven-Year Palestinian Archive Project," Birzeit University, 14 March 2017, www.birzeit.edu/en/news-book-launch-marks-seven-year-palestinian-archive-project, including some of the papers given at the March 2014 conference organized at Birzeit.
32. The list is long and formidable. It is unclear how much of the digitized collection is generally available in the digital commons. For example, the papers and

archives, lack of funds made it hard to go outside Palestine or even far from Ramallah.[33]

If *Awraq*'s resources were all limited, its vision was broad. In the end, some ten thousands digitized document and photographs were collected and borrowed, with thousands more in hold.[34] Documents given to the university over decades made up much of the collection in the initial year and were digitized as well. Further collection has been suspended for some years, and now perhaps for more time while conversion is made to a new metaformat (in accord with rubrics of the Library of Congress) and made ready to move to the Birzeit Museum.[35] Whether *Awraq*'s low visibility is

---

specific cases of abuse and demolition recorded and defended by the Palestinian NGO *El Haq* are available at http://www.awraq.birzeit.edu/en. Palestinian newspapers from the twentieth century are available open access at the Al-aqsa Mosque library in East Jerusalem. For the organizations that were contacted and contributed materials from their collections, see the list provided in Roger Heacock and Caroline Mall-Dibasy, "Liberating the Phantom Elephant: The Digitization of Oral Archives," *Birzeit University Working Paper No. 2011/8* (2011): https://papers.ssrn.com/sol3/papers.cfm?abstract_id=1764253. I thank Suzan Da'an for sharing her nine years of experience collecting, scanning, and digitizing materials for the *Awraq* digital archive, personal communication, October 20–22, 2020.

33. One early *Awraq* report mentions oral history collections acquired from Lebanon and visits made to the Ottoman Archives in Istanbul.

34. Seven years after work had begun, Heacock expressed disappointment at how hard it was to convince people to share the documents they had kept and carefully stored. See "Book Launch Marks Seven-Year Palestinian Archive Project," *Birzeit News*, March 14, 2017, https://www.birzeit/edu/en/news/book-launch. Probably as disappointing was that further collection of materials has been sharply curtailed when he, like many long resident foreigners, was forced to leave in 2018 after thirty-five years living and teaching in Palestine. In 2017, before his departure, the *Awraq* collection was still referred to as "The Palestinian Archive Project" as The Palestinian Museum *digital* archive was only started a year later.

35. The Birzeit University Museum and The Palestinian Museum are not the same institutions (although a Google search of "the museum at Birzeit" brings up only The Palestinian Museum). Information about the Birzeit University Museum and its collections are at: Home, Birzeit's Museum, accessed February 10, 2021, http://www.museum.birzeit.edu/. At the time of writing, there was no reference to the fact that the *Awraq* was to be transferred and housed in the Birzeit University Museum, December 31, 2020.

because its rich range of documents are haphazard and not easy to use, as one Birzeit historian suggested, is hard to say. Minimalist categories of organization too make systematic retrieval on a specific topic difficult.[36]

The "use" of these archives, in the sense of providing an object of study or a "source" that could be used to examine a particular subject is not necessarily the reason why such collections are assembled—it's not what they were intended to inscribe or were imagined to serve. Nonetheless, the *Awraq* archive, still awaiting "use," holds a compelling array of visual and written images. They are not orderly, nor was that the intent. Indeed, they invite less a chronology of events, than a possible *collage* of a living occupation and the chaotic and hazardous ways in which people have maneuvered through and been thwarted in the everyday—permission slips accepted and rejected, court testimonies deemed invalid, court hearings delayed, identity cards greased over with handling, family wedding photos as assault on time warped and lost, curfews imposed. Awraq's unclassified photos and documents may attest to **this** *living occupation and the erratic disruptions in how one lives.*

I think here of the documentary filmmaker Jumana Manna who one admiring reviewer calls a "storyteller of the old school" despite her status of "artist as researcher."[37] Gil Hochberg reads Manna's probably most well-known film, *A Magical Substance Flows Into Me* (2015) to glean how Manna works with the musical archive of a German-Jewish ethnomusicologist from the late 1930s. Rejuvenating the sounds he mixed (that he knew were

---

36. There are a few skeletal lists of archiving by NGOs and non-state associations; for example, *Khazaaen* included *Awraq* on its list of "different archives that contain important documents in Palestinian History," a limited list that has not been updated for some time. The link is dead and now unavailable. Dead links are everywhere, often attesting to ephemeral archiving efforts.

37. Media Farzin, "Jumana Manna; The Violence of Beautiful Things," *frieze*, 197 (August 2018), https://www.frieze.com/article/jumana-manna-violence-beautiful-things.

shared among Arabs and Jews), she remixes them in a new digital musical archive, mimetic of his and of her own making. Manna binds the intertwined histories of displacement through music and the senses. For Hanan Toukan, the film takes "touch, smell and taste as corporeal forces in remembering violence and ultimately surviving it."[38] Manna's visual, aural, and tactile images are imbued with an alternative future and radical vision.[39]

ARCHIVING BAGS OF SEEDS

Manna's gifts are not only evident in her complex treatment of temporalities but in a capacity to animate the politically potent in the materiality and movement of things. Her 2018 feature film, *Wild Relatives*, is a story in and of motion: global industrial agriculture, European benevolence, civil war, and a lost seed bank (created to preserve seeds for posterity) moved from Lebanon to Aleppo, back to Lebanon again and replenished from the Artic. The archiving process is traced in the availability of the seed bank vault, and in the seeds' journey from plush to decimated landscapes and through barren Arctic ones. She documents, as one critic put it, "the violence of beautiful things" with her lens blurring past, present, and future.[40] Her lens and vision make room for all kinds of things; "jars and bags of seeds," a "clay bowl in (a Syrian refugee farmer's) hands." A displaced farmer and the infrastructure of an Artic global seed vault are set against one another.

38. Hanan Toukan, "Music, Borders, and the Sensorial Politics of Displacement /in Jumana Manna's 'A *Magical Substance Flows into Me*'," *Jerusalem Quarterly* 67 (Autumn 2016): 122.
39. Gil Hochberg, "Archival Afterlives in a Conflict Zone: Animating the Past in Jumana Manna's Cinematic Fables of Pre-1948 Palestine," *CSSAAME* 38, no. 1 (2018): 38.
40. Farzin "Jumana Manna." Also see Jumana Manna, "Wild Relatives," interview by Hakim Bishara, *Bomb Magazine*, January 25, 2019, https://bombmagazine.org/articles/wild-relatives-jumana-manna-interviewed/.

Nothing is sentimental about her politics. On the contrary, her camera is steadied with her glare of rage.

THE PALESTINIAN MUSEUM: ARCHIVING AMISS AND "PRECIOUS THINGS"

Efforts to convey the force and vitality of extraordinary ordinary Palestinian lives has been present and absent, extended and suspended, piecemeal and prolific over the last decade. When the historian Beshara Doumani was invited in 2008 to manage the vision and planning of the Palestinian Museum (which he did for two-and-a-half years while working as a history professor at the University of California, Berkeley), he ventured as he put it, "a hundred and eighty degree turn," a "rebuttal of a static museum," away from focus on cultural heritage as a sustainable plan.[41] His vision was for a *mobile, ever-changing set of installations* that were less about heritage than diasporic movement, provocations, and political assertion.[42]

As *Awraq* was gathering and digitizing collections formerly and newly given to Birzeit University, Persekian's *Family Album Project* was in the making. The vision was clear: to collect and digitize "photographs that have for years lain forgotten in cupboards and drawers" and to make a participatory project in which the public was invited to join. By May 2015, the buzz about "museum researchers" already "travelling around the occupied West Bank

---

41. Personal communication with Beshara Doumani, October 19, 2020. One should distinguish a static notion of cultural heritage with the one that Chiara De Cesari celebrates in her treatment of the Palestinian art biennales that attend through NGO's to the "vernacular heritage of historical homes and urban neighborhoods," in "Creative Heritage: Palestinian Heritage NGOS and Defiant Arts of Government," *American Anthropology* 112, no. 4 (2010): 625–637.
42. Personal communication with Beshara Doumani, October 19, 2020.

for months" with rumors of future work reaching to Gaza was in the local and international press.[43]

The Palestinian Museum (PM) was conceived as a curatorial vision in which several archiving projects were embedded. Besides the *Family Album archive* was Persekian's inaugural *pièce de résistance* that never happened, *"Never-Part,"* which was to advocate and enacting rapport between people, memories, and futures. All was centered on what ordinary Palestinians thought of as their "precious things." Some argue that his vision still sustains the museum's agenda. Others hold it to be more symbolically adhered to than realized, removed from any agentive imagining from below, lost in the political glitz that the museum's making attracted and the financial backing that came from magnates in the Arab world. If some hold that the museum embodies and embraces an "emergent political imagination," others in more hushed conversations argue that the early, formative priorities are no longer in sight; that those currently in Palestine being squeezed off their land—not in the past but in the immediate present—have little profile in the archival hub or what were dubbed "its satellite operations."

Doumani's blazing insight, that a people's museum was not for Palestine but for Palestinians, was heard but more as a muffled sound than an urgent warning: it needed to have local and

---

43. Jadaliyya Reports, "The Palestinian Museum's Family Album Project: The Intimate Side of History in Palestine," *Jadaliyya*, May 13, 2015, https://www.jadaili yya.com/Details/32080. According to reports in 2015, they had documented and stored in a digital archive about 3,500 family photographs and conducted over sixty interviews in Jerusalem, Ramallah, Al-Bireh, Bethlehem, Jenin, and Gaza. Also see Gulsah Dark, "Family Album Project at Palestinian Museum Strengthens National Identity Across Country," *Daily Sabah*, June 8, 2015, https://www.dailysabah.com/arts-culture/2015/06/08/family-album. For the ad that was sent out by the not yet opened museum to a diasporic and local Palestinian public about how to preserve, handle, record, and ready their family photos for digitization, see "The Family Album," The Palestinian Museum, accessed February 13, 2021, https://www.palmus eum.org/projects/the-family-album#ad-image-thumb-1651.

diasporic resonance, legibility, participation, and direction. As he wrote at the time:

> The emphasis here is on Palestinian studies, not only Palestine ... There's a distinction I'd like to make between the two ... "Palestinian" shifts the focus from the object, land, to the subject, people ... [a] concern [ed] with Palestinians regardless of the geographic position.[44]

Its making, affiliations, state-like aspirations, numerous resignations, reformulations, and changes in guardianship, curatorial directors, and direction were journalistic fodder: political, artistic, and architectural commentaries have circulated from Jerusalem to New York and back to Ramallah.[45] Some see the museum as having been and remaining a beacon of modernity with local appeal and international cachet. Others criticize its loss of local context and the ways in which it ignores struggles impinging on people every day—though its intent was that a Palestinian common populace, lacking wealth, village bound, camp-crushed, or urban centered, might see themselves as part of a polis with an alternative "beacon of modernity" premised on refusing occupation. If Palestinian artists and academics condemn the museum's top-down dynamics and thus how curatorial decisions are made

---

44. Doumani's first iteration of this argument was in 2007 (when he was part of planning the Palestine Museum), most recently upon receiving the Mahmoud Darwish Chair at Brown University in 2020, quoted above. Elizabeth Redden, "A Milestone for Palestinian Studies," *Inside Higher Ed*, August 11, 2020, https://www.insidehighered.com/news/2020/08/11/brown-establishes-endowed-chair-palestinian-studies.

45. Endorsed by the business leaders of Ramallah and elsewhere in the Middle East and eclipsing lesser ventures, it was expected to garner international expertise and interest as virtually no other "modern" museum in the region had before. Its landscaping with indigenous plants, iterating a Palestinian people in their "natural" socio-ecological setting, is dramatic and received due acclaim. Funded by the nongovernmental Welfare Association, *Taawon*, the museum is on the roster of those with celebrated, dubious, and contentious biographies.

(as many have made clear in private), few are publicly willing to say so.⁴⁶

There are no documents or objects to pull off shelves and out of drawers, though in years when the *Family Album Archive* was being collected, this is exactly what people interviewed for the *Never-Part* project sought to share—items of history, stories of history (a copper coffee maker, a worn backgammon game, an emptied wine bottle of vintage Château Neuf-de-Pape) that were not imagined as candidates for a digital trace. The *Family Album Archival Project*, of which virtually nothing was consulted or displayed for years after Persekian's dismissal, has now been folded into the museum's digital archive.⁴⁷ Its revival would depend on working with Persekian and his early vision of speaking with and through objects. If he remains a persona non grata, it is doubtful how this might happen.

Tension was there nearly from the start: after directing the PM from 2012 to 2016. Persekian and others attribute this to his aesthetic politics. His first intended exhibition, *Never-Part*, was devoted to making patent and glaring the problem of emptiness and the politics that produced it, by leaving the museum empty at its opening. Hanan Toukan succinctly argues that it was to make explicit Palestine's predicament, its lack of control over borders, waters, and skies—and to question the meaning of a museum, the artefacts, and the collecting practices that supposedly define it, in the case of a people violently dispersed all over the globe and prevented from accessing their past and material present.⁴⁸

---

46. The most frequent comment I heard about the Palestinian Museum's agenda and self-declared mandate as an "agent of empowerment" was that the answer depends on whom you speak to, when, and where—in private or public.

47. As reported in "2019 Chicago Architecture Biennial Week #3 Calendar," *Design Applause*, October 5, 2019, https://designapplause/com/architecture2019-chicago.

48. See Hanan Toukan's excellent account of the challenges and triumphs of the museum in "The Palestinian Museum," *Radical Philosophy* 2, no. 3 (December 2018), https://www.radicalphilosophy.com/article/the-palestinian-museum.

It was not an easy sell to those who wanted the materiality of the museum to stand in for and declare the material presence of Palestine as a sovereign body. Although the exhibit never happened, when the museum opened empty in 2016 a rush of snide and disparaging commentaries came from, among others, the BBC, *USA Today*, *The Washington Post*, *The New York Times*, and *The Times of Israel* all gloating over Palestine caught with an "empty building."

Israeli support of the international press was predictably myopic, as if the political and affective force of "unfinished" projects and empty spaces did not have potent political histories elsewhere and of their own. Uriel Orlow's *Unmade Film* (2017) of the Palestinian village of Deir Yassin, disappeared and replaced with an Israeli mental hospital for Holocaust survivors, is a case in point.[49] Hanan Toukan describes Orlow's "horrific realization" that these dual losses, the massacre of Deir Yassin villagers and the mental deterioration of Holocaust survivors were superimposed. She writes: "this impossible film—this not-yet-made film, this fragmented film that never fully becomes despite its 'plan' to do so—has been emerging over an extended and ongoing period of research and production that excavates multiple narratives and layered meanings that converge in [the disappeared village of] Deir Yassin" and its "obliterated geo-histories."[50]

---

49. See the images of this unmade film here at "Unmade Film," Uriel Orlow, accessed February 25, 2021, https://urielorlow.net/project/unmade-film/.

50. Hanan Toukan, "Continuity from Rupture: Deir Yassin's Absent Presence in an Unmade Film," in *Unmade Film*, ed. Uriel Orlow (Zurich: edition fink, 2013). The strategy, the tactic, and the genre invokes ready comparisons, hard not to make. Afghan American Mariam Ghani's film, *What We Left Unfinished* (2019) is at once a quasi-documentary, an exhibition, and a book project. It splices cuts of unfinished films being made during the communist period in Afghanistan (1978–1991) with re-enacted scenes of fear and collaboration in contemporary Afghanistan—a spatial politics casting burnt shadows across the violence of urban and architectural disrepair.

EXHIBITUS INTERRUPTUS

The interrupted exhibition and unfinished project were features of a protracted event, a condensation of conflicts, implicating local and colonial politics, artistic and international metrics of taste, museum politics mixed with a quasi-archiving endeavor to animate political energy, popular sentiment, and civic imagination. Doumani and Persekian shared an early ambition: that "every person should have a say."[51] Part of that vision was realized in the *Family Album Project*, a sort of "pilot" project for *Never-Part*. According to Rana Anani, who managed communications for *Never-Part* and was charged with heading up the *Family Album Project*, objects mattered in multiple ways: as instigation, as prompt to memory, as cueing of relations and political situations, as inspiration. Treasured, banal objects that accompanied a voyage or that called up a scene garnered little interest among those financially and politically invested in capitalizing on how "culture" would serve to realize a future Palestine and how it might be achieved. Not insignificantly, independent archival projects that have been generated from family collections of acoustic, visual, and written recordings have shown themselves to be more agile in making room for the touch and feel of things.

The focus was even stronger and more explicitly on things in *Never-Part*, as it promised to attend to cherished objects with which persons felt "they could *never-part*." Some families offered things that they thought were museum appropriate and not necessarily those to which they were attached. Interviewers say home visits were lively affairs made up of exchanges, arguments, and conversations with several generations often present. Topics ranged from local history, confiscations of land and cultural property, to what should and could remain confined to private lives.

---

51. Jack Persekian, personal communication, October 12, 2020.

ARCHIVING PRAXIS | 223

Such objects as film clips, the photo of a soccer club of friends, the iconic key to the house of which one was dispossessed (a cherished symbolic image on world news), the associations they elicited, the relationships they embodied, and the affect such things stirred (or stirred and immediately squashed) animated those occasions and were at their core. Things were offered that people wanted to share, eager and hesitant, often holding them tight next to their bodies, against their chests. One man pointed to a painting on a wall from a distance—as if it was too fragile and he too brittle to endure or allow touch. A pair of party shoes, an incandescent joy of youth, was offered for view in its original box. With no prepared facilities for storage, objects could not even be borrowed, only photo images and videos recorded the object and owner's touch on digital display. But even these images, stored (it is said) in the museum's digital vaults, have not (yet?) been shown, exhibited, made available to researchers.[52]

How much the museum today still is invested in the extra-territorial imaginative geography of its earlier visionaries is unclear. It could be imagined that the present archival surge across independent archiving projects is just catching up with the earlier quests, including the once possible *Never-Part*. A Facebook and YouTube video intended to announce the museum's inaugural exhibition is still available. It is hard to miss the irony that the actual inaugural event in 2016, absent any exhibition, was mimetic of the political gesture (absent the message) Persekian had intended as part of the Museum's opening. The swift erasure calculated to sweep away the earlier vision had some effect: but it did not disappear wholly. It seemed to remain indelibly inscribed, as the promise of a citizens' contract still casting a long shadow.

52. Availability and open access were requirements for getting funding from the Arcadia Foundation. For an important statement of the history of the museum and on how it is operating and seen by many today, see Hanan Toukan and Adila Laïdi-Hanieh, "Tell the World: Hanan Toukan and Adila Laïdi-Hanieh on the Palestinian Museum," *Art Forum* 59 (Summer 2021): www.artforum.com/print/202106

"COMPULSIVE HABITS"

The statement that was to accompany the YouTube recording for *Never-Part*'s inaugural event is uncanny. It seems to anticipate precisely what emerged among the various independent archiving projects later: individuals excavating their family histories, Palestinian associations setting out to draw on ordinary people, the familial and village threads among their members. The statement reads:

> The protagonists of the Museum's inaugural exhibition are Palestinians from all walks of life and different countries of residence. Each recounts the story of a treasured object s/he would never part with, digging through layers of time, occasionally pausing at an image, *a smell, a ritual, a compulsive habit, or a sound* (emphasis added), and inviting us to join in their sensory experience. This exhibition is a waystation in the lives of personal objects and stories that would not exist in such proximity otherwise.

We might start with the very first word, "the protagonists." What could provide a stronger interpellation for more Palestinians than such a phrase? Protagonists take the stage; the story moves with their movements, stops short when they are assailed, fails to move forward when the protagonists are not actively called upon to engage. What could be closer to the bone than "compulsive habits," "smells," and "sounds"? A halt is impossible to avoid, before this whiff of something wholly other to track. I had written to Jack Persekian when I started the project. This time I wrote startled by the insight that "compulsive habits" could offer.[53] With associations and phrasing that *Never-Part* was intent to perform, incite, and display, no other exhibition in Palestine so directly sought to engage such a full sensorium of things that might matter for an

---

53. An excerpt from my email of January 16, 2021, on reading the introduction to the exhibit that never happened.

exhibition that wanted and enlisted a Palestinian public to think with them.

What might such "compulsive habits" look like? What work would compulsion do in a protracted time of siege? What might a smell do? What might such a compulsive habit be? Could it be the repeated removal of feces thrown on one's car by settlers on the way to work outside of Ramallah? Nails bitten down to the flesh at a checkpoint. Could it be the nutty, herbal, tangy smell of *za'atar* mixed with the acridity of burning tires? Might a compulsive habit reveal the intense stress that repeated glances each second out a window conveys, making sure Israeli soldiers don't move boulders to block a village's one road of entry in the night. Or might it be a rhythmic caress of the trinket that belonged to a person one might never again, see? Or an obsessive checking of one's iPhone to ensure that one's favorite nephew, studying abroad will not be detained on coming home, will not be detained again when he tries to return to his studies in Los Angeles?

Never-Part is not really hard to find on the internet as a promise. But what actually made up the practices of its practitioners, over three hundred interviews, not surprisingly are nowhere to be found. Privacy and copyright rules are invoked. But there may be another reason why they are not there—because the initiative was axed, the vision mangled, the imagined site of a Palestinian populace taking charge as *Khazaaen* would attempt with its allocated "cabinets" just a few years later was hard to reconcile with the museum's agenda. The vision that *Never-Part* never got to convey was not only diagnostic of the tensions within Palestinian corridors of dissent and power, but a disquieting print of what worked and could not work within the archival, artistic, and political landscape of Palestine.

Never-Part is not now included in an accessible archival inventory of the Palestinian Museum (though its digital recordings must be there), nor part of the project of digitization. *Awraq* too found objects hard to incorporate. When *Never-Part* was suspended so was the prospect of transferring objects from Ramallah,

Nablus, Santiago, and Amsterdam. Who knows how they would have been handled and returned after being shown? Those were the discussions in the air.[54] Plans to provide search categories to make the three hundred fifty odd interviews accessible and usable for a public never happened. Those who worked on the project most lamented that those interviewed had been promised that their names and stories would be visible and retrievable. They are not.

Nor is anyone left at the Palestinian Museum in 2021 who worked on the project. Those who did that remember some vaguely, some vividly, where they went and with whom they talked. But there is no written record of their process, what went into their choices, no record of the planned interviews cancelled, or why their efforts have left hardly a trace.[55] If *Never-Part* was never primarily intended as an archiving project, still that is what its small staff were doing all along—bringing together, gathering in from Gaza, Nablus, and what Palestinians refer to as Palestine '48 (within Israel's forced borders) intimate relations between people and things, animating documents and things in the quotidian convergence of object, story, person, and to entice a potential if reticent public to engage the political defiance their own narratives expressed.

---

54. Rana Anani who worked on the *Family Album Archive* for several intense years between 2013–2015 describes an ongoing debate among the staff over whether objects themselves should be collected, or just scanned, and how they would be able to ensure their return if they had found a way to borrow or store them. The project never got that far. Personal communication with the author, January 21, 2021.

55. If we know some of the archiving intentions over the last decade, we know less about their effects on those who worked closely with them, on those whose relationships to objects and material things might differ from those processing the assemblages. Persekian and his staff worked for several years to find a way of enabling people to convey how they related to the objects that mattered to them, to how they might be shared. That effort had little time to garner traction or space to breathe. But one could imagine an extension through the efforts of Fady Asleh, who worked on Persekian's projects early on; Fady's "locker like cabinets" place custodianship in the hands of those who fill them. Small feats of archiving make up the undercurrents of diasporic breadth and political filiations.

Persekian's strategy of working with people and things had its start and was incubated years earlier. In October 2008 at the Palais des Beaux Arts in Brussels, with the very same title, a select group of eight artists was enlisted to share a "precious possession." The exhibit was introduced with a brief description: *There are certain things one would never part with. This intimate relationship, beyond any materials, is what inspires the narration*.[56] But as an opening curation five years later in Ramallah, it required something else: restriction to artists and objects that animated their work seemed too narrow—for the museum and the forging of a more participatory polis.

A different curatorial task emerged as did a more inclusive message. What was to constitute the event (for it would have been an ongoing "event") changed as well. It was to begin before the exhibit was shown, then spread out over different phrases. For the first, the museum would be empty. In the second phase, objects would come into view; in a third, the public would engage with the persons, their narratives, and the objects brought together—gatherings that were to layer multiple displacements and inspirations. Artists were sidelined in favor of a Palestinian populace that might engage one another on an aesthetic and political plane—sharing those things, those objects, those sights and smells and touch, that stayed so intimately close to and distant from them.

NEVER-PART IN THE MAKING

Never-Part as a curatorial project was conceptual, political, and by intention loosely framed. It was experimental, responsive to happenstance, leaving open what would be its ultimate form and range. Tasks changed in the process of finding how visits to

---

56. The statement accompanying the exhibition's YouTube recording seems to anticipate much of what was emergent among independent archiving projects with their mutual focus not on the present or past but the future.

Palestinian homes might best happen. The earliest interviews in 2013 began in Ramallah, on to Nablus. Other volunteer interviewers were recruited in Gaza. Yara Taqhailait, who did the bulk of the interviews and worked on the project for nearly three years, learned as she went along. Her work eventually took her to Chile to meet with Palestinians in Santiago, eager and willing to take part.

The work was ethnographic at heart: people were visited in their homes where multi-generational conversations followed. Researchers made sure to listen far more than they talked. A bare bones staff (with the help of others working part-time and as volunteers) spent some two-and-half years visiting those who had responded to their call, visiting others who offered their objects and assistance after hearing about or listening in on interviews of neighbors. The work was not easy, awkward at times. People offered up objects but also the kinds of stories they imagined the museum staff were seeking. Sometimes the offered objects were those they considered "museum worthy"— a painting or a pottery. It was hard to convey how much more those interviewing sought ordinary objects of the everyday. Sometimes they got them: a comb with no "symbolic" meaning, an item that had accompanied a middle-aged man's travels when he was young, with the PLO to Lebanon, then to Cyprus and Tunis. Exhilarated by the work, the young staff were thrown askew by its abrupt end. When the project was summarily "suspended" and Persekian was asked to leave, many of them resigned, bitter about the work they had put into the project but still in unison with him.

Those objects and their narratives await their time. No one may use any of the material without the museum's permission. Nor may the museum use the materials without working with Persekian, which it has been suggested they undoubtedly would be reluctant to do. Breaking museum contracts (written or not) would leave those assistants who designed and did the work bereft of access to the institutions that would employ them or support their work in the future.

Over the last decade, archiving as praxis and politics has been called upon to activate papers, alliances, arrested friendship, and the sensory pain and pleasure elicited by things. It is as if a radically disruptive optics were being made more available, discerned in a decisive shift in the points of application. Attention is turned more to *the life substances and sustenance of everyday, civilian life*—if one can call it "civilian" in the obdurate face of occupation, those especially vulnerable zones where Israeli military can bulldoze villages and demolish homes by the day and are doing so as I write.[57] More than civilian, the emphasis is on what it takes to *carry through on the ordinary*, to adhere and recast relations of value and care under occupation.

RETURNING TO AWRAQ: THE BEND OF ARCHIVAL LIGHT

We might turn here to an entry from the *Awraq* collection:

> *[T]he fully posed photograph of the statuesque Abdel Aziz Mahmoud Alian Wahdan, explaining to his son and grandson, before the camera, of the dispossession of their family's village land on which the three are standing. How might we approach it, not this photograph but as Ariella Azoulay would insist, this "photographic event" (i.e., the conditions of possibility for the photograph to be taken of these people at this moment in this place.[58] Did Abdel Aziz ask his son and grandson to meet him on the land, and walk with him? Did he stage them in eager pursuit of this lost knowledge, and knowledge of loss?*

---

57. "Special Focus: Sharp High Rate of Property Demolitions since the second half of 2020," Al-Haq: Defending Human Rights, accessed February 16, 2021, https://www.alhaq.org/advocacy/17468.html.

58. Questions that Ariella Azoulay's foundational work with photography would compel us to ask. See Ariella Azoulay, "What is a photograph? What is photography?" *Philosophy of Photography* 1, no.1 (2010), pp. 9–13.

> Was he "explaining" how the land was seized, or was this a re-enactment of what they had to have already known? Who was the absent photographer? A nephew, a brother, a niece at Birzeit University, training in history to study documentation or the geopolitics of land, seized and lost? Might her plunge into these papers and photos kindle something she could imagine being said? How might one manage these trails of lives only partially visible in resistant residence and obstinate flight?

Or we might look to *Awraq*'s digital copy of Harbi Hassan Mustafa's testimony in September 1977 of the sealing up of his home by Israeli military standing with pointed guns, "pulling out windowsills by their sockets," ensuring that the only nearby source of uncontaminated water, the yard's well, was tightly cemented too. The avadavit by Felicia Langer, widely hailed as "the first Israeli lawyer to bring the occupation to court" is probably available elsewhere (indeed Google lists scores of tributes to her).[59] Still, the very presence of this avadavit (poorly typed, uneven keystrokes, on a tired typewriter) in the *Awraq* digital archive (and the fact that it is in Ramallah) provides an immediacy of access, as it puts the temporalities of occupation into recursive light—for these are descriptions that could have been written last month or today.

A countermove would be to defer from and refuse archival work as an extractive enterprise. *Awraq*'s cardinal principle was to resist the winnowing of preferred narratives. Land registration documents with smudged thumb prints, blurry distant photos of rows of Israeli soldiers occupying Gaza, stiff studio portraits of a *pater familias*, reports of student protest at the university were all part of the collection. One of the few researchers who did try to work in its digital collection hesitantly said that s/he was

---

59. Michale Sfard, "In Memory of Felicia Langer, the First Lawyer to Bring the Occupation to Court," *+972 Magazine*, June 24, 2018, https://www.972mag.com/in-memory-of-felicia-langer-the-first-lawyer-to-bring-the-occupation-to-court/.

perplexed by its principles of order, retrieval, and organization in use. But maybe they missed the point.

Rema Hammami astutely suggests that one way to characterize the *Awraq* digital archive might be to see it as replete with "local renditions of a national story."[60] This makes enormous sense. Although some travel was done in the early stages and contact made to digitize the holdings in a range of associations, other collections have not been thwarted by financial constraints as severely as *Awraq*. Coupled with the fact that its founding director, Roger Heacock, was forced to leave Palestine as were other foreigners—just as the Palestinian Museum archival project was moving into digital gear—the overshadowing was no surprise. Still *Awraq*'s partially self-defined mandate to collect unofficial documents was an early and important one, supporting and imagining—if not able fully to realize—a scope of diasporic use and breadth as envisioned in its early formation.

Imagining what The Birzeit University Digital Palestinian Archive can now do or has not been able to do is no longer a point to make. Attempts to animate a public to care, to move beyond fear in contributing their documents is an endurance project, hard to sustain. It has admittedly grown in slow motion. While reformatting its entire digital collection, procuring documents is now on hold. It remains as unordered as intended, but perhaps more random than its categories of access and its website portal on the progress of digitization might suggest. In a current recessive mode, it is a placeholder of sorts for what is still an aspiration. A decade since its inception, archival light is bending elsewhere.

Or maybe that is the point, it always needs to be. Archiving as political practice may only have a half-life, always a provisional project in wait for the next generation to make it into something else. Having long reminded us that archives are not to "annex" but "disrupt," the luminary French historian, Arlette Farge, might

---

60. Rema Hammami, personal communication, October 21, 2001.

well endorse something akin.[61] Namely that countering the conventions of colonial archival production does not produce an imagined opposite. A "counter-archive" neither subscribes to statist projects nor to the authority its documents confer. The "inverse" or "opposite" is not enough. To counter, as Bernard Harcourt reminds, is never the opposite from which it demurs. A new effort is what defeats its force, over time becoming independent of it.[62] Acts of countering may unseat archival authority and reimagine its guardians or counter the conceit of "access" by naming (or ignoring) stop signs, admission requirements, doors marked "no entry." Or one might take on archival authority and their archons—move against their tidy categories and temporal constraints.

In the range of projects elicited here, the principles of valuation reshape archival ecology: excess, ephemera, the unclassified are given a place. Disorder and debris yield potentials that scramble triage since designated "debris" may be where the lineaments of dissensus are forged.[63] The "vitality" of what De Certeau once so valued as "remainders" may be what the current archival surge is seizing upon and what archiving as practice holds in political store.[64]

61. Arlette Farge, *Le Gout de l'archive* [1989] (Paris: POINTS, 1997).
62. Bernard Harcourt, "Counter," in *Thinking with Balibar: A lexicon of conceptual practice*, eds. Ann Laura Stoler, Stathis Gourgoris, Jacques Lezra, 71–84 (New York: Fordham University Press, 2020).
63. Brian Brothman, "Orders of Value: Probing the Theoretical Terms of Archival Practice," *Archivaria* 32, no. 32 (1991): 81. He writes:

> the principal aim of the archivist is to achieve a condition of positive order . . . through the exclusion of what is deemed to be debris . . . Dirt and rubbish continually impinge upon archivists' desire for order and impede their efforts to maintain it . . . as such archival appraisal . . . is a process . . . of value creation and destruction . . . in the context of rubbish theory, destruction strategies are the instruments of an archival ecology.

64. Michel De Certeau, *The Writing of History*, trans. Tom Conley (New York: Columbia University Press, 1992), 78–79. De Certeau, already warning in 1974 against the imposed coherence of the then new digital archives, urged focus on "*deviations*" that give occasion to "*vital remainders*."

Photography can do a new kind of visionary work in this archival fluorescence, capturing comportments of those neither in states of emergency nor under siege: postures at ease, careless poses struck in a safer, less violent world.[65] For what seems at issue is *a new imagining of what kinds of images and documents, soundscapes and materialities could be called on to argue for what could not be destroyed.* In Palestine, where confiscation, pillage, and destruction of documents was a targeted feature of occupation, archives were prize booty. Demolition orders endorsed systematic theft.[66] Within this maelstrom of white-washed destruction—contravening international law and often in the name of development—revisioned archiving practices may act as *forensic inquiry* and do more than endorse restorative justice by putting abuse, surveillance, and denial up for scrutiny and on the line.[67] The imperative is for futures that refuse to be foreclosed.

65. See, for example, the explorative workshops of *Hypotheses*, Editorial Board, "Out of the Archives... New Archival Practices: Toward Alternative Historiographies, Voices and Spaces," *Hypotheses*, December 14, 2018, https://trafo.hypotheses.org/15573. See also "Revisiting Archive in the Aftermath of Revolution," Arab Culture Fund, accessed February 17, 2021, https://www.arabculturefund.org/Projects/6577.

66. Rona Sela's twenty years of research as a curator/activist/researcher attests to the bulge of thousands of visual images and documents looted and confiscated from Palestinians by Israeli military/security forces. See her website and among other essays, "The Genealogy of Colonial Plunder and Erasure—Israel's Control over Palestinian Archives," *Social Semiotics* 28, no. 2 (2018): 201–229; Rona Sela, dir., *Looted and Hidden* (2017).

67. A unique project like Sandi Hillal and Alessandro Petti's *Decolonizing Architecture* has been at the creative and political forefront of joining the forensic, aesthetic, communal, cooperative, and speculative for over a decade. Exhibited worldwide their work has been the subject of extensive and well-deserved attention. Their website provides an excellent introduction at "Home," Decolonizing Architecture Art Research, accessed February 5, 2021, http://www.decolonizing.ps/site/.

PART III

SHATTERZONES OF IMPERIAL DEMOCRACY

7

"All Things Being Equal"

Mobile Extractions in a Carceral World

> Hundreds of forced labor camps *came to exist, scattered throughout the South-operated by state and county governments, large corporations, small-time entrepreneurs, and provincial farmers. These bulging slave centers became a primary weapon of suppression of black aspiration . . . the return of forced labor [w]as a fixture in black life ground pervasively into the daily lives of far more African Americans* (emphasis added).[1]

SHATTERZONES ARE COMMONLY CONSIDERED TO be on the "borderlands of civility," be those in Syria, Afghanistan, or Iraq. Here, I take "shatterzones" beyond their usual designated locations, equally to describe the contemporary carceral history of Europe and the United States. I define these zones as sites of

---

1. Douglas Blackmon, *Slavery by Another Name* (New York: Anchor Books, 2008). A much earlier version of this essay appeared as the epilogue, "In Carceral Motion: Disposals of Life and Labour," in Clare Anderson ed., A *Global History of Convicts and Penal Colonies* (London: Bloomsbury, 2018), 371–380. Research since has prompted revisions, and a new starting point, and in some respects a new essay. Here I more directly address how statecraft, racecraft, and imperial design have shaped the availability and strategic mobility of carceral labor across the histories of the U.S. and Europe's colonial and extra-territorial sites of production, profit, and dispossession.

compressed inequalities, racial cleavages, and racial violences distributing exorbitant inequalities of carceral poverty and derived wealth. Whether in the outer reaches of imperial formations or on the borders of their "democratic" interior frontiers, a constellation of common carceral practices cut across them, marked by regulated, temporary, and provisional carceral labor mobility offset by surveillance and arrest. One of the most striking insights from looking carefully at these forms of coercion is the glaring realization that capitalism has *never been* based only or even primarily and consistently on a beleaguered wage labor force contesting its rights. It has been equally dependent on and *productive* of an unwaged, unpaid labor force without the conditions or means to defend the right to a sustainable life. Carceral containments and coercions are one of those primary sites.

One practice more often overshadowed by focus on the prison industry opens to the recursive histories I consider here; that is, the use of mobile carceral labor, outside and beyond prisons and their fixed locations. "Convict leasing" (the requisition and sale of former slaves, no longer "property," thus fabricated as "criminal," for coerced private and public work) still stands as one of most notorious carceral institutions, a noxious but short-lived solution to post-slavery labor demands. Commonly dated to thirty-three years (1885–1918) and to the southern U.S., the term was reserved for that time and place, but the practice was not. Journalist Douglas Blackmon, in his Pulitzer prize winning book, *Slavery by Another Name*, provides a searing, harsh-grained account of how convict-leasing worked. "Industrial slavery," as he rightly named it, was pursued through WWII providing the labor power that "rebuilt the South." [2]

Blackmon's work is unsurpassed in its attentiveness to the details of greed and brutality in the racial history of the U.S. Still, following his lead, the practice might be considered across

---

2. Blackmon, *Slavery by Another Name*, 30.

a broader geopolitical space and a broader built environment: as a robust extractive industry providing access to unpaid labor and profitability across the imperial globe. Whether named leasing, lending out, "borrowing," or unnamed—its variants fed state enterprises, civic governance, and private profits for more than a century (and sometimes more). Such practice did more than contribute to imperial pursuits.

Much of the hardest physical work performed counted on supplies of a sub-population under sub-human conditions. Tasked with converting earth, trees, granite, and stone into commodities and infrastructure, it could be argued that such coerced unpaid labor made possible the very underpinnings of progress, hailed as signatures of the "modern." In amended form, students of carcerality take "convict leasing" as a source of corporate and municipal profits today.[3]

Penal workers were moved among different state and private projects, fodder for a mobile carceral strategy beyond the U.S. At the turn of the twentieth century, a Dutch colonial prison administration provided convicts to Dutch companies to build shipping crates for one of the most lucrative exported commodities, tea to Europe.[4] Senegalese convicts in the 1930s built the French colony's highways.[5] In colonial Nigeria under British rule, carceral

---

3. See, for example, Charlene Fletcher, "Looking Back: Convict Leasing and the Trusty System," *Black Perspectives*, January 14, 2021, who argues that "penal agribusiness pursued by Texas was similar to that of Kentucky's carceral labor system a hundred years earlier."

4. See Matthias van Rossum, on convict labor of the VOC (the Dutch East Indies Company), "The Dutch East India Company in Asia, 1595-1811," in Anderson, *Convicts and Penal Colonies*, 157-181; Matthias van Rossum, "The Carceral Colony: Colonial Exploitation, Coercion, and Control in the Dutch East Indies, 1810s-1940s," *International Review of Social History* 63, special issue S26 (August 2018): 65-88.

5. See Romain Tiquet, "Connecting the 'Inside' and the 'Outside' World: Convict Labour and Mobile Penal Camps in Colonial Senegal (1930s-1950s)," *International Review of Social History* 64, no. 3 (2019): 473-91. Also see, Ibra Sene, "Colonisation française et main-d'oeuvre carcéral au Sénégal: de l'emploi des détenus des camps pénaux sur les chantiers des travaux routiers 1927-1940," *French Colonial History* 5, no.1 (2004): 153-171.

labor was recruited for public works until independence in 1959.[6] In former Tanganyika unpaid carceral labor were employed in "quarrying, road-making, building work and town sanitation," over a half million "manpower hours of unpaid labour per annum for the government's public works."[7] Mobile penal camps were prevalent in British Kenya as well, first set up in 1933.[8] And for the Cape colony, demand for [unpaid] labor was a "key feature of the South's penal apparatus until 1990."[9] In this wider frame, the U.S. is less an exception than exemplary of a racist history on which both carceral democracy and carceral colonialism thrive.

CONVICT LEASING AND THE 13TH AMENDMENT

A radical shift in the critical study of the U.S. Constitution's 13th Amendment has transformed its import and its historical breadth, producing a cumulative, compelling counter-history of the once celebrated formal, legal end of slavery in 1865. The 13th's key clause has come to be widely seen as the touchstone of what made possible the prolific continuation of entrapped forced labor, the backbone of the racialized carceral economy of the U.S. The

---

6. Belinda Archibong and Nonso Obikili, "Prison Labor: The Price of Prisons and the Lasting Effects of Incarceration," *Journal of African Economic History Working Paper Series* no. 52 (2020): https://papers.ssrn.com/sol3/papers.cfm?abstract_id = 3635484.
7. Stacey Hynd, "'. . . a Weapon of Immense Value'? Convict labour in British Colonial Africa, c. 1850–1950s," in *Global Convict Labor* (London, UK: Brill, 2015), 249–272, see esp. 258–260.
8. Daniel Branch, "Imprisonment and Colonialism in Kenya, c 1930–1952: Escaping the Carceral Archipelago," *International Journal of African and Historical Studies* 38, no. 2 (2005): 239–265, 247.
9. Florence Bernault, "The Politics of Enclosure in Colonial and Post-Colonial Africa," in *A History of Prison and Confinement in Africa*, Florence Bernault, ed. (Portsmouth, NH: Heineman 2003), 1–53. She does note that transferring labor gangs from prison to private enterprises was forbidden in France at the end of the nineteenth century (47). On the other, penal colonies that enforced forced labor, thrived.

"loophole" reads: (for the majority of Americans who neither learned it at school nor yet know it by heart): *"Neither slavery nor involuntary servitude, except as a punishment for crime whereof the party shall have been **duly convicted, shall exist within the United States, or any place subject to their jurisdiction**."* [10]

A "loophole" usually refers to a legal ambiguity or inadequacy, the carceral clause did not. It explicitly made slavery and involuntary servitude legal *as punishment for crime*. That half-sentence has had devastating effects: promoting incarceration, endorsing carceral labor, (re)fortifying racialized relations of violence, all dependent on gross disparities in assessments of human worth. Most importantly, it has set the conceptual and political conditions for a blurring of what constitutes crime and criminality fabricated to supply unfree labor. With jail records from the turn of the century having only vague statistics of those arrested, even the most reputed histories could offer only bald estimates.[11] It took very little to conjure "infractions" that held impoverished Black men and women to forced labor and "lifetime" labor contracts.[12]

More than a single assault, convict leasing and the fictions on which it was sanctioned cast shrapnel, dispersing large and minute shards through the body politic.[13] Prevalent meanings and measures of public insecurity and civic disorder continue to support a racial apparatus, making accusation of "crime" simple, conviction an unfettered act. The "original sin" of U.S. racism, contained in the carceral clause does more than inform a rereading of the

---

10. U. S. Const. amend. XIII, § 1.
11. Thus, even Blackmon could only offer a range from one hundred thousand to "perhaps more than twice that figure" (Blackmon, *Slavery by Another Name*, 7).
12. Blackmon, *Slavery by Another Name*, 27.
13. By the last decade of the nineteenth century, the infamous Black codes (that minimally forbid Black men rights to own property and restricted movement) and vagrancy ordinances (that made it a crime to be unemployed) made forced labor the punishment. Virtually no historian of post-bellum America does not write about the Black Codes, vagrancy ordinances, and "the profits offered by the new trade in labor." Blackmon also suggests that the movement of workers between penal camps in the South was in part a response to the prisons destroyed during the civil war.

13th and its claims to freedom for all. On the contrary it anchors racism as the matrix of white power: its most durable product, a carceral industrial complex feeding more racially targeted incarceration.[14] The conclusion is definitely stark: what constituted crime and what continues to do so, too long *has been tailored and cut to a racialized measure.*

A dense racial apparatus fostered easy entrapment while guarding a white space that local and state-wide ordinances colluded to maintain.[15] With criminality stamped on the flesh, men and women could be "lent out" for weeks, months, or years to companies, individual entrepreneurs, and county and state projects.[16] Procurement was nested in a racialized world: young men walking on a rural road or seen as "idle" in public. Hauled from jails, leased to private coal mines, mills, and quarries, transported and farmed out to work in mines and large agricultural holdings, those seized made the chain of profits long. It extended from cart drivers to white foreman and county sheriffs, and more-—all in avid pursuit of a commodified Black underclass to be "hired" unwaged. Eric Foner suggests that an "empire of prison labor" may not have been the intent of the framers of the 13th amendment.[17]

---

14. See Peter Wagner and Wendy Sawyer, "States of Incarceration: The Global Context 2018," *Prison Policy Initiative*, June 2018, https://www.prisonpolicy.org/global/2018.html.

15. Blackmon, *Slavery by Another Name*, 7.

16. Khalih Gibran Muhammad, *The Condemnation of Blackness: Race, Crime, and the Masking of Modern America* (Cambridge: Harvard University Press, 2010). On the compulsory system of unfree labor to which women were subject, see Mary Farmer-Kaiser, "'Are they not in some sort vagrants': Gender and the Efforts of the Freedmen's Bureau to Combat Vagrancy in the Reconstruction South," *The Georgia Historical Quarterly* 88 (Spring 2001): 25–49, 30. On women and the convict leasing system, see Talitha DeFloria, *Chained in Silence: Black Women and Convict Labor in the New South* (Chapel Hill, NC: University of North Carolina Press, 2015) and Sara Haley, *No Mercy Here: Gender, Punishment, and the Making of Jim Crow Modernity* (Chapel Hill, NC: University of North Carolina, 2016).

17. Eric Foner, "We Are Not Done with Abolition," *New York Times*, December 18, 2020, https://www.nytimes.como/2020/12/15/opinion/abolition-prison-labor-amendement.html.

Still, its lasting product is a legal incentive for carceral labor's proliferation.

IMPERIAL JURISDICTION AND EXTRATERRITORIAL BOUNDS

With so much renewed focus on the 13th's carceral clause, it is striking how narrowly it has been read. Too often its few words have been reduced, usually omitting attention to what the clause stipulated: enforcement "in the U.S. and *in any places within in its jurisdictions.*" Hawaii, Puerto Rico, Samoa, the Philippines, and the Mariana Islands have tended to recede behind national borders in a myopic frame.[18] But even the phrase "within its jurisdiction" calls into question what "jurisdiction" means and has meant, the degrees of imperial sovereignty the United States, Britain, and France confer on themselves beyond law-based sovereignty, and beyond the claims that coerced labor is prohibited by and in the U.S.[19]

Expanding the breadth of racialized criminalization beyond the U.S. opens to a global color line that has run through Europe's imperial projects, with varied degrees of unfreedom a backbone of "modernizing" states and industrial ventures. Carceral and contract labor, indenture, and debt servitude for "unfilled" labor contracts have sustained colonial agribusiness far into the twentieth century. As Lisa Lowe reminds us, degrees of unfreedom

---

18. Benjamin D. Weber's work is one important, notable exception. See his excellent study of the racial violence effected in "the convict clause" with respect to the building of the Panama Canal Zone in "The Strange Career of the Convict Clause: US Prison Imperialism in the Panamá Canal Zone," *International Labor and Working-Class History* 96 (Fall 2019): 79–102. His forthcoming book, a history of race, incarceration, and American empire, will be an essential major contribution to the field of global carceralities.

19. See Ann Laura Stoler, "On Degrees of Imperial Sovereignty," *Public Culture* 18, no. 1 (2006): 125–146.

distribute along *synchronized* racialized lines.[20] Today, unpaid labor "under duress" joins with convict labor in industries that parse out piece work, in fragmented forced labor regimes throughout the globe for work, ostensibly "voluntary." The U.S. did not "invent" vagrancy laws, debt peonage, nor penal servitude as a punishment for purported crime. But it did appropriate those practices, amplify the denigrations that the divisions sharpened between those designated as White and Black by arbitrary and contorted design.

The U.S. was not a new carceral landscape unknown elsewhere. On the contrary, it set up carceral labor camps where and when they were needed, just as Dutch scientists and administrators had done a century earlier to build irrigation works in colonial Java, and U.S. engineers did to build the adjoining roads for the Panama Canal. Across the imperial globe, carceral labor is commonly used for public works, state projects, and for building and maintaining infrastructure. Few calculations measure the cumulative profits it allows, or the "worth" of those subject to that labor. They are not included in official labor market statistics.[21] Even when acknowledged as "an essential input," their contribution to state and private profits comes in and out of focus—often absent from civil and state ledgers—as if kept beyond archival (or legal) bounds.

That absence is less surprising when the specific ties that have bound capital and governance are given dates, locations, and names, as Blackmon so explicitly provides in *Slavery by Another Name*. Robert Perkinson's impressive study of the rise of the prison empire too is one of the few to demonstrate with local sources the astounding levels of corruption and wealth generated. A supreme

---

20. Lisa Lowe, *The Intimacies of Four Continents* (Durham, NC: Duke University Press, 2015).

21. Belinda Archibong and Nonso Obikili, "Convict Labor and the Costs of Colonial Infrastructure: Evidence from Prisons in British Nigeria, 1920–1938," *SSRN*, May 28, 2019 at http://dx.doi.org/10.2139/ssrn.3395458.

court justice could and did own the biggest coal mining company in the U. S. South where carceral labor was the norm. In Texas in the 1880s, where fortunes were made with convict labor, was one of the most prominent owners of twenty-thousand acres in sugar and a mill. A century later the company was still thriving and was to make the *Fortune 500*. One of the largest convict leasing systems in the U.S., it was credited with industrial capitalism's growth and a "principal source of state revenue."[22] The "rule of law" crafted and endorsed the rule of race; the latter at once rigid, arbitrary, and precisely aimed.

State public secrets supported unaccountabilities and deterred counting: that convict leasing was a major source of state revenue; that illegible and illicit profits garnered by state agents, private entrepreneurs, subcontractors, and state agents as private owners of mines, quarries, plantations, and railways were well known but sporadically recorded or ignored. Texas in 1898 provides a portal into complicities that show the very movement of carceral workers from one project to another as common practice, *not* unknown but strategically unnamed.

THE HYPOCRITIC OATH AND IMPERIAL DEMOCRACIES

Despite Loïc Wacquant's claim that the U.S. scale and scope of incarceration is as nowhere else and never before, what he so aptly calls "prisons of poverty" are not confined to the U.S.[23] His use of the plural—"prisons"—did more than gesture to exacerbating inequalities in which contemporary democracies share. He ties those inequalities to "the pathology of the penal state," an "acute

---

22. Robert Perkinson, *Texas Tough: The Rise of America's Prison Empire* (New York: Metropolitan Books, 2010), 105.
23. Loïc Wacquant, *Prisons of Poverty* (Minneapolis: University of Minnesota, 2009) (originally published in French, 1999).

condition spreading from the USA to Europe to Latin America."[24] One might alter the order of that spread, from Europe to the USA to Latin America but again, crime was endowed with a racialized measure. A pervasive crime was to be present at the wrong time—anytime—in a part of a town, city, park, crossroads, street corner where "one did not belong," suspiciously standing at ease, or suspiciously in motion. Wacquant's blunt parsing of "race as a civic felony," precisely made his case: contemporary carceral regimes as systemic sites of " 'race-making'."[25]

Reckoning with the racial specificities of the U.S. as a penal polity with increasing withdrawals of societal care and punishment for fabulated crime obscures the more important knotted relationship to poverty, racism, diminished social provisions, and debt. As Wacquant writes, "the scale and contours of the punishment regime are unrelated to crime."[26] It was a thesis that still needed to be repeated when he wrote it in 2005, and now even more, it needs to be underscored again. Cedric Robinson's coining and condemnation of racial capitalism (1983) reverberates as stark reality today.[27] But it is a subsequent generation of Black studies scholar/activists who has joined Robinson's insights with their assault on the carceral state's complicit current projects.[28]

---

24. Vanessa Barker, "Book Review *Prisons of Poverty*, Wacquant, L.," *The Howard Journal of Criminal Justice* 50, no. 5 (December 2011): https://doi.org/10.1111/j.1468-2311.2011.0695_2.x..

25. Loïc Wacquant, "Race as Civic Felony," *International Social Science Journal* 57, no. 183 (March 2005): 127–142. Wacquant's account of the penal state's development from the U.S. to Latin America covers a short and relatively recent time frame. Earlier colonial models were carceral strongholds with histories of interimperial circuits of carceral policy and practices, often with many forms of coerced labor *simultaneously* in effect.

26. Bruce Western, "Poverty Politics and Crime Control in Europe and America," *Contemporary Sociology* 40, no. 3 (May 2011): 283–286.

27. C. J. Robinson, *Black Marxism: The Making of The Black Radical Tradition* (London: University of North Carolina Press, 1983).

28. Among those are Ruth Gilmore's *Geographies of Racial Capitalism*, An Antipode Foundation film-video; R. D. G. Kelley, "What is Racial Capitalism and Why Does it Matter?", recorded at Kane Hall, University of Washington, Seattle, 2017.

The scope and scale of the U.S. prison-industrial complex surely makes it unique, but its making might better be treated in a conceptual frame less comparative than of convergent filiations. The favored portrayal of the U.S. as a prison-based complex casts prison as its singular form, leaving aside two features of carceral capitalism central to its logic and success: a continuum of unfree labor, and the managed mobilities on which histories of profitable "compulsory but free labor" have thrived. [29]

Distinguishing free and unfree labor in the U.S. becomes messier with respect to the repeated making of captive labor, outside/open air prisons, and on the ambiguous edges of the law. Both have landed disenfranchised Black and colonized persons in labor camps at sites within U.S. "jurisdictions."[30] In the nineteenth-century Netherland Indies "criminalizing restrictions bound workers to their contracts and turned mobility (or 'exit') into a punishable offense."[31] Movement—by whom, when, where, and how—is a managed and unruly process built on calibrated choreographies of penal and forced mobility. De Vito and Anderson write, "empires

---

29. The concept of "managed mobility" describes a signature *dispositif* of imperial colonies and their carceral regimes. See Ann Laura Stoler, "Colony," *Political Concepts: A Critical Lexicon* (2010): https://www.politicalconcepts.org/colony-stoler/ . On the "carceral continuum"—from forced labor in Texas' coal mining industry to British colonial detention camps in Kenya where convicts provided the forced labor for airport construction and public works, see Ann Laura Stoler, *Duress: Imperial Durabilities in our Times* (Durham, NC: Duke University Press, 2016), 108–109. Also see Christian De Vito and Clare Anderson, *Transportation, Deportation and Exile: Perspectives from the Colonies in the Nineteenth and Twentieth Centuries* (Cambridge, UK: Cambridge University Press, 2019), and Noah D. Zatz, "The Carceral Labor Continuum: Beyond the Prison Labor/Free Labor Divide," in *Labor and Punishment*, ed. Erin Hatton (Berkeley: University of California Press, 2021), with attention to its practices and ambiguity in the law.

30. Zatz, "Carceral Labor Continuum," 3.

31. Van Rossum, "The Carceral Colony," 72; G. Roger Knight, "Coolie or Worker? Crossing the Lines in Colonial Java, 1780–1942," *Itinerario*, April 22, 2010, https://www.cambridge.org/core/journals/itinerario/article/abs/coolie-or-worker-crossing-the-lines-in-colonial-java-178019421/A215A9AEB926742271D0BB1A07EBF0A1.

moved colonially convicted imperial subjects and citizens around colonial peripheries to a remarkable degree."[32] Those movements were not confined to the outer ridges of empire or European enterprises in the global south; mobile carcerality was the norm in U.S. pine forests, lumber camps, and mining ventures.

BODIES IN MOTION

A telling set of practices also lie in the conditions of captivity, where and how *catchments of capture* have worked to diminish a capacity to evade subsumption—and its often invisible net. Carceral landscapes of geopolitical breadth equally are evident not in places, but viscerally in the bodies of persons—in the policing of codes, gestures, and purported dispositions that assign them suspect status.[33]

If some carceral landscapes are marked by permanent structure, others depend on mobile arrangements. Relations of domination entail strategic movement, capture, and arrest. They are made possible by *predation*.[34] The ties that bind "predator and prey" make forced and leased labor central to carceral states. A collective prey is identified by character, color, and bodily being, prior to and after capture. Thresholds of susceptibility monitor and track the micro-ecologies of "availability," where acquisitions can best be made.

Grégoire Chamayou's resonant history of centuries of political theory takes as its founding conceptual metaphor and concrete premise that social life and its enmities long have been cast as a

32. De Vito and Anderson, "Transportation, Deportation and Exile."
33. I think here of Helga Tawil-Souri's argument that "Israel's borders then are not easily mapped along any (geographic/territorial) boundary, but on [those people's] mobilities and flows" in "Uneven Borders: Coloured (Im)mobilities: ID Cards in Palestine/Israel," *Geopolitics* 17, no. 1 (2012): 173.
34. Gregoire Chamayou, *Les chasses de l'homme: histoire et philosophie du pouvoir cynegetique* (Paris: La fabrique, 2010).

contest between predator and prey, with the manhunt its enduring motif. Prey status conditions a hypervigilant disposition toward being "tracked"—as much as refusal to engage the rules or the game.[35] Predation is often imagined to be in the southern swamps of escape. But today they are not. Precarious access to jobs, medical care, food, and shelter have long indexed where capture, captivity, and containment thrive. "Being tracked" is not the same as a "tracked existence" ("*une existence traquée*").[36] Nor is "being tracked" a sufficient or particularly accurate translation of "traquer." Its sense in French is to be "hounded," "stalked," "tracked down," each of these variants mark the relentless practices that have made up the racial history of the U.S. and do so today.

In the U.S., carceral landscapes are pervasive and protected from view. Some sites are secluded, clandestine, set apart in the *outer fringes of civil life*. Others occupy dead zones, far from suburbs, tucked away in small town America where jobs are supplied (or promised to be) by the carceral industry. Some sit as violent zones on urbanity's rough edges.

Some were in the heartlands of American capital, such as Andrew Carnegie's U.S. Steel, and Tennessee Coal, Iron, and Railroad, among the largest conglomerates in the early-twentieth-century South. Labor camps were their modus operandi. Over forty years, they together leased "tens of thousands of unpaid, abused, and overworked convicts [who] *cycled through* both (*emphasis added*)."[37] The odd phrase and passive voice speak to a feature of carceral labor often implied but evading measure.[38] How many times and for how long could one be "*cycled through*" different

---

35. Chamayou, *Les chasses*, 101–103, turns to Sartre to ask how the prey "interiorizes" the thoughts of the predator, producing for the one pursued, "*une existence traquée.*" This hypervigilance about being watched is even closer to the conditions DuBois sets out to describe the racial burden of being watched, knowing how one is seen, thereby having to hold to a "double consciousness."
36. Chamayou, Les chasses, 101.
37. See Perkinson, *Texas Tough*, 104.
38. Mentioned once by Perkinson.

camps? Did those persons do the same work, or different work in the same camps? "Outside camps" were rarely visited by public health supervisors; when they were, those reports confirmed the conditions of encampments with partially and precariously able, malnourished, diseased women and men.[39] They did not record names nor make reference to those they had treated elsewhere (nor necessarily would have "remembered" those they did.)

BEYOND THE PRISON MODEL

The term "carceral labor" rather than "prison labor" underscores those arrangements for which prisons are neither the only locus nor model. Carceral labor depends on a more mobile set of practices, more provisional than fixed. Well-worn forms of entrapment exist next to those developed for carceral capitalism's debt coercion or current debt-inducing public finance models.[40] Law reviews detail a spectrum of structural injustices that bleed those of color, selecting for those *where privations most prevail*.[41] Old and new sources of entrapment thread their way through the history of how carceral labor is extracted and "cycled through" the same places, evident in the racial coding of minor infractions, and the hollows of living in recurrent debt.

Marie Gottschalk holds that the U.S. has invested in a "new civil and political order," wed to "governing through crime," one "in the making for decades."[42] Students of colonialisms would only amend the limits on time and place. "Governing through

---

39. An observation of Perkinson's stands more broadly for the imperial democratic model: "All of Texas' principal institutions—its political and legal systems, its economy and culture mores—rested on *a bedrock fractured*: exalted liberty secured through systematic debasement" (*Texas Tough*, 49).
40. Jackie Wang, *Carceral Capitalism* (Cambridge: Semiotext(e), 2017).
41. Zatz, "Carceral Labor Continuum," 3.
42. Marie Gottschalk, "City On a Hill, City Behind Bars: Criminal Justice, Social Justice, and American Exceptionalism," *Nanzan Review of American Studies* 31 (2009): 39.

crime" has a history that exceeds the U.S. and the century. It is difficult to come up with a colonial administration that did not do so. Radically different in the U.S. is the scale of incarceration, the number of prisons and jails, the overwhelming proportion of those of color in them who labor under surveillance outside their walls. Not least are the number of those with lives undone before and long after they have left penal labor regimes or prison grounds.[43]

CONCRETE, IRON, AND STONE

Expansion of state projects, conquest, and "regime maintenance" (a term reserved for counterinsurgency operations outside "the nation") depended on tedious, skilled, and unskilled labor over long hours, or continuous shifts night and day. That work included cutting and clearing trees, moving boulders, hammering stones into gravel, hauling granite, leveling bedrock, clearing swamps, sawing, and hauling lumber, diverting water tributaries, constructing highways from mud and stone, raising and killing chickens, making furniture and fortifications, blasting tunnels, scaling ridges, furrowing land by hand, picking produce, digging out towpaths and canals. The work itself was invariably hard labor but it was the forced conditions under which it was performed, hours stretched, days added, and where food, shelter, clothing, and medical aid could be withheld for hours and days.

State authority was and is partly realized in a monopoly of force as Weber defined it, but it could be argued that as much accrues from the infrastructures built of concrete, iron, and stone—for defense, commodity production, transport, and public

---

43. By Gottschalk's count, the usual figure of 2.2 million people vastly underestimates the numbers in prisons and jails in the U.S.; more than *eight million* people are entrapped by the carceral state. See her "Razing the Carceral State," *Social Justice* 42, no. 2 (2015): 31–51.

works. From the building of irrigation channels in colonial Java, to roadways in the Panama Canal Zone, these infrastructural developments made possible the arteries that moved goods, and militia. To the great profit of the exploding automobile industry, that labor made possible Americana dreams—from continuous commodity flows across the U.S. to long-distance family road trips across the nation.

Coerced, punitive, convict labor did not alone make the "modern"; but it did make possible many of its achievements, from the dockyards of Bermuda and Gibraltar, and the port city of Singapore. Penal labor, resource extraction, and state projects for public works have made up the synergetic histories of carceral labor, capital intensive state and private projects, and investments across the global.

THE ENCRYPTED METRICS OF RACE

The dominant vision of the U.S. as the exceptional carceral state (in the public sphere and academic research) may occlude a broader view that breaches that status. Good reasons might be offered: the U.S. had no penal colonies from its inception; it was considered one. Just as transport of convicts to Australia ended in 1868, ex-slaves in the U.S. were being newly designated as criminals on contrived charges for forced labor they had done as slaves under conditions hardly better. Historians estimate that more than thirty thousand convicts were sent to French Guiana (1854–1931), and forty thousand political prisoners and "common criminals," white and black to New Caledonia (1864–1897), during the precise period in which "convict leasing" was flourishing and a U.S. economy based on it.[44] Colonial Senegal from the 1930s

---

44. See Stephen A. Toth, *Beyond Papillon: The French Overseas Penal Colonies, 1854–1952* (London: University of Nebraska Press, 2006). On the different waves of French political prisoners sent to penal colonies in New Caledonia and Guinea, there

to 1950s had a robust penal system as well.[45] In the Dutch East Indies, the incarcerated population "witnessed a remarkable rise" from ten thousand in 1870 to fifty-seven thousand in 1920. In the 1930s, convicts provided the labor power for roadwork across the inner archipelago.[46] Such uses were state priorities in both sporadic and coordinated restless expansion.

In the U.S., convicts were less often political exiles (though they were that too), or sent to clear new territory for colonization.[47] Instead, the disproportionate black convict population in the U.S. was being leased out to private mining and lumber companies and to build and maintain the expanding roadworks of a budding carceral industrial complex enabled by a racial state.[48] Today the "empire of prison labor" is made up of corporations, private prisons that depend on high incarceration rates, and government "correctional" facilities that lease out those incarcerated or manage in-prison manufacturing of office furniture, military gear, and computer and vehicular components.[49]

---

is an extensive literature not dealt with here. On the "technological ingenuity" that allowed more than thirty-thousand people to come to French Guinea, many of whom inhabited its penal colonies, see Miranda Spieler's incisive study of the work of the law in making people visible and invisible, at once threatening and unmaking them. Miranda Spieler, *Empire and Underworld: Captivity in French Guiana* (Cambridge: Harvard University Press, 2012), 10–11.

45. See Romain Tiquet, "Connecting."
46. Van Rossum, "Carceral Colony," 74.
47. But see Dylan Rodriguez's excellent study, *Forced Passages: Imprisoned Radical Intellectuals and the U.S. Prison Regime* (Minneapolis: University of Minnesota Press, 2006), on imprisoned radical black intellectuals as part of a broader treatment of "black unfreedom," mass-based punishment, and "liquidation." Forming "the grammar and materiality of American society," made unstable by "radical prison praxis" (1–2).
48. Sydney Wilmot, "Use of Convict Labor for Highway Construction in the North," *Proceedings of the Academy of Political Science in the City of New York* 4, no. 2 (January 1914): 6–68. Wilmot's study is not of the South, as most are, but of convict labor used as far Washington and Oregon, where penal workers were housed in stockades that could hold as many as eighty-four men and "were made collapsible for easy removal," (returning to the importance of mobility again) (1914: 17).
49. "Banking on Bondage: Private prisons and mass incarceration," *ACLU*, accessed May 15, 2021, https://www.aclu.org/banking-bondage-private-pris

This is not a history of repetition. If "recursive history" has traction, it is here in tracking the malleable bonds that tie the use of carceral labor to industry and corporate profit.[50] Recurrent techniques of recruitment on domestic and global scales make carceral workers "available" (and eager?) to "escape" for cents an hour, in work for Victoria's Secret, McDonald's, and disease-infested industrial poultry farms.[51] These are not distant versions of the earliest convict leasing programs, providing workers for private lumber and mining companies. Convict leasing was the template for the commodification of what now is named "contract prison labor"—that "$2 billion industry" for which Nordstrom, Target, Whole Foods, among other companies, are (and not) well-known.[52]

Conceptual categories invite a search for semblances, foreclosing others. The historical developments of carceral labor in Europe, and the convict labor requisitioned for U.S. roadways and pine forests were not the same nor were their laboring populations. Still, affinities in governance appear in tactic and intention. Unwaged labor has provided the material underpinnings of

ons-and-mass-incarceration. The Federal Prison Industries, Inc (FPI) is an in-prison machine, in expansion since 1934. For those fashioned as the subjects of crime, who may still receive $0.23 per hour for their work, the response is far closer to rage and indignation than a welcome of the rewards of rehabilitating reform.

50. I describe this recursive process with respect to imperial formations, elsewhere:

recursion is precisely not to imagine that social and political processes ever play out in a repetitive and mimetic fashion. These histories are marked less by abrupt rupture or by seamless continuity and not by repetition of the same . . . Rather they are processes of partial reinscriptions, modified displacements, and amplified recuperation. (Stoler, *Duress*, 27).

51. Poultry farms are a zone of multiple infestations that effect those working in them. See https://www.google.com/url?sa=t&rct=j&q=&esrc=s&source=web&cd= &cad=rja&uact=8&ved=2ahUKEwiE2uSM9tz0AhXtUd8KHQsxAtcQFnoECA UQAQ&url=https%3A%2F%2Fagrilifeextension.tamu.edu%2Flibrary%2Fpoultr y%2Fpoultry-pest-management%2F&usg=AOvVaw0AO-g_SnCIlwhp_aMkxL_B

52. "Calling out Companies that Use Prison Labor," *Global Tel*, accessed May 13, 2021, https://blog.globaltel.com/companies-use-prison-labor/.

statecraft's assertion of sovereign space—and "high modernist" governance since the mid-nineteenth century and earlier.[53]

RACISM'S "UNCIVIL SPACE"

> [T]he convicted man has been treated in two ways, both economic. When economically valueless he has been killed, when economically valuable, he has been enslaved.[54]

This is a biopolitics and geopolitics inscribed in the amended Constitution by a racial logic and opaque metric. What mattered was what was "appropriate" and what was not in a white sovereign space. Little epitomized the aesthetics of white normativity more than the "Ugly Laws," those early twentieth century municipal and state ordinances mentioned in early essays here, that flourished with vagrancy laws. Designed to rid civilian life and an upstanding citizenry of the "unsightly," barely considered among them, these were laws adjudicated through the senses, a *racially inflected sensorium*, hyper-alert to sight, smell, and sounds.[55]

Ugliness was decisive but had no measure. Comportment, dress, cleanliness, motion, or arrest were subject to an arbitrary

---

53. In James Scott, *Seeing Like a State: How Certain Schemes to Improve the Human Condition Have Failed* (New Haven: Yale University Press, 1998), Scott looks at the simplifications that came with "high modernist" states (an "aspiration" to state managed social engineering) and that "citizenship for all" made possible. I see equal investment in the ambiguous categories of racecraft, conducive to mobile attributes and manipulations. See Ann Laura Stoler, "Racial Regimes of Truth," in Stoler, *Duress*, 237–265.

54. E. Stagg Whitin, "Prison Labor," An Address Delivered before the Woman's Department of the National Civic Federation at Washington, January 1914.

55. See Susan Schweik, *The Ugly Laws: Disability in Public* (New York: New York University Press, 2009). They were not applied only to those of color, but to those whose presence in public space was an affront to white sensibilities of aesthetics, decorum, sexual normativity, and race. But see especially Chapter 8, "Race, Segregation, and the Ugly Law," 184–206.

white "common sense." Such statutes fashioned a submetrics of inequality that Susan Schweik describes as having "startling *indeterminancy (emphasis added)*." Assessed by local, capricious criteria, no specification applied. Civilians and reformers, police, county judges, and health officers with "expert" knowledge were its arbiters.[56] The "administration of fear" was and remains prominently a fearful racial one—a white imaginary of precarious, inequitable, and "disproportionate" Black and otherwise subordinate populations.[57]

IMPERIAL DEMOCRACY'S FANTASIES ABOUT WAGE LABOR

In the U.S. and its territories, carceral labor figures as one of the most productive sites of racial inequalities—instantiating a racial history of the present while reproducing the conditions for it. A host of terms attempt to capture how incarceration and capitalism have fed off one another with revision in the present: "carceral capitalism," "barbed wire imperialism," "carceral empire," "prison imperialism," the "global carceral state."[58] Each name a carceral phenomenon wed to capitalism's selective consumption

---

56. Schweik, *Ugly Laws*, 11.

57. On the "administration of fear" see Paul Virilio, *The Administration of Fear* (Cambridge: Semiotext(e), 2012); James Gray Pope, "Mass Incarceration, Convict Leasing, and the Thirteenth Amendment: A Revisionist Account," *NYU Law Review* 94, no. 6 (December 2019): 1528. Again, see Zatz, "Carceral Labor Continuum," for sharp insights on the extra-prison carceral labor extensions that come with the reintroduction of "debtors' prisons," parole or probation violations, nonpayment of child support, or fees related to minor offenses. These are crucial to understanding the continuum today and its similarities and differences to earlier ones.

58. My "carceral archipelago of empire" is among them, an effort to name the conceptual, geopolitical, and racialized qualities of sequestered "undesirables" beyond the rubrics offered by Foucault. See Ann Laura Stoler, *Along the Archival Grain: Epistemic Anxieties and Colonial Common Sense* (Princeton: Princeton University Press, 2009), 130–139.

of certain bodies converted into commodified things. Carceral regimes hover in the grey zone of international and constitutional law, the shallows of citizenship, and meld with other forms of forced labor.[59]

Such namings identify a scale and scope of incarcerations that make private capital and imperial pursuits profitable pairings. A new density of historical and social research tracks broad networks of confinements and camps of unfree workers subject to the logics of mobility and arrest.[60] Some show the calibrations by which forced labor assignments were made by length of a sentence and the nature of a crime. Others show carceral work contingent on where and by whom a sentence was passed.[61] Others focus on the gradation of sentences imposed by the racial order of facts and things. Some show nothing.

The U.S. history of the present assigns carceral labor to the margins of the wage labor market rather than its center. That image and imaginary are fictive at best. That these were workers called on intermittently to "fill in the gaps" in the wage labor market neither makes room for the essential work performed nor the fabulated criminalities it endorsed. *Capitalism has never been confined to "free" wage workers selling their labor power.* Nor was unfree labor an "anomalous necessity arising from labor shortages."[62] Forced labor was neither outside the sphere

---

59. Wang, *Carceral Capitalism*; Aidan Forth, *Barbed-Wire Imperialism: Britain's Empire of Camps. 1876–1903* (Berkeley: University of California Press, 2017).

60. Several recent, excellent volumes and special issues of journals tell us much about the global and historical scale and scope of carceral labor. Christian G. De Vito and Alex Lichtenstein, *Global Convict Labor* (London: Brill, 2015) begins with a bibliographical essay that would seem to make further rehearsals of the temporal and spatial stretch and import of convict labor redundant. Anderson, *Convicts and Penal Colonies*, provides an important account of the long histories of practices attributed to the space and time of what constituted the "modern." This cumulative work represents a collorborative and collective model of scholarship. For reasons already mentioned, the U.S. history of carceral labor tends not to present.

61. See Van Rossum, "The Dutch East India Company," and "The Carceral Colony."

62. Robert Miles, *Capitalism and Unfree Labour: Anomaly or Necessity?* (London: Tavistock, 1987), 197–198 quoted in Sebastien Rioux, Genevieve

of commodification nor made up of a "labor reserve" (as Marx is understood to suggest).[63] Convict labor was and is commodified, negotiated between states and corporations, between county and prison authorities, between the incarcerated and their guards, and within the restricted barter economy of carceral exchange of cash and services among the incarcerated themselves. Unpaid labor, forced labor, coerced labor, indenture (as in the plantations of Southeast Asia), and the equivalent of debt peonage have been core features of carceral capitalism in its national and global instantiations.

Shackles and chain gangs were slave technologies of another time but designed for modernizing state projects and the use of forced labor in outdoor public space.[64] Chain gangs of Black labor in the South in the "roaring twenties" was a brutal twentieth-century practice for building and maintaining roads and highways. Stringent surveillance, scant rations, makeshift shelters, and violence were the norm where penal workers were quartered in "railroad cars and trucks." Decommissioned ships near British and U.S. ports were floating prisons for those

---

LeBaron, and Peter Verovsek, "Capitalism and Unfree Labour: A Review of Marxist Perspectives on Modern Slavery," *Review of International Political Economy* 3 (August 2019): 11.

63. The "lumpenproletariat" in Marx's lexicon, made up of the disenfranchised, unaligned, and socially malignant, was recuperated by the Black Panthers in the 1970s to describe a Black underclass at the political vanguard rather than self-banished from politics. See Errol A. Henderson, "The Lumpenproletariat as Vanguard?: The Black Panther Party, Social Transformation, and Pearson's Analysis of Huey Newton," *Journal of Black Studies* 28, no. 2 (1997): 171–199.

64. The much-reproduced photo (which I choose not to reproduce here) of seven women convicts in Tanganyika doing roadwork, chained together by neck rings, appears in the Carpenter Collection, Lot 1135 (488) at the Library of Congress with the photographer's name (E. M. Santos) and the American collector, Frank G. Carpenter. It was "created/published" between 1890–1930. The women's somber demeanors, some with eyes cast down, some looking straight at the camera/photographer contrasts what seems to be a foreman with a toothy broad smile behind them. The final sentence of the description reads: "Who the convicts in the photograph were and why they were being punished is not known."

doing dock work by day, returning to locked ships by night.[65] In the U.S., they were corralled in boxcars from urban barracks, sailed in as the vanguard shock troops for the clearing (of forests and persons) in the Philippines and the American South. A prize commodity squeezed into the hulls of cargo ships from other shores, they made the infrastructure for private and state profits conceivable and possible.

Benjamin Weber details this point in describing the contribution of convict labor in the building of the Panama Canal Zone and its roads that stretched around it.[66] As importantly, he rightly insists on a point hard to avoid: that the U.S. exported more than convicts to the outer reaches of its imperial locales. It exported its own brand of racial logic.[67] The Panama Canal Zone was a crowning achievement of a U.S. labor regime that conscripted Afro-Panamanian and Caribbean migrants for the chain gangs that made racial capitalism and imperialism such a profitable mix.

Upon U.S. occupation of the Philippines and Puerto Rico, convict labor was used for public works projects as well.[68] Convict labor in what Matthias van Rossum calls "the carceral colony" of the Dutch Indies was crucial to the Indies' modernizing, imperial projects. At its vital center was a mix of coerced, corvée, and indentured labor on which the colony called. Messy distinctions, about which we need to know more, seem to have allowed shipping and lumber companies, and civil engineers to compete in a managed free-market, engineering when and how workers would move between them.[69]

---

65. Prison ships were used extensively in the eighteenth century. "Terrorist" fears resuscitated the use of "floating prisons" in the 21st century. See Duncan Campbell and Richard Norton-Taylor, "US Accused of Holding Terror Suspects on Prison Ships," *The Guardian*, June 1, 2008, https://www.theguardian.com/world/2008/jun/02/usa.humanrights.
66. Weber, "The Strange Career," 79–102.
67. Weber, "The Strange Career."
68. Weber, "The Strange Career," 99, fn. 37.
69. Van Rossum, "The Dutch East India Company." A passing description of the convicts recruited in Wonosobo, Java to make six hundred wooden shipping boxes (mentioned above) might invite more questions: were they "gifted" by a government

Mobility and transience required neither shelters of brick nor stone. Makeshift barracks and flimsy shacks barely protected from the elements were as much fixtures in the U.S. carceral complex as were the brick and mortar penitentiaries. As Blackmon writes (the epigram for this essay), "Hundreds of forced labor camps came to exist, scattered throughout the South—operated by state and county governments, large corporations, small-time entrepreneurs, and provincial farmers."[70]

Angela Davis and Mike Davis together sharpened a weapon in the fight against Black incarceration in developing the concept of the prison-industrial complex.[71] They opened a space for political analysis, producing a virtual revolution in understanding of how prisons operated and the slave history that produced them. It would be hard to be more prescient with respect to the range of industries that now profit from those arrangements. Still, thinking with a *carceral* (rather than prison) industrial complex might provide more global purchase, making room for its stretch beyond prison and national bounds.

Carceral profitability resides in the movement of bodies in temporary stasis and motion, forcing labor to the locations where it was needed. Penal labor in Indochina under French colonial rule, in Florida in the 1920s, and for roadwork in Georgia as late as the 1960s were contexts unamenable to fixed confinement or immobile labor. The mining of Georgia's Bellwood Quarry is paradigmatic, key to similar practices and their proliferation elsewhere. Convict labor camps were temporary and built with *provisionality* in mind: hundreds of men were housed in covered pens. Most significantly the camps at

---

prison to only certain private Dutch entrepreneurs Were they "gifted" to other entrepreneurs as need arose? How dependent was the sugar industry on penal labor?

70. Blackmon, *Slavery*, 7.
71. See Angela Davis, "The Prison Industrial Complex," in *Are prisons obsolete?* (New York: Seven Stories Press, 2003), 84-104.

the Bellwood quarries were "*developed around the extraction of granite.*"⁷²

Throughout the imperial world, regimes of coercions were built around extractive industries and infrastructural priorities.⁷³ Penal mobilities are part of a counter-history in the making.⁷⁴ Extraction and work camps went hand in hand. This was a history that both preceded the widespread emergence of prisons and penitentiaries and remained strategically important long after. Mobile forms of incarceration were subject to sparse oversight. The costs of provisions were made minimal, as were the costs of deaths.

STATE POWER AND THE PROFITS OF CARCERAL LABOR

> *[M]odern statecraft is largely a project of internal colonization, often glossed, as it is in imperial rhetoric, as a "civilizing mission." The builders of the modern nation-state do not merely describe, observe, and map; they strive to shape a people and landscape that will fit their techniques of observations.*⁷⁵

---

72. Convict labor at Bellwood Quarry, Atlanta Rail Corridor Archive, accessed 23 January 2017, http://atlrailcorridorarchive.org/exhibits/show/bellwood-quarry/convict-labor-at-bellwood-quar.

73. The Bellwood quarry camps were closed in the 1960s, not because of the exposés written about them, but because the water tables were considered dangerously polluting of Atlanta's water supply.

74. See for the example, the introductions to two special issues of *International Review of Social History*, De Vito and Anderson, "Transportation, Deportation and Exile; and Zhanna Popova, "Dissecting Sites of Punishment: Penal Colonies and Their Borders," *International Review of Social History*, August 7, 2019, https://www-cambridge-org.libproxy.newschool.edu/core/journals/international-review-of-social-history/article/dissecting-sites-of-punishment-penal-colonies-and-their-borders/638465268443A0AAB1E504B98E0E5526.

75. Scott, *Seeing Like a State*.

Understanding Black incarceration as one of the most powerful political institutions in the U.S., a point Loïc Wacquant argues, opens to broader claims.[76] For it figures in the material architecture of governance in ways that need to be further explored. Carceral labor, the "uncounted workforce" of the contemporary global order, hides in the seams of state allocations and the geopolitics of spatial control.[77] Some students of statecraft would argue that it is more central today than in the past, precisely for those tasks that expand, enhance, fortify, and perform state governance projects.[78]

Governance is dependent on the capacities to make powerful conversions: water into irrigation, fields into highways, boulders into gravel, forests into railroads, persons into things fitted as prosthetics to machines. Conversions of labor power into profits, pine trees into turpentine, quarries mined for ore are among the extractions in these shatterzones where imperial power has harnessed both nature and persons. Again, the principle of "managed mobility" is fundamental to imperial governance. Whether called "penal mobility" or "carceral mobility," one of its consequential features is often mentioned only in passing; namely that this model of movement and its control derives from what "seeing like a state" entails, and what expectations thinking like a state place on its experts, agents, and profiteers to realize and efficiently perform.[79]

---

76. Wacquant, *Prisons of Poverty*.

77. Darius Rafieyan and Cardiff Garcia, "The Uncounted Workforce," *WBUR*, June 29, 2020, https://www.wbur.org/npr/884989263/the-uncounted-workforce.

78. Rioux, LeBaron, and Verovsek, "Capitalism and Unfree Labor," 1: "Contrary to the expectations of liberal and neoclassical economists, as well as many Marxist theorists, the deepening and extension of capitalism seem to have reinforced unfree labor rather than diminished it . . . remain(ing) resilient in the global economy."

79. See the special issue of the *International Review of Social History* 64 (2019): 415–425, especially Popova, "Dissecting Sites of Punishment" and Zhanna Popova and Francesca Di Pasquale's introduction.

UNFREE LABOR IN WORKING THE WOODS

> [S]tate simplifications, the basic givens of modern statecraft, were ... rather like abridged maps ... They represented only that slice of [the actual activity of society] that interested the official observer ... They were maps that, when allied with state power, would enable much of the reality they depicted to be remade.[80]

Seeing Like a State is crisp, uncluttered with jargon. A condemnation of capital, corporations, and state engineers from beginning to end, showing not only how and what states see but what they don't. States simplify the categories of persons and things in a visionary pursuit of making enumeration, measurement, design, and control more rapid and accessible—if not always possible. At issue are visions and their failures. Scott's opening, a seemingly benign set of state projects to improve "forest hygiene," is the scene of a catastrophe in the making and telling. In his reading, forest hygiene was committed to a metric that shaped what forests would look like, by what and by whom they would be populated, how they would be converted into profits, and remade. This commitment to measure is what defines seeing like a state, rationalized measures dependent on a "political simplification of the modern era, the concept of a uniform, homogeneous citizenship."[81]

But this is also where the models and measures break down. Making the world legible to governance goes with making it illegible to what authorities imagine might thwart their plans. The harvesting of turpentine with convict labor is one of those exemplary sites in which enormous profits were garnered with a practice from which health and forest officials looked away.

---

80. Scott, *Seeing Like a State*, 3.
81. Scott, *Seeing Like a State*, 32.

The labor that went into working the woods, the profits accrued, the racially marked convict labor deployed, and the use and abuses of carceral labor are part of a racial history only partially measured. Seeing like a state demanded omissions. The numbers of convict workers, "freely" procured from county, regional holding pens for men of color fell outside state calculations. So did their deaths.

If "convict leasing" was banned by the early 1920s (as debt peonage had been in 1867), the turpentine industry ignored it. Between 1880 and 1950, a majority of work in the industry devoted to extracting resin from pine trees from South Carolina, Georgia, Florida, and through to Texas was performed by a captive forced labor of "vagrants" culled by local officials from local jails.[82] Resin was a valued commodity for sealing hulls on wooden boats, for protecting rigging from salt water, and for lamps and streetlights before the advent of petroleum.

The turpentine industry was lucrative, brutal, and destructive. Dependent on the longleaf pine forests that once covered almost five million acres of North Carolina, the process called for regular weekly slices into a tree's bark to release the sap, which increasingly exhausted a tree's production. Widening scars made it harder to tap. A tree could be "turpentined" for little more than three years.

From the late-nineteenth to mid-twentieth century, the industry moved south from North Carolina to Georgia and finally to Florida. In "a frenzied half century of exploitation," millions of acres were reduced to less than sixty thousand.[83] Private penal camps followed: shacks in u-shape formation, barbed-wire

---

82. Jerrell H. Shofner, "Forced Labor in the Florida Forests, 1880–1950," *Journal of Forest History* 25, no. 1 (1981): 14–25.

83. David Cecelski, "The Turpentine Trail," January 11, 2021, https://davidcecelski.com/2019/07/29/the-turpentine-trail/; Mark Andrews, "For Decades, Turpentine Industry sapped Florida Forest, Workers," *The Orlando Sentinel*, August 20, 1993, https://www.orlandosentinel.com/news/os-xpm-1993-08-29-9308270659-story.html.

perimeters patrolled by dogs and white guards.[84] It was in Florida's pine glades, where turpentine distilleries and convict camps became one of the densest sites of convict leasing, where vagrancy laws "manufactured convicts" for unpaid labor.[85] Patrols along the barbed wire perimeters kept people in the camps, and inaccessible to outsiders. Bare life was produced in the mobile space of a commodity production beyond the prison and with gradations of violence and profit that made prisons conduits to penal labor.[86]

CARCERAL LABOR AND THE CONCEITS OF DEMOCRACY

The 13th amendment served to place convicts outside the pale of protection from enslavement, removed from the moral economy of democratic rights. Étienne Balibar points to two ways of destroying the capacity to act on one's own behalf: one reduces the person to "the status of things that can be eliminated or instrumentalized at will in a world of commodities." The second destroys "the conditions of possibility of politics."[87] Incarceration

---

84. Black workers were shackled at night to their huts. Labor camps of the Putnam Lumber Company (where testimonies reported daily flogging and forced prostitution) were under repeated federal investigation in the 1920s and 1930s.

85. Alexandra D. Mahibir, "Slavery by the Name of Turpentine: The Lynching of Odis Price," Northeast University School of Law, Summer 2015, https://repository.library.northeastern.edu/downloads/neu:m0428561f?datastream_id = content. Throughout northern Florida, none of these camps were more reviled than the largest twenty-thousand acre concession owned by a State Senator, T. J. Knabb. See Matt Marino, "The Brutality of Florida's Turpentine Industry," *FloWriter*, November 9, 2018, https://flowriter.net/2018/11/09/the-brutality-of-floridas-turpentine-industry/ . It was only in 1970 that the scarred trees were abandoned. See Knabb Turpentine, Wikipedia, https://en.wikipedia.org/wik/Knabb_Turpentine, accessed February 2, 2021. His camps were notorious even at the time. Over decades, courts accused him of "inhumane treatment." He was acquitted every time.

86. Robert N Lauriault, "From Can't to Can't: The North Florida Turpentine Camp, 1900–1950," *The Florida Historical Quarterly* 67, no. 3 (January 1989): 310–28.

87. Étienne Balibar, *Violence and Civility: On the Limits of Political Philosophy* (New York: Columbia University Press, 2015), 142.

attempts to do both by making the cost of a retort, a claim, and a non-acquiescence exorbitant—torture, banishment, or death.

Carceral labor did not create the conditions for political banishment but once having put convicts out of reach of public debate and public space, they were effectively excised from the polities in which they otherwise might imagine they tangentially belonged. In U.S. history, those excisions have provided the ballast and means for white sovereign claims. Like the carceral circuits of penal colonies and transport of convicts, carceral practices in the U.S. and its jurisdictions have produced prolonged and/or permanent conditions of political banishment, some at a distance, some right at home.

Removal from the polis does not mean removal from the law. Indeed, it is the law that has provided the processes that produce disenfranchisement, dislocation, and dispossession. Current debates focus on voting rights and the prior conditions of eligibility. But removal still operates as a governing logic directed at those deemed precariously at odds with civil norms. An encrypted metric adjudicates on those to be banished. Nineteenth-century idioms of the deserving and undeserving poor reverberate through social policy as "compassionate conservatism" did in the 1980s, and again in the submetrics of inequalities today.

Tracing unfree labor over a *longue durée* upsets both political fictions and historical narratives. Carceral labor has not been marginal to nation-state formation or a peripheral form of capital accumulation. It has been both a paradigmatic site of profit and state power. If a linear story of modernity from coerced to free labor was ever viable, it is not now. The conventional wisdom that capitalist expansion was forged by waged labor is challenged by the racialized unfreedoms and a racial state that hold it in place. A global perspective on carceral regimes' recursive history should alter our optics on a corporate and state powerhouse, lucrative at so many scales. Private investors, sub-contractors, lowly state officials, and county judges all profited. Contemporary histories of these collusions are at a new pitch. Defying the received narratives of penal history and imagining a new conceptual and concrete vocabulary registers penality as a central instrument of power and penal mobility, part of a broader contemporary history of inequalities, disenfranchisement, forced movement, containment, and forced arrest.

THE HYPOCRITIC OATH AND THE CARCERAL CLAUSE TODAY

Once imagined in the shadows of the law, the 13th's carceral clause has emerged at the forefront of abolition advocacy. A larger populace than ever is staking a new future on interpretative action, holding *that while the 13th formally and legally ended the institution of slavery in the U.S., it perpetuated and endorsed it by multiple other means in force today*. Variants of that last sentence have been written over and again by journalists, historians, sociologists, artists, prison abolitionists, and civil rights activists in and outside the carceral system. Still, the observation is often prefaced by the disclaimer that the clause was "easy to overlook." Legal scholars bent on reinterpreting it refer to it being "neglect[ed] by courts and scholars."[88]

Books, essays, radio programs, and award-winning documentaries have sought to restate its effects.[89] Michelle Alexander's

---

88. Scott Howe, "Slavery as Punishment: Original Public Meaning, Cruel and Unusual Punishment and the Neglected Clause in the 13th Amendment," *Arizona Law Review* 51 (2009): 984–1034. Eric Foner reminds us that it did not go unnoticed by white Southerners who, when it was passed, immediately pushed for the Black Codes, consigning and confining African-Americans to involuntary labor. Eric Foner, "We are Not Done with Abolition."

89. Blackmon's book was headlined by the *New York Daily News* some eight years later, when PBS aired a documentary of the same name. Authored by the notoriously unreliable Shaun King, "How the 13th Amendment Didn't Really Abolish Slavery, But Let it Live on in U.S. prisons," *New York Daily News*, 21 September 2016, https://www.nydailynews.com/news/national/king-13th-amendment-didn-abolish-slavery-article-1.2801218.

tracing of the history of Jim Crow to black incarceration and the prison industrial complex has fueled dispute, as has Ava DuVernay's award winning documentary, *13th*, which opened the 2016 New York Film Festival.[90]

Still, the capacity to "see" the clause recedes from view as often as it erupts to account for the carceral present. Film critic Odie Henderson's rave review of the *13th* made the "easily missed clause" news.[91] Other critics wrote of Duvernay's "startling" findings, and the film's "cathartic" revelations.[92] Proper outrage and inattention attest to our warped knowledge-worlds where the clause is a testament to a racial logic that need never use the word race, nor speak its name. The clause can disappear, deactivated as it recedes from view—and then re-emerge, visible, telling, and newsworthy for a prolonged or brief "shocking" moment, much as colonial "atrocities" continue to surface and recede from attention today.

The racial politics of incarceration and the politics of disregard produce the clause's occlusion—to the rage of some and purported ignorance of others. In anti-racist activist spaces and an increasing number of academic disciplines, the 13th now stands for the oath of a democratic polity at odds with itself. Debate and mobilization around the carceral clause are igniting a resurgent and unprecedentedly broad abolitionist campaign.[93] Still, the

90. Michelle Alexander, *The New Jim Crow: Mass Incarceration in the Age of Colorblindness* (New York: The New Press, 2009). On the background history to the documentary, *13th*, directed by Ava DuVernay (2016, Los Gatos, Netflix)

91. Roger Ebert, "*13th*," rogerebert.com, accessed February 2, 2021, https://www.rogerebert.com/reviews/13th-2016.

92. Manohla Dargis, "The Journey from Shackles to Prison Bars," *The New York Times*, September 30, 2016, https://www.nytimes.com/2016/09/30/movies/13th-review-ava-duvernay.html.

93. Some argue that the 13th is more present because Black incarceration is under scrutiny as part of a broader complex for which the abolish prison movement has fought. The "13thism" movement emerges from both. See Daryl Michael Scott, "The Social and Intellectual Origins of 13thism," *Fire!!!* 5, no.2 (Spring 2020): 2–39. Reactivating the call made two decades ago by Angela Davis, Ruth Gilmore, and others for "Abolition democracy" (a term borrowed with tribute to W.E.B. DuBois) their manifesto calls for prison abolition and deletion of the clause. Gilmore's longstanding, outspoken advocacy for abolition is now receiving deserved attention. See

13th's presence in juridical debate pales next to the 14th's. In contrast to the one hundred and twenty-five thousand law review articles on the 14th (providing "equal protection") over the last fifty years, the 13th is said to "stand in the shadows, seemingly invisible to legal scholars."[94]

One could posit that the carceral clause is the ultimate violent "distraction" from Americana's fabulation about itself—a distraction for and from a polity and populace's dreams of white sovereignty.[95] That racial imaginary makes sense of refusal to adjust vision and gaze—or to recognize that the U.S. has built not only its highways but its reformist and "progressive" projects on unfree carceral labor and on a continuum of conditions of coerced underpaid (migrant farmworkers), quietly abusive domestic labor,

---

the *New York Times* profile on how she might change your mind about how prison abolition should and can happen. Rachel Kushner, "Is Prison Necessary? Ruth Wilson Gilmore Might Change Your Mind," *The New York Times*, April 17, 2019, https://www.nytimes.com/2019/04/17/magazine/prison-abolition-ruth-wilson-gilmore.html.

94. Michelle Goodwin, "The Thirteenth Amendment: Modern Slavery, Capitalism, and Mass Incarceration," *Cornell Law Review* 104 (2019): 899–992. See Pope, "Mass Incarceration," 1465–1554, for a history of the debates over the carceral clause and its constitutionality at the time it was passed. Pope addresses how those debates figure and might refigure the dominant reading of the clause and forced labor in carceral sites today. In a recent search on Google and Google Scholars, the 13th amendment was referenced in 12,200 articles and 45,600 books and newspapers since 2000, reported March 10, 2021. For the "carceral/exception clause" that number descends to three hundred and fifty-six books and sixty-one articles since about 2000, reported March 17, 2021.

95. Barnor Hesse develops this key concept in "White Sovereignty and Black Life Politics: The N* * **r They Couldn't Kill," *South Atlantic Quarterly* 116, no. 3 (2017): 581–604, building on Frederick Douglas and W.E. B. DuBois' "white citizenship democracy" to describe the machinations of racecraft in the U.S. Also see Hesse's podcast, "White Sovereignty: The Law of Racial Rule," October 7, 2020, in *Building Sustainable Futures: Global Challenges and Possibilities*, produced by Northwestern Buffett Institute for Global Affairs, podcast, MP3 audio, https://www.audible.com/pd/White-Sovereignty-The-Law-of-Racial-Rule-Podcast/B08KXMSRDM.

Risa L. Goluboff, "The Thirteenth Amendment and the Lost Origins of Civil Rights," *Duke Law Review* 50 (2001): 1609–1685 is a forceful reminder that notwithstanding legal injunctions against forced servitude and peonage, the latter avidly indicted in the 1940s, remains.

barely paid, illegal workers. Wage labor and forced labor of those of color were and remain Americana's shatterzone, its corrosive and curative core.

Jackie Wang's uncompromising study of carceral capitalism in the U.S. details profit for states and municipalities of fines (unpaid taxes, bail costs) imposed on urban Black populations, subsidizing municipal coffers. The contemporary debt peonage system has long fed off the inability of the poor to pay the fees and fines that come with being targeted for petty crime.[96] The ubiquity of the "company store/town model" places debt as one the most effective carceral *dispositifs* in prison and outside.[97]

Legal activists are now challenging not only how the 13th amendment applies to the imperial sovereign places that the U.S. has claimed; an even more brazen charge challenges the forms of labor that a U.S. citizen legally can endorse and profit from, whether inside or outside imperial bounds. A new generation of critical lawyers is confronting the "extra-territorial" use of forced labor in those places around the globe where the U.S. state is *not* sovereign.[98]

Public interest groups have called for boycotts of companies that have used and continue to endorse and use forced labor. What may be new is how the 13th's carceral clause is being pressed into radical contemporary service. Reinterpreted more expansively,

---

96. Wang, *Carceral Capitalism*.
97. Pope, "Mass Incarceration," describes today's prison as "the ultimate company town," where management can force inmates to work, unilaterally set their wages (at zero, if desired), unilaterally set rent, force inmates to buy necessities from the company store, compel inmates to work beyond their normal release date by driving them into debt, and them to obtain public money for housing, punishing and rehabilitating them. Colonial agribusiness and mining companies honed that form of entrapment, producing constricted movement of workers by paying them not in cash but in kind at inflated prices. Up through the 1930s, indenture was the norm. Ann Laura Stoler, *Capitalism and Confrontation in Sumatra's Plantation Belt* (New Haven: Yale University Press, 1985).
98. Tobias Barrington Wolff, "The 13th Amendment and Slavery in the Global Economy," *Columbia Law Review* 102 (2002): 973–1050.

the aim is not "reform" but to produce a radical break that challenges the narrow interpretation of "forced" and "involuntary servitude" and the racial histories of their making.

Critical historiography of incarceration is impatient with worn-out stories. It is intent on making more visible and legible both the substantive and subjacent forces of a retrograde punitive system—in mutating processes of profiting-making, war-making, depoliticization, and duress. Most importantly, its sights are set on abolition, undoing myths that incarceration can be a "solution" for social disorders that are its effect. The carceral industry has produced a shatterzone whose veins are bursting with dissent, smashing rock.

* * *

8

Colonial Diffractions in (Il)liberal Times

Diffraction in physics is broadly defined as a "bending of light around the corners of an obstacle" into the obstacle's shadow.[1] *The obstacle is key to how the light is bent, effecting the resulting intensity of the light and what remains in the shadows. Might diffraction capture some of the conditions under which colonial idioms and relations appear in dim or glaring light, depending on what and with whom they come into contact as they "bend"? Might this bending of light capture how matters colonial diffract through an illiberal present, intensifying or diffusing around some human kinds, not others? Do these deflections cloud or clarify the illiberal disorder of things?*

IN THIS CURRENT FRAUGHT—FIERCELY INEQUITABLE and environmentally precarious—world order, it is hard to miss a striking surge of new densities around what could be construed as wholly disparate or related phenomena.[2] Popular

---

1. "Diffraction," Wikipedia, accessed February 2, 2021, https://en.wikipedia.org/wiki/Diffraction. Diffraction is a concept in physics with numerous variations in how it operates. This Wikipedia site is as comprehensive in its definition as any I have read.

2. First delivered in September 2019 as the Firth Memorial Lecture for the 2020 Association of Social Anthropology, it later appeared in *Public Culture* 33, no.1 (January 2021): 65–86. This version is a rethinking of its founding premise and the nature of its provocation. It was written in summer 2019 before COVID-19, and Black

mobilizations and occupations of public space come up against right-wing retrenchment and xenophobias. Toxic sinkholes and gutted landscapes name a damaging imperial present. Calls for the restitution of stolen objects join managerial performances of colonial apology by European and North American heads of state. Not least, are burgeoning initiatives and mandates to decolonize classrooms, public institutions, disciplines, speech, and behavior, exceeding confines of academic worlds.

Celebrations of contemporary distance from and nostalgia for the colonial order of things—erupt and disrupt, surface, and recede. How they do so is typically contradictory, recurrent, and recursive. Within this maelstrom, colonial imaginaries, principles, and unwelcome practices come endowed with enormous weight and political currency. Ever more magical wisdom and show of good faith seem to place one on the good side of history that colonial condemnations are imagined to offer. How to make sense of this cumulative accretion of demands, assertions, and denials that enlist and press on the colonial from so many quarters and with such a range? Are patterns discernable in the forms these invocations take? Is there an available conceptually adequate political grammar to do so? And why the profusion now?

This final essay pursues an admittedly unwieldy set of propositions, identifying two radical shifts in how colonialism is politically positioned and temporally framed. Most broadly, colonial invocations are covering a more capacious ground than ever before—the archive stretches across the academe, public education, indigenous communities, activist blogs, the mainstream press, splaying high-pitched over museum curation. These shifts alter what is labeled colonial and where that accusation is directed, and what it is implicitly or explicitly called upon to do.

For one, colonial histories today have a decidedly different cast than before; many are deep *histories of the present, not allusions to*

Lives Matter gave long belated urgency to questions of racial injustices in the U.S. and across the world.

vague legacies and residual damage but demand for accountabilities of sustained, durable subordinations now. But as many are not. Some are focused, often vaguely, more on what "colonial-like" conditions are imagined to do and be, rather than conditions built into infrastructures of today's polities. Asymmetries of exposure and precarity sometimes seem addressed to enduring historical inequalities, some seem abstractly tied to whatever inequites are here and now.

A question hard not to ask: are those demands seen as colonial-sourced addressing what needs to be repaired and redressed? Should protest again paeans to colonial agents (feted or unacknowledged), to racist *bas-reliefs* (defended as "art") and museum exhibits be distinguished from protests targeting toxic deposits, land grabs, dispossesions (past and present) and scarred landscapes? How do the former figure the substance of continued duress? And how do these weigh against other inequities of imperial democracies, racialized practices, not protected by "the rule of law," but propagated by it? Some might see these practices as surfacing sporadically from the underside of these polities. I see them as foundational to what these polities do, their affective politics casting illiberalisms as that which they only tolerate but indeed invest. Limited access, contingent permissions, no trespass zones are the barricades that cut across this broader polity, falling disproportionately across the bodies of the immigrant, refugee, brown and black poor.[3]

A second radical shift is temporal. Here certain features of colonial regimes where profits have been wagered on coerced and confined labor are rendered not as violating histories of the present, but as premonitions, foreboding forecasts—*as histories of the global future*. This unprecedented invocation works off a cumulative archive in the remaking, one extending its extractive

---

3. See a complementary essay to this one by Adela Taleb, "Europe in focus: Imperial formations in the fabric of the European Union," *Ethnic and Racial Studies* 44, no.10 (2021) 1755-1788.

core to a longer historical and wider planetary arc.[4] An adequate conceptual vocabulary is still in formation, at times unsure of its mark. Temporality is key: time frames out of sync jostle longer and shorter durée; slow violence and accelerated extraction waver in their measures of accrued inequalities, disrepair, disregard, and degraded care.[5]

"Illiberalism" is a political term commonly reserved for polities at the far end of the democratic spectrum and indeed outside it, openly and proudly repressive of freedom of speech and assembly, popular social movements, visual and verbal forms of dissent. Such a term, like shatterzone, should not be reserved for the "European periphery"—Turkey's Erdoğan, Hungary's Orban, Israel's Netanyahu, and Brazil's Bolsonaro. Wendy Brown argues that the saturating values of neoliberalism have undermined "democratic provisions" in recent decades while commitments to political equality and social justice have been swept aside incrementally with terrifying speed and ease.[6] I think she is right. Still, I would hold that the label "illiberal" holds "liberal" firmly in place, capturing a part of the liberal spectrum secure at the Euro-American "core." The United States under Trump was exemplary: a democratic polity with illiberalism etched into the protean principles of inclusion and exclusion, a normative capacity that

---

4. Dipesh Chakrabarty makes the most incisive argument for a planetary scale of analysis in "The Climate of History: Four Theses," *Critical Inquiry* 35 (2009): 197–222; "Postcolonial Studies and the Challenge of Climate Change," *New Literary History* 43, no. 1 (2012): 1–18; "Planetary Crises and the Difficulty of Being Modern," *Millenium: Journal of International Studies* 46, no. 3 (2018): 259–282. From the press, see Robin Mckie, "How Our Colonial Past Altered the Ecobalance of an Entire Planet," *The Guardian*, June 10, 2018, https://www.theguardian.com/science/2018/jun/10/colonialism-changed-earth-geology-claim-scientists.

5. The cartographic imaginary here is broad but the actual map is not: I'm focusing here on the Euro-American matrix of imperial design, of those at the center of these polities and those rendered invisible at their center or shunted to their margins.

6. Wendy Brown, *In the Ruins of Neoliberalism: The Rise of Antidemocratic Politics in the West* (New York: Columbia University Press, 2019).

liberalism produces and protects, part of its central repertoire—not an exception.⁷

If this essay is in part a disquieting reflection on how a lived condition and a trope—at once tired and enlivened—are commonly conflated and converged, its underlining disquiet lies elsewhere. The first part builds the evidence of ever more colonial references and distillations. The second part reflects on the colonial as a *diagnostic* that turns less to the effects of the past than to a threatening future. As a diagnostic of the immediate future it is at once effective and misleading. On the line is what contemporary liberal polities do to not diminish confinements, to fortify "interior frontiers" and to uphold the "deepening divides" of border and boundedness on which they depend. Piece-meal and massive appropriations of land, mineral, and water resources—siphoned, redirected, and extracted --create and expand the racialized zones of differential micro-ecologies and the sustainabilities of those who live in them.⁸

The old and new terms suggest a revised scale and scope of colonial effects, a template of empire and a vision spilling beyond colonialism's once imagined edges. Terms like "global apartheid" are neither metaphors nor euphemisms. Such a phrase speaks across a range of contexts, from state endorsed racisms to the accretion of renewed vocabularies marking out contaminating, sullied, invasive and evasive, disdain-worthy populations. It is a lexicon that feeds off quests for immunity and purity, the bedrock of racialized regimes of truth and their grammars.⁹

---

7. On illiberal democracy by the self-declared "centrist," Fareed Zakaria, *The Future of Freedom: Illiberal Democracy at Home and Abroad* (New York: Norton, 2007); Ashutosh Varshney, "Narendra Modi's Illiberal Drift Threatens Indian Democracy," *Financial Times*, August 18, 2017.

8. Ann Laura Stoler, "Interior Frontiers," *Political Concepts: A Critical Lexicon* 4 (2018), https://www.politicalconcepts.org/interior-frontiers-ann-laura-stoler/; Didier Fassin ed., *Deepening Divides: How Physical Borders and Social Boundaries Delineate Our World* (London: Pluto Press, 2019).

9. Ghassan Hage mines an adjacent lexical vein to capture what he sees for the future: "a savage colonization" may be an unfortunate misnomer, but his point is not. The phrase entreats us to calibrate intensified forms of enmity, unequally disabling

These diffractions of colonial conditions make for a temporality that defies linearity. Colonial entailments (at once residual and emergent) provide anxious forebodings and forecasts across a broad space and future tense. In these efforts to locate and name the sorts of distress and duress on the horizon, colonialisms of the imagined, occluded, and imaginary are not confined to the academe; the arts, and popular and public reckonings describe degraded, precarious conditions in the lowlands of social life, on the shifting borders of land and sea, in unprotected, distressed, flooded, parched, and leached environments.[10]

Calling on colonial practices and principles to account for today's social failures is an effective deflection and perhaps misguided weapon, by assigning as colonial what increasingly brash and brazen illiberal policies produce and which democratic institutions so skillfully hide. The question seems simple but it's multiplex: does a current and insistent turn to "decolonize" misrecognize the embedded and ubiquitous inequities that are written into liberalism's own dossier on itself? Are illiberal and colonial formations not both forged in racial disparity and disposability? This is neither a new question nor new observation. Some thirty years ago, numbers of those working on colonial history

---

and dispossessing, targeting specific social kinds. See Ghassan Hage, "État de siege: A Dying Domesticating Colonialism?" *American Ethnologist* 43, no. 1 (2016): 38–49.

10. Mega-plantations are in takeover mode. As Tania Li slyly puts it—refusing any resort to linear imperial history, "plantations are back." See Tania Li, "After the Land Grab: Infrastructural Violence and the 'Mafia System' in Indonesia's Oil Palm Plantation Zones," *Geoforum* 96 (2018): 328–327. My own work on North Sumatra's palm oil plantations decades ago suggests they were never gone. Even in the late 1970s monoculture was expanding in a World Bank-endorsed, authoritarian (post) colonial period. See Stoler, *Capitalism and Confrontation in Sumatra's Plantation Belt, 1879–1979* (New Haven: Yale University Press, 1985). Still, it was hard to see then that palm oil and the industrial plantation industry would explode the global commodity market from Sumatra to New Jersey truck companies substituting it for ethanol. See Burton English and Daniel de la Torre Ugarte, "A Decade Later: Corn Ethanol's Broken Promises," *The Hill*, October 22, 2015, http://thehill.com/blogs/congress-blog/energy-environment/257635.

argued that conduct, comportment, and competence carved out the exclusions on which liberalism's and imperial formations depend.[11] The current consequences of that observation again invite pressing questions about colonial invocations, prompted by new demands for visibility and new forms of political dissent.[12]

Colonial invocations often carry a similar political valence, often as a shorthand for injustice, in familiar and new ways. The proliferation cuts across the disciplines and those who consider themselves its renegade and recalcitrant members. Its interpellators and publics cross boundaries as well; those whose life worlds have been directly affected by colonialisms and actively remain so; politicians and their pundits who make themselves "relevant" by speaking to "colonial memories" on lofty moral ground; scholars of colonialisms now more apt to address the contemporary detritus of what was once treated as past. Activists are defacing monuments and reclaiming sacred grounds. An avid liberal press primes a public, "shocked" at the exposé news of colonial dispossessions of people, places, and things.[13]

"Newly" informed publics may register momentary outrage or disbelief, but share a common discursive thread: how often can one hear, "Could these colonial massacres really have been the case?" or "Could their children really have been taken by force?" or "Did 'we,'—our Dutch/German/Belgian/U.S./British/Italian/Portuguese/Canadian/French/Japanese government—really do

---

11. See Frederick Cooper and Ann Laura Stoler eds., *Tensions of Empire: Colonial Cultures in a Bourgeois World* (Berkeley: University of California Press, 1997), 1–56, 198–237; Uday Mehta, *Liberalism and Empire: A Study in Nineteenth Century British Liberal Thought* (Chicago: University of Chicago Press, 1999).

12. The surge in France for and against thinking how the colonial matters from Houria Bouteldja, *Whites, Jews, and Us* (Paris: Découverte, 2019), to the assault on "postcolonial studies" and their tiresome "barkers." See Texte collectif, "Les bonimenteurs du postcolonial business en quête de respectabilité academique," *L'Express*, December 26, 2019, https://www.lexpress.fr/actualite/politique/les-bonimenteurs-du-postcolonial-business-en-quete-de-respectabilite-academique_2112541.html.

13. Think France's *Le Monde*, Britain's *The Guardian*, The Netherlands' *De Volkskrant*, and, in the United States, *The New York Times* and *The New Yorker*.

that to those people, right there/here, in this place?" And from academic corridors: "Did the celebrated French avant-garde anthropologist Michel Leiris and his guys really steal those ritual objects in North Cameroon in the 1930s (and celebrate it as a rescue operation)?"[14] But many museum trustees in their rarefied worlds, are finding themselves unable to avoid what others find hard not to ask.[15] "Can restitution really repair what is actually lost?" Does a frenzied focus on "returning" objects (to whom?) displace other losses? And is the fact of dispossession assuaged by the exchange of things?

Does it matter that "decolonial" projects draw on the currency of colonialism to make broader claims, often with little pretense that what they are protesting is covered by the rubric of *colonial* at all?[16] Initiatives are thick and thin: some amplify how specific, located colonial histories matter; others skirt the dark coordinates of colonial effects. Both may be diffracting newly renewed illiberalisms, below the radar of denunciation, inequities hidden and sanctioned by law. Colonial idioms resonate in a space of intensifying inequalities of resource and opportunity.[17] As both figure and ground, colonial citation and objects seem to surface

14. See, for example, Phyllis Clark-Taoua, "In Search of New Skin: Michel Leiris's *L'afrique fantôme*," *Cahiers d'études africaines* 167 (2002): 479–498.
15. There are notable exceptions: Wayne Modest's work at the Tropen Museum in Amsterdam. See Words Matter, Tropen Museum, accessed February 7, 2021, https://www.tropenmuseum.nl/en/about-tropenmuseum/words-matter-publication; Also see the work of Clementine Deliss, as discussed in Edward M. Gómez, "Shaking Up the Ethnographic Museum," *Hyperallergic*, July 18, 2020, https://hyperallergic.com/577138/shaking-up-the-ethnographic-museum/.
16. See "Decolonize this place" that describes itself as an "action-oriented movement, centering Indigenous struggle, Black liberation, free Palestine, global wage workers, de-gentrification, and dismantling patriarchy"; Decolonize this Place, accessed February 3, 2021, https://decolonizethisplace.org/contact.
17. Although Piketty's world map of inequalities is not an imperial one, he has written on the colonial inequalities with respect to metropolitan France. See Facundo Alvaredo, Denis Cogneau, and Thomas Piketty, "Income Inequality under Colonial Rule: Evidence from French Algeria, Cameroon, Indochina and Tunisia, 1920–1960," *World Inequality Database* (2018), http://wid.world/wp-content/uploads/2017/12/118-Alvaredo-Cogneau-Piketty.pdf.

as an emphatic and endowed descriptive for protracted inequities, named and unnamed.

DEMOCRATIC EXPECTATIONS

New fields mark recognitions of new and old collusions. Neologisms—"technocolonialism," "digital colonialism," and "data colonialism" seem to reach for inequities of wide breadth, imperial effects on a scale that weighs heavily on the Global South, particularly in the effects of uneven access in technological domains.[18] Each term calls out enduring and hardening asymmetries in relations of power that depend on exemptions and exclusions. The practices can differ, as can the sites of pressure and "points of application."[19] But a more important element may be shared: that these inequities are imagined to be tenaciously robust, *above and beyond the normative democratic order of things.*

Some expectation about what contemporary liberal and illiberal polities are, do, promise to do, and fail to do seems on the line. May this indeed be what distinguishes today's from earlier colonial inflections that speak, if indirectly, to illiberalism's priorities reshaping global democracies now? Some are categorical indictments: the U.S. not as a democracy but as "the first modern settler state,"[20] Israel's "settler state" as a democratic apartheid with its Islamophobic

---

18. Mirca Madianou, "Technocolonialism: Digital Innovation and Data Practices in the Humanitarian Response to Refugee Crises," *Social Media and Society* 5, no. 3 (2019): 1–13; Michael Kwet, "Digital Colonialism is Threatening the Global South," *Al-Jazeera*, March 13, 2019, https://www.aljazeera.com/indepth/opinion/digital-colonialism-threatening-global-south-190129140828809.html. On the ethnocolonial museum, Clementine Deliss, "On the Necropolitics of Sequestered Colonial Collections," Lecture, The New School for Social Research, New York City, November 28, 2018; E. Guitiérrez Rodríguez, "The Coloniality of Migration and the 'Refugee Crisis'," *Refuge: Canada's Journal on Refugees* 34, no.1 (2018):16–28.
19. David Scott, "Colonial Governmentality," *Social Text* 43 (1995): 198–199.
20. Mahmood Mamdani, "Settler Colonialism: Then and Now," *Critical Inquiry* 41, no.3 (2015): 608.

racialized governance.[21] The targets may be whole colonies in an imperium, but more often "colonial sorts" of governing practices that democratic orders have incorporated as their *modus vivendi* and treat as state secrets. Imperial democracies harbor a resilient fiction that only their archons and governing agents know the extent and technologies of the inequities on which they depend.[22]

THE POLITICS OF TENSE

One thing is clear: colonialisms are no longer as assuredly relegated to the *passé composé*.[23] Nor do the terms colonial "remnants" and "leftovers" come as easily unfettered, even if the press still affords such terms *caché*. Claims are of an actively entrenched colonial matrix that is present and proximate. Resources, opportunities, and access are distributed through affective and economic relations, rippled through with trespassing signs, rife with imperial strategies of confinement that extend a logos and pathos committed to inequities. These effects course through the liberalisms in which an unspecified "we" protect and invest.

Denigrations can settle in the ether of affronts and abrasions, around sensibilities that look, sound, and smell like a colonial ethos of derision and distaste. Senegalese street sellers in Paris or Chagossians living on London's outskirts, both at the inner borders of Europe's illiberal enclaves, would have little trouble recognizing what John Jackson describes as *"de cardio racism"* in

---

21. Magid Shihade, "Global Israel: Settler Colonialism, Mobility, and Rupture," *Borderlands* 14, no.1 (2015): 1–16; Rachel Busbridge, "Israel–Palestine and the Settler Colonial 'Turn': From Interpretation to Decolonization," *Theory, Culture & Society* 35, no. 1 (2018): 91–115.

22. Ann Laura Stoler, *Duress: Imperial Durabilities in Our Times* (Durham: Duke University Press, 2016); Martin Thomas, *Empires of Intelligence: Security Services and Colonial Disorder after 1914* (Berkeley: University of California Press, 2007).

23. *Passé composé* is the French tense for a definitely completed action.

the U.S.—working furtively, and in passing.[24] But sometimes the language and gestures only seem furtive. Consider this ugly scene, one I was enlisted, "passively," to join.

> *Paris metro, early evening February 16, 2019. Startled by the sound. The hiss was loud and clear, emanating from several women seated in a metro, disapprovingly watching a young Roma mother, squirming infant on her lap, a toddler swiping her hands across the grimy subway floor. Condemnation was pointed: such sorts not knowing how to care for their young. Wordless but not silent; an audible disdaining hiss exhaled . . . under their breaths. Those of us in seats close-by, faces squashed in newspapers and iPhones were intended to sanction and to hear.*

Such registers of dissonance reside glaring, blinding, and unseen in urban surroundings, some more palpably inhere in those bodies defiant of norms and comportments of discomfort. Most take hold, depending on the hue of flesh.

Still, what is deemed colonial or "colonial like" is often hard to decipher. What liberal polities are expected to protect and foster can be as well. For naming a relationship or set of practices as colonial with respect to liberalism may capture two very different expectations: one may position illiberalism as an excess in liberalism's otherwise tempered bearing—an excess, a temporary discrepancy between prescription and practice. Or it may signal something less innocuous: that state violence, confinements, incarcerations, and their distribution are the ready apparatus of liberal regimes, their "preserved possibilities" to be animated as inherent features, inescapably present.

The act of naming here waivers as unstable and ambiguous—as absent presence, as metaphor or stark reality depending on how extended the temporality of colonial disorders is conceived to be.

---

24. John Jackson, Jr., *Racial Paranoia: The Unintended Consequences of Political Correctness* (New York: Basic Civitas Books, 2008), 78.

What constitutes "pastness" in the colonial disorder of things? The luminous philosopher Alia Al-Saji—Henri Bergson and Maurice Merleau-Ponty much before—invites us to take "pastness" as *"so close to the present as to be its lining (emphasis added)."*[25] Verb tenses matter a lot and come with their own politics. Whether considered in the definitely finished *passé composé*, or the ongoing past imperfect, or the present, the conditional, the visionary ("if only"), or the apocalyptic future, colonial invocations are at once conceptual, personal, and political. These are perceptions and practices that in turn shape dispositions of coerced and compromised choice, creating a "cleft" (*clivé*) habitus fashioned and remade.[26]

The militancy of verbal tense can be exactly what makes news stories "hot" and what they are "about." Colonial effects are forefront in the 2018 Intercept podcast, "Hurricane Colonialism: The Economic, Political and Environmental War on Puerto Rico"; *Le Monde* derides a New Caledonian *independantiste* leader for "diatribes" against "the colonial state." A ballistic missile alert in 2018, plastered on flashing signs on a Hawaiian highway is reported as "Life, Death and Politics in Hawaii: 125 years of Colonial Rule."[27]

Those asserting indigenous demands in Australia, the U.S., and Canada are at the forefront of making temporal claims.[28] Nailing settler colonialism to the Israeli state's door and apartheid to its policies re-announces not only the violent displacements of the Nakba but of the recursive continuity of more newly

---

25. Alia Al-Saji, "The Past," Lecture, Political Concepts Annual Conference, The New School for Social Research, New York City, NY, April 18, 2014.

26. Pierre Bourdieu, *Esquisse pour une auto-analyse* (Paris: Raison d'agir, 2004), 127.

27. Andrea Freeman, "Life, Death and Politics in Hawaii: 125 Years of Colonial Rule," *The Conversation*, January17, 2018, https://theconversation.com/life-death-and-politics-in-hawaii-125-years-of-colonial-rule 90273.

28. Audra Simpson, *Mohawk Interruptus: Political Life Across the Borders of Settler States* (Durham: Duke University Press, 2014); Glen Sean Coulthard, *Red Skin, White Masks: Rejecting the Colonial Politics of Recognition* (Minneapolis: University of Minnesota, 2014).

crafted obstructions and modes of crushing restrictions on life and labor.[29] Here the past imperfect and present tense express an insistent acknowledgement that some of the world remains subsumed by (as they refuse) a vital hypermodern colonial governing apparatus now.

ILLIBERAL INEQUITIES AND COLONIAL LININGS

Nomenclatures are battlefields in these Gramscian wars of position, sites of conceptual and political struggle in this imperial democratic space. The target may be as diffuse as global capitalism—or unspecified as in "Empire by Its Other Names."[30] Wrestling too with what's in a name, Elizabeth Povinelli seizes on "settler liberalism" to get at the exacerbating conditions of Australian intervention in Aboriginal governance.[31] Illiberalism in my own use is a current inherent to imperial democracies. I use democratic polity as a vernacular, ethnographic term to describe the forms of governance in which some of a U.S. populus imagine that those bereft of homes, jobs, and social services live.

Call outs of a colonial condition are political claims: from Chirac's endorsement of the benefits of colonialism in 2005, to Sarkozy's refusal to apologize for colonial atrocities, to Macron's "stunning" acknowledgement of colonialism as a "crime against

---

29. https://www.google.com/url?sa=t&rct=j&q=&esrc=s&source=web&cd= &cad=rja&uact=8&ved=2ahUKEwjV0pL6keL0AhVkmeAKHUHHBAkQFnoE CAwQAQ&url=https%3A%2F%2Fapnews.com%2Farticle%2Freligion-race-and-ethnicity-israel-mediterranean-sea-west-bank-3c9adae04858a7735b031e58e3419c6 4&usg=AOvVaw2SK6kM4X5JjuD6OcNHT11J

30. "Empire by Its Other Names," Conference, The Heyman Center for the Humanities at Columbia University, New York City, NY, April 5–6, 2019.

31. Elizabeth Povinelli, *Economies of Abandonment: Social Belonging and Endurance in Late Liberalism* (Durham: Duke University Press, 2011); "Elizabeth Povinelli," Wikipedia, accessed February 26, 2020, https://en.wikipedia.org/wiki/Eli zabethPovinelli.

humanity," a disturbing message remains; one claiming innocence at its righteous core. "We" run our polities differently (Macron), these histories really have little to do with us, so don't harp on them (Sarkozy), and most importantly "we" can show our good will in publicized spectacles of apology, despite the fact the real French-Dutch-Belgians-Americans-Canadians-Australians are not to blame.[32] Here history matters as solace, inscriptions of a circumscribed "we" in the face of a set of acts "we" no longer endorse, conventions of violence so different from the ones "we" hold today.

Verbal tenses mark sacred acts of absolution. But not always. Colonial-era laws can be sources of new repressions, revitalized (not vestigial) in national legal codes (as they are in those against gay sex in Singapore). Gay rights activists in India last year made them the object of public protest, mocking those laws as the "colonial hangover."[33]

Restitution and reparation projects—documenting theft and extraction of people, labor, resources, art, and artifacts—are being

32. On Chirac, see Julio Godoy, "FRANCE: Recasting Colonialism as a Good Thing," *Inter Press Service*, July 5, 2005, http://www.ipsnews.net/2005/07/france-recasting-colonialism-as-a-good-thing/. On Sarkozy see Diadie Ba, "Africans Still Seething over Sarkozy Speech," *Reuters*, September 7, 2007, https://uk.reuters.com/article/uk-africa-sarkozy/africans-still-seething-over-sarkozy-speech-idUKL05130 34620070905. On "Macron's Stunning Acknowledgement of Torture in Algeria" (and the fact that "he stopped short of making a formal apology") see Yasmeen Serhan, "Emmanuel Macron Tries—Slowly—To Reckon with France's Past," *The Atlantic*, September 14, 2018, https://www.theatlantic.com/international/archive/2018/09/emmanuel-macron-acknowledges-torture-algeria/570283/.

33. "The colonial hangover" and "post-colonial hangover" have become ubiquitous terms of self-deprecation in South Asia and Southeast Asia politics and the press, but also in snide favor among conservative journals like *Foreign Affairs*. See Amy Qin, "Inspired by India, Singaporeans Seek to End Gay Sex Ban," *New York Times*, December 16, 2018, https://www.nytimes.com/2018/12/16/world/asia/singapore-gay-sex-ban.html; Rupa Subramanya, "The Colonial Hangover of India's Rape Law," *The Washington Street Journal*, January 4, 2013, https://blogs.wsj.com/indiarealtime/2013/01/04/the-colonial-hangover-of-indias-rape-law/; Joshua E. Keating, "The Post-Colonial Hangover: Some Empires Really Were Worse than Others," *Foreign Policy*, January 3, 2012, https://foreignpolicy.com/2012/01/03/the-post-colonial-hangover/.

fought over in the Caribbean, the U.S., across Africa and Asia, and in EU conferences, not for the first time but with an ever more secure moral warrant. "Statue wars" have been mobilizing dramatically documented topplings that have become media events for some time. As many following the 2015 movement "Rhodes Must Fall" would argue, it was not about a monument or Rhodes, but about the durability of continuing inequalities and the refusal to acknowledge them.[34]

Culling an initial inventory with a set of spare tableaus that veers between salience and silence, again prompts my earlier question: What distinguishes a racial democracy from its colonial "lining"? As touchstone of moral injury and redemption, what are these sightings acting upon? Is it the tenets of governance or an *imperial democratic* disorder, reconfigured, dominant, and on the horizon?

Wendy Brown's take on "the rise of antidemocratic politics in the West" adds ballast to an argument that a dismantling of democracy is confluent with the colonial coordinates of contemporary states.[35] Does her understanding (and Bonnie Honig's notion of a "democracy in disrepair") point to features of democracy that foster the continued production of a global imperial underclass, something colonial-like, disenfranchised and desperately and generally invisibly poor?[36] Do references to undo the colonial (rather than the *demos*) address how much current illiberal polities barter in a sustained, racially marked, underclass of those in precarity? A governance geared to "managed mobility," detention of the invisible, disappearance of the overworked, death of the superfluous "workless poor" hinges on a matrix of racial disparities.

---

34. As Amit Chaudhuri put it, "unequal access to opportunity and mobility is structurally embedded as the norm." See "The Real Meaning of 'Rhodes Must Fall'," *The Guardian*, March 16, 2016, https://www.theguardian.com/uk-news/2016/mar/16/the-real-meaning-of-rhodes-must-fall.

35. Brown, *Ruins of Neoliberalism*, 23, 24.

36. Bonnie Honig, *Public Things: Democracy in Disrepair* (New York: Fordham University Press, 2017).

THE COLONIAL INTERPELLATION: A DIAGNOSTIC

Colonial evocations are at once symptomatic and diagnostic of the shatterzones in which we live. They register the re-amplified exclusions long built into the very principles of liberal orders. How colonial histories are positioned is up for grabs. How they matter has long marked out political positions: *"exaggerated"* (says the right and ultra-right), inadvertently sidelined, and *forgotten* (*"oubli"*) says a well-meaning liberal left, systematically *ignored* (say anti-colonial movements and their fervent academic supporters).

This preliminary inventory is a *bilan* in the French sense of an audit, a taking stock of the canonical Kantian question—what is this present and what distinguishes this semipublic colonial presence as a social and political phenomenon? Perhaps more surprising still is that questions about the timing and placements of these interpellations are not even being asked. An absence of the question in itself is strange. Across the imperial globe occluded colonial histories are decidedly not new, but they are big news. Think the Windrush generation scandal that rocked British politics in 2018 when it was made public that hundreds of adults and children from the Caribbean were wrongly detained and threatened with deportation from the UK by the Home Office.[37] Or look to the 2018 exposé of one thousand six hundred children from the former French colony of Réunion, taken from their parents in the 1950s and 1960s, to work as farmhands in depopulated rural France.[38]

---

37. Amelia Gentleman, "Windrush Scandal: No Passport for Thousands Who Moved to Britain," *The Guardian*, May 4, 2018, https://www.theguardian.com/uk-news/2018/may/04/windrush-scandal-no-passport-for-thousands-who-moved-to-britain; Maya Goodfellow, "The British Government's Racist Heart," *The New York Times*, May 3, 2018, A23.

38. BBC, "Réunion Island and the 'Stolen Children' of France," *BBC World News*, January 30, 2018, https://www.bbc.com/news/av/world-42879241/reunion-island-and-the-stolen-children-of-france.

The politics of government apologies demands a political and moral history of its own. Right now, it reads as a passion play restaged. Think the formal televised apologies of the tearful Prime Minister of Canada in 2017 to the thousands forced to attend Indian residential schools.[39] In 2021 were front-page "exposés" on the two hundred and fourteen graves of native children attending those schools.[40] A half-hearted 2008 apology by Australian Prime Minister Kevin Rudd to the "Stolen Generations," is now joined by Belgium's early 2019 public apology to those from its former African colonies for removing some fifteen thousand "métis"— mixed children of African mothers and Belgian fathers from their parents and placing them in orphanages.[41] Apologies are merely distractions. Ugly replacements for the longterm allocation of what should be large allocations of redistributed resources now.

But disobeying zoning ordinances as to what counts as knowledge and what unseats common sense are, too, on the public agenda. Frontpage news of a member of the Cherokee Nation, drawing on the first treaty in 1795 to assert a right to a seat in the U.S. Congress, is not calling for an apology but speaking to a contract reneged.[42] The expulsion of the local population of the

---

39. Ian Austen, "Trudeau Apologizes for Abuse and 'Profound Cultural Loss' at Indigenous Schools," *The New York Times*, November 14, 2017, https://www.nytimes.com/2017/11/24/world/canada/trudeau-indigenous-schools-newfoundland-labrador.html.

40. On May 28, 2021, representatives of the Tk'emlúps te Secwépemc Nation reported finding the remains of two hundred and fourteen children buried at the former Kamloops Indian Residential School, run by the Catholic Church in British Columbia from 1890 until 1978, Reuters reported.

41. "Apology to Australia's Indigenous Peoples," Government of Australia, accessed February 13, 2020, https://www.australia.gov.au/about-australia/our-country/our-people/apology-to-australias-indigenous-peoples; Milan Schreuer, "Belgium Apologizes for Kidnapping Children from African Colonies," *The New York Times*, April 4, 2019, https://www.nytimes.com/2019/04/04/world/europe/belgium-kidnapping-congo-rwanda-burundi.html; Milan Schreuer, "Belgium Apologizes for a Racist Atrocity in Its African Colonies," *The New York Times*, April 5, 2019, A6.

42. Jose A. Del Real, "Cherokee Nation Seeks to Send First Delegate to Congress," *The New York Times*, August 27, 2019, https://www.nytimes.com/2019/08/27/us/cherokee-nation-delegate-congress.html.

Chagos Archipelago to make way for the Diego Garcia U.S. military installation on its largest island, Maurice, is CNN and BBC worthy news today as it was in 2011, when Wikileaks made public that the island was designated a protected "nature reserve" to make it impossible for Chagossians to ever return.[43] It took until 2019 for the UN to call out Britain's illegitimate "colonial" occupation. Chagossians remain in Mauritanian slums and many are still without British citizenship in dismal quarters next to Gatwick Airport.[44]

CRITIQUE AND DISSENSUS

What's the work of critical social inquiry in this world of appearances and shadows where the term "colonial" mobilises condemnations of anti-democratic politics and the durability of inequities and the distributed toxins of imperial debris? Are these colonial references in illiberal times rebukes of what and who democratic polities do not defend today? Are these rebukes redundant for imperial democracies whose very warp and weft are secured by those very inequalities? Or are some of these brazen and bellicose

---

43. John Pilger, "How Britain Forcefully Depopulated a Whole Archipelago . . . and Managed to Cover It Up," *Al Jazeera*, February 25, 2019, https://www.aljazeera.com/indepth/opinion/britain-forcefully-depopulated-archipelago-190225082624527.html; "Chagos Archipelago," Wikipedia, accessed February 12, 2020, http://en.wikipedia.org/wiki/Chagos; "HMG Floats Proposal for Marine Reserve Covering Chagos Archipelago (British Indian Ocean Territory)," Wikileaks Cable: LONDON1156_a, May 15, 2009, https://wikileaks.org/plusd/cables/09LONDON1156_a.html; "General Assembly Welcomes International Court of Justice Opinion on Chagos Archipelago, Adopts Text Calling for Mauritius' Complete Decolonization," United Nations General Assembly, accessed May 22, 2020, https://www.un.org/press/en/2019/ga12146.doc.htm.

44. Alexi Demetriadi, "Lost in Exile: The Forgotten Chagos Islanders," *New Internationalist*, June 22, 2017, https://newint.org/features/web-exclusive/2017/06/22/lost-in-exile-chagos-islanders-of-west-sussex; Katie McQue and Jamie Doward, "Chagos Children 'Stuck for Years in Unsafe Lodgings'," *The Guardian*, August 10, 2019, https://www.theguardian.com/world/2019/aug/10/chagos-children-stuck-years-unsafe-lodgings.

indictments that transgress protocol and interrupt proprieties hallmarks of a new political now?[45]

A proud claim two decades ago that anthropology is the comparative study of common sense seems to have expired.[46] The task now rivets more on the breach of common sense—on a tracking of the collective conditions that produce the disjointed, schizophrenic temporalities in which those on the move, quartered off, and confined must live. The Palestinian poet/activist Raja Shahadeh identifies a "rift in time" to describe the multiple conflicting temporalities of living under Israeli mandates and the everyday of Palestine.[47] Breaches offer the unexpected exposure of something out of sync. They disrupt the seamless order of a scene played as if in sharp focus, expose distorted truth claims, pierce through political fictions indifferent and unaligned.

The recursive quality of imperial form directs attention to likenesses but often misses the connectivities that unevenly secure and concentrate weathered and new zones of containment. How much is the figure and fear of the migrant and refugee—imagined to be contaminating and contagious, sullying white immunity and storming the gates—evidence of a master principle of imperial governance? Do these fears make no room for even thinking what it takes to endure the waiting, the pacing, the makeshift shelters, abrupt movements to evade arrest? Those connections are starkly evident in recent work of Benjamin Stora, famed historian of the French-Algerian war, in his pointed claim: "Today, the damned of the earth have molted into the damned of the sea." It's a riveting statement that opens to several interpretations, depending on

---

45. Jacques Rancière, *Dissensus: On Politics and Aesthetics* (New York City: Continuum, 2010).

46. Michael Herzfeld, *Anthropology: Theoretical Practice in Culture and Society* (Oxford: Blackwell, 2001).

47. Michel Foucault, "Questions of Method," in *The Foucault Effect: Studies in Governmentality*, ed. Graham Burchnell, Colin Gordon, and Peter Miller, 73-86 (London: Harvester, 1991); Raja Shehadeh, *A Rift in Time: Travels with my Ottoman Uncle* (London: Profile, 2011).

how literally it is thought that Stora imagines the process of "molting" to be. Is it that those same colonized populations about which Fanon wrote as the *Wretched of the Earth* are literally drawn from the same populations of the global south, risking, and losing their lives today? Or that the "damned" or "wretched" of the earth of one generation have been replaced by others, with similar histories, drawn from other pools of workless and vulnerable populations who are and are not the same?

The title that the "centrist" magazine *L'Express* gave to Stora's essay was telling: "Current migrations *revive the colonial question*."[48] Does "revival" mean here that the colonial question was imagined to be dormant and that the migrant crisis—refugee drownings, these persons stateless and starving—reflect a resurgent precarity and resilience? This is a searing tableau in the making: "The wretched of the earth and sea." Gilmore's riveting definition of racism as "exposure to premature death" speaks to a colonial and contemporary nexus, which might animate Jochen Schmon's pointed question: how the Mediterranean has become a mass grave and why deaths considered "tragic" and "catastrophic" are not considered and named as the "deliberate deployment of life-threatening policies." Is this not genocide, he asks, not by totalitarian states but by liberal democratic ones?[49]

---

48. Benjamin Stora, interview by Alexis Lacroix, "Les migrations actuelles réveillent la question coloniale," *L'Express*, October 30, 2018, https://www.lexpress.fr/culture/les-migrations-actuelles-reveillent-la-question-coloniale_2044964.html. See the conference call and debate, "Migrant de Mediterranée, qui sont ces damnés de la mer?", Conference, Musée national de l'histoire de l'immigration, Paris, June 19, 2015, http://www.canal-u-tv/video/histoire_immigrations/migrants_de_la_mer.

49. Jochen Schmon, "'Migration Crisis' or 'Mass Killing'—The Mediterranean Sea as a Mass Grave of Imperial Genocide?" Unpublished manuscript, The New School for Social Research, 2019. Ruth Wilson Gilmore, *Golden Gulag: Prisons, Surplus, Crisis, and Opposition in Globalizing California* (Oakland: University of California Press, 2007), 247.

"TO DECOLONIZE": SUBSTANCE AND GESTURE

"To decolonize" is clearly one of the galvanizing political calls of the moment that may target any number of sites and protracted situations: this media outlet, this club, this art forum, this business plan, this field of inquiry, and this oppressively homophobic space. As a favored motto of public and private educational institutions it can be appeasing and depoliticizing as often as it can serve as a call to arms. It gains credibility as more than an active verb but as a mobilizing call to action in which everyone can participate and choose how they do so. The smooth glide into carefully curated curriculum reforms is compelling when the stakes and risk are low, and no one is threatened.[50] But irreverent projects strike closer to the bone: like those discussed earlier with respect to the archival surge in Palestine that embraces improprieties of aesthetics and politics that redefine dissent and refuse policing categories in their collaborative practice.

What politicality comes with the decolonial citation can be intense or inactive. Cynical reason might cast proliferating decolonial callouts as political correctness gone awry, an academic fashion exponentially raised, invocations replacing practical conceptual labor. "Colonial!" as an exclamation and moral accusation can bear the quality of an interpellation that too easily may be ignored and miss its mark. Differentiating between radically disruptive and mild reformist gestures may offer one way to ask what a colonial interpellation is imagined to leverage and politically activate now.

---

50. Eve Tuck and K. Wayne Yang, "Decolonization is Not a Metaphor," *Decolonization: Indigeneity, Education & Society* 1, no. 1 (2012): 1–40; Walter D. Mignolo and Catherine E. Walsh, *On Decoloniality: Concepts, Analytics, Praxis* (Durham: Duke University Press, 2018).

THE MOLECULAR OF DEMOCRATIC INEQUALITIES

Imperial democracies provide the foundational and formative lineaments of hazardous, life-endangering conditions. Colonial indictments pull in two directions: doing the dirty work of exposing colonialism's inherently inequitable currents, while masking how much anti-democratic impulses shape democratic polities now.

The carceral archipelago of empire marks out the disposabilities on which confinements, detentions, and incarceration have thrived to mine ore, tap turpentine in Florida forests, build highways, man the industrial chicken slaughterhouses of Costco and other low-cost industrial brands. In tracing the (carto)graphic history of disposabilities, it is hard to miss that the distribution of carceral institutions and the logics of their placements allowed for mobilization of deployable, disposable labor and "precariously able men."[51] Jodi A. Byrd refers to a "zombie imperialism" that creates a "living dead" in a liberal state that makes "freedom available for some and not others."[52]

Whose deaths are consistently premature, whose presence is deemed superfluous, where disasters will most brutally strike are products of an imperial consolidating machine, crushing together a convergence of earthly risks, political contagions, and bodily contaminations.[53]

---

51. Ann Laura Stoler, "In Carceral Motion: Disposals of Life and Labour," in *A Global History of Convicts and Penal Colonies*, ed. Clare Anderson (London: Bloomsbury, 2018).

52. Jodi A. Byrd, *The Transit of Empire: Indigenous Critiques of Colonialism* (Minneapolis: University of Minnesota Press, 2011), 262.

53. Disproportionately skewed against the disenfranchised, extractions mediate what and who will be in demand or abruptly converted to a burdensome surplus. Hannah Arendt described the making of surplus men as a hallmark of totalitarian states, but today's illiberal policy makers know better. French philosopher Elsa Dorlin specifies further, a "necroliberalism" where corporate computations are barely expended on the range of persons, non-persons, and social ecologies laid to waste. See Elsa Dorlin, "Démocratie suicidaire," *Esprit* (December 2018), https://

This splaying out of an imperial archive expands the limits of a colonial watermark, as it etches out the history of institutions once seen as totally distinct from the imperial "laboratories" where their signature molds were cast. Here one might look to the relationship between policing and the military in the Philippines under U.S. rule in the early-twentieth century with Alfred McCoy's meticulous tracking of the direct adoption of the same configuration of techniques and tactics in the urban U.S.[54]

The colonial archive—as an imaginary and curated set of multimedia documents—looks both very much and nothing like it did before, in part because colonial and liberal orders converge in uncannily similar ways. Both indelibly mark where some people know they do not have the real right to walk, to sit, to eat, to breathe, to belong. Racial lines are drawn in tangles of invisible and visible barbed wire. Colonialism as conceptual metaphor and material relationship is forged in the careful design that Foucault once accorded sexuality—a *"dense transfer point of power . . . charged with instrumentality."*[55] It may be the very obviousness of that instrumentality that confers traction. Colonial invocations may be turned into disruptive interpellations for restorative justice in civil wars over redistributive demands—or go astray.

Sometimes the colonial template signals more a new forecast of what is to come. As mandate for the future, it often fixes on the accrual of thin excuses and unaccountabilities. Colonialism in this vein gets recruited to serve as a summons of sorts—a subpoena to attend. Here the history and concept of the lie are tightly tethered to imperial democracy's lie, an organically collusive one. In revising Arendt's understanding of the political lie as a central

---

esprit.presse.fr/article/elsa-dorlin/democratie-suicidaire-41832 in tribute to Achille Mbembe, *Necropolitics* (Durham: Duke University Press, 2019).

54. Alfred McCoy, *Policing America's Empire: The United States, the Philippines, and the Rise of the Surveillance State* (Madison: University of Wisconsin Press, 2009).

55. Michel Foucault, *The History of Sexuality, Vol I: an introduction*, trans. Robert Hurley (New York: Random House, 1990).

node of totalitarian regimes, it is not a stretch to argue that democratic fictions—equity before the law, protection from predatory policing, a rehabilitative carceral system, are elements of a racial formation, political lies of their own. Virulent racial currents at the heart of liberal polities, despite strong anti-colonial ones, remain amplifying and robust even when shredded again and again.[56]

The argument that "neo-authoritarians" (Trump, Johnson, Orban, Erdoğan, Modi, Le Pen) need not destroy democratic aspirations, because they are so successfully hollowing them out, is hard to refute.[57] The indictment prompts a collective project: to ask what sorts of instruments gut social security and public space, to identify the excisions that make care—and care for the polis—no longer deemed essential or required. The "vital lie" of imperial democracies nourishes the dissimulations required to lie to oneself about what one knows and does not know simultaneously, about the structural inequities etched in the present.

In this vein again, this colonial presence is a summons to attend, rather than a detailed road map, how the fictive histories of imperial democratic governance have been drawn. Liberal democratic and colonial governance are sometimes billed as separate, lived by some as though two entities, by others endured and lived as one. The invocation of colonialism as warrant can come with a metric as well, deployed to ferret out collusions between colonial promises ("full sovereignty," "not yet" ready, autonomy deferred, and/or delayed), and liberal promises (of representation, social justice, and the rule of law) for some and not others. Both are invariably in the conditional tense, contingent promises held in suspension, not intended to be kept.

---

56. Hannah Arendt, "Lying in Politics" in *The Crisis of the Republic* (New York: Harcourt, 1979).
57. Vijay Prashad, "Hybrid Wars and US Imperialism," *The People's Forum NYC*, posted November 1, 2019, YouTube video, https://www.youtube.com/watch?v=D-uxISFZbG8.

A DARK DIAGNOSTIC: SENSORIUMS OF DISTRESS

These are times of impending and current distress. Spare tableaus with new folds can make for newly visible planes. One such tableau might attend to how a colonial reference seems to be picking up frequencies of distress, attuned to a broader sensorium. Sharper soundings, irritants, abrasive substances, toxicities that were not as audible or visible—available to the senses and political sensibilities, speaking to distaste, defining disgust as they had not been attended to before. Destruction, disfigurement, disgust, and contagion are familiar to colonial lexicons, but one could argue that more subjects and substances are being called up as sites of damage, to be dismissed, made ineligible, rejected across a wider range of scales.

Identifying damage requires juxtaposing measures that appear or disappear as too minute or too massive depending on how they're scaled. They are also easily confused with "other" undervaluatios and overloads in the air: micro pollutants, air quality so bad it has no grade, diminished water tables, fish dead and animals gagging on plastics, selectively located electronic trash and garbage dumping, nuclear waste unevenly permeating micro and macro ecologies. In this ever-wider span of earth and sea, critical social inquiry is neither of interest nor bears credibility without underscoring the often-prior measures and alternate metrics people subjected take of the damages subsuming them and consuming the planet.

This last, still ambiguous casting of the colonial ties it to a future—a dark diagnostic of where the world is heading on a planetary scale. In this latter scenario, colonialism extends as an entwined phenomena. It is envisioned as an expanding condition, as warning, and as strategic accusation. A buildup of xenophobic states has become a norm.[58] Ghassan Hage speaks to a "feeling of

---

58. Eric Fassin's references to the current state of xenophobia are too many to name. See his, "Xenophobia from Above and Precarious Democracy," Lecture

being 'under siege'" in a "savage colonialism" that has "become increasingly pervasive in the contemporary Western world" with "a similar sense of ecological besiegement and crisis."[59] Here "a settler colonial and neocolonial ethos" "tend to converge" into a "global apartheid-like" situation.[60] This bifurcated world is, as he writes, a "toxic modern colonial order itself."[61] But it is not equally present to all: some people are suffocating from air that is fetid and thin and deadlocked in colonial histories that assault and refuse to detach from their bodies.

Achille Mbembe turns to a divisive Schmittian politics of pure enmity, pushing imperial democracies beyond their comforting liberalisms to their most illiberal extremes and precarious edge.[62] This is a state of permanent war of a new world order with calibers of hate and animosity bred by an expansive capitalism without limits and planetary apartheid as an immediate future. Characterization of "liberal democracies" as riven with multiple "forms of exclusion, hostility, [and] hate movements" could be construed as excessive but that would miss the point.[63] With prose that gravitates from extravagant global strokes to the smell of burnt flesh, Mbembe identifies obscenities of power and a fantasy annihilation of the enemy. It is not unlike what the Department of Homeland Security (DHS) called "the universal adversary" (for which it seriously first sought the defining attributes in 2003).[64] The DHS makes Mbembe's hyperbolic imagery seem almost like an understated rendition of the imminent, if not yet the real.

Course, Visual Culture Research Center, Kyiv, June 1–2, 2012, http://vcrc.org.ua/en/eric-fassin-xenophobia/.
    59. Ghassan Hage, "État de siège," 38.
    60. Hage, "État de siege," 42.
    61. Hage, "État de siège," 48.
    62. Mbembe, *Necropolitics*.
    63. Achille Mbembe, "The Society of Enmity," *Radical Philosophy* 200, no. 1 (2016): 23–35.
    64. National Planning Scenarios, Washington Post Media, accessed February 4, 2020, https://media.washingtonpost.com/wp-srv/nation/nationalsecurity/earlywarning/NationalPlanningScenariosApril2005.pdf.

The vision is recursive, a "desire for an enemy" among "democratic regimes" buttressed by a hyper-walled world and vigilant zoning of gates, barriers, and checkpoints that reads as an imperial logic through and through. Its colonial technologies and democratic regimes are distinct from and folded through one another in the same breath.[65] Again, that naming is a political act, part of an alert system diffused across new platforms and planes. And the alert is pointed: to intensified, accelerated differentiations, manifest in more blatant forms of expulsions, erasures, predatory policing, and selective disposabilities. These rival those lineaments of power that conferred the right to kill "to defend society" at another time—endorsed as exceptions and urgencies but never on an imperial wide scale. Today the accretions are seen to be more encompassing, *a division of the earth* as *empire* with sites of damage and reward, vulnerability and security marking out an unprecedented clarity of catastrophic differentiation and difference on a planetary scale.

One could argue that the colonial call only harks back to Fanon in part, but more to the principles written into imperial democratic practices and policies. It's a conceptual and concrete impulse which from the beginning has specified the non-persons for whom democratic precepts would be inapplicable—they would have no part.[66] Mbembe wrestles as well with the conditions of possibility that endorse *the murderous qualities of liberal states.* Those qualities course within the corridors of colonial regimes and the racist underbelly of democratic liberal ones. Jasbir Puar names "debility" as that sought by liberal settler states as part of a "biopolitical scripting of populations available for injury," a "debilitation" "caused by the exploitative capital and imperial

---

65. Mbembe, "The Society of Enmity," 26. Also see Achille Mbembe, *politiques de l'inimitié* (Paris: La Découverte, 2016).

66. Edmund S. Morgan, *American Slavery, American Freedom: The Ordeal of Colonial Virginia* (New York: W.W. Norton & Company, Inc., 1975).

structures of the global north."⁶⁷ Liberal democracy's discriminatory infrastructures are entangled with colonial ones in this unacknowledged political frame. Each of these efforts to set out the parameters of liberal states should act as compelling reminders that imperial democracies from their start depended on setting aside those with no part and with no possibility of having one.

The forecast is maybe too dark. What a colonial-like ecologically devastating future might look like is a space of contest: a dark future met by bold dissent from the uneven distribution of choices, resources, possibilities that the carceral archipelago of empire imposes and illiberal affiliations of imperial democracies so stealthily hone. Naming how interior frontiers are assured in wars over who belongs does work to de-mask conjured contagions, to breach fictive differences, to deflate racist postures by those refusing to accept the categories and constraints imposed unevenly on us all. The conditions and promises of white *immunitas* do explicit and surreptitious work to mark the contagioius.⁶⁸ *Immunitas* hides itself as comparative concept, with "focus [more] on difference from the condition of others than on the notion of exemption itself." But exemption is decidely there—a severing of that reciprocity on which *communitas* depends. A committed imaginary of white *immunitas*, its colonial idioms and interior frontiers have a formidable adversary that refuses the mandate that these are the terms that will continue to shape how, where, and who constitutes the "we."

Colonial idioms and call outs can challenge entrenched disparities of possibility in ways that breach democratic barriers. They also put up for public scrutiny what democratic polities

---

67. Jasbir Puar, *The Right to Maim: Debility, Capacity, Disability* (Durham: Duke University Press, 2017), 94.
68. Roberto Esposito, *Immunitas: The Protection and Negation of Life* (Malden: Polity Press, 2011), 6–7.

promise, who they most damage and fail. What conditions enable a participatory and radical demolition project is harder to tell. These are the shatterzones of imperial democracies, stone walling racisms with high pressured veins internal to those polities, fissions within themselves.

Bibliography

Abizadeh, Arish. "Was Fichte an Ethnic Nationalist? On Cultural Nationalism and Its Double." *History of Political Thought* 26, no. 2 (Summer 2005): 334–359.

Abu-Lughod, Lila. "Palestine: Doing Things with Archives." *Comparative Studies of South Asia, Africa and Middle East* 38, no. 1 (2018): 3–5.

Abu-Lughod, Lila. "Imagining Palestine's Alter-Natives: Settler Colonialism and Museum Politics." *Critical Inquiry* 47 (Autumn 2020): 1–26.

Acharya, Amitav, and Tan See Seng, eds. *Bandung Revisited: The Legacy of the 1955 Asian-African Conference for International Order.* Singapore: NUS Press, 2008.

ACLU. "Banking on Bondage: Private Prisons and Mass Incarceration." November 2, 2011. Accessed May 15, 2021. https://www.aclu.org/banking-bondage-private-prisons-and-mass-incarceration.

Adorno, Theodor W. *Negative Dialectics*, translated by E.B. Ashton. London: Routledge, 1973.

Agamben, Giorgio. *Gusto.* Macerata: Quodlibert, 2017.

Agee, James. *Let Us Now Praise Famous Men* [1939]. Boston: Houghton Mifflin, 2001.

Ahmed, Sara. *Strange Encounters: Embodied Others in Post-Coloniality*. London: Routledge, 2000.

Ahmed, Sara. *The Cultural Politics of Emotion*. New York: Routledge, 2006.

Aissaoui, Mohammed. "Houellebecq et *Plateforme:* 'La region la plus con, c'est quand même l'islam'." *Le Figaro*. December 10, 2014, https://www.lefigaro.fr/livres/2014/12/30/03005-20141230ARTF IG00159-houellebecq-et-plateforme-la-religion-la-plus-con-c-est-quand-meme-l-islam.php.

Ako, Edward O. "*L'Etudiant noir* and the Myth of the Genesis of the Négritude Movement." *Research in African Literatures* 15, no. 3 (Fall 1984): 341–354.

Alexander, Michele. *The New Jim Crow: Mass Incarceration in the Age of Colorblindness*. New York: The New Press, 2009.

Al-Haq: Defending Human Rights. "Special Focus: Sharp High Rate of Property Demolitions since the second half of 2020." January 2020. Accessed February 16, 2021. https://www.alhaq.org/advocacy/17468.html.

Alhelou, Yousef. "Palestinian Archives: A Reflection of a Rich History." *Middle East Monitor*. February 7, 2019. https://www.middleeastmonitor.com/20190207-palestinian-archives-a-relfection-of-a-rich-history.

Allen, Danielle. *The World of Prometheus: The Politics of Punishing in Democratic Athens*. Princeton: Princeton University Press, 2000.

Allison, H.E. *Kant's Theory of Taste: A Reading of the Critique of Aesthetic Judgment*. New York: Cambridge University Press, 2001.

Alloula, Malek. *The Colonial Harem*. London: University of Minnesota Press, 1986.

Althusser, Louis, Étienne Balibar, Roger Establet, Pierre Macherey, and Jacques Rancière. *Reading Capital: The Complete Edition*, translated by Ben Brewster and David Fernbach. London: Verso, 2016.

Althusser, Louis. *For Marx*. New York: Verso, 1965.

Alvaredo, Facundo, Denis Cogneau, and Thomas Piketty. "Income Inequality under Colonial Rule: Evidence from French Algeria, Cameroon, Indochina and Tunisia, 1920–1960." *World Inequality Database* (2018). http://wid.world/wp-content/uploads/2017/12/118-Alvaredo-Cogneau-Piketty.pdf.

Anderson, Benedict. *The Spectre of Comparisons*. New York: Verso, 1998.
Anderson, Clare, ed. *A Global History of Convicts and Penal Colonies*. London: Bloomsbury, 2018.
Andrews, Mark. "For Decades, Turpentine Industry sapped Florida Forest, Workers." *The Orlando Sentinel*, August 20, 1993. https://www.orlandosentinel.com/news/os-xpm-1993-08-29-9308270659-story.html.
Appadurai, Arjun. "Topographies of the Self." In *Language and the Politics of Emotion*, edited by Catherine Lutz and Lila Abu-Lughod, 92–112. New York: Cambridge University Press, 1990.
Arendt, Hannah. "Truth and Politics." *The New Yorker*, February 25, 1967.
Arendt, Hannah. *The Crisis of the Republic*. New York: Harcourt, 1979.
Al-Saji, Alia. "The Past." Lecture, Political Concepts Annual Conference, The New School for Social Research, New York City, NY. April 18, 2014.
Althabe, Gérard. *Production de l'étranger, xénophobie et couches populaires* [1985]. Paris: Sorbonne, 2017.
Apter, Emily. "Afterword: Towards a Theory of Reparative Translation." *Cultural Inquiry* 19 (2020): 209–228.
Anzieu, Didier. *Le Moi-Peau*. Paris: Editions Dunod, 1985.
Arab Culture Fund. "Revisiting Archive in the Aftermath of Revolution." October 18, 2018. Accessed February 17, 2021. https://www.arabculturefund.org/Projects/6577.
Archibong, Belinda, and Nonso Obikili. "Prison Labor: The Price of Prisons and the Lasting Effects of Incarceration." *Journal of African Economic History Working Paper Series* no. 52 (2020). https://papers.ssrn.com/sol3/papers.cfm?abstract_id=3635484.
Atlanta Rail Corridor Archive. "Convict Labor at Bellwood Quarry." Accessed January 23, 2017. http://atlrailcorridorarchive.org/exhibits/show/bellwood-quarry/convict-labor-at-bellwood-quar.
Austen, Ian. "Trudeau Apologizes for Abuse and 'Profound Cultural Loss' at Indigenous Schools." *The New York Times*, November 14, 2017. https://www.nytimes.com/2017/11/24/world/canada/trudeau-indigenous-schools-newfoundland-labrador.html.
Austin, John L. "A Plea for Excuses: The Presidential Address." *Proceedings of the Aristotelian Society* 57 (1956–1957): 1–30.

Azoulay, Ariella. "What is a photograph? What is photography?" *Philosophy of Photography* 1, no.1 (2010): 9–13.

Azoulay, Ariella. "Archive." *Political Concepts* 1, no. 1 (2011). http://www.politicalconcepts.org/archive-ariella-azoulay/.

Ba, Diadie. "Africans Still Seething over Sarkozy Speech." *Reuters*, September 7, 2007. https://uk.reuters.com/article/uk-africa-sarkozy/africans-still-seething-over-sarkozy-speech-idUKL0513034620070905.

Bachelard, Gaston. *La philosophie du non*. Paris: Presses Universitaires de France, 1940.

Backstrom, Per, and Benedikt Hjartarson, eds. *Decentering the Avant-Garde*. Amsterdam: Rodolpi, 2014.

Baldwin, James. *The Evidence of Things Not Seen*. New York: Henry Holt and Company, 1985.

Balibar, Étienne. "Suffrage Universel!" *Le Monde*, May 4, 1983. https://www.lemonde.fr/archives/article/1983/05/04/suffrage-universel_2833939_1819218.html.

Balibar, Étienne. "Racism as Universalism." *New Political Science* 8, no. 1–2 (1989): 9–22.

Balibar, Étienne. "Fichte et la frontière intérieure: A propos des *Discours à la nation allemande*." *Cahiers de Fontenay* 58/59 (June 1990).

Balibar, Étienne. *Les frontières de la démocratie*. La Découverte: Paris, 1992.

Balibar, Étienne. *Masses, Classes, Ideas: Studies on Politics and Philosophy Before and After Marx*, translated by James Swenson. London: Routledge, 1994.

Balibar, Étienne. "The Infinite Contradiction," translated by Jean-Marc Poisson and Jacques Lezra. *Yale French Studies* 88 (1995): 142–164.

Balibar, Étienne. "Émancipation, transformation, civilité." *Les temps modernes* 587 (May 1996): 409–449.

Balibar, Étienne. *La crainte des masses: Politique et philosophie avant et après Marx*. Paris: Galilée, 1997.

Balibar, Étienne. *Politics and the Other Scene*, translated by Christine Jones, James Swenson, and Chris Turner. New York: Verso, 2002.

Balibar, Étienne. "World Borders, Political Borders," translated by Erin M. Williams. *PMLA* 117, no. 1 (January 2002): 71–78.

Balibar, Étienne. "Election/Selection." Keynote, *tRACEs*, University of California, Irvine. April 10-11, 2003. https://vimeo.com/album/1631670/video/25691025.

Balibar, Étienne. *We the People of Europe: Reflections on Transnational Citizenship*, translated by James Swenson. Princeton: Princeton University Press, 2003.

Balibar, Étienne. "Strangers as Enemies: Further Reflections on the Aporias of Transnational Citizenship." Lecture, The Institute on Globalization and the Human Condition, McMaster University Hamilton, May 2006. https://globalization.mcmaster.ca/research/publications/working-papers/2006/ighc-wps_06-4_balibar.pdf.

Balibar, Étienne. "Europe as Borderland." *Economic Planning and Social Space* 27, no. 2 (2009): 190-215.

Balibar, Étienne. "Civic Universalism and Its Internal Exclusions: The Issue of Anthropological Difference." *boundary 2* 39, no. 1 (2012): 207-229.

Balibar, Étienne. "At the Borders of Europe: From Cosmpolitanism to Cosmpolitics." *Translation* 4 (Spring 2014): 83-103.

Balibar, Étienne. "Can We Say: After the Subject Comes the Stranger?" November 2014 Columbia Maison Française. Posted November 20, 2014. YouTube video. https://www.youtube.com/watch?v=ACaXH-WW6Fo.

Balibar, Étienne. *Violence and Civility: On the Limits of Political Philosophy*. New York: Columbia University Press, 2015.

Bandes, Susan A. "Remorse, Demeanor, and the Consequences of Misinterpretation: The Limits of Law as a Window into the Soul." *Journal of Law, Religion and State* 3 (2014): 170-199.

Bandes, Susan A. "Remorse and Demeanor in the Courtroom: Cognitive Science and the Evaluation of Contrition." In *The Integrity of Criminal Process: From Theory to Practice*, edited by Jill Hunter, Paul Roberts, Simon N. M. Young, David Dixon, 309-326. Portland: Hart Publishing, 2016.

Barker, Vanessa. "Book Review *Prisons of Poverty*, Wacquant, L.," *The Howard Journal of Criminal Justice* 50, no. 5 (December 2011): 1-5. https://doi.org/10.1111/j.1468-2311.2011.0695_2.x.

Barthes, Roland. *The "Scandal of Marxism": and Other Writings on Politics, Essays and Interviews, Vol 2*. Calcutta: Seagull Books, 2015.

Bartov, Omar, and Edward Weitz, eds. *Shatterzones of Empire: Co-existence and Violence in Eastern European's Borderlands*. Bloomington: Indiana University Press, 2013.
BBC. "Réunion Island and the 'Stolen Children' of France." *BBC World News*, January 30, 2018. https://www.bbc.com/news/av/world-42879241/reunion-island-and-the-stolen-children-of-france.
Beard, Mary. "Democracy According to the Greeks." Produced by The New Statesman. *New Statesman*, October 14, 2010. Audio. https://www.newstatesman.com/ideas/2010/10/athenian-democracy-athens.
Behdad, Ali. *Belated Travelers: Orientalism in the Age of Colonial Dissolution*. Durham: Duke University Press, 1994.
Bengson, John, and Marc A. Moffett, eds. *Knowing How: Essays on Knowledge, Mind and Action*. New York: Oxford University Press, 2011.
Benjamin, Walter. "Theses on the Philosophy of History." In *Illuminations*, edited by Hannah Arendt, 253-264. New York: Schocken, 1976.
Bernstein, Richard. *Beyond Objectivism and Relativism: Science, Hermeneutics and Praxis*. Philadelphia: University of Pennsylvania Press, 1983.
Brewes, Timothy. *The Event of Postcolonial Shame*. Princeton: Princeton University Press, 2011.
Bijl, Paul. "Colonial Memory and Forgetting in the Netherlands and Indonesia." *Journal of Genocide Research* 14, no. 3–4 (2012): 441–461.
Bilgrami, Akeel. "Identity." *Political Concepts* 1 (2011). http://www.politicalconcepts.org/identity-akeel-bilgrami.
Birzeit University. "Book Launch Marks Seven-year Palestinian Archive Project." *Birzeit News*, March 14, 2017. https://www.birzeit.edu/en/news/book-launch-marks-seven-year-palestinian-archive-project.
Birzeit Museum. "Home." Accessed February 10, 2021. http://www.museum.birzeit.edu/.
Blanchard, Pascal, and Nicolas Bancel, eds., *Sexe, race et colonies*. Paris: La Découverte, 2018.

Blackmon, Douglas. *Slavery by Another Name: The Re-Enslavement of Black Americans from the Civil War to World War II*. New York: Anchor Books, 2010.
Boltanski, Luc. *Distant Suffering: Morality, Media and Politics*. New York: Cambridge University Press, 1999.
Boom, Joeri. "Nieuw bewijs van massa-executie in Indonesie, *Archiefmap 1304*." *De Groene Amsterdammer*, October 10, 2008, nr. 41.
Bourdieu, Pierre. *La distinction: critique social du jugement*. Paris: Minuit, 1979.
Bourdieu, Pierre. *Distinction: A Social Critique of the Judgement of Taste*. Cambridge: Harvard University Press, 1984.
Bourdieu, Pierre. *Esquisse pour une auto-analyse*. Paris: Raison d'agir, 2004.
Bouteldja, Houria. *Les Blancs, les Juifs et nous*. Paris: Découverte, 2019.
Breton, André. "Un grand poète noir." In *Cahier d'un retour au pays natal*. Paris: Arthème Fayard, 1947.
Breton, André. "A Great Black Poet." In *Notebook of a Return to the Native Land*, edited and translated by Clayton Eshleman and Annette Smith, ix-xix. Middletown: Wesleyan University Press, 2000.
Brody, Richard. "The Uses of 'Mythologies'." *The New Yorker*, April 19, 2012. https://www.newyorkers/com/culture/olumbi-brody/the-uses-of-mythologies.
Brothman, Brian. "Orders of Value: Probing the Theoretical Terms of Archival Practice." *Archivaria* 32, no. 32 (1991): 78–100.
Brown, Wendy. *In the Ruins of Neoliberalism: The Rise of Antidemocratic Politics in the West*. New York: Columbia University Press, 2019.
Bsheer, Rosie. *Archive Wars: The Politics of History in Saudi Arabia*. Stanford: Stanford University Press, 2020.
Buck-Morss, Susan. *Dreamworld and Catastrophe: The Passing of Mass Utopia in East and West*. Cambridge: MIT Press, 2000.
Bulson, Erick. *Little Magazine, World Form*. New York: Columbia University Press, 2019.
Busbridge, Rachel. "Israel–Palestine and the Settler Colonial 'Turn': From Interpretation to Decolonization." *Theory, Culture & Society* 35, no. 1 (2018): 91–115.
Butler, Judith. *Senses of the Subject*. New York: Fordham, 2015.

Byrd, Jodi A. *The Transit of Empire: Indigenous Critiques of Colonialism*. Minneapolis: University of Minnesota Press, 2011.
Campbell, Duncan, and Richard Norton-Taylor. "US Accused of Holding Terror Suspects on Prison Ships." *The Guardian*, June 1, 2008. https://www.theguardian.com/world/2008/jun/02/usa.humanrights.
Carruthers, Mary. *The Craft of Thought: Meditation, Rhetoric, and the Making of Images, 400–1200*. New York: Cambridge University Press, 1998.
Cassin, Barbara. *Vocabulaire européen des philosophies: Dictionnaire des intraduisibles*. Paris: Seuil, 2004.
Cassin, Barbara, ed. *Dictionary of Untranslatibles: A Philosophical Lexicon*. Princeton: Princeton University Press, 2014.
Caswell, Michelle. *Archiving the Unspeakable: Silence, Memory, and the Photographic Record in Cambodia*. Madison: University of Wisconsin Press, 2014.
Cecelski, David. "The Turpentine Trail." January 11, 2021. https://davidcecelski.com/2019/07/29/the-turpentine-trail/.
De Certeau, Michel "The Historiographical Operation." In *The Writing of History*, translated by Tom Conley, 56–110. New York: Columbia University Press, 1992.
Césaire, Aimé. *Discourse on Colonialism* [1955], translated by Joan Pinkham. New York: Monthly Review Press, 2000.
Césaire, Aimé. *Negre je suis, negre je resterai*. Paris: Albin Michel, 2005.
Césaire, Aimé. *Non a l'humiliation*. Arles: Actes du Sud, 2014.
Césaire, Aimé. *Aimé Césaire: Ecrits politiques, 1935–1956*. Paris: Jean Michel, 2016.
Césaire, Aimé. *Resolutely Black: Conversations with Françoise Vergès*. New York: Polity, 2020.
Césaire, Suzanne. *The Great Camouflage: Writings of Dissent (1941–1945)*, edited by Daniel Maximin and translated by Keith Walker. Middleton: Wesleyan University Press, 2012.
De Cesari, Chiara. "Creative Heritage: Palestinian Heritage NGOS and Defiant Arts of Government." *American Anthropology* 112, no. 4 (2010): 625–637.
De Cesari, Chiara. "The Paradoxes of Colonial Reparation: Foreclosing Memory and the 2008 Italy–Libya Friendship Treaty." *Memory Studies* 5, no. 3 (2012): 316–326.

De Cesari, Chiara. "Anticipatory Representation." In *Reimagining the State*, edited by Davina Cooper, Nikita Dhawan, and Janet Newman, 153–170. London: Routledge, 2019.
Chakrabarty, Dipesh. "The Climate of History: Four Theses." *Critical Inquiry* 35 (2009): 197–222.
Chakrabarty, Dipesh. "Postcolonial Studies and the Challenge of Climate Change." *New Literary History* 43, no. 1 (2012): 1–18.
Chakrabarty, Dipesh. "Planetary Crises and the Difficulty of Being Modern." *Millenium: Journal of International Studies* 46, no. 3 (2018): 259–82.
Chamayou, Gregoire. *Les chasses de l'homme: histoire et philosophie du pouvoir cynegetique*. Paris: La fabrique, 2010.
Chapman, Herrick, and Laura Fader, eds. *Race in France: Interdisciplinary Perspective on the Politics of Difference*. New York: Bergahn, 2004.
Chaudhuri, Amit. "The Real Meaning of 'Rhodes Must Fall'." *The Guardian*, March 16, 2016. https://www.theguardian.com/uk-news/2016/mar/16/the-real-meaning-of-rhodes-must-fall.
Childers, Kristen Tromberg. "Aimé Césaire's *Notebook of a Return to the Native Land*." 2016. *Fiction and Film for Scholars of France*. https://h-france.net/fffh/tag/cesaire-aime/.
City University of New York. "Christian Palestinian Archive: A Project by Dor Guez." Accessed May 20, 2020, https://www.gc.cuny.edu/About-the-GC/Building-Venues-Particulars/James-Gallery/Exhibitions/Detail?id=35554.
Clark-Taoua, Phyllis. "In Search of New Skin: Michel Leiris's *L'afrique fantôme*." *Cahiers d'études africaines* 167 (2002): 479–498.
Clark-Taoua, Phyllis. *Forms of Protest: Anti-Colonialism and Avant-Gardes in Africa, the Caribbean, and France*. Portsmouth: Heinman, 2002.
Clifford, James. *The Predicament of Culture: Twentieth-Century Ethnography, Literature, and Art*. Cambridge: Harvard University Press, 1988.
Cole, Lori. "*Légitime défense*: From communism and Surrealism to Caribbean Self-Definition." *Journal of Surrealism and the Americas* 4, no. 1 (2010): 15–30.
Collier, Stephen, and Andrew Lakoff. "Regimes of living." In *Global Assemblages: Technology, Politics, and Ethics as Anthropological*

Problems, edited by Stephen Collier and Aihwa Ong, 22-39. Hoboken: Wiley, 2005.

Cooper, Frederick, and Ann Laura Stoler. *Tensions of Empire: Colonial Culture in a Bourgeois World*. Berkeley: University of California Press, 1997.

Coulthard, Glen Sean. *Red Skin, White Masks: Rejecting the Colonial Politics of Recognition*. Minneapolis: University of Minnesota, 2014.

Crawford, Donald W. *Kant's Aesthetic Theory*, Madison: University of Wisconsin Press, 1974.

Culver, Anniker. *Glorify the Empire: Japanese Avant-Garde Propaganda in Manchuko*. Vancouver: University of British Columbia Press, 2013.

Dar Yusuf Nasri Jacir for Art and Research. "About Us." Accessed May 21, 2020. https://darjacir.com/About-Us.

Dargis, Manohla. "The Journey from Shackles to Prison Bars." *The New York Times*, September 30, 2016. https://www.nytimes.com/2016/09/30/movies/13th-review-ava-duvernay.html.

Dark, Gulash. "Family Album Project at Palestinian Museum Strengthens National Identity Across Country." *Daily Sabah*, June 8, 2015. https://www.dailysabah.com/arts-culture/2015/06/08/family-album.

Davidson, Arnold, "In praise of counter-conduct," *History of the Human Sciences* 24, no.4, 2011, 25-41.

Davis, Angela. "The Prison Industrial Complex." In *Are Prisons Obsolete?* 84-104. New York: Seven Stories Press, 2003.

Decolonizing Architecture Art Research. "Home." 2021. Accessed February 5, 2021. http://www.decolonizing.ps/site/.

Decolonize this Place. "Contact." 2019. Accessed February 3, 2021. https://decolonizethisplace.org/contact.

Deleuze, Gilles, and Felix Guattari. *What is Philosophy?* New York: Columbia University Press, 1994.

Deliss, Clementine. "On the Necropolitics of Sequestered Colonial Collections." Lecture, The New School for Social Research, New York City. November 28, 2018.

Del Real, Jose A. "Cherokee Nation Seeks to Send First Delegate to Congress." *The New York Times*, August 27, 2019. https://www.

nytimes.com/2019/08/27/us/olumbia-nation-delegate-congress.html.

Demetriadi, Alexi. "Lost in Exile: The Forgotten Chagos Islanders." *New Internationalist*, June 22, 2017. https://newint.org/features/web-exclusive/2017/06/22/lost-in-exile-chagos-islanders-of-west-sussex.

Design Applause. "2019 Chicago Architecture Biennial Week #3 Calendar." *Design Applause*, October 5, 2019. https://designapplause/com/architecture2019-chicago.

De Vito, Christian G., and Alex Lichtenstein. *Global Convict Labor*. London: Brill, 2015.

De Vito, Christian G., and Clare Anderson. *Transportation, Deportation and Exile: Perspectives from the Colonies in the Nineteenth and Twentieth Centuries*. Cambridge: Cambridge University Press, 2019.

Donadio, Rachel. "The Dark Consequences of Poland's Holocaust Law." *The Atlantic*, February 8, 2018. https://www.theatlantic.com/international/archive/2018/02/olumb-holocaust-law/552842/.

Dorlin, Elsa. "Démocratie suicidaire." *Esprit* (December 2018). https://esprit.presse.fr/article/elsa-dorlin/democratie-suicidaire-41832.

Doumani, Beshara, and Mayssun Soukarieh. "A Tribute Long Overdue: Rosemary Sayigh and Palestinian Studies." *Journal of Palestine Studies* 38, no. 4 (Summer 2009): 6–11.

Du Bois, W.E.B. *The Souls of Black Folk* [1903], edited by Brent Hayes Edwards. Oxford: Oxford University Press, 2007.

Duncan, Martha Grace. "So Young and So Untender: Remorseless Children and the Expectations of the Law." *Columbia Law Review* 102 (2002): 1469.

Duras, Marguerite. *Un barrage contre le Pacifique*. Paris: Gallimard, 1986.

Dussel, Enrique. *The Underside of Modernity: Apel, Ricoeur, Rorty, Taylor, & the Philosophy of Liberation*. London: Humanities Press, 1998.

DuVernay, Ava, dir. *13th*. 2016; Los Gatos, CA: Netflix Productions.

Ebert, Roger. "*13th.*." rogerebert.com, September 13, 2016. Accessed February 2, 2021. https://www.rogerebert.com/reviews/13th-2016.

Edens, John F, Shannon E. Kelley, Scott O., Lilienfield, Jennifer L. Skeem, and Kevin S. Douglas. "DSM-5 Antisocial Personality Disorder: Predictive Validity in a Prison Sample." *Law and Human Behavior* 39, no. 2 (April 2015): 123–129.

English, Burton, and Daniel de la Torre Ugarte. "A Decade Later: Corn Ethanol's Broken Promises." *The Hill*, October 22, 2015. http://thehill.com/blogs/congress-blog/energy-environment/257635.

Erasmus University Rotterdam. "When Breathing is Political." 2020. Accessed May 13, 2021. https://www.eur.nl/en/news/when-breathing-political.

Eslava, Luis, Michael Fakhri, and Vasuki Nesiah. "The Spirit of Bandung." In *Bandung, Global History, and International Law: Critical Pasts and Pending Futures*, edited by Luis Eslava, Michael Fakhri, and Vasuki Nesiah, 3–32. New York: Cambridge University Press, 2017.

Esposito, Roberto. *Immunitas: The Protection and Negation of Life*. London: Polity, 2011.

Eversley, Melanie. "Running While Black: Ahmaud Arbery's Killing Reveals Runners' Shared Fears of Profiling." *The Undefeated*, May 8, 2020. https://theundefeated.com/features/running-while-black-ahmaud-arberys-killing-reveals-runners-shared-fears-of-profiling/.

Fabian, Johannes. "Forgetful Remembering: A Colonial Life in the Congo." *Africa: Journal of the International African Institute* 73, no. 4 (2003): 489–504.

Facuhereau, Serge. *Avant-Gardes du Xxe siècle: Arts & Littérature 1905–1930*. Paris: Flammarion, 2010.

Fanon, Frantz. *Les damnés de la terre*. Paris: Maspero, 1961.

Fanon, Frantz. *Black Skin, White Masks*. London: Pluto Press, 1986.

Fantl, Jeremy. "Knowledge How." *The Stanford Encyclopedia of Philosophy* (Spring 2021 Edition), edited by Edward N. Zalta. https://plato.stanford.edu/archives/spr2021/entries/knowledge-how/.

Farge, Arlette. *Le Gout de l'archive* [1989]. Paris: POINTS, 1997.

Farley, Anthony. "The Poetics of Colorlined Space." In *Crossroads, Directions, and A New Critical Race Theory*, edited by Francisco

Valdes, Jerome Culp, and Angela Harris, 97–158. Philadelphia: Temple University Press, 2002.

Farmer-Kaiser, Mary. "'Are they not in some sort vagrants?' Gender and the Efforts of the Freedmen's Bureau to Combat Vagrancy in the Reconstruction South." *The Georgia Historical Quarterly* 88, no.1 (Spring 2004): 25–49.

Farzin, Media. "Jumana Manna; The Violence of Beautiful Things." *Frieze* 197 (August 2018). https://www.frieze.com/article/olumb-manna-violence-beautiful-things.

Fassin, Didier, and Eric Fassin, eds. *De la question sociale à la question raciale*. Paris: La Découverte, 2006.

Fassin, Didier, ed. *Deepening Divides: How Physical Borders and Social Boundaries Delineate Our World*. London: Pluto Press, 2019.

Fassin, Eric. *Démocratie précaire*. Paris: La Découverte, 2012.

Fassin, Eric. "Xenophobia from Above and Precarious Democracy." Lecture Course, Visual Culture Research Center, Kyiv. June 1–2, 2012. http://vcrc.org.ua/en/eric-fassin-xenophobia/.

Fassin, Eric, Carine Fouteau, Serge Guichard, and Aurelie Windels. *Roms & riverains: une politique olumbia de la race*. Paris: La fabrique, 2014.

Feldman, Leah. "Global Souths: Toward a Materialist Poetics of Alignment." *Boundary 2*, 47, no. 2 (2020): 199–225.

Fejzula, Merve. "Women and the 1956 Congress of Black Writers and Artists in Paris." *Black Perspectives (AAIHS)*, November 3, 2016 https://www.aaihs.org/women-and-the-1956-congress-of-black-writers-and-artists-in-paris/.

Fenn, Elizabeth A. "Biological Warfare in Eighteenth-Century North America: Beyond Jeffery Amherst." *The Journal of American History* 86, no. 4 (March 2000): 1552–1580.

Ferguson, Bruce. "Preface." In *Otherwise Occupied*, Venice Biennale 2013, edited by Ryan Bishop and Gordon Han. Jerusalem: Palestinian Art Court—al Hoash, 2013.

Fernando, Mayanthi L. *The Republic Unsettled: Muslim French and the Contradictions of Secularism*. Durham: Duke University Press, 2014.

Ferraris, Maurizio. *Documentality: Why It Is Necessary to Leave Traces*, translated by Richard Davies. New York: Fordham University Press, 2013.

Fichte, Johann Gottlieb. *Addresses to the German Nation*, translated by R.F. Jones and G.H. Turnbull. Chicago: The Open Court Publishing Company, 1922.

Fichte, Johann Gottlieb. *Addresses to the German Nation*, translated by Isaac Nakhimovsky, Bela Kapossy, and Keith Tribe. Cambridge: Hackett Publishing, 2013.

Fields, Barbara, and Karen Fields. *Racecraft: The Soul of Inequality in American Life*. New York: Verso, 2012.

Foner, Eric. "We Are Not Done with Abolition." *New York Times*, December 18, 2020. https://www.nytimes.como/2020/12/15/opinion/abolition-prison-labor-amendement.html.

Ford, Derek R. "Air and the Politics of Resistance." *The Aggregate Website* 2 (March 2015). http://www.we-aggregate.org/piece/air-and-the-politics-of-resistance.

Forth, Aidan. *Barbed-Wire Imperialism: Britain's Empire of Camps. 1876–1903*. Berkeley: University of California Press, 2017.

Foucault, Michel. *Archaeology of Knowledge*. New York: Pantheon, 1972.

Foucault, Michel. *Il faut défendre la société: Collége de France lectures*. Paris: Gallimard, 1976.

Foucault, Michel. *The History of Sexuality, Vol 1*. New York: Vintage Books, 1976.

Foucault, Michel "Les rapports de pouvoir passent à l'intérieur des corps, entretien avec L Finas, *La Quinzaine littér*aire, no. 247, (January 1977) in Michel Foucault, *Dits Ecrits*, vol 3, (under the direction of Daniel Defert and François Ewald) pp. 228-236.

Foucault, Michel, Collège de France lectures, 1 March 1978 (Paris: Gallimard, 2004), p. 205

Foucault, Michel. "About the Concept of the 'The Dangerous Individual,' in 19th-century Legal Psychiatry." *International Journal of Law and Psychiatry* 1 (1978): 1–16.

Foucault, Michel. "Nietzsche, Genealogy, History." In *The Foucault Reader*, edited by Paul Rabinow, 76–100. New York: Pantheon, 1984.

Foucault, Michel. *The History of Sexuality, Vol I: An Introduction*, translated by Robert Hurley. New York: Vintage Books, 1990.

Foucault, Michel. "Questions of Method." In *The Foucault Effect: Studies in Governmentality*, edited by Graham Burchnell, Colin Gordon, and Peter Miller, 73–86. London: Harvester, 1991.

Foucault, Michel. *The Essential Foucault: Selections from the Essential Works of Foucault, 1954–1984*, edited by Paul Rabinow and Nikolas Rose. New York: The New Press, 2003.

Foucault, Michel, *Securité, territoire, populations, Leçon du 1 mars 1978, Cours au Collège de France 1977-1978* (Paris: Gallimard, 2004), 197- 219.

Foucault, Michel. *The Government of the Self and Others: Lectures at the Collège de France 1982–1983*, translated by Graham Burchell and edited by Frédéric Gros. New York: Picador, 2010.

Foucault, Michel. *Wrong-Doing and Truth-Telling: The Function of Avowal in Justice*, edited by Fabienne Brion and Bernard E. Harcourt. Chicago: University of Chicago Press, 2014.

Foucault, Michel. *Discourse and Truth and Parresia*, edited by Henri-Paul Fruchaud and Daniele Lorenzini. Chicago: Chicago University Press, 2019.

Foulcher, Keith. "A Survey of Events Surrounding Manikebu: The Struggle for Cultural and Intellectual Freedom in Indonesian Literature." *Bijdragen tot de Taal-. Land-en Vokenkunde* 125, no. 4 (1969): 429–465.

Foulcher, Keith. *Pujangga Baru: Literature and Nationalism in Indonesia, 1933–1942*. Adelaide: Flinders University, 1980.

Foulcher, Keith. "Culture and Colonialism in the Essays of Armijn Pane, 1933–1953." In *Lasting Fascinations: Essays on Indonesia and the Southwest Pacific to Honour Bob Hering*, edited by Harry Poeze and Antoinette Liem, 131–152. Stein: Yayasan Kabar Sebarang, Yayasan Soekarno, 1998.

Freeman, Andrea. "Life, Death and Politics in Hawaii: 125 Years of Colonial Rule." *The Conversation*, January17, 2018. https://thec onversation.com/life-death-and-politics-in-hawaii-125-years-of-colonial-rule 90273.

Gadamer, Hans-Georg. *Truth and Method* [1960]. New York: Continuum, 1999.

Geertz, Clifford. "Common Sense as a Cultural System." *Local Knowledge* 33, no. 1 (1975): 73–93.

Geertz, Clifford. *Local Knowledge*. New York: Basic Books, 1983.

Gentleman, Amelia. "Windrush Scandal: No Passport for Thousands Who Moved to Britain." *The Guardian*, May 4, 2018. https://www.theguardian.com/uk-news/2018/may/04/windrush-scandal-no-passport-for-thousands-who-moved-to-britain.

Gestenfeld, Manfred. "How the Netherlands Hid Its War Crimes for Decades." *Besa Center*, August 31, 2020. https://besacenter.org/perspectives/olumbias-war-crimes.

Gigerenzer, Gerd. *Gut Feelings: The Intelligence of the Unconscious.* New York: Viking Press, 2007.

Gikandi, Simon. *Slavery and the Culture of Taste.* Princeton: Princeton University Press, 2011.

Gilman, Sandra. *The Jew's Body.* New York: Routledge, 1991.

Gilmore, Ruth Wilson. *Golden Gulag: Prisons, Surplus, Crisis, and Opposition in Globalizing California.* Oakland: University of California Press, 2007.

Glissant, Eduardo. *Traite du Tout-monde.* Paris: Gallimard, 1997.

Glissant, Eduardo. *La Cohée du Lamentin.* Paris: Gallimard, 2005.

Global Tel. "Calling out Companies that Use Prison Labor." October 25, 2019. Accessed May 13, 2021. https://blog.globaltel.com/companies-use-prison-labor/.

Godoy, Julio. "FRANCE: Recasting Colonialism as a Good Thing." *Inter Press Service*, July 5, 2005. http://www.ipsnews.net/2005/07/olumb-recasting-colonialism-as-a-good-thing/.

Goebel, Michael. *Anti-Imperial Metropolis: Interwar Paris and the Seeds of Third World Nationalism.* New York: Cambridge University Press, 2015.

Goluboff, Risa L. "The Thirteenth Amendment and the Lost Origins of Civil Rights." *Duke Law Review* 50 (2001): 1609–1685.

Gómez, Edward M. "Shaking Up the Ethnographic Museum." *Hyperallergic*, July 18, 2020. https://hyperallergic.com/577138/shaking-up-the-ethnographic-museum/.

Goodfellow, Maya. "The British Government's Racist Heart." *The New York Times*, May 3, 2018, A23.

Goodwin, Michelle. "The Thirteenth Amendment: Modern Slavery, Capitalism, and Mass Incarceration." *Cornell Law Review* 104 (2019): 899–992.

Google. "Remorseless." Google Dictionary. Accessed 12 May 2021. https://www.google.com/search?q=google+dictionary&rlz=1C5CHFA_enUS840US840&oq=google+dictionary&aqs=chrome..69i57j0i512l3j0i131i433i512j0i512l5.2244j0j4&sourceid=chrome&ie=UTF-8#dobs=remorseless.

Google. "English Translation of 'Oubli'." Google Translate. Accessed May 15, 2021. https://www.google.com/search?client=safari&rls=en&q=oubli+olumbi&ie=UTF-8&oe=UTF-8.

Gordon, Lewis. "Of Illicit Appearance: The L.A. Riots/Rebellion as a Portent of Things to Come." *TruthOut*, May 12, 2012. http://truthout.orgr/articles/of-illicit-appearance.

Gottschalk, Marie. "City On a Hill, City Behind Bars: Criminal Justice, Social Justice, and American Exceptionalism." *Nanzan Review of American Studies* 31 (2009): 33–58.

Gottschalk, Marie. "Razing the Carceral State." *Social Justice* 42, no. 2 (2015): 31–51.

Gourgouris, Stathis. *Nothing Sacred* (forthcoming).

Government of Australia. "Apology to Australia's Indigenous Peoples." 2008. Accessed February 13, 2020. https://www.australia.gov.au/about-australia/our-country/our-people/apology-to-australias-indigenous-peoples.

Green, André. *La folie privée: Psychanalyse des cas-limites*. Paris: Gallimard, 1990.

Green, André. *On Private Madness*. Abingdon: Taylor and Francis, 2018.

Grey Art Gallery NYU. "Baya: Woman of Algiers." 2017. Accessed June 15, 2021. https://greyartgallery.nyu.edu/exhibition/baya-woman-algiers.

Grossman, Evelyne. *Eloge de l'Hypersensible*. Paris: Les Editions de Minuit, 2012.

Hage, Ghassan. "*État de siège*: A Dying Domesticating Colonialism?" *American Ethnologist* 43, no. 1 (2016): 38–49.

Haley, Sara. *No Mercy Here: Gender, Punishment, and the Making of Jim Crow Modernity*. Chapel Hill: University of North Carolina Press, 2016.

Halim, Hala. "Lotus, the Afro-Asian Nexus, and Global South Comparatism." *Comparative Studies of South Asia, Africa and the Middle East* 32, no. 3 (2012): 563–583.

Halim, Hala. "Afro-Asian Third-Worldism into Global South: The Case of Lotus Journal." *Global South Studies*, November 22, 2017. https://globalsouthstudies.as.virginia.edu/key-moments/afro-asian-third-worldism-global-south-case-lotus-journal.

Hanan, M. Eve. "Remorse Bias." *University of Nevada, Las Vegas School of Law* 83, no. 1144 (2018): 302–56.

Harcourt, Bernard. "Aimé Césaire: Poetic Knowledge, Vitality, Négritude, and Revolution." *Columbia Law Blog*, December 22, 2016. http://blogs.law.columbia.edu/nietzsche1313/aime-cesaire-poetic.

Harcourt, Bernard. "Contre/Counter." In *Thinking with Balibar: A Lexicon of Conceptual Practice*, edited by Ann Laura Stoler, Statis Gourgouris, Jacques Lezra, 71-84. New York: Fordham, 2020).

Hardot, Pierre. *Philosophy As A Way of Life*. London: Blackwell, 1995.

Harrison, Olivia C., and Teresa Village-Ignacio, eds. *Souffles/ANFAS*. Palo Alto: Stanford University Press, 2016.

Hartman, Saidiya. *Wayward Lives, Beautiful Experiments: Intimate Histories of Riotous Black Girls, Troublesome Women, and Queer Radicals*. New York: Norton, 2019.

Hause der Kulturen der Welt. "The Whole Life: Archives and Reality." 2019. Accessed May 13, 2021. https://www.hkw.de/en/programm/projekte/2019/the_whole_life/das_ganze_leben.php.

Havel, Vaclav, and John Keane. *The Power of the Powerless: Citizens Against the State in Central Eastern Europe*. Armonk: M.E. Sharpe, 1985.

Heacock, Roger, and Caroline Mall-Dibasy. "Liberating the Phantom Elephant: The Digitization of Oral Archives." *Birzeit University Working Paper No. 2011/8* (2011). https://papers.ssrn.com/sol3/papers.cfm?abstract_id=1764253.

Henderson, Errol A. "The Lumpenproletariat as Vanguard?: The Black Panther Party, Social Transformation, and Pearson's Analysis of Huey Newton." *Journal of Black Studies* 28, no. 2 (1997): 171–199.

Henghold, Laura. "Between Bodies and Pleasures: A Territory without a Domain." *Foucault Studies* 15 (February 2013): 148–163.

Herzfeld, Michael. *Anthropology: Theoretical Practice in Culture and Society*. Oxford: Blackwell, 2001.

Hesse, Barnor. "White Sovereignty and Black Life Politics: The N* * **r They Couldn't Kill." *South Atlantic Quarterly* 116, no. 3 (2017): 581–604.

Hesse, Barnor. "White Sovereignty: The Law of Racial Rule." October 7, 2020, in *Building Sustainable Futures: Global Challenges and Possibilities*, produced by Northwestern Buffett Institute for

Global Affairs, podcast, MP3 audio. https://www.audible.com/pd/White-Sovereignty-The-Law-of-Racial-Rule-Podcast/B08KXMSRDM.

The Heyman Center for the Humanities. "Empire by Its Other Names." Conference. Columbia University, New York City, NY. April 5–6, 2019.

Hirschfeld, Lawrence. "Art in Cunaland: Ideology and Cultural Adaptation." *MAN* 12, no. 1 (1977): 104–123.

Hirschman, Albert. *The Passions and the Interests*. Princeton: Princeton University Press, 1977.

Hochberg, Gil. "Archival Afterlives in a Conflict Zone: Animating the Past in Jumana Manna's Cinematic Fables of Pre-1948 Palestine." *CSSAAME* 38, no. 1 (2018): 30–42.

Hochschild, Adam. *King Leopold's Ghost: A Story of Greed, Terror, and Heroism in Colonial Africa*. Boston: Houghton, Mifflin, Harcourt, 1999.

Honig, Bonnie. *Public Things: Democracy in Disrepair*. New York: Fordham University Press, 2017.

Howe, Scott. "Slavery as Punishment: Original Public Meaning, Cruel and Unusual Punishment and the Neglected Clause in the 13th Amendment." *Arizona Law Review* 51 (2009): 984–1034.

Hypotheses Editorial Board. "Out of the Archives . . . New Archival Practices: Toward Alternative Historiographies, Voices and Spaces." *Hypotheses*, December 14, 2018. https://trafo.hypotheses.org/15573.

Jadaliyya Reports. "The Palestinian Museum's Family Album Project: The Intimate Side of History in Palestine." *Jadaliyya*, May 13, 2015. https://www.jadailiyya.com/Details/32080.

James, Susan. *Passion and Action: The Emotions in Seventeenth-Century Philosophy*. Oxford: Clarendon Press, 1997.

Jedamski, Doris. "*Balai Pustaka*—a Colonial Wolf in Sheep's Clothing." *Archipel* 44 (1992): 23–46.

Jackson Jr., John. *Racial Paranoia: The Unintended Consequences of Political Correctness*. New York: Basic Civitas Books, 2008.

Joseph-Gabriel, Annette K. "Subverting Empire: Gendered Narratives of Anti-colonial Resistance in Francophone Literature and Politics, 1939–1960." PhD Diss., Vanderbilt University, 2015.

Joseph-Gabriel, Annette K. "Beyond the Great Camouflage: Haiti in Suzanne Césaire's Politics and Poetics of Liberation." *small axe* 20, no. 2 (July 2016): 1–13.

Joyeux-Prunel, Beatrice. *Les avant-gardes artistiques, 1918–1945.* Paris: Gallimard, 2017.

Joyeux-Prunel, Beatrice. "Provincializing Paris: The Center-Periphery Narratives of Modern Art in Light of Quantitative and Transnational Approaches." *Artl@s Bulletin*, 4, no. 1 (2015): 40–64.

Judy, R. A. *Sentient Flesh, Thinking in Disorder, Poesis in Black.* Durham: Duke University Press, 2020.

Kant, Immanuel. *Critique of Judgement* [1951], translated by J.H. Bernard. New York: Hafner Press, 1974.

Kazan, Helene. "Dossier\Decolonizing Archives and Law's Frame of Accountability." *Documentary World-Making* 4, no. 17 (2020). https://vols.worldrecordsjournal.org/04/17.

Keane, John. "Does Democracy Have a Violent Heart." In *War, Democracy and Culture in Classical Athens*, edited by David Pritchard, 378–408. Cambridge: Cambridge University Press, 2010.

Keating, Joshua E. "The Post-Colonial Hangover: Some Empires Really Were Worse Than Others." *Foreign Policy*, January 3, 2012. https://foreignpolicy.com/2012/01/03/the-post-colonial-hangover/.

Khazaaen. "Who Are We?" 2016. Accessed February 21, 2021. http://www.khazaaen.org/en/node/1113.

King, Shaun. "How the 13th Amendment Didn't Really Abolish Slavery, but Let It Live On in U.S. prisons." *New York Daily News*, 21 September 2016. https://www.nydailynews.com/news/national/king-13th-amendment-didn-abolish-slavery-article-1.2801218.

Knight, G. Roger. "Coolie or Worker? Crossing the Lines in Colonial Java, 1780–1942." *Itinerario*, April 22, 2010. https://www.cambridge.org/core/journals/itinerario/article/abs/coolie-or-worker-crossing-the-lines-in-colonial-java-178019421/A215A9AEB926742271D0BB1A07EBF0A1.

Koriat, Ashere, and Morris Goldsmith. "Memory Metaphors and the Laboratory/Real-Life Controversy: Correspondence versus

Storehouse Concepts of Memory." *Behavioral and Brain Sciences* 29, no. 2 (1996): 167–228.

Kostelantz, Richard. *Dictionary of the Avant-Gardes*. London: Routledge, 2001.

Kramer, Paul. *The Blood of Government: Race, Empire, the United States, and the Philippines*. Chapel Hill: University of North Carolina Press, 2006.

Kreiss, Daniel, Alicee Marwick, Francesca Bolla Tripoli. "The Anti-Critical Race Movement Will Profoundly Affect Public Education." November 20, 2021. https://www.google.com/url?sa=t&rct=j&q=&esrc=s&source=web&cd=&cad=rja&uact=8&ved=2ahUKEwiQ2oug9Oj0AhWtkokEHSDVCbgQFnoECAMQAQ&url=https%3A%2F%2Fwww.scientificamerican.com%2Farticle%2Fthe-anti-critical-race-theory-movement-will-profoundly-affect-public-education%2F&usg=AOvVaw1DSU7db6TXZwhxrmeX2HKh.

Kushner, Rachel. "Is Prison Necessary? Ruth Wilson Gilmore Might Change Your Mind." *The New York Times*, April 17, 2019. https://www.nytimes.com/2019/04/17/magazine/prison-abolition-ruth-wilson-gilmore.html.

Kwet, Michael. "Digital Colonialism is Threatening the Global South." *Al-Jazeera*, March 13, 2019. https://www.aljazeera.com/indepth/opinion/digital-colonialism-threatening-global-south-190129140828809.html.

Lacasse, Katherine. "Going With your Gut: How William James' Theory of Emotions Brings Insights to Risk Perception and Decision-making Research." *New Ideas in Psychology* 46 (October 2015): 1–7.

Lauriault, Robert N. "From Can't to Can't: The North Florida Turpentine Camp, 1900–1950." *The Florida Historical Quarterly* 67, no. 3 (January 1989): 310–328.

Lee, Christopher, ed. *Making a World after Empire: The Bandung Moment and its Political Afterlives*. Athens: Ohio University Press, 2010.

LeFlouria, Talitha L. *Chained in Silence: Black Women and Convict Labor in the New South*. Chapel Hill: University of North Carolina Press, 2015.

Léno, Etienne, Thelus Léno, Réne Ménil, Jules-Marcel Monnerot, Michel Pilotin, Maurice-Sabas Quitman, et al. *Légitime defense* (June 1, 1931).
Léno, Etienne, Thelus Léno, Réne Ménil, Jules-Marcel Monnerot, Michel Pilotin, Maurice-Sabas Quitman, et al. *Légitime défense* (1932).
Li, Tania. "After the Land Grab: Infrastructural Violence and the 'Mafia System' in Indonesia's Oil Palm Plantation Zones." *Geoforum* 96 (2018): 328–327.
Lorenzini, Daniele, "From Counter-Conduct to Critical Attitude: Michel Foucault and the Art of Not Being Governed Quite so Much," *Foucault Studies* no.21, (June 2016): 7-21.
Lotem, Itay. "A Decade After the Riots, France has Rewritten its Colonial History." *The Conversation*, January 25, 2016. https://theconversation.com/a-decade-after-the-riots-france-has-rewritten-its-colonial-history-50499.
Lowe, Lisa. *The Intimacies of Four Continents*. Durham: Duke University Press, 2015.
Lowry, Michael. *Walter Benjamin: Avertissement d'incendie: une lecture des thèses "Sur le concept d'histoire"*. Paris: Presses Universitaires de France, 2001.
Lugo, Grace. "Shatter-belt Countries: They Affect the Rest of the World, Too." *StoryMaps*, February 2, 2020. https://storymaps.arcgis.com/stories/8cf2192b87cd4ad787086c30467e7d48.
Mack, Arien, and Miriam Ticktin, eds. "The Invasive Other." *Social Research* 84, no. 1 (2017). https://www.socres.org/post/841-spring-2017-invasive-other.
Mackreath, Helen. "Interview with Dor." *The White Review*, November 2015. https://www.thewhitereview.org/features/interview-with-dor-guez/.
Maculiffe, Sam. "The Imagination of Detail: Barthes and the Politics of Utopia." Paper presented at the London Conference in Critical Thought, London South Bank University, London, UK, June 2017.
Madianou, Mirca. "Technocolonialism: Digital Innovation and Data Practices in the Humanitarian Response to Refugee Crises." *Social Media and Society* 5, no. 3 (2019): 1–13.
Mahibir, Alexandra D. "Slavery by the Name of Turpentine: The Lynching of Odis Price." Northeast University School of Law,

Summer 2015. https://repository.library.northeastern.edu/downloads/neu:m0428561f?datastream_id=content.
Maier, Hendrik, M.J. "Phew! Europeesche beschaving! Marco Kartodikromo's *Student Hidjo*." *Southeast Asian Studies* 34, no. 1 (June 1996): 184–210.
Mamdani, Mahmood. "Settler Colonialism: Then and Now." *Critical Inquiry* 41, no. 3 (2015): 596–614.
Manna, Jumana. "Wild Relatives." Interview by Hakim Bishara. *Bomb Magazine*, January 25, 2019. https://bombmagazine.org/articles/wild-relatives-jumana-manna-interviewed/.
Marcokartodikromo, Mas. *Mata Gelap* [1914]. Yogyakarta: Pataba Press, 2021.
Marino, Matt. "The Brutality of Florida's Turpentine Industry." *FloWriter*, November 9, 2018. https://flowriter.net/2018/11/09/the-brutality-of-floridas-turpentine-industry/.
Masilela, Ntongela. "The Very Beautiful African-ness in Baldwin: In Memoriam." *Pitzer*, 1998. Accessed May 13, 2021. http://pzacad.pitzer.edu/NAM/general/essays/baldwin.pdf.
May, Ernest R. *Imperial Democracy: The Emergence of America as a Great Power*. New York: Harcourt and Brace, 1961.
Mbembe, Achille. *On the Postcolony*. Durham: Duke University Press, 2003.
Mbembe, Achille. *Politiques de l'inimitié*. Paris: La Découverte, 2016.
Mbembe, Achille. "The Society of Enmity." *Radical Philosophy* 200, no. 1 (2016): 23–35.
Mbembe, Achille. *Necropolitics*. Durham: Duke University Press, 2019.
Mbembe, Achille. "SPRC In conversation with Achille Mbembe." Interview by Paul Gilroy. UCL Sarah Parker Remond Centre, June 25, 2020. Audio. https://www.ucl.ac.uk/institute-of-advanced-studies/publications/2020/jun/sprc-conversation-achille-mbembe.
McCoy, Alfred. *Policing American Empire: The United States, the Philippines, and the Rise of the Surveillance State*. Madison: University of Wisconsin, 2009.
McGranahan, Carole, and John Collier, eds. *Ethnographies of U.S. Empire*. Durham: Duke University Press, 2018.

Mckie, Robin. "How Our Colonial Past Altered the Ecobalance of an Entire Planet." *The Guardian*, June 10, 2018. https://www.theguardian.com/science/2018/jun/10/colonialism-changed-earth-geology-claim-scientists.
McNally, R.J. "The Science and Folklore of Traumatic Amnesia." *Clinical Psychology Science and Practice* 11, no. 1 (2004): 29–33.
McQue, Katie, and Jamie Doward. "Chagos Children 'stuck for years in unsafe lodgings'." *The Guardian*, August 10, 2019. https://www.theguardian.com/world/2019/aug/10/chagos-children-stuck-years-unsafe-lodgings.
Mehta, Parvinder. "Repressive Silences and Whispers of History: Lessons and Legacies of 1984." *Sikh Formations* 11, no. 3 (2015): 366–396.
Mehta, Uday. "Liberal Politics of Exclusion." *Politics and Society* 18, no. 4 (1990): 427–454.
Mehta, Uday. *Anxiety of Freedom*. Ithaca: Cornell University Press, 1992.
Mehta, Uday. *Liberalism and Empire: A Study of Nineteenth-Century British Social Thought*. Chicago: Chicago University Press, 1999.
Meldrum, Ryan Charles, Alex R. Piquero, Turgut Ozkan, and Zachary A. Powell. "An Examination of the Criminological Consequences and Correlates of Remorselessness During Adolescence." *Youth Violence and Juvenile Justice* 16, no. 3 (2018): 279–298.
Memmi, Albert. *Dominated Man: Notes toward a Portrait*. New York: Orion Press, 1968.
Ménil, René. *Preface, Légitime défense*. Paris: Editions Jean-Michel Place, 1978.
Menon, Dilip. "Bandung is Back: Afro-Asian Affinities." *Radical History Review* 119 (Spring 2014): 241–245.
Michaelian, Kourken. "The Epistemology of Forgetting." *Erkenntnis* 74, no. 3 (2010): 399–424.
Michel, Jean-Claude. *The Black Surrealists*. New York: Peter Lang Publishers, 2000.
Mignolo, Walter D., and Catherine E. Walsh. *On Decoloniality: Concepts, Analytics, Praxis*. Durham: Duke University Press, 2018.
Miles, Robert. *Capitalism and Unfree Labour: Anomaly or Necessity?* London: Tavistock, 1987.

Miller, William I. *The Anatomy of Disgust*. Cambridge: Harvard University Press, 1997.
Mills, Charles. "White Time: The Chronic Injustice of Ideal Theory," *Du Bois Review* 11, no.1 (2014), 27–42.
Mintz, Sidney. *Sweetness and Power: The Place of Sugar in Modern History*. New York: Penguin, 1985.
Morgan, Edmund S. *American Slavery, American Freedom: The Ordeal of Colonial Virginia*. New York: W.W. Norton & Company, Inc., 1975.
Morse, Stephen J. "Commentary: Reflections on Remorse." *Journal of the American Academy of Psychiatry and the Law* 42 (March 2014): 49–55.
Mrazek, Rudolf. *The Complete Lives of Camp People: Colonialism, Fascism, Concentrated Modernity*. Durham: Duke University Press, 2020.
Muhammad, Khalil Gibran. *The Condemnation of Blackness: Race, Crime, and the Making Modern America*. Cambridge: Harvard University Press, 2010.
Muldoon, Paul. "The Power of Forgetting: *Ressentiment*, Guilt, and Transformative Politics." *Political Psychology* 38, no. 4 (2017): 669–683.
Musée national del'immigration. "Migrant de Mediterranée, qui sont ces damnés de la mer?" Conference. Paris. June 19, 2015. http://www.canal-u-tv/video/histoire_immigrations/migrants_de_la_mer.
Ngai, Sianne. *Ugly Feelings*. Cambridge: Harvard University Press, 2005.
Nietzsche, Frederick. *Untimely Meditations*, translated by R.J. Hollingdale. New York: Cambridge University Press, 1996.
Nietzsche, Frederick. *On the Genealogy of Morals II*, translated by Maudemarie Clark and Alan Swensen. Indianapolis: Hackett Publishing, 1998.
Nowlan, Amica Sciortino. "Who was Wifredo Lam?" *1843 Magazine*, September 19, 2016. https://www.economist.com/1843/2016/09/19/who-was-wifredo-lam.
Nussbaum, Martha. *Upheavals of Thought: The Intelligence of Emotions*. Cambridge: Cambridge University Press, 2001.

Nussbaum, Martha. *Hiding from Humanity; Disgust, Shame, and the Law*. Princeton: Princeton University Press, 2004.
Nussbaum, Martha. *From Disgust to Humanity: Sexual Orientation and Constitutional Law*. New York: Oxford, 2010.
Nuzzo, Angelica. *Ideal Embodiment: Kant's Theory of Sensibility*. Bloomington: Indiana University Press, 2008.
Oglivie, Bertrand. *L'Homme jetable: Essai sur l'exterminisme et la violence extreme*. Paris: Editions Amsterdam, 2012.
O'Malley, Vincent. "What A Nation Chooses to Remember and Forget: The War for New Zealand's History." *The Guardian*, October 17, 2016. https://www.theguardian.com/commentisfree/2016/oct/18/what-a-nation-chooses-to-remember-and-forget-the-war-for-new-zealands-history.
Onuoha, Mimi. "When Proof is Not Enough." *Five Thirty Eight*, July 1, 2020. https://fivethirtyeight.com/features/when-proof-is-not-enough/.
Orlow, Uriel, ed. *Unmade Film*. Zurich: edition fink, 2013.
Orlow, Uriel. "Unmade Film." Accessed February 25, 20212P Foundation Wiki. "Amador Fernandez-Savater, Amador. "War of Maneuver vs. War of Position." 2016. Accessed May 13, 2021. https://wiki.p2pfoundation.net/War_of_Maneuver_vs_War_of_Position.
Oxford English Dictionary. 2nd ed. 20 vols. Oxford: Oxford University Press, 1996, continually updated at https://www.oed.com.
Peguine, Sarah. "Profile of the Artist: Dor Guez." *The Seen*, April 23, 2014. https://theseenjournal.org/profile-artist-dor-guez/.
Perkinson, Robert. *Texas Tough: The Rise of America's Prison Empire*. New York: Metropolitan Books, 2010.
Petersson, Fredrik. "Prelude to Bandung: Anti-colonialism Between the Wars." *Imperial and Global Forum*, October 20, 2014. https://imperialglobalexeter.com/2014/10/20/prelude-to-bandung-the-interwar-origins-of-anti-colonialism/.
Pham, Quynh N., and Robbie Shilliam, eds. *Meanings of Bandung: Postcolonial Orders and Decolonial Visions*. London: Rowman and Littlefield, 2016.
Pilger, John. "How Britain Forcefully Depopulated a Whole Archipelago . . . And Managed to Cover It Up." *Al Jazeera*, February 25, 2019. https://www.aljazeera.com/indepth/opin

ion/britain-forcefully-depopulated-archipelago-190225082624
527.html.
Plenel, Edwy. "Refoulement et persistence de la question colonial." *Mediapart*, November 27, 2021. http://www.mediapart.fr.
Pope, James Gray. "Mass Incarceration, Convict Leasing, and the Thirteenth Amendment: A Revisionist Account." *NYU Law Review* 94, no. 6 (December 2019), 1465-1554.https://www.nyulawreview.org/issues/volume-94-number-6/mass-incarceration-convict-leasing-and-the-thirteenth-amendment-a-revisionist-account/.
Popova, Zhanna. "Dissecting Sites of Punishment: Penal Colonies and Their Borders." *International Review of Social History* 64 (2019), 415-425. August 7, 2019. https://www-cambridge-org.libproxy.newschool.edu/core/journals/international-review-of-social-history/article/dissecting-sites-of-punishment-penal-colonies-and-their-borders/638465268443A0AAB1E504B98E0E5526.
Poulantzas, Nicos. *State, Power, Socialism*, translated by Patrick Camiler. London: Verso, 1978.
Povinelli, Elizabeth. *Economies of Abandonment: Social Belonging and Endurance in Late Liberalism*. Durham: Duke University Press, 2011.
Premack, David, and Guy Woodruf. "Does the Chimpanzee Have a Theory of Mind?" *Behavior and Brain Sciences* 1, no. 4 (1978): 515–526.
Price, Richard. *The Convict and Colonel: A Story of Colonialism and Resistance in the Caribbean*. Durham: Duke University Press, 1998.
Price, Sally. *Paris Primitive: Jacques Chirac's Museum on the Quai Branly*. Chicago: Chicago University Press, 2010.
Puar, Jasbir. *The Right to Maim: Debility, Capacity, Disability*. Durham: Duke University Press, 2017.
Qato, Mezna, "Forms of Retrieval: Social Scale, Citation and the Archive of the Palestinian Left." *International Journal of Middle East Studies* 52, no. 2 (2019): 312-315. "Returns of the Archive," The Nakba Files, 1 June 2016. Nakbafiles.org/2016/06/01/returns-of-the-archives.
Qin, Amy. "Inspired by India, Singaporeans Seek to End Gay Sex Ban." *New York Times*, December 16, 2018. https://www.nytimes.com/2018/12/16/world/asia/singapore-gay-sex-ban.html.

Raben, Remco. "On Genocide and Mass Violence in Colonial Indonesia." *Journal of Genocide Research* 14, no. 3/4 (2012): 485–502.

Rabinow, Paul. *Anthropos Today: Reflections on Modern Equipment.* Princeton: Princeton University Press, 2003.

Rafieyan, Darius, and Cardiff Garcia. "The Uncounted Workforce." *WBUR*, June 29, 2020. https://www.wbur.org/npr/884989263/the-uncounted-workforce.

Rahkonen, Keijo. "Bourdieu and Nietzsche: Taste as a Struggle." In *The Legacy of Pierre Bourdieu: Critical Essays*, edited by Simon Susen and Bryan S. Turner. London: Anthem Press, 2011, 125–144.

Redden, Elizabeth. "A Milestone for Palestinian Studies." *Inside Higher Ed*, August 11, 2020. https://www.insidehighered.com/news/2020/08/11/brown-establishes-endowed-chair-palestinian-studies.

Rancière, Jacques. *Dissensus: On Politics and Aesthetics*, translated by Steven Corcoran. London: Bloomsbury, 2010.

Rieff, David. *In Praise of Forgetting: Historical Memory and Its Ironies.* New Haven: Yale University Press, 2011.

Rheinberger, Hans-Jörg. *An Epistemology of the Concrete: Twentieth-Century Histories of Life.* Durham: Duke University Press, 2010.

Rheinberger, Hans-Jörg. *Toward a History of Epistemic Things.* Stanford: Stanford University Press, 1997.

Rigouste, Mathieu. *L'ennemi intérieur: la généalogie coloniale et militaire de l'ordre sécuritaire dans la France contemporaine.* Paris: La Découverte, 2009.

Rioux, Sebastien, Genevieve LeBaron, and Peter Verovsek. "Capitalism and Unfree Labour: a Review of Marxist Perspectives on Modern Slavery." *Review of International Political Economy* 3 (August 2019): 709–731.

Rizal, José. *Noli Me Tangere.* Manila: Institute Nacional de Historia, 1978.

Roberts, Brian Russell, and Keith Foulcher, eds. *Indonesian Notebook: A Sourcebook on Richard Wright and the Bandung Conference.* Durham: Duke University Press, 2016.

Roberts, Mary. *Intimate Outsiders: The Harem in Ottoman and Orientalist Art and Travel Literature.* Durham: Duke University Press, 2007.

Rodriguez, Dylan. *Forced Passages: Imprisoned Radical Intellectuals and the U.S. Prison Regime*. Minneapolis: University of Minnesota Press, 2006.
Rodríguez, E. Guitiérrez. "The Coloniality of Migration and the 'Refugee Crisis'." *Refuge: Canada's Journal on Refugees* 34, no.1 (2018): 16–28.
Rosenfeld, Sophia. *Common Sense: A Political History*. Cambridge: Harvard University Press, 2011.
van Rossum, Matthias. "The Dutch East India Company in Asia, 1595–1811." In *A Global History of Convicts and Penal Colonies*, edited by Clare Anderson, 157–181. London: Bloomsbury, 2018.
van Rossum, Matthias. "The Carceral Colony: Colonial Exploitation, Coercion, and Control in the Dutch East Indies, 1810s–1940s." *International Review of Social History* 63, special issue S26 (August 2018): 65–88.
Ruas, Charles. "'Long Live Degenerate Art': In 'Art et Liberté,' an Egyptian View of Surrealism Addresses Contemporary Issues." *ARTNews*, March 6, 2017. https://www.artnews.com/art-news/reviews/subjective-realism-an-egyptian-view-of-surrealism-as-an-expression-of-contemporary-issues-7905/.
Ryle, Gilbert. "Knowing How and Knowing That: The Presidential Address." Meeting of the Aristotelian Society at the University of London Club. November 5, 1945, 1–16.
Ryle, Gilbert. *The Concept of Mind*. New York: Penguin, 1949.
Said, Edward. *Orientalism*. New York: Pantheon, 1978.
Saint Augustine. *The Confessions*, translated by Henry Chadwick. Oxford: Oxford University Press, 1992.
Salih, Ruba. "From Bare Lives to Political Agents: Palestinian Refugees as Avant-Garde." *Refugee Survey Quarterly* 32, no. 2 (2013): 66–91.
Schmitt, Carl. *The Concept of the Political* [1932]. Chicago: Chicago University Press, 1996.
Schmon, Jochen. "'Migration Crisis' or 'Mass Killing'—The Mediterranean Sea as a Mass Grave of Imperial Genocide?" Unpublished manuscript. The New School for Social Research. 2019.
Scholar, Richard. "The Archipelago Goes Global: Late Glissant and the Early Modern Isolario." In *Globalizations in the Making*,

edited by Eva Sansavior and Richard Scholar, 33–57. Liverpool: Liverpool University Press, 2015.

Schreuer, Milan. "Belgium Apologizes for Kidnapping Children from African Colonies." *The New York Times*, April 4, 2019. https://www.nytimes.com/2019/04/04/world/europe/belgium-kidnapping-congo-rwanda-burundi.html.

Schreuer, Milan. "Belgium Apologizes for a Racist Atrocity in Its African Colonies." *The New York Times*, April 5, 2019. A6.

Schuller, Kyla. *The Biopolitics of Feeling: Race, Sex, and Science in the Nineteenth Century*. Durham: Duke University Press, 2018.

Schweik, Susan. *The Ugly Laws: Disability in Public*. New York: New York University, 2009.

Scott, Daryl Michael. "The Social and Intellectual Origins of 13thism." *Fire!!!* 5, no. 2 (Spring 2020): 2–39.

Scott, David. "Colonial Governmentality." *Social Text* 43 (1995): 191–220.

Scott, James. *Domination and the Arts of Resistance: Hidden Transcripts*. New Haven: Yale University Press, 1990.

Scott, James. *Seeing Like a State: How Certain Schemes to Improve the Human Condition Have Failed*. New Haven: Yale University Press, 1998.

Scott, James. *The Art of Not Being Governed*. New Haven: Yale University Press, 2009.

Seikaly, Sherene. *Men of Capital: Economy and Scarcity in Mandate Palestine*. Palo Alto: Stanford University Press, 2016.

Seikaly, Sherene. "How I Met My Great-Grandfather: Archives and the Writing of History." *Comparative Studies of South Asia, Africa and the Middle East* 38, no. 1 (2018): 6–20.

Sela, Rona. "The Genealogy of Colonial Plunder and Erasure—Israel's Control over Palestinian Archives." *Social Semiotics* 28, no. 2 (2018): 201–229.

Serhan, Yasmeen. "Emmanuel Macron Tries—Slowly—To Reckon with France's Past." *The Atlantic*, September 14, 2018. https://www.theatlantic.com/international/archive/2018/09/emmanuel-macron-acknowledges-torture-algeria/570283/.

Setia, Sophia. *Provisional Avant-Gardes: Little Magazine Communities from Dada to Digital*. Stanford: Stanford University Press, 2019.

Sfard, Michael. "In Memory of Felicia Langer, the First Lawyer to Bring the Occupation to Court." *+972 Magazine*, June 24, 2018. https://www.972mag.com/in-memory-of-felicia-langer-the-first-lawyer-to-bring-the-occupation-to-court/.

Shapin, Steven. *The Social History of Truth: Civility and Science in Seventeenth Century England*. Chicago: Chicago University Press, 1994.

Sharpe, Jenny. *Immaterial Archives: An African diaspora Poetics of Loss*. Evanston: Northwestern University Press, 2020.

Shehadeh, Raja. *A Rift in Time: Travels with my Ottoman Uncle*. London: Profile, 2011.

Shihade, Magid. "Global Israel: Settler Colonialism, Mobility, and Rupture." *Borderlands* 14, no. 1 (2015): 1–16.

Shiriashi, Takahashi. *An Age in Motion: Popular Radicalism in Java, 1912–1926*. Ithaca: Cornell University Press, 1990.

Shofner, Jerrell H. "Forced Labor in the Florida Forests, 1880–1950." *Journal of Forest History* 25, no. 1 (January 1981): 14–25.

Sief, Ola. "Hotspots of Inspiration: Art Hubs that Transformed the Egyptian Art Scene." *Rawi Magazine* (2016). https://rawi-magazine.com/articles/hotspots_of_inspiration/.

Silverblatt, Irene. *Modern Inquisitions: Peru and the Colonial Origins of the Civilized World*. Durham: Duke University Press, 2004.

Simpson, Audra. *Mohawk Interruptus: Political Life Across the Borders of Settler States*. Durham: Duke University Press, 2014.

Slater, David. "Exporting Imperial Democracy: Critical Reflections on the US Case." *Human Geography* 2, no. 3 (2009): 1–13.

Slavin, David. "The French Left and the Rif War, 1924–25: Racism and the Limits of Internationalism." *Journal of Contemporary History* 26, no. 1 (Jan 1991): 5–32.

Sleiman, Hana, and Kaoukab Chebaro. "Narrating Palestine: The Palestinian Oral History Archive Project." *Journal of Palestine Studies* 47, no. 2 (2018): 63–76.

Sloterdijk, Peter. *The Art of Philosophy: Wisdom as Practice*. New York: Columbia University Press, 2012.

Smith, Barry C. "The Nature of Sensory Experience: The Case of Taste and Tasting." *Phenomenology and Mind* 4 (2013): 212–227.

Solomon, Robert. "On Emotions as Judgments." *American Philosophical Quarterly* 25, no. 2 (April 1988): 183–191.

Sommer, Doris. *Proceed with Caution, When Engaged by Minority Writing in the Americas*. Cambridge: Harvard University Press, 1999.
Spahr, Juliana. *DuBois's Telegram: Literary Resistance and State Containment*. Cambridge: Harvard University Press, 2018.
Sperber, Dan, and Deidre Wilson. *Relevance*. Hoboken: Wiley Blackwell, 1986.
Spieler, Miranda. *Empire and Underworld: Captivity in French Guiana*. Cambridge: Harvard University Press, 2012.
Spillers, Hortense. "Mama's Baby, Papa's Maybe: An American Grammar Book." *Diacritics* 17, no. 2 (1987): 64–81.
Steedman, Carolyn. *Landscape for a Good Woman*. London: Virago Press, 1986.
Stein, Rebecca. *Screen Shots: State Violence on Camera in Israel and Palestine*. Stanford: Stanford University Press, 2021.
Stephens, Michelle Ann. *Skin Acts*. Durham: Duke University Press, 2014.
Stewart, Kathleen. *Ordinary Affects*. Durham: Duke University Press, 2007.
Stoler, Ann Laura. *Capitalism and Confrontation in Sumatra's Plantation Belt*. New Haven: Yale University Press, 1985.
Stoler, Ann Laura. "Sexual Affronts and Racial Frontiers: European Identities and the Cultural Politics of Exclusions in Colonial Southeast Asia." *Comparative Studies in Society and History* 34, no. 3 (1992): 514–551.
Stoler, Ann Laura. *Race and the Education of Desire: Foucault's History of Sexuality and the Colonial Order of Things*. Durham: Duke University Press, 1995.
Stoler, Ann Laura. *Carnal Knowledge and Imperial Power: Race and the Intimate in Colonial Rule*. Berkeley: University of California Press, 2002.
Stoler, Ann Laura. *Along the Archival Grain: Epistemic Anxieties and Colonial Common Sense*. Princeton: Princeton University Press, 2009.
Stoler, Ann Laura. "Colony." *Political Concepts* 1 (2011). https://www.politicalconcepts.org/colony-stoler/.
Stoler, Ann Laura. *Duress: Imperial Durabilities in Our Times*. Durham: Duke University Press, 2016.

Stoler, Ann Laura. "Introduction: The Dark Logic of Invasive Others." *Social Research* 84, no. 1 (Spring 2017): 3–5.

Stoler, Ann Laura. "Interior Frontiers." *Political Concepts: A Critical Lexicon* 4 (2018). https://www.politicalconcepts.org/interior-frontiers-ann-laura-stoler/.

Stoler, Ann Laura, Stathis Gourgouris, and Jacques Lezra, eds. *Thinking with Balibar: A Lexicon of Conceptual Practice*. New York: Fordham University Press, 2020.

Stora, Benjamin. *La gangrene et l'oubli: La memoire de la guerre d'Algérie*. Paris: La Découverte, 1991.

Stora, Benjamin. "Les migrations actuelles réveillent la question coloniale." Interview by Alexis Lacroix. *L'Express*, October 30, 2018. https://www.lexpress.fr/culture/les-migrations-actuelles-reveillent-la-question-coloniale_2044964.html.

Strassler, Karen, and Ann Laura Stoler. "Casting for the Colonial: Memory Work in 'New Order' Java." *Comparative Studies in Society and History* 42 (2000): 4–48.

Subramanya, Rupa. "The Colonial Hangover of India's Rape Law." *The Washington Street Journal*, January 4, 2013. https://blogs.wsj.com/indiarealtime/2013/01/04/the-colonial-hangover-of-indias-rape-law/.

Sutherland, Heather. "Pudjangga Baru: Aspects of Intellectual Life in the 1930s." *Indonesia* 6 (October 1968): 106–127.

Taleb, Adela. "Europe in focus: Imperial formations in the fabric of the European Union." *Ethnic and Racial Studies* 44, no.10 (2021): 1755–1788.

Taoua, Phyllis. *Forms of Protest: Anti-Colonialism and Avant-Gardes in Africa, the Caribbean, and France*. Portsmouth: Heinman, 2002.

Tawil-Souri, Helga. "Digital Occupation: Gaza's High-Tech Enclosure." *Journal of Palestine Studies* XLI, no. 2 (Winter 2012): 27–43.

Tawil-Souri, Helga. "Uneven Borders: Coloured (Im)mobilities: ID Cards in Palestine/Israel." *Geopolitics* 17, no. 1 (2012): 153–176.

ten Brinke, Leanne, and Sarah Macdonald. "Crocodile Tears: Facial, Verbal and Body Language Behaviors associated with Genuine and Fabricated Remorse." *Law and Human Behavior* 36, no. 1 (2012): 51–59.

Texte collectif. "Les bonimenteurs du postcolonial business en quête de respectabilité academique." *L'Express*, December 26, 2019. https://www.lexpress.fr/actualite/politique/les-bonimenteurs-du-postcolonial-business-en-quete-de-respectabilite-academique_2112541.html.

Thesaurus.com. "Remorselessness." Accessed May 13, 2021. https://www.thesaurus.com/browse/remorselessness.

Thomas, Martin. *Empires of Intelligence: Security Services and Colonial Disorder after 1914*. Berkeley: University of California Press, 2007.

Ticktin, Miriam. *Casualities of Care: Immigration and the Politics of Humanitarianism in France*. Durham: Duke University Press, 2011.

Tiquet, Romain. "Connecting the 'Inside' and the 'Outside' World: Convict Labour and Mobile Penal Camps in Colonial Senegal (1930s–1950s)." *International Review of Social History* 64, no. 3 (2019): 473–491.

Toth, Stephen A. *Beyond Papillon: The French Overseas Penal Colonies, 1854–1952*. London: University of Nebraska Press, 2006.

Totten, Michael J. "Shatter Zones." *Australia/Israel & Jewish Affairs Council Review*, July 31, 2015. https://aijac.org.au/australia-israel-review/shatter-zones/.

Toukan, Hanan. "Continuity from Rupture: Deir Yassin's Absent Presence in an Unmade Film." In *Unmade Film*, edited by Uriel Orlow. Zurich: edition fink, 2013.

Toukan, Hanan. "Music, Borders, and the Sensorial Politics of Displacement in Jumana Manna's 'A Magical Substance Flows into Me'." *Jerusalem Quarterly* 67 (2016): 117–123.

Toukan, Hanan. "The Palestinian Museum." *Radical Philosophy* 2, no. 3 (December 2018): 11–22. https://www.radicalphilosophy.com/article/the-palestinian-museum.

Tropen Museum. "Words Matter." Accessed February 7, 2021. https://www.tropenmuseum.nl/en/about-tropenmuseum/words-matter-publication.

Tuck, Eve, and K. Wayne Yang. "Decolonization Is Not a Metaphor." *Decolonization: Indigeneity, Education & Society* 1, no. 1 (2012): 1–40.

Twain, Mark. *King Leopold's Soliloquy: A Defense of His Congo Rule*. Boston: The P. R. Warren Co., 1905. https://digitalcollecti

ons.amnh.org/asset-management/2URM1TE32PY?FR_=1&W=1150&H=919.

Tye, Michael. "Knowing What It Is Like: The Ability Hypothesis and The Knowledge Argument." In *Reality and Human Supervenience: Essays on the Philosophy of David Lewis*, edited by Gerhard Preyer and Frank Siebelt, 223–238. Lanham: Rowman & Littlefield, 2000.

United Nations General Assembly. "General Assembly Welcomes International Court of Justice Opinion on Chagos Archipelago, Adopts Text Calling for Mauritius' Complete Decolonization." 2019. Accessed May 22, 2020. https://www.un.org/press/en/2019/ga12146.doc.htm.

Utama, Wildan Sena. "From Brussels to Bogor: Contacts, Networks and the History of the Bandung Conference, 1955." *Journal of Indonesian Social Sciences and Humanities* 6, no. 1 (2016): 11–24.

Varshney, Ashutosh. "Narendra Modi's Illiberal Drift Threatens Indian Democracy." *Financial Times*, August 18, 2017. https://www.ft.com/content/0015a59e-80e2-11e7-94e2-c5b903247afd.

Virilio, Paul. *The Administration of Fear*. Cambridge: Semiotext(e), 2012.

Wacquant, Loïc. "Race as Civic Felony." *International Sosical Science Journal* 57, no. 183 (March 2005): 127–142.

Wacquant, Loïc. *Prisons of Poverty*. Minneapolis: University of Minnesota, 2009.

Wagner, Peter, and Wendy Sawyer. "States of Incarceration: The Global Context 2018." *Prison Policy Initiative*, June 2018. https://www.prisonpolicy.org/global/2018.html.

Wang, Jackie. *Carceral Capitalism*. Cambridge: Semiotext(e), 2017.

Ward, Bryan H. "Sentencing Without Remorse." *Loyola University of Chicago Law Journal* 38 (Fall 2006): 131–167.

Wark, McKenzie. *The Beach beneath the Street: The Everyday Life and Glorious Times of the Situationist International*. New York: Verso, 2011.

Warr, Mark. "Crime and Regret." *Emotion Review* 8, no. 3 (2016): 231–239.

Washington Post Media. "National Planning Scenarios." 2005. Accessed February 4, 2020. https://media.washingtonpost.com/wp-srv/nation/nationalsecurity/earlywarning/NationalPlanningScenariosApril2005.pdf.

Weber, Benjamin D. "The Strange Career of the Convict Clause: US Prison Imperialism in the Panamá Canal Zone." *International Labor and Working-Class History* 96 (Fall 2019): 79–102.
Weber, Samuel. *Benjamin's—abilities.* Cambridge: Harvard University Press, 2008.
Weheliye, Alexander G. *Habeas Viscus.* Durham: Duke University Press, 2014.
Weil, Simone. "Les membres palpitants de la patrie." *Vigilance* 63, no. 10 (1938).
Weil, Simone. *Contre le colonialisme.* Paris: Payot & Rivage, 2018.
Weisman, Richard. *Showing Remorse: Law and the Social Control of Emotion.* Burlington: Ashgate, 2014.
Western, Bruce. "Poverty Politics and Crime Control in Europe and America." *Contemporary Sociology* 40, no. 3 (May 2011): 283–286.
Whitin, E. Stagg. "Prison Labor." An Address Delivered Before the Woman's Department of the National Civic Federation at Washington, January 1914.
Wieviorka, Michel. *La France Raciste.* Paris: Seuil, 1992.
Wikileaks Cable. "HMG Floats Proposal for Marine Reserve Covering Chagos Archipelago (British Indian Ocean Territory)." LONDON1156_a. May 15, 2009. https://wikileaks.org/plusd/cables/09LONDON1156_a.html.
Wikipedia. "Chagos Archipelago." Accessed February 12, 2020. http://en.wikipedia.org/wiki/Chagos.
Wikipedia. "Diffraction." Accessed February 2, 2021. https://en.wikipedia.org/wiki/Diffraction.
Wikipedia. "Elizabeth Povinelli." Accessed February 26, 2020. https://en.wikipedia.org/wiki/Elizabeth_Povinelli.
Wikipedia. "John Keane (political theorist)." Accessed June 13, 2021. https://en.wikipedia.org/wiki/John_Keane_(political_theorist).
Wikipedia. "Knabb Turpentine." Accessed February 2, 2021. https://en.wikipedia.org/wik/Knabb_Turpentine.
Wilder, Gary. *Freedom Time: Negritude, Decolonization, and the Future of the World.* Durham: Duke University Press, 2015.
Williams, Chatterton. "The French Origins of 'You Will Not Replace Us'": The European Thinkers Behind the White-Nationalist Rallying Cry." *The New Yorker*, December 4, 2017. https://www.

newyorker.com/magazine/2017/12/04/the-french-origins-of-you-will-not-replace-us.

Williams, Raymond. *Keywords: A Vocabulary of Culture and Society.* London: Fontana, 1976.

Williams, Raymond. *Marxism and Literature.* Oxford: Oxford University Press, 1977.

Wilmot, Sydney. "Use of Convict Labor for Highway Construction in the North." *Proceedings of the Academy of Political Science in the City of New York* 4, no. 2 (January 1914): 6–68.

Wilson, Deirdre, and Dan Sperber. "Relevance Theory." In *The Handbook of Pragmatics*, edited by L. R. Horn and G. Ward, 607–632. London: Blackwell, 2004.

Wittgenstein, Ludwig. *Philosophical Investigations*, translated by G.E.M. Anscombe. New York: Macmillan, 1968.

Wolff, Tobias Barrington. "The 13th Amendment and Slavery in the Global Economy." *Columbia Law Review* 102 (2002): 973–1050.

Wright, Richard. *Black Power: Three books from Exile: Black Power; The Color Curtain and White Man, Listen!* New York: Harper, 2008.

Zatz, Noah D. "The Carceral Labor Continuum: Beyond the Prison Labor/Free Labor Divide." In *Labor and Punishment: Work in and out of Prison*, edited by Erin Hatton, 133-178. Berkeley: University of California Press, 2021.

Zakaria, Fareed. *The Future of Freedom: Illiberal Democracy at Home and Abroad.* New York: Norton, 2007.

Zerelli, Linda M.G. "The Turn to Affect and the Problem of Judgment." *New Literary History* 46 (2015): 261–286.

Zhong, Rocksheng, Madelon Baranoski, Neal Geigenson, Larry Davidson, Alec Buchanan, and Howard V. Zonana. "'So You're Sorry?' The Role of Remorse in Criminal Law." *Journal of the American Academy of Psychiatry and Law* 42, no.1 (2014): 39–48.

Zhong, Rocksheng. "Judging Remorse." *New York Review of Law and Social Change* 39 (2015): 133–172.

Index

13th Amendment, 240–243, 265
13th Amendment: Subordinate
  Clause, 267–71

abolition, 267–271
Adorno, Theodor, 144
aesthetics, 99, 100, 182
  choice, 143, 175
  commitments, 142
  conventions, 31
  of dissent, 143, 161, 163, 165, 206
  innovation, 143, 150, 166
  inspiration, 178
  Kant, xxviii, 73–74
  philosophy, 81
  politics, 150, 157, 183–84
  practice, 141, 193
  sensibility, 156–57
  and taste, 78–81, 90
affect
  affective states, 35, 58
  anger, xi, 51, 66, 76
  compassion, 62, 65, 104
  contempt, 36, 43–44, 49, 55, 83

disdain, xxvii, 41–42, 52, 67–68,
  71, 78, 83, 137
envy, 37, 47, 50, 52, 54, 71
fear, xi, xii, 22–23, 33, 47,
  163, 256
guilt, 48
hate, xxviii, 41, 297
humiliation, xi, 22, 39, 45–46,
  66, 71
jealousy, 37, 50–51
as judgement, longing, xxvii, 22,
  55–56
pity, 39, 41–42, 49–50,
  55, 62
pride, 40–41, 45, 52
rage xi, 44, 46, 50, 58, 119, 141,
  171, 183–85, 197–98 (see also
  sentiment; sensibility)
Agamben, Giorgio, 82–83
Agee, James, 33
Ahmed, Sara, 47
Ako, Edward, 147
Al-Saji, Alia, 283
Alexander, Michelle, 267–68

Algeria, 134, 208
  Algerian, 150
  colonial, 112
Algerian War, xxx, 92n68, 92, 112, 134, 290 (*see also* France, French-Algerian War)
Alisjahbana, Sutan Takdir, 151, 174
Althusser, Louis, 10–11, 27, 136
Anani, Rana, 222, 226n54
Ananta Toer, Pramoedya, 179–80, 197
Anderson, Georgette, 167
Appadurai, Arjun, 183–84
Arab National Committee, 213
archive, 100, 141, 143–44, 195–96, 199, 212, 216–217
  access, anti-colonial, 142, 165, 273
  archival practice, 203–09
  archival surge, 202, 223, 232, 292
  colonial, 92, 294
  counter, 150, 232
  digitization, 213–16, 230–31
  objects as, 217–221
Arendt, Hannah, xxxvii, 50, 102, 294
Aristotle, 51
Asleh, Fady, 207–209 (*see also* Khazaeen*)
Augustine, 123
Austin, John, xxiii, 109–10
avant-garde, xxxi, 141–4
  anti-colonial, 141
  Antilles, 147, 153
  Brazilian, 153–54, 156
  Cuban, 148, 150, 196
  Egyptian, 142, 151, 164, 196
  Martiniquais, 45, 141, 146, 169, 187
  Mexican, 143, 156
  Moroccan, 147, 170, 187, 192–94
Awraq, 199–200, 202n5, 203–04, 213–15, 229–32
Azoulay, Ariella, 210,

Bachelard, Gaston, xxi
Balai Pustaka, 171
Baldwin, James, 39, 116, 197–98
Balibar, Étienne, xviii, xxvi, 3n1, 3–4, 7–11, 14–15, 20, 21, 22–28, 32–34, 265
Bandes, Susan, 61
Bandung Conference, 1955, 163, 176–182
Barthes, Roland, xix–xx
Bedoiun, 121, 211
Belgium, 120, 288
  Belgian Congo, 119–20
Benjamin, Walter, 113–14, 130–31, 135
Bergson, Henri, 283
Bernstein, Richard, 106, 112
Berrada, Omar, 159n32
Birzeit University, 199, 202n5, 217, 230,
Black Lives Matter, xxxiii, 184
Black Panthers, 155, 194, 195, 258n62
Black Power, 163
"Black Surrealists," 168, 195
Blackmon, Douglas, 238–39, 244
Blackness, 170
Boltanski, Luc, 50
borders xxxvii, 14, 39, 86, 91, 106, 238, 243, 277, 281
  borderlands, xiii, xxxiv, xxxvii–xxxviii, 51, 55, 70
  borderlands of civility, xxxv, 238
  borderlands of inequality, 37, 44
  checkpoints, 12, 225, 298
  fictive 143
  frontiers, xvii–xviii
  internal, xxx, 7–8. 15–16, 27, 32–33
  invisible, xix
Israel/Palestine, 200, 220, 226

national, xiii
not a line, 21–22
territorial, 30
toxic frontier 23
boundaries, 4, 77, 97, 100, 104, 278
of bodies, 165
of the self, xxxvii
of states, 13
social, 91
Bourdieu, Pierre, xxviii, xxx, 67–70, 71, 72, 73–77, 82–86, 91, 94–97, 99, 100, 105, 106
Boven Digul, 154, 179, 180
breath, 44, 45–46, 95, 193, 294, breathing, 45–46
Breton, André, 150, 154, 160–62, 170, 186–87
Britain, 120, 287, 289
  Australia, 120, 125, 252, 283–84, 288
Brown, Wendy, 275
Brussels Conference 1927, 176
Buck-Morss, Susan, 158
bureaucracy, technologies of, 189
Butler, Judith, 30
Byrd, Jodi A., 293

Calais Refugee Camp, 31
camps
  carceral, 244
  concentration, 119, 121
  labor, 247–50, 260–61
  penal, 154, 180, 240, 264–65
  refugee, 31
  Roma, 106 (see also Boven Digul; carceral labor; coercion; turpentine)
Camus, Albert, xxix, 133–35
Canada, 120, 125, 283, 288
Cape Colony, 240

capital, 244, 252, 263,
  aesthetic, 150
  accumulation, 266
  American, 249
  cultural, x, 180
  private, 257
captivity, xxxvi, 248–49, (see also carceral; containment; slavery)
carceral, 180
  archipelago, 293, 299
  capitalism 241, 247, 256, 258, 270
  clause, 241, 243, 267–71
  colonialism, 240
  democracy, 240, 253, 257–61, 265–67
  histories, 237, 244, 254
  institutions, 238
  landscapes, 248–249
  as mobile, 239, 248–50, 262
  poverty, 238
  and race, 241–42, 246, 260, 267–68
carceral labor, 238, 243–45, 247–48, 250–52, 261–62, 265–67
  in British Kenya, 240
  in colonial Nigeria, 239–40
  convict leasing, 240–43, 252
  in New Caledonia, 252
  in Papua, 154
  in Tanganyika, 240
  in the United States, 253, 256–61, 264–65 (see also 13th Amendment; camps)
Caribbean, xxxiv, 146, 147, 171, 185, 192–93
  French Caribbean, 152
  migrants, 259
  pan-Caribbean, 169, 195
  restitution, 286
  Windrush Generation, 287

Carnegie, Andrew, 249
Carruthers, Mary, 123, 126, 127n49
categories, 3, 15, 41, 70, 100, 118,
    215, 231–32, 263, 292, 299
  aesthetic, 80
  conceptual, 254
  categorization, political, 6
  racial, 35, 59, 72
  of worth, 102
Césaire, Aimé, xxv, xxx, 37–38,
    45–46, 146, 150, 160, 161–62,
    166–67, 169, 170, 184–85, 197
Césaire, Suzanne, 149, 151, 169–70,
    184–87, 190, 197
Cesari, Chiara, 120–21
Chagos Archipelago, 281, 288–89
Chairil, Anwar, 174
Chakrabarty, Dipesh, 181
Chamayou, Grégoire, 248–49
charm, 75, 95n76
Chirac, Jacques, 284
citizen, xiii, 9, 17–18, 22, 129, 188
  citizenship, xxxvi, 20, 257, 263,
    289
  non-citizen, xiii
class, xxx, 51, 53–57, 70, 73–74, 80,
    83, 91, 93–94
  knowledge, 104
  middle-class, 69, 104
  working-class, 70
classification 118, 14
Clifford, James, 187
coercion, 88, 175, 238, 250,
  and care, 38
  forced labor, 174, 237, 240–44,
    252, 257–58, 260, 264, 270 (*see
    also* carceral labor)
colonial
  administration, 251
  anti-, 143–45, 149, 151, 157, 160,
    172, 176–177, 182–84

aphasia, xxiii, 71, 114
archives, 4, 19–20, 36, 202, 210
common sense, 4, 160, 185
counter, 142, 149, 190, 196
critical colonial studies, 188–89
detentions, 143
as a diagnostic, 276, 287–89
diffractions, 272
disorder, 108, 153, 282–83
enduring conditions, xxxii
governance, 35, 143, 153, 295
hangover, 285
histories, x, 113, 121, 134, 273–74,
    287
imaginaries, 273
impositions, 148
inequities, x, 284–86
knowledges, 118, 126, 133
lexicon, xxxiii
neo-colonial, 174, 297
peripheries, 248
as police action, 112
post-, xxxii
regimes of truth, 64, 201
remnants, 281
repressions, 141
settler, 297
surveillance, 143, 166
violences, 109, 112, 126, 129
white colonial privilege, 19, 41
Colonial Java, 244, 252
colonialism 149, 151, 157, 172, 190
  anti-, xxx–xxxi
  carceral, 121, 240
  as conceptual metaphor
  data, digital, as feature of French
    society, 284–85
  folklorization of, 122
  hidden, 133–4
  invocation of, 273, 278, 283,
    294–95

nostalgia for, 10, 183, 273
race and, 16–20
savage, 297
settler, 283
social metabolisms of, 46
as subpoena, 294
techno, 280
colonization, 253, 260
de-colonization, 167, 187
colony, 145
carceral, 259
and metropole, 195
common sense, xxii, 31, 78, 85, 102–03, 106, 112, 119, 144, 159–61, 256, 288, 290
colonial, 4
Kant, 78n26, 89
racial, xxix
concept work, 75, 79, 83, 132, 144, 148, 184, 188, 212, 273, 284
conceptual failure, 137
conceptual labor, 292
Conference of Black Writers and Artists 1956, 170
contagion, xxvii, 95–96, 293, 296, 299
contaminating, 83–84, 86, 96–98, 101, 276, 290
contamination 10, 30, 43
of race, 98
containment, x, 249, 267 (*see also* enclosure)
carceral, 238
zones of, 290
COVID-19, xxxiii, 184
credibility, 64, 88, 103, 117, 121, 296,
hierarchies of, xxi–xxii
crime, 100, 241–42, 244, 250–51, 257, 270
against humanity, 284–85

and race, 65, 246
criminal, 28, 60–66, 119, 238
criminality, xxxv, 241–42
Critical Race Theory, 6

Daoud, Kamel, 133–35
Davis, Angela, 260
Davis, Mike, 260
De Andrade, Oswald, 148, 154
De Certeau, Michel, 132n57, 232
death, xxxiii, 40–41, 43, 66, 197, 261, 266, 291
penalty, 65
premature, 291, 293
sentences, xii, 48, 63–64,
debris
as archive, 125, 144, 210, 232
imperial, 289 (*see also* imperial, detritus)
Deebi, Aissa, 210
Deleuze, Gilles, 112, 113
democracy, xii, 31, 265–67, 280–81, 286
carceral, 240, 265–67
as imperial, xiii, xix, xxiii, xxxiii, xxxvi–xxxvii, 256–61
liberal, xi, 291, 295297–99
as justice, xviii
and labor, 256–61
as settler state, 280, 283
Denmark's People's Party, xxxiii
derision, 41, 43, 68, 281,
Derrida, Jacques, 212n28
diagnostic, xxii, 117, 276, 287–89
dark, 296–300
of futures, 276
of imperial politics
interior frontiers as, 6, 8, 11, 23
jealousy as, 51
in reserve, 37 (*see also* dispositif; jealousy; remorse)

diffraction, xxiii, 123, 272, 277
digitization, 204, 213-16
dis-ease, 11, 18, 36,
disgust, xxviii, 11, 43, 49, 55, 68, 70-71, 80-84, 86-87, 94-98, 99-101, 105-06, 296
  gut feeling, 101-05
  moral, 26
  and race, 99-101 (see also contagion, contamination)
disinteredness, 73-75, 87, 94 (see also Kant, Immanuel)
displacements, xii, 14, 117-18, 149, 170, 216, 227, 283 (see also Nakba)
dispositif, 4, 174
  carceral, 270
  of empire, xxxv
  of governance, 23, 143
  interior frontier as a, 6, 11, 17, 30
  racial, 85
  taste as a, 88 (see also diagnostic)
dispossession, xxxvii, 117, 266
  colonial, xi, 279
  Palestine, 201, 204, 229
disproportion, 161, 195
disregard, xxii, xxiii, 123-24, 127, 137, 186, 212, 275
  dis-regard, 123
  politics of, 18, 123, 135, 268
  as violence, 124-25
dissent, xxxiii, 9, 150, 157, 165, 177, 193, 201, 209, 271, 275, 278, 292, 299,
  aesthetics of, 143, 145, 152, 206
  and the avant-garde, 160-62
  poetics of, xxx, xxxiii, 168, 186, 198
distaste, xxviii, 19, 68, 70-72, 73, 79-80, 80-84, 87, 93, 101, 105-07

dégôut, xxviii, 94, 104
  and disgust, 102-104, 296
  disgusto, 82-83
  embodied force, 101
  as a metric, 86
  racialized sensibilities, 68 (see also Bourdieu, Pierre; Kant, Immanuel; Gadamer, Hans-Georg; taste)
Do Amaral, Tarsila, 148, 154
documentality, 211n26 (see also evidence; witnessing)
documents, xxiv, 206, 212, 213-16, 226, 233, 294
  colonial, 19, 36
  destroyed, xxxi, 3, 120
  military, 109
  objects as, 201-02, 207-08, 211
  and politics, 211
  unofficial, 231-32
double-consciousness, 18
Doumani, Beshara, 217, 222
Du Bois, W.E.B., 18
Duras, Marguerite, 37, 40-44, 54
duress, xxvi, 44, 165, 274, 282
Dussel, Enrique, 189
DuVernay, Ava, 268

enclosure, 101, 213 (see also containment)
enmity, xii, xxviii, 24, 297
erasure, xxxviii, 118, 131, (see also forgetting)
Esposito, Roberto, 98n87
evidence, xxi, 36, 39, 101-02, 117, 205, 210, 212, 276
  of remorse, 59-60, 63, 65
exclusion, xxix, 8-9, 11, 20, 27-28, 100, 188, 275,
extraction, xii-xiii, 189, 252, 261, 275, 284-285

Fanon, Frantz, ix, xxxvi–xxxvii, 29, 46, 92, 93, 147, 170, 181, 191, 193, 194, 291,
Farge, Arlette, 231–32
Farley, Anthony Paul, 98, 101
fashion, 21–22, 41–42, 55, 77, 90, 97, 132, 183, 188, 255
Fassin, Eric, 106
feeling, x, 15, 22, 39, 48, 50, 59, 61, 74, 76, 79, 85–87, 102–03,
structures of, xix, 36, 54, 83, 135
(*see also* affect; gut feelings; sensibility; sentiment)
Fichte, Johan Gottlieb, xxvi, 12–16, 19–20
Fields, Barbara, 27
Fields, Karen, 27
First Surrealist Manifesto, 187
flesh, ix, 13, 29, 39, 55, 67–68, 74, 77, 99, 136–37, 164, 242, 282, 297
Foner, Eric, 242, 267n87
forgetting, xxxii, 108–10, 115–17, 121, 129, 131, 134
colonial, 108–09
forget-ability, 113–15
forgetfulness, 136–37
The Great Forgetting, 119–20
as political concept, 111–13
scenes of making, 117–20
as structured violence, 124–26
Foucault, Michel, 111, 117, 148, 194, 294
Foulcher, Keith, 175
France, xxxiii, xxxviii, 93
archive, 4, 19, 92
banned in, 92, 147, 185
carceral labor, 239, 252–53, 261, 287
colonial, 20, 44, 71, 93, 112, 125, 129, 134–35, 187, 197
exiled from, 161
French-Algerian War, 92n68, 112, 290

French Caribbean, 152, 192
French Communist Party, 10
French Indochina, 40
French surrealists, 152
French taste, 70–71, 72
immigration, 10, 17, 31–32
imperial, xxxviii, 32, 92, 120, 169, 243
racism, xxix–xxx, xxxviii–xxxix, 10–12, 69–70, 72, 92, 106, 197–98
republican, 72
Vichy 143, 147, 167, 185
Front National, 5n4, 31

Gadamer, Hans-Georg, 71–72, 78–80, 85, 87–89, 106
Garner, Eric, 45
Geertz, Clifford, 103, 160,
geopolitics, xxxv, xxxviii, 86, 142, 230, 262
of race, 16, 71, 255
Germany, xxxv, 120
Gigerenzer, Gerd, 102
Gilmore, Ruth Wilson, 268n92, 291
Glissant, Eduardo, 170, 195
global apartheid, 276, 297,
Gottschalk, Marie, 250–51
Gourgouris, Stathis, 181
government apology, 108, 273, 285, 288
Gramsci, Antonio, 103, 149,
Green, André, xvii–xviii, 22, 25, 29–30
Grossman, Evelyne, xx
Guattari, Félix, 112, 113
Guez, Dor, 206
gut feelings, xxviii, 75–77, 101–105

Hage, Ghassan, 276n9, 296–97
Hammami, Rema, 231
Harcourt, Bernard, 232

Harrison, Olivia, 193
Heacock, Roger, 199, 213, 214n34
Henderson, Odie, 268
Hirschman, Albert, 57–58,
Hochberg, Gil, 203n7, 215
Hochschild, Adam, 120–21
Holocaust, 110, 116, 221
home, 31–34, 59
Honig, Bonnie, 286,
Hornsby, Jennifer, 128
Houellebecq, Michel, 69
human-kinds, xxvii, 25, 136, 272
   value of, 16, 97, 101, 105, 107
humanism
   anticolonial, 180
   radical, 162–66, 177, 181–82
   universal, 180

ignorance, 18, 57, 110, 121,
   137, 268
illiberalism, xxxiii, 46, 272, 275,
   277, 280–82, 284–86, 297 (see
   also liberalism)
imagination, 75–76, 167–68, 183,
   187, 222
   colonial, 118, 273
   geographies of, xxxvi
   political, 130, 202, 218
   racial, xxxii, 4, 85, 92
imperial
   archives, 294
   democracies, x, xi, xxiii, xxxii,
   256–61
   designs, x
   detritus, 148
   domains, xiii
   formations, x, 125, 187–89, 238,
   278
   governance, 122, 142, 148, 262,
   290
   histories, xxxvi, 120

   politics, 94
   sovereignty, 153, 243
   spaces, xiii
   ventures, xviii
imperialism, xi, 92, 176, 181, 186,
   256, 259, 293
incarceration, 240–43, 245, 251,
   253, 256, 260–62, 265–66, 268,
   271, 293,
   anti, xxxvi
   imprisonment, 48
   industry, xxxvi, xxxvii, 27 (see
   also abolition)
Indonesia, xxxiv, 178–80
   avant-garde, 171–176
   independence, 112–13
inequality, xxiii, xxvii, 6, 33, 52,
   134, 202, 238, 245–46, 274–75,
   289, 293–95
   currencies of, x
   and *dispositifs*, 9
   racial, xxxii, 16, 18, 60, 197, 256
   shatterzones of, xxxiv–xxxvi
   sub-metrics of, xii, xxii, xxv,
   xxxii, 39, 71, 88, 256, 266–67
infrastructures, xiii, xxix, 100, 148,
   251, 274, 299
   racial, x, xxxv, 4
   of violence, 25
interior frontiers, xiii–xviii, xxvi,
   4, 6–9, 16–20, 28–34, 45, 72,
   197, 238, 276, 299 (see also
   diagnostic; *dispositif*)
irreverence, xxxvi–xxxix
Islamaphobia, 6, 26, 93, 280–81
Israel, 200, 202
   archives, xxxi, 207, 209
   atrocities, 207
   borders, 226
   Deir Yassin, 221
   illiberalism, xxxiii

Jaffa, 206
occupation, 225, 229–33, 290
response to Palestine
 Museum, 221
settler state, 202–03, 280–81, 283
as a shatterzone of inequality, xxxv

Jacir, Emily, 207
Jackson, John, 281
James, Susan, 57
jealousy, 37
 as a diagnostic, 50–51
Jim Crow, 99, 267–68
Jordan, xxxiv, 208
Joyeux-Prunel, Béatrice, 156
justice, 211–12
 democracy as, xviii
 racial, 44
 restorative, 233, 294
 social, 174, 275, 295
 system, 61

Kahir-Eddine, Mohammed, 194
Kant, Immanuel, xxviii, 73–77,
 79–81, 86, 89, 91, 94, 95,
 101, 102
Kazan, Helene, 205
Keane, John, xii
Kelley, Robin, 162n39
Khazaeen, 207–09
Kostelantz, Richard, 159–60

Laabi, Abdellatif, 193, 194–95
labor, 53–54, 189
 affective, 42, 52, 58
 archival, 203, 206
 camps, 249
 carceral, 238, 240–45, 247,
  250–54, 261–63, 265–67
 extraction, xii, 284
 forced, 174–75, 237

unfree, 263–65
unwaged, 238–39
wage, 238, 256–61, 270
Lam, Wilfredo, 150, 196
Langer, Felicia, 230
Latif, Abedellah, 170
Lebanon, xxxi, xxxiv, 204, 208, 216,
 228
Lebanese Civil War, 205
Leiris, Michel, 279
LEKRA, 175, 179
Leopold II, 119–20
Lévi-Strauss, Claude, 82
liberalism, xi, xxiii, 46, 188,
 276–278, 282, 284–86, 289,
 293, 295, 297
Lowe, Lisa, 243–44
Lubis, Mochtar, 179

Madness, 21–22, 198 (*see also*
 Green, André; Marco, Mas)
Mahieddine, Baya, 150
Maier, Henk, 172, 174
Manifesto, xxiii, 152, 154, 166,
 177, 187 194–95 (*see also* First
 Surrealist Manifesto)
 anti-colonial, 92
Manna, Jumana, 215–17
Marco, Mas, 154, 172–73, 197
Mariana Islands, 243
Martinique, 146 (*see also*
 avant-garde)
Marx, Karl, 258n62
Marzon, Egidio, 141
Maskhoul, Bashir, 210
Matisse, Henri, 150
Mbembe, Achille, xii, 46n16,
 297–98
Mehta, Uday, xvn4, 188
Memmi, Albert, 105–06
Ménil, René, 146, 161, 167

Merleau-Ponty, Maurice, 283
metrics, xxiv, 48, 78, 86, 263-64, 296
 of inequality, xxxii
 of race, 252-55
 sub-metrics, xii, xxiv-xxx, 39-40, 60, 71, 76, 88, 160, 266
 of taste, 84, 86, 222
Miller, William, 43, 80, 97,
mobility, 86, 238, 247, 257, 260, 262, 267, 286,
modernity, xxxv, 180, 188, 219, 266
 laboratories of, 189
Montag, Warren, 136-37
morality, 61, 153
Mrazek, Rudolph, 180
Mufti, Amir, 181
Mustafa, Harbi Hassan, 230

Nakba, 283-84
Napoleanic Wars, 12
nationalism, 14, 18
necropolitics, xii
negritude, 146, 162-63, 168-70, 193, 195, 197 (*see also* avant-garde; "Black Surrealists")
 anti-, 162
Nehru, 177
neo-authoritarian, 295
 Jair Bolsonaro, 5, 48, 295
 Recip Tayyip Erdogan, 5, 48, 295
 Marine Le Pen, 5, 48, 295
 Donald Trump, 5, 275, 295
 Geert Wilders, 5, 48, 295
Netanyahu, Benjamin, 275
Ngai, Sianne, 52-53
Nietzsche, Friedrich, 115, 118, 125, 136
Nissabouri, Mostafa, 192-93
North Africa, 31, 187, 193

Nussbaum, Martha, 81, 85, 97, 100, 101-02, 104, 105,

objects, 92, 98, 123, 227-28
 in archives, 212, 220, 225
 precious, 201, 222-24
 stolen, 273, 279-80
occupation, 174, 219, 229, 230, 233, 259, 289
 digital, 213
 living, 215
October 1961 Vigil, 69
Orbán, Viktor, 275
Orlow, Uriel, 221

Palestine, xxxiv, 141, 220-21, 225, 233, 290
 archival terrain, 200-09, 292
 authority, 213
 Deir Yassin, 221
 family histories, 224-25, 227
 Gaza, 204-05, 213, 226, 228, 230
 Palestine Museum, xxxi, 199, 201, 207, 217- 21, 225-26, 231
 Palestine Poster Project Archives, 204n10
 Palestinian Oral History Archive, 203-04
 Ramallah, xxxi, 199, 225, 227, 228, 230
 refugees, 166, 204
 as shatterzone, 203
Pan-African Movement, 195
Panama Canal Zone, 244, 252, 259
Pane, Armijn, 151, 174, 196
Péguy, Charles, 167
Pergerakan, 171
Perkinson, Robert, 244-45
Persekian, Jack, 199, 220, 222-23, 224, 226n55, 228
Philippines, 243, 259, 294

photographs, 202, 205–06, 214, 217, 233
PKI, 175
poetic, 162, 167, 184, 193
  Knowledge, 150, 169, 190–91
  Rage, 141, 191, 197–98
  Truth, 167–68, 194
poetics, xxx, 142, 148, 150, 157, 159, 163, 166, 169–70, 171, 184, 187, 191, 193
  of dissent, xxx, 186, 198
  of politics, xxiv
police, 45, 85, 112, 256
political concept, xxvii, 26, 49, 160
  envy as a, 54
  forgetting, 111–13, 117–18, 136
  interior frontier as a, xxvi, 6, 8–9, 11 (*see also* affect, envy; forgetting; interior frontiers; taste)
politicality, xx, 44, 55, 88, 111, 129–30, 142–43, 149, 151, 166, 172, 190, 292
  of the senses, 36–37, 40
politics, xxxvii, 49, 145, 150, 174
  aesthetics and, 157, 169, 292
  anticolonial, 182
  archival, 213–16, 229
  avant-garde and, 158–59, 172, 183
  biopolitics, of the body, of comparison, xviii, xxxvii
  conditions of possibility of, 265–66
  of disgust, 94–99
  of disregard, 18, 123, 135
  of gut feelings, 101–05
  identity, 116
  of inspiration, 192–94
  of knowledge, 35–36
  and poetic rage, 191
  political manifesto, 194–95
  and race, xxxiii, 41, 48, 177, 268–70

of sentiment, 36, 47, 55, 137
of tense, 281–84
of wanting, 55
Port-au-Prince, xxv, 37, 143,
Poulantzas, Nicos, 26
poverty, xviii, xxxiii, 43, 53, 100, 116, 246, 266, 270, 274, 286
Povinelli, Elizabeth, 284
power, xxxii, 8, 46, 74, 195–98
  digital, 213
  and forgetting, 115–17, 125
  imperial, 145, 150
  labor, 239–40, 253, 257
  political, 118
  and race 35, 45
  relations of, 23, 47, 101, 280
  and the state, 261–62, 266
  of taste, 72, 78–80, 83, 88, 105–06
Price, Richard, 122, 125–26
Price, Sally, 122
prison, 64, 125–26, 183, 197, 239, 250–51, 258, 270
  abolition, 267
  empire, 242, 244, 256
  industry, 238, 247–48, 260–61, 268
  labor, 242, 253–54 (*see also* Boven Digul; camps; carceral)
Puar, Jasbir, 298

race
  aesthetics of, 81
  being raced, 149
  as civic felony, 27, 246
  and comportment, 256
  and contamination, 98
  crafting of, 77, 10
  critical race theory, 6
  and the death penalty, 65
  as entrapment, 242
  geopolitics of, 71, 255

race (cont.)
  metrics of, 252–55
  and nationalism, 18
  "the race question," 163
  racecraft, xxvii, xxxvi, 27, 165
  raceless, xxvi, xxxviii
  race-making, 246
  racial capitalism, 246, 259
  racial cleavages, xxxv, 238
  racial formations, xxi–xxvi
  racial imaginaries, xxxii
  racial law, 43, 64
  racial logics, xxxii, 259, 268
  racial order, 43, 168, 257
  racial subordinations, 196
  and taste 84–86
  and the ugly, 99–101
racism, xxix, xxx, xxxiv, 61, 95,
    105–07, 168, 198, 246, 291
  anti-, 162, 186
  and colonialism, 16–20, 163
  de cardio, 281
  and (dis)taste
  in France, 10, 71, 93
  state, 189
  in *Tropiques*, 168
  uncivil space, 255–56
  as universalism, 18
  United States, 240–43
  and white power, 242
Rancière, Jacques, 30, 165, 210
Rassemblement National, xxxiii
Rawagede 1947, 120
refugee, xiii, xxxv, 31, 70, 106, 274,
    290–91
  Palestine, 166, 204
refusal, 12, 39, 94, 96, 112, 177, 190,
    195, 209
  to acknowledge, 116, 125, 284–86
  anti-colonial, 183
  to comply, 62

dissidence, 148, 165
recalcitrance, xxii, xxxi, 145, 157,
    159, 165, 177
remorse, xxxii, 47, 48, 59–61, 134
  as a diagnostic, 63
  and the law, 60–61, 63–64
  pardon, 64
Remorselessness, 61–66
Restitution, xi, 273, 279, 285, (*see
    also* objects)
Réunion, 287
Rheinberger, Hans-Jorg, xx–xxi
Rif War, 187
Rizal, José, 144–45
Robinson, Cedric, 246
Roma, 106, 282
Ryle, Gilbert, 78, 127–29

Said, Edward, xxxvi, 91, 183
Saigon, 19, 40–41
Salih, Ruba, 166
Sarkozy, Nicolas, 116n25, 285
Sayigh, Rosemary, 202
Schmitt, Carl, xxxvii
Schweik, Susan, 99–100, 256
Scott, James, 47, 263
Security regimes, 9, 28, 32, 191,
Seikaly, Sherene, 205–06
Senghor, Léopold, 146, 167,
    169, 170
senses, xxvii–xxviii, 30, 35, 40, 43,
    47, 66, 75, 95–96, 150, 216, 296
  politicality of, 36–37
  sensorium, 55, 104, 224, 255, 296
  sensory regimes, xxii, 102, 137,
    164
sensibility, 130
  grids of, 48–49
sentiment, xxii, xxvii, 35–37, 39, 43,
    48–49, 56–59, 78, 130
  community of, 138

as epistemology, 56
as measures of value, xxvii
   49–53
and power, 39, 47, 58
politics of, 36, 58, 66, 137
racial grammar of, 35
Setia, Sophie, 175n77
Shahadeh, Raja, 290
shame, xi, 22, 36 41–42, 45, 47,
   49–50, 52, 63, 109, 119, 163
shameless, 41
shatterzone, xxxiv–xxxv, 203, 237
   and affect, 37
   carceral industry, 238, 262, 271
   of compressed inequalities, xxxv
   illiberalism, 275
   Middle East, 238
   Sudan, United States, xxxiv, 238,
      270
Shiriashi, Takahashi, 172
Silverblatt, Irene, 189
Situmorang, Sitor, 179, 180
skin, ix, 68, 99 (see also flesh)
slavery, xviii, xxxvi, 191, 238,
   240–44, 265–67
   post-, 169, 238
"Small review," 143, 146, 151, 175,
   185
   Art et Liberté, 155, 164
   Dunia Bergerak, 172
   Étudiant noir, 146–47
   Légitime défense, 146, 152–53,
      195
   Lotus, 182
   Pujangga Baru 151, 174
   Souffles-Anfas, 147, 155, 192–95,
      197
   Tropiques, 151, 160–62, 167–69,
      185–86, 193
social kinds, xxviii, 87, 105
Soeharto, 180

Solomon, Robert, 50
Sperber, Dan, 122
Staatiche Kuntsammlungen
   Dresden, 141
state, 16, 18, 118, 129, 189, 260,
   261–62, 263–64, 280
   carceral, 252, 256
   documents, 212
   fiction, 21–22
   institutions of, 23, 200, 239
   racial, 253, 266
   secular, 60
   statecraft, 57–58, 261–62
   stateless, xviii, 22–23, 291
   state project, 26, 120, 242–45,
      251–52, 258
Steedman, Carolyn, 37, 53–56
Stewart, Kathleen, 47
Stora, Bejamin, 290–91
Sukanta, Putu Oka, 148, 196
Sukarno, 177
Syria, xxxiv, 208, 237
   Syrian poetry, 182

Taqhailait, Yara, 228
Tarazi, Monaster, 204–05
taste, xxviii, xxxii, 67
   bad, 69n7
   and community, 72, 78–80
   and disgust, 85, 87–88, 97, 102
   as *dispositif*, 88
   as feeling, 85–86
   good, 69, 78, 82, 87, 97, 104
   gout, 80, 83–84
   grammars of, 71
   gusto, 82–83
   as judgement, 103
   made flesh, 68
   pure, 73–75, 95
   race and, 70, 71, 84–86, 89–90,
      93, 105–06

taste (cont.)
  of reflection, 91
  sense of, 216
  as social hierarchy
  tasteless, 84
  as unknowable, 79
  and violence, 94
  vulgar 70, 73, 75, 95–96 (see also Agamben, Giorgio; Bourdieu, Pierre; distaste; Gadamer, Hans-Georg; Kant, Immanuel; Williams, Raymond)
Tawil-Souri, Helga, 213
The Netherlands, xxxiii, 5, 113
  carceral labor, 239, 244, 253, 259
  Dutch colonial, 32, 49, 123–24, 146, 154, 171–73, 180, 188, 197, 259
  Dutch colonial archives, xxi, 4, 19
  The Netherlands Indies, 121, 183
torture, 189, 266
  Algerian War, xxx, 112
  documents of, xxiv
Toukan, Hanan, 216, 220, 221
toxicities, xxvi, 198, 296
  of racecraft, xxvii
  toxic deposits, 274
  toxic frontiers, 23
  toxic waste, 102
transgression, 29, 90–91
truth, 57–58, 131, 290
  parrhessia, 65–66, 194
  poetic, 167–68, 184, 194
  political, 103
  regime of, 25, 48, 64, 77, 87, 90, 137, 166, 201, 276
  of the self, 51
truth claims, 65, 129, 290
turpentine, 262–65, 293 (see also camps; labor, forced)
Twain, Mark, 120
Ugly Laws, xviii, 99–101, 106, 255

unfinished Projects
  Deir Yassin, 121; *Never-Part*, 218, 220–21, 222–27, 227–29
United States, 241,
  Constitution, as a carceral state, 238–40, 244–45, 247, 249, 267–71
  carceral labor, 240–43, 244, 247–48, 250–52, 256–57, 261–65
  dispossession, 121
  illiberalism, 275
  as imperial democracy, xxxiii, 125, 243
  racial injustice, 45, 197, 246, 252–54, 256–261
  as a shatterzone of inequality, xxxv–xxxvi

vagrancy laws, 241n12, 244, 255, 265, (see also carceral labor, convict leasing)
van Rossum, Matthias, 259
veridiction, xxxvii, 51
Villa-Ignacio, Teresa, 193
violence, x, 25, 63, 88, 97, 117, 135, 216, 285
  democratization of, xii
  racial, 45, 241, 265
  slow, 275
  structured, 124–26, 132
vulnerability, 40, 104, 298

Wacquant, Loïc, 27, 245–46, 262
Walsh, Daniel, 204
Wark, McKenzie, 164
Weber, Benjamin, 259
Weber, Samuel, 113–114
white
  arrogance, 41, 43, 94
  imaginaries, 53, 256
  immunitas/immunity, 98, 290
  fantasies, 191

fictions, 53, 191
paranoia, 163
sovereignty, 191, 269
supremacy, xxxiii, 4, 89, 147
Wilder, Gary, 167, 169
Williams, Raymond, xix, 36–37, 54, 83,
witnessing, 117, 137, 207 (*see also* documentality; evidence)

worth, 16, 40, 49–53, 77, 87, 97, 102, 107, 110–111, 212, 241, 244,
metrics of, xxiv–xxvi
unworthiness, 105–06 (*see also* human-kinds)
Wright, Richard, 163, 170, 178–80, 197

Yoyotte, Pierre, 196

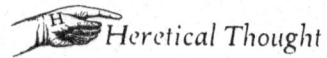

HERETICAL THOUGHT

Series editor: Ruth O'Brien,
The Graduate Center, City University of New York

Call Your "Mutha": A Deliberately Dirty-Minded Manifesto for the Earth Mother in the Anthropocene
Jane Caputi

Assembly
Michael Hardt and Antonio Negri

The Rise of Neoliberal Feminism
Catherine Rottenberg

Insurgent Universality: An Alternative Legacy of Modernity
Massimiliano Tomba